ESSENTIALS

OF

CONTEMPORARY LITERATURE

ESSENTIALS OF
CONTEMPORARY LITERATURE OF
THE WESTERN WORLD

VOLUME **1**

Continental European

BY

DONALD HEINEY
Professor of Comparative Literature
University of California, Irvine, California

LENTHIEL H. DOWNS
Professor of English
Denison University, Granville, Ohio

BARRON'S EDUCATIONAL SERIES, INC.
New York • London • Toronto • Sydney

All inquiries should be addressed to:
Barron's Educational Series, Inc.
250 Wireless Boulevard
Hauppauge, New York 11788

Library of Congress Catalog Card No. 73-75772

Paper Edition
International Standard Book No. 0-8120-0447-7

PRINTED IN THE UNITED STATES OF AMERICA

789   500   98765432

TABLE OF CONTENTS

Foreword

Preface to the Second Edition

Foreword

The literature of the western world during the past hundred years has been remarkable for a number of reasons: its profusion, its diversity, its exciting experimentation, its successes and failures. Spengler may have been right in his prediction of the decline of the west, but literary creativity has burgeoned rather than declined since his thesis was enunciated some fifty years ago. Of course the profusion has not all been good. Printing presses have worked overtime, and we may be in danger from the inundation of the mediocre and the banal, even the trash which threatens cultural pollution. It has been estimated that an average of ten novels are published each day in the United States and Europe, and the figure is probably still on the rise. Now more than ever a guide is useful to keep head above paper. Prior to 1870 literature pretty much winnowed itself; it had to be reasonably good to be worth printing in the first place and time took care of whatever sneaked through on false merits. But the cries for relevance and the modern and technological progress have complicated our world. We cannot afford to let time do the job alone, because there are hidden voices that can speak to our condition now and we do not have that much time for waiting.

One of the most interesting facets of modern literature is the interrelatedness of its practitioners. It is impractical and too narrowly provincial to study English writers or American writers or French writers in isolation. It is even impossible. What do you do with a man like Samuel Beckett, ostensibly an Irishman for most of his life, who writes his most important works in French for the absurdist theatre in Paris and then translates them into English? Or Vladimir Nabokov, who might be claimed by Russian, English, German, French, or American literatures? (*Lolita* seems clearly American, if Humbert and Nabokov do not.) Or any of a dozen others? Nationality just isn't that important any more. Movements cross borders without passport or visa: realism, naturalism, expressionism, Theatre of the Absurd—all of them. Therefore cross reference is a necessity, lest doors be closed rather than opened. Yet in these fluid times, when generic, historic, and national lines dissolve so easily, we must set up tentative boundaries even as we invite their crossing. Continental Europe, Britain, and America are recognizable in large outline as the areas of the Western World which have contributed most to the literature of our times, and with the sometimes admittedly arbitrary forcing of bedfellows we shall look at them in that order. The addition of new material to the first editions of *Contemporary Literature* and *Recent American Literature* has made advisable a reorganization into the following volumes: I, Continental European; II, British; III Recent American (to 1930); IV, Recent American (post 1930). For a fuller understanding of movements, ideas, and innovative techniques, the reader of one volume is invited to refer to the others.

Although again somewhat arbitrarily, the discussion of contemporary criticism is reserved for the end of Volume III and Volume IV, not because there are no European or British critics but because literary criticism in our time has become rather surprisingly something of an American-Canadian industrial complex, with transatlantic voices as somewhat adjunct even when innovative. The big business of criticism, with its journals, Modern Language and College English Associations and institutes, has carved out its empire even if it has not yet created a monopoly.

Preface to Second Edition

The gratifying and continuous response to the original version of *Contemporary Literature* and *Recent American Literature* has prompted this revised edition, in which the entire text has been reviewed and brought up to date and a substantial body of new material has been written. Since 1954 five more of the authors treated in the book have been recognized by the Swedish Academy with the Nobel Prize. Of the others so recognized only three have been added to this new edition. For the Nobel Prize, even though it is the most prestigious of literary awards, is no absolute indication of merit or significance. It has passed by too many of the great writers of the twentieth century—Proust, Kafka, Joyce, Rilke, and Brecht, to name only a few—and it has been awarded to others out of national or geographical considerations, or simply out of confusion of the good with the best. The classics of contemporary literature are not those awarded the prominent prizes, or those treated in textbooks; they are those that are read and continue to be read, and those that profoundly influence the spirits and intellects of their readers. This is the primary criterion that has been followed in writing this new edition of *Contemporary Literature*.

No survey of recent literature can remain up to date very long. Writers, like other people, have a way of dying and being born at inopportune times—for instance just after a book has gone to press. (During the preparation of this preface Erich Maria Remarque and John Dos Passos have died toward the end of September 1970, and the Nobel Prize has been offered to Alexander Solzhenitsyn with unpleasant reactions in the Soviet press.) Twenty-seven authors of the first edition are now no longer living. Many or most of them have been retained, but it has been necessary to revise and bring up to date information about them. And many new writers have appeared; more than enough, it seems, to replace those who are no longer on the scene. The authors of this new edition had some anguishing choices to make. It was relatively easy to decide, for example, on the inclusion of two movements which have sprung up in the fifties and sixties: the Nouveau Roman or Anti-Novel and the Theatre of the Absurd. It was with the exclusions that the anguish began. It was not easy to leave out some of the writers one would like to include, many of them personal favorites of the present authors. The process of selection demands rigor and risk. Nobody will be entirely happy with this matter of exclusion and inclusion, the present authors least of all. What we have tried to make is a handbook of workable size. Like a suitcase for a journey on which one must travel light, it lacks a number of luxuries one would like to have. But we hope, and believe, it contains at least the necessities. The reader who knows something of the authors treated in this book will have little difficulty reading and comprehending other twentieth-century writers who may fall within his sphere of interest.

There is also the question of classification, often of putting writers in company they would not choose for themselves. But they have to be somewhere, and as long as we are tentative and not rigidly categorical about it we can show relationships, influences, and points of contact that legitimately help us understand each author's originality and major impact. The lines of demarcation are not firm but flexible, sometimes even highly elastic. It is amazing to observe how little modification of interpretation and prediction made in 1954 was needed in 1970. Two brief examples will suffice. Of Herman Hesse it could then be said that "he has not achieved the fame of a Mann or a Gide," that "he probably never will, in fact, become a popular author in the broadest sense." But Hesse is now pouring from the American presses in paperbacks and is widely read even among persons who do not ordinarily read European novels; not only has he become a kind of literary folk hero, but he has as well many serious, competent, and dedicated readers—undoubtedly more, today, than Gide, Of Jean Anouilh it was true that he was "relatively little known in America," but today that awareness of Anouilh has been expanded. There are a number of other examples of such rises and falls in reputation. We have sought to take account of them, to an extent; but our primary measuring-stick has been our own subjective—and fallible—evaluation of the importance of writers.

Another measure of importance may be the influence of writers on subsequent literary generations. The genuinely seminal writers of the twentieth century (and by seminal we mean those whose ideas and methods moved other writers to carry these ideas and techniques further, or to develop new literary methods through their influence) are all here. First of all, five recognized masters: Proust, Joyce, Kafka, Mann, and Faulkner. Then another group of only slightly less significance: Pirandello, Gide, Rilke, Brecht, Sartre, Camus. And a third ranking (and the present authors begin to quake a little at making such peremptory and autocratic judgments on their betters): Gertrude Stein, Dos Passos, Ford Madox Ford, D. H. Lawrence, Yeats, Eliot, Pound, W. H. Auden, Sherwood Anderson, Samuel Beckett, Ionesco. Even below this level we are still in the realm of the important, and sometimes even of the great. To make the selections for such a book is a humbling experience: it makes one realize how many great and important things our time has contributed to the course of centuries.

Summaries or analyses of an author's chief works can never be a substitute for reading them; there is no substitute for this experience. But after a work has been read—as one of us remarked in the preface to another book—"a concise synopsis which includes a well-judged critical evaluation is often helpful in recalling details and in making the pattern or theme of the whole work apparent." The reader is invited to disagree to his heart's content with our critical evaluations, to substitute his own summaries, to sharpen the edge of his critical apparatus on our work as on a honing stone. We do not expect always to be agreed with. We hope, at best, that our book will become a familiar companion on the reader's bookshelf and the recurring guide of his exploration of modern literature.

We should like to acknowledge our indebtedness to several student generations and to colleagues present and absent for their insights into the infinite and various richness of contemporary literature. The greatest satisfaction of the teacher is to learn from those he teaches, and to talk of what he has learned with his friends. It is for these friends, and these students, that this book has been written.

DONALD HEINEY   LENTHIEL H. DOWNS
UNIVERSITY OF CALIFORNIA, IRVINE   DENISON UNIVERSITY

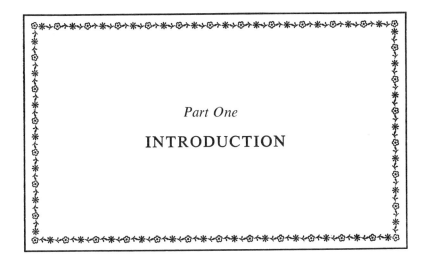

Part One

INTRODUCTION

1. THE LEGACY OF THE NINETEENTH CENTURY

Literature is an organic development; its present is always connected to its past. Each literary generation derives from the preceding one just as human generations succeed each other. At the same time the process of evolution in literature is in a sense more complex: literary movements long dormant are frequently revived and renovated to fit the age, and thus the influence of a literary movement may be felt across the gap of centuries. Medieval art, neglected since the Renaissance, was revived in various romantic movements of the nineteenth century; the themes of Greek mythology often served as sources for the dramatist of the twentieth century. To comprehend the background of twentieth-century literature we must give a certain attention to the whole of literary history, and especially to the literature of the century preceding.

Undoubtedly the dominant phenomenon in nineteenth-century literature was the emergence of REALISM. From a literary point of view the triumph of realism was the triumph of the novel, in which it found its most apt expression. In its social aspect realism was a manifesta-

1

tion of the faith in science and liberalism which grew constantly during the century and only began to waver towards 1900. In content realistic literature is generally concerned with the affairs of the middle and lower classes; it treats economic, social, and technical matters in addition to the traditional literary themes of love and gallantry, and it purports to utilize the vernacular of daily life instead of the artificial poetic diction of previous literatures.

The beginnings of realism can naturally be traced as far back as Homer; but in modern times a convenient arbitrary point of departure is to be found in the work of STENDHAL (pseud. of Henri Beyle, 1783-1842). This brilliant French novelist, who wrote far ahead of his times, treated themes of the utmost romanticism, but he did so in a sparse, objective, and ironic manner which was greatly to influence subsequent realistic authors.

HONORE DE BALZAC (1799-1850) carried Stendhal's realism into the realm of subject matter as well as style. His *Comédie humaine,* a vast panorama of French society under the Empire and the Restoration, comprises twenty-four novels and a score of stories and tales. GUSTAVE FLAUBERT (1821-80) brought to the novel an even greater objectivity, a scientific penetration, and a painstaking exactitude in style. His *Madame Bovary* and the short tale *A Simple Heart* represent the high-water mark in French realism.

In England the realistic movement, latent in Defoe, Fielding, and Richardson, begins in earnest with CHARLES DICKENS (1812-70). Although Dickens had no such pseudo-sociological vision as Balzac's "Human Comedy" in mind, he nevertheless created a similar panorama of early nineteenth-century Britain. WILLIAM MAKEPEACE THACKERAY (1811-63) and ANTHONY TROLLOPE (1815-82) are the chief remaining figures of the British realistic movement.

Perhaps the most powerful of the European realistic novels were those of the great Russian triumvirate: FYODOR DOSTOYEVSKY (1821-81), IVAN TURGENEV (1818-83), and LEO TOLSTOY (1828-1910). Tolstoy's novels *Anna Karenina* and *War and Peace* are worthy of especial mention as examples of Russian realism. ANTON CHEKHOV (1860-1904), whose short fiction and plays (*The Sea Gull, The Three Sisters, The Cherry Orchard*) were both important in turn of the century Russia, is regarded almost equally as realist (slice-of-life and realism of the apparently irrelevant) and impressionist. His deep influence on contemporary English literature is to be seen particularly in the short stories of James Joyce and Katherine Mansfield. In the Scandinavian countries the chief of several important realistic authors was the Norwegian dramatist HENRIK IBSEN (1828-1906), whose work is dominated by biting criticsm of the middle class as well as antagonism toward bourgeois Philistinism and materialism. Ibsen's work was especially influential in Germany, where it served as one of the focal points of the naturalistic movement in the theatre, and in England, where it found a formidable champion and publicist in Bernard Shaw.

Toward the end of the century the realistic movement began to metamorphose into the school known as NATURALISM. Compared with mid-century realism, naturalism tended to be more militantly pseudo-scientific in its approach and even more concerned with degraded, often sordid levels of human existence. EMILE ZOLA (1840-1902) shares with the critic Hippolyte Taine the honor of founding the French naturalist school. Zola sought to make literature into a branch of social science; the novel in his view was to study social behavior as the chemist studies the behavior of compounds in a testtube. His formidable *Rougon-Macquart* series, an integrated novel sequence similar to Balzac's *Comédie humaine,* purported to present "a natural and social history of a family under the Second Empire." Zola was especially fascinated with the operation of heredity, which he felt to be the dominant motivating force in human destiny.

In Germany naturalism, as noted above, received a great impetus from the work of Ibsen. The chief German naturalists of the nineteenth century are the novelist THEODOR FONTANE (1819-98); the collaborators ARNO HOLZ (1863-1929) and JOHANNES SCHLAF (1862-1941), who wrote chiefly criticism, drama, and short stories; and GERHART HAUPTMANN (1862-1946), a versatile author who in the twentieth century turned to Symbolism and expressionism. Naturalism was less prominent in nineteenth-century English literature. Its chief exponent was THOMAS HARDY (1840-1924), whose novels are marked by a deep deterministic pessimism. Other important European naturalists are the Spaniard BENITO PEREZ GALDOS (1843-1920) and the Italian GIOVANNI VERGA (1840-1922). In

America and Britain, and in a certain sense in Germany, naturalism was to reach its true climax only in the twentieth century.

At the same time, markedly different literary movements were developing independently of the realistic-naturalistic mainstream. The weird tales of the German E. T. A. HOFFMANN (1776-1882) and the strangely obsessive poems and tales of the American EDGAR ALLAN POE (1809-49) formed the seed from which another literary movement was to grow: the highly artificial, often ingrown and perverted school of DECADENCE. This generic term, embracing several sub-movements whose general tendencies are similar, implies the themes of the linking of love and death, pleasure and pain; an obsession with corpses, ghosts, and torture; and the pessimism or *Weltschmerz* of a hero who finds no satisfaction in earthly activity. Adumbrations of this tendency are apparent in the eighteenth-century Gothic novel; in the nineteenth century the movement centers around the work of the French poet CHARLES BAUDELAIRE (1821-67). Baudelaire, himself greatly influenced by Poe, was to exert a powerful spell over French poetry for the remainder of the century. Similar in tone, and possibly even more neurotic, were the plays and novels of the Swedish AUGUST STRINDBERG (1849-1912), an erratic genius whose eccentricities expressed themselves as much in his personal life as they did in his work. Strindberg's weirdly chaotic dramas of the later period were especially important as an influence on the early twentieth-century expressionistic school. Two more important decadents, both of whom wrote toward the end of the century, are the French novelist JORIS KARL HUYSMANS (1848-1907) and the British novelist and playwright OSCAR WILDE (1856-1900).

A third literary current of the nineteenth century, in some aspects connected with the decadent movement, was the school of SYMBOLISM. Its starting point was the rejection of bourgeois-capitalistic materialism and the realistic literature which grew out of it. Foreshadowings of the movement are to be found in the British PRE-RAPHAELITE movement, a repudiation of humanism and a revival of medievalism headed by JOHN RUSKIN (1819-1900), and the French PARNASSIAN school of poetry, a neoclassic and aesthetic revolt centering around the poet CHARLES LECONTE DE LISLE (1818-94). The Symbolist school properly speaking began to form around 1880 and reached its climax in the eighteen-nineties. Its leading poets were STÉPHANE

MALLARMÉ (1842-98), JOSÉ MARIA DE HEREDIA (1842-1904), PAUL VERLAINE (1844-96), and HENRI DE RÉGNIER (1864-1936). The Symbolists sought to extirpate all narrative, exposition, and didacticism from poetry, to form each poem around a single image or sensation, and to utilize the newly-discovered subconscious associations of the human mind to lead the reader along the path from the concrete to the intangible. In addition there was a certain element of decadence in Symbolistic poetry: a conscious cult of beauty for its own sake, and an obsession with sensory or erotic experience. Several of the leading poets of the twentieth century, including W. B. Yeats, T. S. Eliot, R. M. Rilke, W. H. Auden, and Stephen Spender, were palpably influenced by French Symbolism.

Two additional influences on twentieth-century literature should be mentioned even though they themselves are not specifically literary. The socialist-radical movement, culminating in the work of KARL MARX (1818-83), began to find literary expression in the late nineteenth century and became even more prominent after 1900. Not only did authors like André Malraux frankly profess Marxism, but a large number of twentieth-century authors consciously or unconsciously presented Marxian concepts such as the conflict of social classes or the intransigence of the bourgeois-capitalistic ruling classes.

Lastly, the Viennese psychoanalyst SIGMUND FREUD publicized the importance of the subconscious life in forming human motivation and, even more important, by his revelation of the suppressed sexual element in human activity, paved the way for a franker and more revealing treatment of erotic themes in literature. There is scarcely an author in the twentieth century who can be said to have escaped the influence of Marx or Freud or both.

2. MAIN CURRENTS OF THE TWENTIETH CENTURY

The year 1900 is more than an arbitrary chronological milestone in literary history: it marks the onset of a new era in literature as it does in the field of social activity. On first examination the striking characteristic of twentieth-century literature is its extreme diversity. There is no one single school, no one tendency, which can be said to typify the age. Never before in literary history have there been so many cénacles, so many schools, circles, and movements existing simultaneously. This diversity is naturally only an aspect of a wider heterogeneity in social development: the twentieth century, having no one dominant social philosophy, cannot hope for unanimity in literature.

In addition, an important minority of twentieth-century authors show a tendency to lose themselves in obscurantism and esotericism. Literature has never, except in rare instances, been the preoccupation of the great masses of the population; but never before has literature been written for such a small and clannish group of *cognoscenti*. Comparatively speaking, the public which enjoys the poetry of Rainer Maria Rilke, Paul Valéry, T. S. Eliot or Ezra Pound is an infintely smaller percentage of the total population than the public which read the poems of Tennyson or Hugo or even that which patronized the plays of Shakespeare. Certain schools of poetry especially in the twentieth century tend to be difficult, heavy with allusion, and highly technical in construction.

At the same time the opposite tendency is discernable: many twentieth-century authors seek deliberately to create a literature for the masses, a literature which sacrifices none of its artistic quality in being presented in terms comprehensible to the man in the street. This experiment has, of course, been carried forth on a wide scale and in a highly organized manner in Soviet Russia, but the attitude is also apparent in the work of such contemporary naturalists as Theodore Dreiser and Roger Martin du Gard. Along with the tendency to broaden the basis of all the arts—music, the opera, drama, and painting—to make them assimilable by the mass of the population, there has been a comparable effort to democratize literature. Literature, however, is a verbal art requiring a certain background and vocabulary for proper appreciation; it is inherently a more difficult art to popularize than painting or music. Thus the democratization of literature has been accompanied by a simplifying, sometimes even a vulgarizing, of literary standards.

Amid the complex diversity of twentieth-century literary schools it is possible to discern two basic tendencies. The first of these, the realistic-naturalistic movement, continues the current which began in the nineteenth century with Stendhal, Balzac, Tolstoy, and Ibsen.

In the twentieth century this movement tends to become more militantly political, more liberal in outlook, and at the same time more consciously scientific in technique.

The second great movement might be roughly termed "the reaction to realism." It comprises the various forms of repudiation of external objectivity: psychological literature, Neo-romatncism, impressionism, expressionism, and other forms of anti-realistic experimentation.

The realm of ideological or intellectual literature is treated in a separate section. The authors in this section agree more in content than they disagree in technique, and in general the chief importance of their work lies in its ideological content. Poetry, in the twentieth century concerned chiefly with technique, is also treated in a separate section, as is Soviet literature, isolated from the West and proceeding according to dogmatic and highly specialized literary principles.

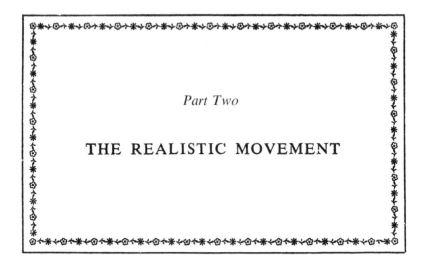

Part Two

THE REALISTIC MOVEMENT

3. REALISTS AND STORY-TELLERS

The dominant realistic movement which began in the middle of the nineteenth century and which reached its climax with Flaubert, Tolstoy, and Ibsen continued well into the twentieth century. Where the main body of European novelists had turned to naturalism and subsequently reacted against it in the early nineteen-hundreds, an important minority, including figures of the stature of Thomas Mann and Arnold Bennett, continued to write in the traditional and realistic style of the mid-nineteenth century.

These writers as a group manifest a strong feeling of artistic vocation; they consider themselves professional authors whose business it is to write books, and they are generally wary of engaging in politics, lending their services to groups, or promulgating doctrines. At the same time they tend to be broadly liberal and humanitarian in outlook; several of their number suffered exile for their opposition to totalitarian regimes. Generally speaking, these authors can be classed as antagonistic to bourgeois conventions of morality or respectability; they frequently portray sensitive and artistically talented young persons whose lives are devoted to the struggle against middle-class

Philistinism. As artists all of them are concerned with the delineation of character, especially eccentric, impassioned, or sensitive character; and with the exception of Benavente all find the novel the best vehicle for this sort of content. Many realists demonstrate an almost devout respect for the art of writing; they are consecrated craftsmen who construct books with a careful and perspicacious attention to detail. Of the group treated, Bennett and Maugham are primarily story-tellers whose work contains no dominant or consistent message, while each of the others demonstrates some *Leitmotif* in his work.

Thomas Mann (German, 1875-1955)

Mann is probably the most widely read of the great authors of the twentieth century; his work is well known even among many readers whose backgrounds are relatively limited. At the same time he is often considered a profound and stylistically formidable author. It is true that his books contain little plot in the ordinary sense, and are often filled with involved theological, philosophical, and aesthetic discussions. His style, especially in his major works, tends to be amorphous and discursive. It is not without justice that his work is considered difficult.

Yet Mann is not a profound philosopher, a daring literary innovator, or a prophet like his own heroes Adrian Leverkühn and Joseph. As a thinker he is content to synthesize the intellectual materials of his time. He draws from many sources—Goethe, Nietzsche, Stefan George, Freud, Jung, the Russian novelists—and organizes their concepts into new and interesting intellectual patterns. The same motifs recur throughout his work and seem to develop and solidify throughout his career, and in this sense he may be said to have a personal philosophy.

The most striking intellectual characteristic of Mann's work is his preoccupation with contrasts and antitheses, or perhaps in one great antithesis with many forms. Born into the prosperous and respectable merchant society of Lübeck, he later discovered another way of life in creative art; and during the rest of his career he viewed his personality in terms of the conflict of these two influences. The extent of the conflict can be shown in a diagram in which the key concepts of this struggle are arranged in parallel columns:

Lübeck (home life)	cosmopolitanism
Germany; Teutonism	Italy; France; the Slavic races
the bourgeois	the bohemian
bourgeois democracy	fascism
business	art, music, poetry
efficiency; practicality	romanticism
health; life	sickness; death
the average man	genius
blondness	dark or red hair
sacred love	profane love
the serene (Apollonian)	the demonic (Dionysian)
the rational	the irrational
Puritanism	hedonism

It is important to note that Mann associates both genius and the arts with disease and mysticism; this linkage occurs constantly in his work. It should also be noted that "Teutonism" here signifies German stability and honor, and that this stands in sharp contrast to the demonic romanticism of Germany's Hölderlins, Nietzsches, and Wagners.

In many of Mann's works these concepts are personified in antithetical characters. In *Tonio Kröger* Hans Hansen and Ingeborg are obviously of the left column, and Lisabeta Ivanovna of the right. In *The Magic Mountain* Settembrini and Naphta respectively personify the rational and the demonic. In *Doktor Faustus* the bourgeois Zeitblom is contrasted with the demonic Leverkühn. Other characters, like Tonio Kröger and Hans Castorp (and like Mann himself) stand somewhere in the middle and are pulled by both extremes.

Within this basic framework the more important of Mann's subconcepts should be distinguished:

(1) One of the most important aspects of the dichotomy is manifested in Mann's preoccupation with SOUTHERN EUROPE; he well demonstrates the tendency termed in German the *Drangnachsuden*. In Mann's case he associates the southern countries, especially Italy and Greece, not only with artistic creativity (cf. Wincklemann and Goethe) but also with hedonism, passion, violence, and death. He sees classic Greece mainly in terms of the ecstatic Dionysian element, ignoring or deprecating the Apollonian element which was also present. In one work the situation remains intact but is transferred bodily

to a new locale: in the *Joseph* tetralogy Israel is the land of Puritanism and law and Egypt the realm of passion, violence, and the cult of death.

(2) To Mann the ARTIST is the epitome of genius, demonism, and disease. The artist is divinely touched; to him bourgeois happiness is denied, but he achieves the higher, more ecstatic pleasures of creativity. In a sense he becomes God through his creative power. A genius, he nevertheless fails to achieve the simplest rewards of life: love of woman, comfort, home, and serenity. Mann has a profound respect for the craft of writing and for artistic standards in general, and he is constantly aware of the apartness of the artist from the rest of mankind. In this connection the influence of the aesthetic Stefan George circle upon Mann is evident.

(3) Mann views SICKNESS (right column) as more interesting than HEALTH (left column); moreover he feels that sickness is somehow mystically connected with passion and creativity. It is only after Hans Castorp, the hero of *The Magic Mountain,* contracts tuberculosis that he experiences true sensual love, and it is only after the Leverkühn of *Doktor Faustus* is afflicted with syphilis that he achieves his greatest musical creativity. Music is especially associated with disease and violence in Mann; to him the operas of Wagner and the symphonies of Mahler are only a step from the irrational mystique of Nazism. Thus, although Mann is extremely sensitive to music, he mistrusts its power and often seems to view it as a diabolic force. This tendency to regard art, music, and romanticism in general with suspicion increases throughout Mann's career.

(4) Mann early became interested in MYTHOLOGY and MYTHO-LOGICAL PSYCHOLOGY; this interest grew throughout the thirties until it reached a climax in the *Joseph* series (1933-44). He is especially influenced by the theory of the recurrence of the myth, propounded both by Jung and by Nietzsche. Jung expounded the concept of the "archetype," the universal myth which emerges in slightly different forms in all human cultures. Nietzsche described the "Eternal Return" or "Eternal Recurrence," the rebirth of the myth in successive epochs of the same or different cultures. Thus Mann extracted his belief in the universality and timelessness of the myth. In the tale *Death in Venice* a mysterious gondolier ferries the hero across the Venetian lagoon; the student of classic mythology will recognize him as Charon, the boatman who conducts the traveller across the Styx to the under-

world. In *Doktor Faustus* Mann resurrects the medieval Faust legend and clothes it in modern dress. The Eternal Return theme is most prominent in the *Joseph* tetralogy, but appears in some form in most of Mann's works.

Freudian symbolism, Freudian dreams, and psychoanalytic concepts also play a large part in Mann's work. He accepts the concept of the subconscious existence implicitly; in many of his works, e.g. *The Magic Mountain,* the hero's conflict is connected with his effort to reach awareness of his own true nature, which is buried in his subconscious. At the same time Mann often views psychoanalysts as characters skeptically. This is especially true in *The Magic Mountain,* where the psychoanalyst Krokowski is treated as a grotesque charlatan although psychoanalytic concepts play a large latent part in the novel. In the *Joseph* series psychoanalytic concepts form one of the basic themes of the work; in *The Holy Sinner* Mann seems to return to a skeptical and satirical attitude toward the subject.

Irony and satire are present in most of Mann's work, although their part is often only incidental and secondary. There are satirical portraits in most of his novels and in all but a few stories. *The Transposed Heads* and *The Holy Sinner,* two short novels from his later period, rely upon irony as their principal device; certain stories written in the thirties belong in this same class. Readers and critics who approach Mann with excessive earnestness often miss his lighter side.

Mann is an expert creator of character in the nineteenth-century tradition. His characters fall roughly into two groups: the heroes, who are often transmuted personifications of the author's own attitudes; and his secondary characters, who tend toward the grotesque and eccentric. He is at his best in sketching originals, geniuses, Bohemians, and demonics: the clownish Herr Grünlich in *Buddenbrooks,* the anonymous musician who passes so strangely through *Death in Venice,* the antithetical philosophers Settembrini and Naphta in *The Magic Mountain,* and the garrulous narrator of *Doktor Faustus,* Professor Serenus Zeitblom. He is adroit at depicting the enthusiasm, the fervor, and the desperation of youth, as he does in Tonio Kröger; and he is particularly successful in establishing strange and haunting moods, of which the best-known example occurs in *Death in Venice.*

LIFE: Mann was born in 1875 in the old North German trading town of Lübeck, the son of a respectable middle-class commercial family. His mother, however, had certain exotic qualities; she was a fiery and sensitive woman partly of Creole extraction. Mann became early aware of the contrasting influences of his mother and father on his character, and the dichotomy is apparent throughout his life and work. When, still an adolescent, he determined upon his vocation as a writer, he developed a profound contempt for middle-class respectability and all the Puritanism its code demands; but he never quite succeeded in making the transition to Bohemianism. His Tonio Kröger, consecrated to the artistic life and yet somehow ashamed of it, is not without resemblance to Mann himself.

As a young man of bourgeois background inclined to literature Mann joined the staff of *Spring Storm,* a short-lived review of verse and prose, and presently became its principal contributor. After a trip to Italy and a series of short stories, he produced his first important work, the immense novel *Buddenbrooks.* This earned him a certain fame, which he confirmed with the tale *Tonio Kröger* in 1903. In 1911 appeared *Death in Venice,* the masterpiece among his shorter works. The war produced *Reflections of an Unpolitical Man* (1918), an essay on current politics later attacked as anti-democratic by Mann's critics. From 1912 to 1924 he worked intermittently at *The Magic Mountain,* his best-known and perhaps his greatest long work. In 1929 he was awarded the Nobel Prize for Literature, chiefly in recognition of this novel. A long tetralogy on the Joseph legend, *Joseph and his Brothers,* appeared in successive volumes from 1933 to 1944, and in 1947 he published *Doktor Faustus,* which he seemed to consider the culminating work of his career. Meanwhile his life had become involved in current German politics. He opposed Nazism even before it had become a major force in German society, and in 1933 he abandoned Germany to take up a voluntary exile in Switzerland. During the entire period of his exile, and continuing into the war years, he was active in anti-fascist movements in Europe as well as in America. In 1938 he moved semi-permanently to the United States, where he remained through the war; he eventually installed himself in a suburb of Los Angeles. In 1953, however, he expressed grave suspicion of the direction American culture was moving, and after stating that he felt his freedom to be abridged in America announced his determination to return to Europe permanently.

Mann took up residence near Zurich in Switzerland, that haven of the central European mind that would remain free of political pressures. He resumed work on *The Confessions of Felix Krull, Confidence Man,* the first fragment of which had been written as a novella in 1911, and published his novel, over three hundred pages of additional narrative (still potentially unfinished), in 1954. On June 6, 1955 Thomas Mann celebrated his eightieth birthday with world homage. Shortly thereafter he took sick and died of thrombosis in Zurich on August 12. *Felix Krull* published in English translation in 1955 was widely acclaimed as a bravura performance at the final curtain.

CHIEF WORKS: *Tonio Kröger* (novella, 1903), of all Mann's works, best symbolizes the antitheses which went to make up his own personality. The hero Tonio is the child of a temperamental Latin mother and a practical and business-like German father. The story falls roughly into three sections. The first of these is chiefly concerned with Tonio's school days. As an adolescent, shy and sensitive, he is afflicted with an obsession that he is different from his companions, that they are healthy and normal in a way he can never be. His best friend, Hans Hansen, is athletic and vigorous; he is interested only in sports and horses, and when Tonio tries to interest him in Schiller's *Don Carlos* he is unimpressed. Tonio's awkward attempts at love are equally unsuccessful; he admires Ingeborg Holm, the blond daughter of the local doctor, but is humiliated in her presence through an incident at a dancing-school.

The second section transpires in Munich a number of years later. Tonio, now a young man, goes to visit his friend Lisabeta Ivanovna, a talented young painter. He pours out his inner torments and feelings of inadequacy to her, but she refuses to accept him as a fellow artist. She tells him he is a *bourgeois manqué,* a hopeless misfit who can never hope to escape his middle-class background.

In the third section Tonio, restless and disillusioned, returns to his old home town, where he is almost arrested as a vagabond (symbol of the bourgeois society's rejection of the artist it has produced). He then wanders off on a trip to Denmark. He puts up at a remote country hotel where, by an unfortunate coincidence, Hans Hansen and Ingeborg Holm arrive, evidently on their wedding trip. Tonio, in despair, realizes that he belongs neither to the conventional society of Hans and Ingeborg nor to the bohemian cénacle of Lisabeta; he is condemned to wander, forever homeless, between two worlds.

Der Tod in Venedig (Death in Venice, novella, 1913) is a more complex tale; the various strands are interwoven so skillfully as to be almost imperceptible. Gustave von Aschenbach, a successful German writer whose career somewhat resembles Mann's own, comes to Venice, world-weary and bored, in search of some interest or excitement which will stimulate him to creation. There, almost without his knowing it, he falls in love with Tadzio, a beautiful Polish youth he encounters playing on the beach. Aschenbach is infatuated to the point of insanity; he culls allusions from Homer and Plato to justify his passion, and contrives an elaborate system for watching the boy without being detected. When he is warned that cholera is spreading through Venice, he stays on, reckless of his own fate, and is seized with the fatal disease as he sits on the beach watching Tadzio, who seems to beckon to him from the waves.

Tadzio, of course, is a symbol of death, of evil, and of degeneration, a satanic force which attracts Aschenbach in spite of the admonition of his reason. In addition to the antithesis between reason and vice, there are many similar dichotomies in the story. Youth is contrasted with age, Southern Europe to Teutonic Europe, classicism to modern Christianity, and love is contrasted to death—or rather the subtle and antagonistic connection between love and death is symbolically demonstrated. *Death in Venice* is the most decadent of Mann's works, and at the same time one of the most powerful and convincing.

Buddenbrooks (novel, 1901) is a long and heavily documented work somewhat influenced by French naturalism. The novel demonstrates the decline of a German merchant family through four generations. In 1835 the clan, headed by the old grain merchant Johann Buddenbrook, is prosperous and vigorous; it dominates the political and economic life of the town. But the strain soon begins to weaken and degenerate. Johann's son Thomas dabbles in aesthetics and philosophy, and his brother Christian relapses into insanity. The line eventually ends in little Hanno, a delicate and sensitive "artist type" who dies of the typhus. The Buddenbrook clan, having declined from the vigor of Johann, the "self-made man," to the total decadence of aestheticism, passes from the scene and is replaced by another more vigorous line.

Buddenbrooks is infinitely more complex than the usual naturalistic novel. There are many interlinking motifs and symbols which appear again and again throughout the action. It stands apart from the usual naturalistic saga of heredity as well by its subtle presentation of character and by the sensitive and perceptive understanding with which Mann analyses his more refined characters. *Buddenbrooks* was said to be the most popular of Mann's works in Germany before Hitler.

Der Zauberberg (The Magic Mountain; novel, 1924) is partly a *Bildungsroman* or novel of personal development and partly a philosophical allegory. Hans Castorp, a young German engineer, comes to a tuberculosis sanitorium at Davos in the Swiss Alps to visit his cousin. Although he plans to stay only three weeks, he discovers traces of the disease in himself and is forced to remain for seven years. In the intellectual microcosm of the sanitorium Castorp discovers a world of idea and spirit of whose existence he had previously been unaware. Each of the persons who influence him during his stay is a carefully-chosen personification of some broader force; at the end of his stay Castorp has come into contact with every aspect of European culture, and has become a synthesis of these opposing forces. The chief influences on his development are as follows:

(1) His erotic awakening, accomplished first through his immature love for Pribislav Hippe and later through his attraction to the fascinating Russian patient Clavdia Chauchat. Clavdia, red-headed, wilful and erotic, yet intelligent, well personifies Mann's concept of the attraction of a sensual love, evil and yet quasi-divine. Clavdia may also be interpreted as a personification of the Slavic east, one of the chief exterior influences on Germany (personified in Castorp). It is noteworthy also that Castorp, like Mann, thinks of sexual love as connected with disease or even as a disease itself.

(2) Settembrini, an eccentric Italian scholar, is the *Homo humanus,* the personification of humanism, clarity, rationalism, and the bourgeois libertarianism of the eighteenth century. Settembrini is the opponent both of the mystic sensualism of the east (Clavdia) and of the irrationalism of Naphta (see below).

(3) The philosopher Naphta, Jewish by birth but Jesuit-educated, is the *Homo dei,* a personification of mysticism, the irrational, the

romantic, medievalism, passion, and death. Mann is particularly interested in this tendency because of its ambiguity; it is present both in his own personality and in the mystique of German Nazism. Yet Naphta is no Nazi; his attitude is more subtle, more highly intellectualized, and he proves the winner in most of the arguments he conducts with Settembrini. In the sense that the sanitorium is a microcosm of Germany, this amounts to a prediction by Mann that the irrational and demonic will triumph over the rational in German culture.

(4) The psychoanalyst Krokowski, like Naphta, is one of the "apostles of darkness"; he explores a hidden and none too savory region in the human mind. Mann's tacit disapproval of Krokowski is obvious. Yet it should be noted that he condemns the psychoanalyst as a man rather than psychoanalysis as a system; indeed Mann propounds psychoanalytic concepts positively elsewhere in the book. Another medical man who influences Castorp is Hofrat Behrens, the physician in charge of the sanitorium, who introduces him to the splendors and intricacies of the human body. Behrens is a complex figure; scientific detachment is mingled with avarice and cynicism in his character.

The climax of Castorp's education, and the integration of these influences, occurs in the episode titled "Snow" in Chapter V. Wandering alone on skis in a snowstorm, he becomes drowsy and experiences a mythological dream in which he visits the serene and voluptuous "People of the Sun"—obviously the classical Greeks. Castorp at first perceives the Apollonian aspect of Hellenic culture, the moderation and serenity of their life in the sunshine amid beautiful objects of art. Passing into a temple, however, he discovers the underlying Dionysian element: grotesque and evil priestesses are engaged in dismembering the corpse of a child. This revelation of the brutal and elemental forces underlying civilization and art serves to complete Castorp's intellectual development and to climax the theme of antitheses previously seen in Settembrini-Naphta and Pribislav-Clavdia. Castorp now realizes the significance of man's struggle with nature, both within his own body and without in the external world. As the novel ends the author hints that Castorp is killed in the First World War; yet he dies in full understanding of his position in the universe, and his engagement with death is a sort of victory.

Joseph und seine Brüder (Joseph and his Brothers; novel tetralogy,

1933-44) consists of *Die Geschichten Jaakobs* (translated as *Joseph and his Brothers*, 1933), *Der junge Joseph* (*Young Joseph*, 1934), *Joseph in Aegypten* (*Joseph in Egypt*, 1938), and *Joseph, der Ernährer* (*Joseph the Provider*, 1944). Mann, attracted to the subject when he was asked to write a commentary on a set of pictures illustrating the life of Joseph, at first planned a short novella. The project eventually expanded into a tetralogy of over 2,100 pages.

The plot is built around the framework of the story as related in *Genesis* XXXff. The first volume begins with a "Prelude" in which Mann sketches out the mythological themes of the work (see below). The remainder of the volume is devoted to the story of Jacob and other predecessors of Joseph. The hero himself is introduced as a talented *Wunderkind* who has intense religious and psychological insights; his "Freudian" dreams are a particularly important source of his wisdom. Betrayed by his brothers, he is taken from the pit into which they cast him by a Midianite merchant and eventually sold into bondage in Egypt. There he becomes a servant of Potiphar, who in contrast to the Biblical characterization is shown as a highly complex, cultivated, and sympathetic character. Joseph is tempted by Eni or Mut, the wife of Potiphar; he stirs in her an almost maternal passion which overcomes her natural chastity and reserve. Rejected, she accuses Joseph before her husband; but he, civilized and lenient, condemns the youth to a quite nominal imprisonment under pleasant conditions. In the last volume Joseph, called before the Pharaoh (the historical Amenhotep IV, also known as Ikhnaton), uses his power of dream to assist the monarch in a program of social welfare, and achieves fame through forestalling the seven-year famine.

This plot, however, is only the framework of the tetralogy; its real interest lies in its presentation of mythological themes. Mann published essays on Freud in 1929 and 1936; during this era he also became interested in Jung's theory of archetypes, Goethe's concept of primal types, and Nietzsche's idea of the Eternal Return. These four thinkers share a belief that there is a tendency to recurrence in the myths of mankind; Jung defined the archetype as a myth (e.g. the Adonis-Tammuz pattern of death and rebirth) which seems to break out in parallel form in many cultures. The story of Joseph is taken as an archetypical situation, and many minor archetypes are interwoven into the plot. Some of the mythical elements of the tetralogy are as follows:

(1) The Adonis-Tammuz-Osiris situation: the hero dies and is perpetually resurrected, usually in a manner connected with sexual reproduction and the renewal of life. Joseph himself, thrown into the pit, "dies" and is "resurrected" by the Midianite merchant. Later he discovers the same myth in the story of the Egyptian Osiris.

(2) The brother-feud, a Freudian situation in which one blood brother kills another out of jealousy. Examples treated in the tetralogy are Cain-Abel, Jacob-Esau, Isaac-Ishmael, the Egyptian god-brothers Osiris and Set, and Joseph himself attacked by his own brothers. In some cases the murder is not actually carried out, but its Freudian significance is no less important.

(3) The Eternal Mother concept, in which an older woman appears to a young man simultaneously as lover and as mother—i.e. the Oedipus Complex. The mystical concept of the renewal of life is involved. The chief example is the incident of Joseph and Mut.

(4) The mythical significance of the dream as a revealer of archetypes. Joseph is presented as a "moon-wanderer," an intuitive dreamer adept at "moon-grammar" or mystical insight. Many dreams containing Freudian symbols are recounted.

In structure the work unites these many complex themes in a pattern akin to musical composition, a technique Mann was to explore more fully in *Doktor Faustus* (see below).

Lotte in Weimar (translated as *The Beloved Returns;* novel, 1939) utilizes the figures of Goethe and several of his contemporaries to form an unusual novel of psychological analysis. In 1772 the young Goethe, studying law in Wetzlar, fell in love with Charlotte (Lotte) Buff, who was informally engaged to a young official named Kestner. Although Charlotte necessarily rejected Goethe's love, the three remained friends until his departure from Wetzlar. From this experience Goethe constructed the novel *The Sorrows of Young Werther,* one of the most successful works of his early period. Years later, in 1816, Lotte, now Charlotte Kestner, paid a visit to the aging Goethe at Weimar. Around this incident is built Mann's novel.

When Charlotte, a widow and mother of nine children, comes to Weimar her memories of her youth are awakened, and in spite of herself she feels some resentment toward Goethe for his part in the affair. In 1772 his love had been the greater, yet this had not pre-

vented him from making opportunistic use of his emotions; he had
utilized the affair as material for the novel which brought him his
first fame. But to Goethe this seems only natural; an artist must
utilize all the deepest emotions of his own life if his art is to achieve
authenticity. Thus one of the themes of the novel: that to the artist
the line between life and art is an amorphous one which must be
crossed continually.

Her arrival at Weimar causes a temporary nostalgia to invade
Charlotte which for a time almost conquers her resentment over
Goethe's making literary use of the Wetzlar affair; for a moment she
is half in love with the Goethe she remembers from her youth. But
she soon learns that the past cannot be recaptured; Goethe is now a
personage, surrounded by toadies and admirers and genially distinguished in manner. Also present at Weimar, however, is August,
Goethe's young son by his wife Christine (née Vulpius). To Charlotte the figure of August is curiously ambivalent: she sees in him
the Goethe of 1772, yet he seems to her like her own son, a child
born of the unconsummated love Goethe bore for her. Likewise
Goethe himself, somewhat stirred by the news of the arrival of his
old love, nevertheless sees the eternal Lotte incorporated in August's
young blonde fiancée; here again is the concept of the recurrence of
experience which Mann utilized in the *Joseph* series. Reminded of
each other, both Goethe and Charlotte feel they are reliving an old
experience, yet each feels the other has changed, grown old, respectable, and uninteresting.

The technique of the novel is one of gradual revealment. Goethe
is not presented directly until the seventh chapter, when he emerges
in a long internal monologue. In style this chapter, the most original
one of the novel, resembles the stream-of-consciousness technique of
Joyce or Virginia Woolf. Mann uses fragments and quotations from
Goethe's works, well known to German readers, to give the poet's
thoughts an air of authenticity. The climax of the action is the dinner
given by Goethe to celebrate Frau Kestner's visit. Defending himself
before Charlotte's reproaches, he protests that if she has been damaged
by their love like a moth drawn into a flame, he as the candle has
been equally consumed; this image is drawn from Goethe's lyric
"Holy Longing." Thus the final theme is introduced: the poet is eter-

nally consumed by his creative activity and must be constantly reborn in other bodies. As Charlotte departs, the novel ends on a conciliatory note consistent with Goethe's known character in his old age.

Die vertauschten Köpfe (*The Transposed Heads;* short novel, 1940) is a work of virtuosity rather than a major statement; Mann himself refers to it as a "metaphysical jest." However it is among the most engaging of his works; his talent as a story-teller and his skill in irony are here most apparent. The story, an adaptation of an Indian myth, concerns a voluptuous maiden, Sita, who loves two youths, Shridaman (symbol of spirit) and Nanda (symbol of flesh or life). As a result of her "Freudian" wish to incorporate both these qualities in a single lover, the heads of the youths become exchanged; "spirit" is governed by the mind of "life" and vice versa. In relation to Mann's other work Shridaman stands for rationality and Nanda for instinct or passion; this repeats Mann's favorite antithesis.

Doktor Faustus (novel, 1947) is the major work of Mann's later period. It purports to be the biography of Adrian Leverkühn, a German composer who dies in 1940, related by his friend Serenus Zeitblom. The account is written during the closing years of the Second World War, but Adrian's career is covered from 1885 to 1930, when he becomes incurably insane. Leverkühn is a tragic genius who renounces normal human life to devote himself fervently to his music. He contracts a real or symbolic pact with the Devil by which he is to achieve his artistic goals and create whatever he wishes, provided only that he never experiences human love. Willful and passionate, Leverkühn contracts syphilis in his youth in an almost deliberate act of folly; he seems to feel subconsciously that the disease will heighten his artistic sensitivity. When he dies his goals are achieved, yet he has paid a terrible price for his triumph.

This apparently discursive narrative is actually one of the most intricately constructed of Mann's novels. Many themes are introduced and interwoven as the novel proceeds. The chief thematic threads to be noted are as follows:

(1) The novel is a political allegory; Leverkühn's career parallels the history of Germany from 1870 to 1940. He becomes insane in 1930, approximately the era of the emergence of Nazism, and dies in 1940 with the onset of the Blitzkrieg. Germany too, to gain its

place in the sun, has signed a pact in blood with the "Devil" (Nazism) and is later sacrificed to this bargain. Much of the description of Adrian's character must be interpreted as analysis of the German temper of the twentieth century.

(2) The Faust legend is presented in modern dress. Mann bypasses the optimistic Goethian version of the story to go back to the weird and romantic medieval *Faustbuch*. Both Faust and Leverkühn dabble in theology in their youths; both sign a compact with the Devil, and in both lives love is followed by tragedy and death. The climax of the novel, the final interview of Leverkühn with his friends in a Bavarian lodge, is taken directly from the *Faustbuch*. Other details, down to the Faustian poodle, are copied with fidelity. As in the *Joseph* series, here again Mann makes use of the Eternal Recurrence concept of Jung and Nietzsche.

(3) On the personal level Leverkühn's story involves the problem of the artist vs. society. Adrian, a highly creative, demonic personality, rebels against stable bourgeois society. Yet he cannot leave it entirely behind; Zeitblom, in many respects a symbol of German respectability, remains his friend all his life. The Artist, personified in Adrian, is condemned to inevitable unhappiness; cut off from normal human intercourse, he is sacrificed to his art, which can never be a wholly adequate substitute for the love and understanding of his fellow humans. Yet his unhappy ecstasy is of a higher order than the complacent contentment of the bourgeois. Among the artists who allegedly influenced the portrait of Leverkühn in this respect are Nietzsche (who is also said to have contracted syphilis deliberately, and whose death parallels Adrian's), Beethoven, Hugo Wolf, Gustav Mahler, and Schönberg, who like Leverkühn invented a new multitonal musical scale.

(4) Technical discussion of music plays a large part in the novel. There are many discussions of musical works, both the imaginary compositions of Leverkühn and the actual work of Bach, Haydn, Chopin, and Beethoven. A noteworthy example is the discussion of Beethoven's piano sonata opus 111 in Chapter VIII. Structurally the novel is based on a musical, almost symphonic pattern. Themes are introduced in the early chapters, restated as the action proceeds, and combined and integrated in the climax of the novel. Mann throughout his career associates music with rebellion, insanity, violence, irrational-

ity, and the demonic personality; thus it was natural for him to choose
a musician as the hero of a tragedy.

The somewhat pedantic Gymnasium professor Zeitblom relates the
novel in a pedestrian, sometimes convoluted style. The pace of the
novel increases toward the end in a quasi-musical climax.

Many names in the novel are significant. Zeitblom ("flower of his
time") suggests a complacent bourgeois who accepts the conventions
of society; his first name is Serenus. Leverkühn ("keen in liver")
apparently alludes to the medieval theory of the liver as the seat of
passions and lusts.

The Holy Sinner (in German *Der Erwählte;* novel, 1951) is an
ingenious and witty parody of the medieval romance, based partly
on the verse epos *Gregorius vom Stein* by the Middle High German
poet Hartmann von Aue (ca. 1165-1210), who in turn borrowed his
legend from the French. The hero, Gregorius or Grigorss, is born of
the incestuous union between noble-born twins in the castle of Beaure-
paire, in Flanders. His life is a series of ludicrous coincidences and
implausible triumphs: he is set adrift in a boat, rescued by an abbot
who educates and rears him, travels to Flanders where he unwittingly
marries his own mother (thus going Oedipus one better by becoming
his own father's brother-in-law), discovers his colosssal sin and retreats in horror to a hermit's rock, and is at last chosen Pope by divine
revelation. The tale is related by Clemens the Irishman, a garrulous
monk who interlards his narrative with snatches of Norman, Middle
High German, Anglo-Saxon, and liturgical Latin. The novel is one of
Mann's wittiest and most sparkling works; the best parts of it resemble
Rabelais or Sterne. The chief technique used is that of parody; Mann
makes medieval society appear ridiculous by exaggerating its more
ludicrous literary conventions. Another interpretation is that the novel
is a semi-serious mythical treatment of certain human archetypes:
e.g., the Oedipus complex. The English translation by H. T. Lowe-
Porter is ingenious and accurate.

*Bekenntnisse des Hochstaplers Felix Krull (The Confessions of Felix
Krull, Confidence Man;* the novel, 1954) is a loose, wandering story
of a young rogue, swindler, cheat, which makes use of and parodies
at least three traditions of the novel, the picaresque, the confessional
and the *bildungsroman* or developmental narrative. Above all it is a
great comic novel. After having presented the artist in many guises,

as violinist, novelist, magician, composer, hero, and priest, we have here a portrait of the artist as a young thief or charlatan.

Felix (the happy born, "of finer clay") makes an art of fraud. Above all the costume boy likes to play roles, to assume disguises. Mann himself seems to be confessional, to be playing the role of Felix whose adventures stop abruptly but joyously in Portugal at the age of twenty in 1895 (Mann's own age at the time) although he is writing from the perspective of forty and retirement, a forced retirement one gathers. There are all sorts of artists who practice deception in this account: from the father of Felix, Engelbert Krull, who manufactured cheap, unpalatable German champagne but marketed it in handsome bottles with gilt cords, silver wire and foil around the compressed corks and a handsome label with a female figure clad only in bangles and necklaces announcing *Loreley extra cuvée;* his godfather, the painter Schimmelpreester (high priest of mould and corruption), for whom young Felix modeled; perhaps most important of all the actor-singer, Müller-Rose, to whom his father introduced him, and who knew the art of transfiguring his pustule covered body by greasepaint and costume and gesture into charm and fame and applause.

After his father's bankruptcy and suicide, Felix moves with his mother from his childhood home near Mainz to Frankfurt. On the godfather's advice the mother starts a small boarding hourse, older sister Olympia goes to the music halls for a theatrical career, and Felix, after ingeniously avoiding compulsory military service at eight-een by a prodigious display of epileptoid symptoms all the while declaring his fitness for service, goes to Paris to become an elevator boy and subsequently a waiter at the Saint James and Albany Hotel. He is happy at this point to change his name to Armand at the direc-tor's request. At customs inspection on the train to Paris he had stolen a box of jewelry from a wealthy lady, the writer Diane Philibert, whose husband Houpflé has made his money manufacturing toilets in Strassburg. As a guest of the hotel, Diane makes a play for Armand in his handsome lift-boy's uniform, and she is delighted when she finds out he's a thief, a perfect Hermes. She insists on pretending to be violated and on his stealing more. Building up a bank account Armand permits himself to lead judiciously a double life, waiter giv-ing perfect service at the Saint James and sometimes customer at the

Grand Hotel des Ambassadeurs with a perfect air of *noblesse oblige*.

One of the regular patrons of the Saint James dining room, the young Marquis Louis de Venosta from Luxemburg whose parents arrange for him to take a world tour to forget his girl friend, Zaza, persuades Armand-Felix to take the trip in his place, and assuming his name, Felix plays the role of Marquis Loulou with perfection and quiet joy. In the dining car of the train to Lisbon, the first stop on the tour, Armand-Felix-Venosta meets Professor Kuckkuck, Paleontologist, Director of the Museum of Natural History in Lisbon, and the founder of that institution. During the dinner conversation and later at the museum Felix senses that it is in astrophysics, comparative evolution, paleontology, and microbiology that we may find our future myths and the terms of our metaphors. He is excited by the theory of three spontaneous generations: the emergence of Being out of Nothingness, the awakening of Life out of Being, and the birth of Man. What was added when Man emerged was the knowledge of Beginning and End. In Lisbon Felix is a great success. He has an audience with the king and receives a medal from him, honors highly pleasing to Loulou's aristocratic family in Luxemburg. He climaxes his adventures by making love to Zouzou (short for Susanna), Kuckkuck's daughter, and almost simultaneously achieving intimacy with her mother, the majestic Iberian, Dona Maria Pia, who shouts "Holé" as she rushes into his arms, the perfect way to go.

Felix Krull as a novel is not as somber as Herman Melville's *The Confidence Man;* it is more consequential than Thackeray's *Barry Lyndon;* yet it suggests an interesting comparison with both. Critics have noted a possible parody of Goethe's *Dichtung und Wahrheit*. It is youthful in tone, and written by a man who seems to grow younger as he grows older, much like the effect of Yeats' late poetry. One reviewer of Mann's last novel noted that the writer seems to be making merry at the expense of his own magic but fortunately he also makes magic out of his merriment.

Heinrich Mann (German, 1871-1950)

There are many parallels between the careers of Heinrich Mann and his more famous brother Thomas. Both were strongly influenced by their conservative and traditional family background in the Hanseatic

trading city of Lübeck; both inherited a romantic strain from their
mother, and both as novelists are concerned with the situation of the
artist torn between the demands of his creativity and the inhibitions
inherited from his middle-class background. Heinrich, however, is
even more extreme in his antagonism toward bourgeois culture. Radically humanistic and individualistic in personality, he has demonstrated
himself to be a courageous anti-fascist in public life. Like his brother,
he went into voluntary exile after the advent of Nazism in 1933; he
lived for a time in Nice, and eventually settled in the United States.
During his exile he was active in anti-fascist work; he held the office
of President of the World Committee Against War and Fascism, and
contributed to several other such activities. He visited Germany in
1949, but returned after a short stay to California, where he died in
1950.

WORK: Heinrich Mann's fictional satire is directed, not against
Nazism, which is perhaps too close to his own experience, but against
the mores of the German Empire in the period before 1914. In *Das
Kaiserreich* (novel trilogy, 1914-25) he drew a caustic picture of
prewar Germany including portraits of living statesmen and officials.
The trilogy is actually a record of an age in the style of Dos Passos'
U.S.A. rather than a conventional work of fiction. The chief works
produced during Mann's period of exile were the two historical novels
on the life of the seventeenth-century French King Henry IV: *Die
Jugend des Königs Henri Quatre,* (1935) translated as *Young Henry
of Navarre;* and *Die Vollendung des Königs Henri Quatre* (1938),
translated as *Henry, King of France.*

Heinrich Mann's best-known work, however, is the novel *Professor
Unrat* (1904), translated as *Small Town Tyrant.* This story achieved
an enormous popular success and was made into a motion picture,
The Blue Angel, which introduced Marlene Dietrich to the cinema
public. The novel is a tragic and biting satire on two separate aspects
of the society of the Kaiserreich; the supercilious arrogance of the
Gymnasiumprofessor class, and the hypocritical virtue of middle-class
morality. The protagonist, Professor Raat, is a pompous secondary-
school teacher whose name suggests the German word *Unrat*—"garbage" or "rubbish" (the connotation is conveyed in English translation
by calling the Professor Dr. Gaubage). The Professor, whatever his
name, is an insufferable tyrant. Unsatisfied with browbeating his pupils

in the classroom, he maintains a rigid supervision over the morality of their private lives. This activity leads him into an investigation of a music-hall actress named Rosa Fröhlich (literally "gay") who he rightfully suspects is exerting an undesirable influence over several of his students. He resolves to chastise Rosa for this in the name of his academic prestige. But the wily and seductive Rosa soon dazzles him into helplessness; he becomes madly infatuated with her and is covered with ridicule when his students and the townsfolk learn of the affair. Soon his career is destroyed; he marries Rosa and runs off with her on a wild excursion through Europe. At length they return to establish an eccentric ménage in the very town where the Professor has formerly taught; they set up a sort of amateur gambling den and house of pleasure, and the Professor amuses himself tormenting his former pupils when their gambling losses lead them into debt with him. But Rosa betrays him; he is desperately ineffectual and unhappy, and at length turns to petty crime and is led off to jail. The Professor, an insufferably stiff and arrogant character in the early pages of the novel, becomes through his degeneration a pathetic and moving figure.

Jacinto Benavente y Martínez (Spanish, 1866-1954)

Benavente is the chief Spanish dramatist of the twentieth century. His plays became standard production pieces in Spain in the period before the First World War, and after the Nobel Prize award in 1922 at least two or three of them have found acceptance in the world theatrical repertory.

Benavente's career has passed through several points of transition; in fact his published work is so large and he has participated in so many movements that he is almost impossible to classify. His work may nevertheless be grouped roughly into two periods. The first group includes translations, historical dramas, romantic sketches, and satirical comedies written before 1905, and the second group comprises the more mature, serious, and original work written after that date. He has been active in the theatre as a professional playwright, and his life has had little incident apart from his writing career. His best works are the half-realistic, half-romantic social dramas of the type of *La Malquerida* and the fantastic comedies like *The Bonds of Interest* and *The Prince Who Learned Everything Out of Books*. This bifurcation may be compared to a similar one in the work of Ibsen;

La Malquerida is Benavente's *Ghosts,* and the fantasies are his *Peer Gynt.* Benavente is not a radical modernist, although he participated in the liberal movement of '98; he is essentially, like most of the writers in this section, an author of the nineteenth century temper. Certain of his dramas, especially his erotic tragedies, show the influence of modern psychiatry, but the basic conservatism of his style remains unchanged.

Benavente has a high respect for the craft of the artist. "I do not make my plays for the public; I make the public for my plays." At the same time he feels sincerely that drama must be reestablished on a popular basis, even at the cost of subtlety; several of his plays, especially *His Widow's Husband* (comedy, 1908) were deliberately conceived as modern folk dramas. Benavente wrote little of importance after he was awarded the Nobel Prize for Literature in 1922. He died at his home in the Antocho district in Spain in 1954.

CHIEF WORKS: *Los Malhechores del Bien (The Evil Doers of Good;* drama, 1905) is a transitional play, one of Benavente's first productions in his new and more mature manner. The subject is the hypocrisy of organized philanthropy, especially the variety practiced by wealthy old ladies. The Marchioness of Casa Molina, a bigoted and condescending tyrant, exerts a total control over her family and indeed over the lives of the entire village. She forces her niece Teresa into a loveless marriage with the Marquis of San Toribio, a smug Tartuffe old enough to be her father; she browbeats her brother, Don Heliodoro, an eccentric freethinker who is forced to depend on her for charity; and she ruthlessly drives apart a young peasant couple, Nativity and Jesus, because she disapproves of Jesus's gipsy ways. The Marchioness surrounds herself with a coterie of gossiping prudes who flatter her shamelessly and repeat to her, with exaggerations, the more spicy bits of scandal they unearth in the village. At length Teresa and Don Heliodoro revolt against this insufferable tyranny. Their own lives are irremediably ruined, but at least they can do something to save Nativity and Jesus. Teresa tells Nativity how her own life has been smothered by a forced marriage and encourages her to follow her own heart, and Heliodoro provides Jesus with the necessary funds for their elopement. Although Teresa and Heliodoro know they have brought down the rage of the Marchioness upon themselves, they are content to have frustrated her plans in at least this one matter. This drama of moral conflict owes something to Molière, especially to *Tartuffe* and *Le Misanthrope,* as well as to Ibsen's studies of hypocrisy in bourgeois society. Its chief defect is its reliance on set speeches rather than on action to convey its message.

Los Intereses Creados (*The Bonds of Interest;* comedy, 1907) is a farcical fantasy utilizing the stock characters and situations of the Italian *Commedia dell'arte.* Leander and Crispin, a pair of penniless rogues just released from the galleys, come to "an imaginary country" determined to make their fortunes through some sort of genteel rascality. They pretend to be servant and master, and Crispin, boasting of the wealth of his noble employer, secures lodging, fine clothes, and cash for them on credit. At length they enter into a plot to marry Leander to Silvia, the daughter of the wealthy Polichinelle. Aided by the poet Harlequin and the braggart Captain, they insinuate themselves into Polichinelle's household. The plans hit a snag, however, when Leander falls madly in love with the girl he is supposed to seduce. Silvia returns his love, and the two rascals plot to win her from her father by pretending to be beaten up by his minions and raising a mob against his house. At the crucial moment Polichinelle discovers that Crispin and Leander have fled from Bologna to escape justice. He prepares a case against them, and soon invades their apartment accompanied by a comic judge, a bevy of constables, and a great crowd of Leander's creditors. Leander hides, and Crispin extricates the pair from the trap by proving to the creditors that they can hope to collect their debts only if Leander marries Silvia and claims her dowry. The creditors, realizing where their interest lies, clamor for Polichinelle to allow the marriage, and at last he is forced to give in. Leander, refined by his love, confesses the sins of his past and swears to embrace a life of virtue, and only Polichinelle, the miser, is discontent as the curtain falls. *The Bonds of Interest* is not only a witty and entertaining farce, but an interesting revival of a historic dramatic form: the Italian comedy of the XVI century.

La Malquerida (sometimes translated *The Passion Flower;* tragedy, 1913) is a domestic tragedy somewhat resembling Ibsen but marked by a characteristic Spanish intensity. Acacia, the daughter of Raimunda and step-daughter of Esteban, has rejected a passionate suitor, Norbert, and is about to marry Faustino, a young man from a neighboring village. On the eve of their engagement Faustino is ambushed and killed. Suspicion at first falls on Norbert; he is arrested, and even when he is acquitted by the court Tío Eusebio, father of Faustino, swears he and his sons will kill him. Gradually it becomes evident, however, that the actual murderer was one Rubio, a companion of Esteban. Esteban discouraged Acacia's first engagement because he could not bear to think of her leaving the house. He shortly came to realize he was hopelessly in love with her; and when her marriage appeared inevitable, he paid Rubio to murder Faustino. Now he is afraid of the threats of Rubio, who has become the real master of his house. For her part Acacia loathes and detests Esteban, and will not even allow him to embrace her. This, as we shortly see, is because she herself secretly loves him and is fighting desperately against her own passion. In the climactic scene Esteban confesses his love and his crime to Raimunda; Acacia, unable to resist her passion any longer, flings herself into Esteban's arms. A wild struggle breaks out in which Esteban shoots Raimunda and gives himself up to the law; Acacia at the last moment is reconciled with her dying mother. *La Malquerida* is chiefly a study in perverted love, and in the ferocious passions which underlie ordinary family relationships.

Ivan Bunin (Russian, 1870-1953)

Bunin is a realist in the manner of the great nineteenth-century Russian novelists; his literary antecedents are Chekhov, Tolstoy, and Turgenev. Not only is his style detailed and conservative, but his themes are personal and metaphysical rather than social. In this one respect he follows Tolstoy rather than Gorky and the Soviet novelists. His chief work *The Village* has certain satirical elements in it, but it is the Russian soul and indeed all mankind which is satirized rather than any one social class. Bunin was evidently greatly influenced by Ivan Goncharov (1812-91) whose *Oblomov* he imitated in a story, "A Dream of Oblomov's Grandson." In addition he drew inspiration from Western European literature, especially in his youth; he translated Longfellow and read widely in French literature. Thus he is profoundly cosmopolitan in outlook even though he is Russian in temperament. Like Turgenev, he has little patience with the cult of the "Russian soul" and its supposed mystic virtues.

LIFE: Bunin's background is aristocratic. He was born in 1870 to an old and respectable landowning family in Voronezh. He began to write as a student in the University of Moscow; in 1903 he was awarded the Pushkin Prize, and in 1909 he was elected a member of the Academy. He travelled widely in the years before the First World War; many of his stories are laid in Italy. In 1917 he publicly denounced the Revolution and has remained in exile since, eventually settling in Paris. He has been active in emigré circles, although he has produced very little of importance since 1917. In 1933 he was awarded the Nobel Prize for literature. Ivan Alexeyevich Bunin died at the age of eighty-three in Paris of a heart attack.

CHIEF WORKS: *The Village* (Russ. *Derevnya;* novel, 1910), usually considered Bunin's masterpiece, is a novel of rural life greatly resembling Goncharov's *Oblomov,* although it lacks the salty wit of the earlier novel. The narrative centers around the two Krasoff brothers, Tikhon and Kuzma, who live out their lives in the region of the grubby and poverty-stricken village of Durnovka. Tikhon is a mean and grasping storekeeper who browbeats his servants and charges the peasants exorbitant prices for necessities, and his brother Kuzma is an unsuccessful dreamer and wanderer in the tradition of Pushkin's Aleko. Life in the village is completely stupefying; Bunin portrays the peasants, so fondly poetized by Turgenev and Tolstoy, as depraved and stunted beasts too lazy to better their own lot and too selfish to cooperate in opposing the landowners. At the same time *The Village* is not naturalistic. The details, however moving, are never shocking or distasteful, and there are many passages of a high lyrical beauty. A notable scene is the seduction of a servant-girl, "the Bride," by Tikhon; the passage admirably combines Goncharov's pessimism and Tolstoy's transcendental *Weltschmerz.*

The Gentleman from San Francisco (Russ. *Gospodin iz San Frantsisko;* tale, 1915) has been widely translated and reprinted. The theme is similar to that of Tolstoy's *The Death of Ivan Ilyitch;* the resemblance to Mann's *Death in Venice* might also be remarked. The hero, the unnamed "gentleman from San Francisco," dies in Capri in the splendor of a fine hotel, surrounded by his family and a corps of obsequious servants. A moving contrast is drawn between the splendor and wealth of the gentleman's life and the emptiness of his worldly gains when he is at last confronted by death. The gentleman, for all his dollars and power, is at last packed into a tarred box and shipped back to America like any other piece of freight, half-forgotten even by his family.

Sigrid Undset (Norwegian, 1882-1949)

Sigrid Undset is known in America and England mainly for *Kristin Lavransdatter,* and she is thus thought of chiefly as a writer of historical novels. But her approach is far from the romantic escapism of the commercial historical novel of our time. Her attitude toward human life is essentially a realistic one, and her method is the careful and penetrating documentation of the psychological realist. In technique *Kristin Lavransdatter* resembles Tolstoy's *Anna Karenina* more than it does any twentieth-century novel, and there are even some parallels in content: both novels are concerned with relations between man and woman, both center about the heroine, and both take a broadly tolerant but conservative attitude toward sexual mores.

Sigrid Undset has little sympathy with the liberal, socialistic, and feminist ideas of the twentieth century. She is not a political reactionary, but she is a deeply feminine personality who feels that the results of political agitation are seldom worth the misery they cause. It is Elend's vain effort to revolt against what he considers an evil regime that wrecks the marriage of Elend and Kristin; and it is only Kristin's warm feminine sympathy and her ability to transcend political strife that rebuild the marriage in the end. Sigrid Undset is the antithesis of Ibsen, and her heroines inevitably revert back to an age before the time when Ibsen and his plays helped them to revolt.

In style the typical Undset novel is a subtle mixture of external documentation and internal psychology. Sigrid Undset is no naturalist, nor does she affect the complete objectivity of a realist such as Flaubert. At the same time she is not a writer of psychological woman-novels in the manner of Virginia Woolf or Katherine Mansfield. Her novels are copiously documented, and her heroines live a detailed and complex external life in addition to their mental existence. Here again the best comparison is that with Tolstoy, whose novels are closely detailed but who is chiefly interested in inner conflicts. In plot Sigrid Undset is refreshingly original; she seems to be entirely unaffected by the hackneyed conventions of the popular love-novel. In *Kristin Lavransdatter* the love affair of Kristin and Elend goes well in the first years of their marriage, then turns sour after several children have been born; this reverses the usual formula of love triumphing over obstacles. It is true that the pair eventually come to a reconciliation, but the author contrives this not to finish off the plot but because she believes the power of female affection is greater than the power of male pride.

LIFE: Sigrid Undset was born in Denmark in 1882 of a distinguished family of intellectuals; her father was an eminent Norwegian professor and archeologist and her mother a Danish gentlewoman. Her parents, mistrusting the liberal coeducational schools of the time, sent her to board with a private tutor, Mme. Ragna Nielsen. From this lady the young Sigrid derived inspiration and encouragement, although Mme. Nielsen was disappointed in her plans for a university and scientific career for her pupil. The death of Sigrid's father reduced the family to poverty, and she was forced to struggle for her own living in an engineering office. This she did until 1907, when the success of her first novel, *Fru Martha Oulie,* determined her to continue in a literary career. From 1907 to 1911 she continued in the vein of her first book: these early works are simple and realistic, in sharp contrast to the Neo-romanticism of Scandinavian letters of the day. Her first historical novel, *Vigaljot og Vigdis* (translated as *Gunnar's Daughter*) appeared in 1909. Thenceforth she continued to turn out novels at a slow but steady rate, all the time working toward the personal style which was to emerge triumphant in *Kristin Lavransdatter.* She married in 1911; her husband was A. C. Starsvad, a Norwegian painter. Three children resulted from this union, which she raised along with her husband's three children from a former marriage. From 1920 to 1922 she published sections of her masterpiece, the trilogy *Kristan Lavransdatter,* and in 1928 she was awarded a Nobel Prize for this work. In its citation the Swedish Academy rightfully termed her the leading female Scandinavian writer of the century. In 1924 occurred another turning point in her life: Sigrid Undset, who had struggled for years with an uneasy agnosticism, was received into the Catholic Church. This event completed her evolution toward self-realization and climaxed the essentially conservative and emotional tendencies which had grown throughout her career.

Divorced in 1922, she lived in her own home at Lillehammer, Norway until 1940, when the Second World War forced her to Sweden and thence to America. She returned to Norway after the war. Sigrid Undset died in her home in Lillehammer in the late spring of 1949 and was given a State funeral in recognition of the influence of her writings. Although she wrote more than thirty other books of fiction and non-fiction after *Kristin Lavransdatter,* this trilogy remains her most conspicuous success. It gives a sense of the continuity of history and more importantly the nobility of human beings.

CHIEF WORKS: Although a large number of Sigrid Undset's works have been translated into English, the only one to enjoy a wide popularity is *Kristin Lavransdatter* (novel trilogy, 1920-22). The action is laid in Norway in the fourteenth century. The first novel, *The Bridal Wreath,* tells the story of Kristin's courtship and marriage. Marked by her father to marriage with Simon Andressön, a neighboring farmer, Kristin nevertheless falls in love with the dashing Elend Nikulaussön. The lovers are often separated, but at last Simon and Kristin's father, Lavrans Björgulfsön, agree grudgingly to the marriage.

The Mistress of Husaby follows the young couple through the first fifteen years of their married life. Kristin bears seven sons, including a pair of twins, and learns to manage her husband's estate of Husaby while Elend engages in military and political intrigues. Kristin sometimes feels a pang of conscience to think that her marriage has been built on the misery of Simon and the anger of her father, and soon this sin is punished in God's own way. Elend, resentful against a corrupt and inefficient monarchy, becomes involved in a treasonable plot against the crown. He is arrested and tried for his life, and escapes only after surrendering all his lands to the state. Thenceforth he is forced to live on the bounty of Kristin, who has inherited the small farm of Jörundgaard from her father.

The Cross, the final novel of the trilogy, concerns the new life of Kristin, Elend, and their sons at Jörundgaard. Kristin is forced to labor unceasingly to make both ends meet, and Elend is bitterly resentful against the fate which has made him dependent on a woman. At last Elend runs away to a mountain lodge where he can cherish his pride in isolation. After some time Kristin, compassionate and forgiving, visits Elend to try to persuade him to return. He refuses, but a son is born to Kristin of this meeting. Kristin, who is known not to be living with her husband, is accused of adultery with her steward Ulf. Lavrans, a son, rides to warn Elend of this crisis, and the husband returns to defend his wife. Her name is vindicated, but Elend dies in a brawl with the calumniators. Later, after the marriage of her sons, Kristin turns over her estate to her son Gaute and his wife Jofrid and enters a convent. There she dies in an epidemic of the Black Plague.

The predominant theme of the trilogy is the contrast between the warm, understanding feminine nature of Kristin and the foolish masculine pride and pugnacity of her husband. From Elend's "heroism" arise all the travails of their life together, and from Kristin's femininity come all the rewards.

4. TWENTIETH-CENTURY NATURALISTS

The naturalistic movement, which reached its climax in continental Europe around 1890 but continued to exert an influence well into the twentieth century, arose chiefly out of an endeavor to apply to literature the method of the physical and social sciences. Although naturalism is foreshadowed in the work of Stendhal, Balzac, Ibsen, and others, the school properly speaking was established by Emile Zola (1840-1902), who not only laid down the theoretical basis for naturalistic literature but proceeded to follow his own precepts by creating some of the chief naturalistic works of the nineteenth century.

Zola, inspired by Claude Bernard's *Introduction to the Study of Experimental Medicine* (1865) and by Hippolyte Taine's deterministic and socio-eugenic theories, published in 1880 *The Experimental Novel,* a long essay or manifesto calling for the creation of a new scientific literature. The influence of heredity upon characters was to be demonstrated with a scientific exactitude; literature was to observe and record life rather than to interpret it or to create a world of the imagination. Vice and virtue were "products like sugar and vitriol"; they were to be utilized as a chemist uses reagents for the discovery of scientific truth. In his *Rougon-Macquart* series Zola actually created a vast cycle of novels dissecting the rise, triumph, and degeneration of a single family and the operation of the principles of heredity on its members. Several units of this cycle, especially *L'Assommoir* (*The Dram-Shop,* 1877), *Nana* (1880), *Germinal* (1885), and *La Terre* (*Earth,* 1887) must be classed along with the greatest novels of the nineteenth century. The cycle, comprising twenty volumes in all, was widely imitated in the twentieth century.

Around Zola formed a school of young authors determined to exterminate the literature of the past and create an idiom "worthy of the age of the locomotive." Edmond de Goncourt (1822-96) and Jules de Goncourt (1830-70), Alphonse Daudet (1840-97), and Henry Becque (1837-99) produced work of first rank, and the circle also included many minor literary figures. The dramatic headquarters of the movement was the Théâtre Libre, an experimental theatre group managed by a former gas-company employee, André Antoine. During a seven-year period from 1887 to 1894 this group produced a hundred and twenty-four new plays, many of them destined to earn a permanent place in world literature.

Spreading from France, the naturalistic movement reached its height in Germany and Russia around the turn of the century; Arno Holz, Gerhart Hauptmann, and Maxim Gorky became the champions about whom the disciples rallied. In the Anglo-Saxon countries the movement caught on somewhat more slowly. Although Thomas Hardy and George Gissing are sometimes considered naturalists, English literature during the fin-de-siècle was actually dominated by the Pre-Raphaelite revival and by the "cult of decadence" of Swinburne and Wilde. The height of British naturalism was to occur in the twentieth century with John Galsworthy and his contemporaries. In America the movement was heralded by Frank Norris (1870-1902) and by Theodore Dreiser, who published his first novel in 1900, but it reached its climax only in the period after the First World War.

Eventually American naturalists, particularly Dos Passos and Faulkner in so far as he may be considered naturalistic, were to be important influences on the European novelists of the mid-twentieth century, bringing the impulse and ideas of Zola full circle and adding certain cinematic perspectives.

Naturalism differs from the realism of Flaubert and the great Russian novelists in several aspects, none of which are clear-cut and definitive. It tends to be more doctrinaire in its exposition of pseudo-scientific principles, it is less interested in character and more in the conflict of social forces, and it is concerned to a greater extent with the sordid, the shocking, and the depressing aspects of existence. By these criteria, however, there are naturalistic elements in Dostoyevsky, and Galsworthy and Scott Fitzgerald demonstrate many qualities of typical realists. Some further suggested qualities of literary naturalism are as follows:

(a) Naturalism is scientific or pseudo-scientific in its approach; it attempts to treat human beings as biological pawns rather than agents of free will. The author does not attempt to judge his characters or to comment upon their actions; he merely inserts them into a crucial situation and then pretends to stand back and watch them with the impassivity of the scientist. Although Zola and Martin du Gard apply this principle with some success, it has generally remained a synthetic theory and has only infrequently been applied to actual literary works.

(b) The naturalist attempts to make literature into a document of society. He writes "novel cycles" purporting to cover every aspect of modern life, or creates characters who are personifications of various social classes. Many naturalists gather copious data from actual life and include it in their literary works; they write novels around specific occupations such as railroading or textile manufacturing in which they utilize technical details of the trade for story-interest. This aspect of naturalism represents an attempt to remove literature from the realm of the fine arts into the field of the social sciences.

(c) Because of the above-described documentary nature of naturalism, the technique often involves the conscious suppression of the poetic elements in literature. The prose style is flat, objective, and bare of imagery; it includes copious details and explanations, and is wary of highly literary metaphors. It endeavors to imitate scientific, technical or sociological writing rather than the *belles-lettres* of the past, and in doing so ignores the great part of what is ordinarily considered literary beauty. Like the pseudo-scientific dogma described in (a) above, this quality is often more theoretical than practical. The best naturalists are those who do not totally abandon the literary traditions of the past. On the other hand some naturalists are merely writers lacking in the poetic instinct; they avoid a highly literary prose because they have little feeling for style and imagery. For this reason many naturalistic novels seem gauche and awkwardly written to one familiar with the novels of Tolstoy, Flaubert, or Thackeray.

(d) Naturalistic literature tends to be concerned with the less elegant aspects of life; its typical settings are the slum, the sweatshop, the factory, or the farm. Where the romantic author selects the most pleasant and idealistic elements in his experience, the naturalistic author often seems positively drawn toward the brutal, the sordid, the cruel, and the degraded. This tendency is in part a reaction against earlier literature, especially against the sentimentalism of the Dumas school where vice is invariably made to appear romantic. The real motivating forces in a naturalistic novel are not religion, hope, or human idealism; they are alcohol, filth, disease, and the human instinct toward bestiality.

It will be immediately apparent that there are important exceptions to this principle. Dreiser and Baroja fastidiously avoid shocking detail, Galsworthy's scenes are laid in the middle class, and Scott Fitzgerald prefers to do his slumming at the Ritz.

(e) Naturalism is sometimes, but not always, socialistic or radical in attitude. The sympathy of the typical naturalist lies with the proletariat, and he sees social evolution mainly in terms of the conflict of classes. Industrial strife plays a large part in the naturalistic novel, as does description of the exploitation of the worker, male and female, by the boss. Many critics have held that there is a strong romantic element in naturalism, and the liberalism of the naturalist, when it occurs, tends to be of an intellectual, quixotic, and impassioned variety. In spite of their purported objectivity, in fact, many naturalists seem less detached than angry. Naturalism is the literature of revolt, both political and literary.

A Pathfinder: Henrik Ibsen (Norwegian, 1828-1906)

Ibsen, a key figure in the evolution of modern Scandinavian literature, is important in another aspect as an influence on the broader development of the European realistic and naturalistic movements. He is not a model naturalist as the term later came to be understood, but his importance as a predecessor of later German, British, and American naturalists is great. In Germany and France his work exerted its main effect on the naturalist school in the eighteen-eighties; in England and America his influence was reserved to the period immediately before the First World War. In this era, publicized by Bernard Shaw and others, his dramas excited a tremendous social and literary controversy. Today, after the triumph of feminism and the dying out of chauvinistic Norwegian nationalism, many of his social dramas seem to have lost their point, and he is viewed chiefly as a master of dramatic psychology. Yet his attacks on Philistinism and hypocrisy are just as significant today as they were when they were written.

The most important of Ibsen's plays may be considered in two groups. The first includes the poetic dramas of the period up to his visit to Norway in 1874; *Brand* and *Peer Gynt* are the most important of these. The tone of these early dramas is romantic: the settings are fantastic or exotic, and the characterization tends to be symbolic or allegorical rather than naturalistic. The later social dramas, which actually begin with *The League of Youth* (1869), are written in prose; their settings are contemporary, and they treat naturalistic heroes involved in modern social or political conflicts. The main difference between these two groups of plays is in technique; Ibsen's content is relatively consistent throughout his work. The most important social and philosophical concepts to be found in Ibsen's dramas are as follows:

(1) Ibsen strongly defends the SOVEREIGNTY OF THE INDIVIDUAL, especially his right to develop his personality along its natural lines. In such dramas as *The Wild Duck* and *An Enemy of the People* he speaks out strongly for the individual whose standards are not those of a hypocritical and selfish society. The motto of this attitude is "Be yourself"; the greatest sin for the individual is to betray his nature in an endeavor to become what society wants him to be.

(2) On the other hand Ibsen defends ILLUSORY HAPPINESS against its natural enemy, abstract truth. The philosophy is best expressed in *The Wild Duck,* where the raisonneur Relling argues convincingly that it is only through illusion that life is made bearable. The concept is implied in *Brand,* where the hero brings misery to his family and himself through his fanatic quest for truth. In *Peer Gynt* Ibsen writes, "Truth, when carried to excess, ends in wisdom written backwards." This clarifies the apparent incompatibility with Ibsen's above-mentioned plea for idealism and integrity; it is only when carried to excess that idealism becomes fanaticism.

(3) Ibsen is antagonistic toward MIDDLE-CLASS MORALITY, which in his dramas often takes the form of a malicious persecution of gifted individuals. Bourgeois society, purporting to maintain its ideals of justice. freedom, and equality, is actually interested only in defending its property; it savagely attacks any individual who seems to menace it. The "pillars of society" in Ibsen are stuffed shirts whose wealth

and power has been built on the work of others; thus they subconsciously fear true creativity and idealism when they encounter it. Yet this hatred of the bourgeoisie does not lead Ibsen into socialism; he demonstrates in *The League of Youth* that the ideals of reformers are just as hypocritical as those of capitalists. Criticism of the bourgeoisie is present in most of Ibsen's later work, but it is most obvious in *Pillars of Society, A Doll's House,* and *An Enemy of the People.*

(4) As a champion of FEMINISM Ibsen argues for the liberation of woman from the bonds of middle-class marriage, although his position is by no means identical to that of the organized feminist movement. *A Doll's House* probably did more than any other single literary work to better the social position of women in Europe and America. Yet in *Hedda Gabbler* Ibsen shows the perils which await the emancipated woman in a society which is not ready to accept her. It is the "superior woman," the woman of intellect and imagination, for whom Ibsen battles, but none of his heroines of this type (Nora Helmer, Mrs. Alving, Hedda Gabbler) achieve happiness through their revolt or attempted revolt. Thus Ibsen battles to emancipate woman but fails to offer a convincing picture of her taking her place alongside man and achieving her proper intellectual and social fulfillment. It is here that Ibsen parts company with Bernard Shaw and with the dogma of organized feminism.

LIFE: Henrik Ibsen was born at Skien, Norway, in 1828; his father belonged to that respectable and comfortable merchant class the author was later to attack. Apprenticed to an apothecary, he was frustrated and unhappy, and his sensitive nature rebelled; in his youth he developed that resentment of oppression he was to retain all through his career. His first drama, *Cataline* (published in 1850), was immature in technique but showed the iconoclastic and rebellious tendencies of his later work. In 1850, still undecided whether to pursue a literary career, he accepted an offer to serve as stage manager of the newly-established Norwegian theatre at Bergen. In 1862 he published his first important work, the satirical *Kaerlighedens komedie (Love's Comedy).* Shortly after writing *The Pretenders* (1864) he left his native country for Germany and Italy; he returned to Norway only twice between 1864 and 1891. During this long, voluntary exile Ibsen became familiar with the broad stream of European culture, but remained faithful to his Norwegian background. His foreign residence was a period of great productivity. His best poetic dramas, *Brand* and *Peer Gynt,* appeared in 1866 and 1867 respectively, and most of the major works of his career were written before 1892. Great fame came to him after the publication of his dramas in Europe during the eighties; the production of *Ghosts* and *A Doll's House* provoked violent opposition from religionists and Puritans.

In 1891 Ibsen returned to Norway and took up his residence at Christiania, where he remained until his death. His later dramas, not as well-known as his social-problem plays, are moody and philosophical in tone; *When We Dead Awaken* (1899) is an amorphous allegory of his own career. Stricken with illness in 1901, Ibsen suffered after a time from mental collapse, in which he remained until his death in 1906.

CHIEF DRAMAS: *Brand* (verse drama, 1866) is a study of a fervent idealist who sacrifices himself and those he loves to his fanatic pursuit of perfection. Brand is a Protestant minister who believes that all compromise is the work of Satan. He allows no consideration of personal comfort or safety to halt him; he risks his life crossing the ice in dangerous weather to visit a dying girl, and sallies forth in a storm to bring consolation to a murderer on his deathbed. When a fisherman refuses to accompany him on this second mission a woman, deeply stirred by his idealism, agrees to steer the boat for him; she later becomes his wife. She bears him a child which dies because of the austere conditions in which Brand insists on living; she clings pitifully to the garments of the dead child, but Brand makes her give even these tokens to a needy gypsy. The sorrowing mother, deprived of everything that held her to life, dies of a broken heart.

At last the people, awed by Brand's fervent consecration, recognize him as a saint. But he, ambitious for yet greater spiritual heights, calls upon them to leave their church and come to worship God in the mountains. The people grow tired of his inhuman sternness, and finally come to the point of rejecting him with imprecations and stones. Leaving them, he departs into the mountains, God's own church, and is killed in an avalanche. But before he dies he hears a voice announcing that "God is Love"—the truth he has overlooked in his fanatic devotion to the ideal of perfection.

Peer Gynt (verse drama, 1867) is similar in style but totally different in theme; Peer is an insouciant and blundering rascal who spends all his life running away from reality. When we first meet him his mother Ase is upbraiding him for his worthlessness. He retorts by threatening to run off with a local girl on her wedding night, and when Ase remonstrates he picks her up and sets her on the roof of their house. At the wedding Peer kidnaps the bride as he has threatened; he soon grows tired of her and runs off into the forest where he meets the Trolls, repulsive semi-human elves. He asks to become one of their number, but when the Trolls prepare to slit his eyes (i.e. to make his self-deception and his flight from reality complete) he balks.

After a time Solveig, a girl who has fallen in love with him at the wedding, comes to live with him in the forest. When the Trolls come to menace him over his promise to join their band, he heartlessly abandons Solveig, flees from the forest, and goes to visit his mother, whom he finds dying. He then sets off on an adventurous trek through the world. In America he grows prosperous in the slave trade; in Asia he sells idols. In every country he becomes wealthy through pandering to the local folly, be it religion or rum. Reaching the deserts of northern Africa, he is greeted as a prophet, and a life of luxury is opened to him but he falls in love with Anitra, a dancing girl, and she robs him of his wealth and leaves him stranded. He then wanders to Egypt, where he lectures to a club of learned gentlemen who turn out to be inmates of an asylum; here in the madhouse Peer is crowned Emperor of Himself.

At last he is old and tired of wandering; he returns to Norway and meets the Button Molder (Death), who informs him that he is unworthy to enter either Heaven or Hell because his sins have been as trivial as his virtues. The Button Molder therefore proposes to melt him down and return him to the storehouse of human material to be made over again. But Solveig, who has been waiting for years for Peer's return, arrives; he takes refuge in her arms and her love protects him. In addition to its satire on its superficial and cynical hero, *Peer Gynt* contains a latent criticism of the Norwegian character, or at least one aspect of it. Many events and incidents in Norwegian history are alluded to, and Peer's rescue points the way to Norway's regeneration.

Samfundets Stötter (*Pillars of Society;* drama, 1877) marks Ibsen's definite abandonment of the poetic style; it is also his first important drama of social criticism. This transitional work, however, is not of the quality of the great plays which follow it. A vivid picture of the corruption of small-town society, the play centers around the person of Consul Karsten Bernick, inheritor of a famous shipbuilding concern. Bernick has allowed another man to bear the disgrace for his own love-affair as well as the guilt for a theft that was never committed. His excuse is that, being a pillar of society, he cannot weaken the social structure by admitting his guilt and thus inviting a total lack of respect for the class he represents.

Et Dukkehjem (*A Doll's House;* drama, 1879) contains Ibsen's chief statement of his attitude toward the position of women and Victorian marriage. Nora Helmer, the heroine, is a middle-class housewife in a typical Norwegian town. Her husband Torvald treats her in an affectionate but condescending manner; he calls her by pet names and chides her gently for excessive spending, and in general forces her to live in a "doll's house" as a spoiled and incompetent darling. But as the play progresses it becomes apparent that Nora is the real backbone of the family. In fact, although he does not know it, Torvald owes his life to her. Years before she borrowed money for a trip to Italy which doctors said was necessary to save Torvald's life. At the time she explained to him that the money came from an inheritance; ever since then she has scrimped and saved to pay off the debt. These previous events are established when Christine Linde, a childhood friend of Nora's, visits her unexpectedly. Christine, now widowed, begs Nora to help her find a job; Nora persuades her husband, a banker, to fire one Krogstad, an incompetent official, and put Christine in his place. But Krogstad is the usurer who secretly loaned Nora the money for her husband's trip years before. Now he threatens that unless his job is protected he will reveal to Torvald a particularly unsavory aspect of the affair. When Nora borrowed the money she gave her father's signature as surety for the loan; but Krogstad has discovered that the bond is dated three days after the old man's death, and that the signature is forged—obviously by Nora herself.

In Act II, soon after Torvald sends off a letter discharging Krogstad, Nora attempts to pay off her debt by borrowing from an old friend, Dr. Rank. But when Dr. Rank, who is in love with her, makes advances to her, she realizes this is impossible. Krogstad shortly arrives, threatens Nora, and drops into the letter-box outside the door a letter exposing the whole affair. Christine, apprised of the situation, promises to dissuade Krogstad from tne denunciation by appealing to his old love for her; now Nora's only problem is to keep Torvald from the letter-box until this can be done.

But in Act III Torvald finds the letter in the box; enraged, he accuses Nora of being a liar and a cheat. When a second message arrives from Krogstad promising not to publicize the scandal, Torvald, who is mainly concerned for his personal reputation, forgives Nora and attempts to make up to her. But she has been driven to the breaking-point by this demonstration of his lack of faith in her; in a long climactic speech she bares to him the false basis on which their marriage has been built. She protests that she lives in a "doll's house," and that after eight years she and Torvald are still strangers to each other. Perhaps, she says, he will realize the gravity of the situation if his "doll" is taken away from him. She adds that if both of them could be so much changed that their life together "would be a real wedlock," a reconciliation is barely possible. On this faintly hopeful note she departs, slamming the door behind her and symbolically repudiating the whole fabric of her marriage. Thus Ibsen calls for a progressive approach to marriage based on mutual love, respect, and confidence between man and wife.

Gegangere (*Ghosts;* tragedy, 1881) is a study of the catastrophic consequences of a marriage not based on true affection and respect; it is also one of the first European dramas to treat the subject of venereal disease. The scene is laid in the house of the widowed Mrs. Alving. As the action opens she is planning the dedication of an orphanage built to the memory of her husband out of the money he left her. Pastor Manders, an old family friend, comes to go over the ceremony and to review business details of the project. Meanwhile Oswald, Mrs. Alving's only son, has recently returned from Paris, where he has been an art student; he is to be present at the ceremony in honor of his father. A sub-plot is established when Engstrand, the carpenter who has built the orphanage, an alcoholic and hypocritical rascal, comes to persuade Mrs. Alving's housemaid Regina to come away and live with him. Regina passes locally for his daughter, and he wants her to serve as hostess in a "sailors' home" (actually a tavern) he plans to set up. Regina indignantly rejects this proposal, but when Manders arrives he urges her to accept Engstrand's offer.

Manders also counsels Mrs. Alving against taking out fire insurance on the orphanage; to do so, he warns, would cause the public to doubt her faith in divine protection. In the conversation between Mrs. Alving and Manders the history of the former's marriage comes out. Married too young to the characterless and dissipated Alving, she ran away from him after a year, but was persuaded to return to her conjugal duties by Manders. This, as it turns out, was the great mistake of her life; from her forced and unnatural marriage with Alving have come all the catastrophes of the family. Regina, Mrs. Alving reveals, is actually her husband's illegitimate daughter; she has raised the girl herself out of a sense of obligation. Moreover, Oswald was sent away to study in Paris precisely so that he might not be corrupted by his father. As the first act ends Mrs. Alving is terrified to overhear Oswald making amatory overtures to Regina; it seems to her that she sees the ghost of her husband enacting the same scene with Regina's mother.

In Act II Oswald reveals to his mother that he is suffering from a serious disease. At first, he says, he believed this to be a congenital venereal disease, but was reassured when his mother's letters told what a fine man his father had been. He proposes to marry Regina and take her away. Just as Mrs. Alving is preparing to tell him the truth about Regina's parentage, the news comes that the Orphanage has caught fire and is in danger of burning down.

Act III takes place just before dawn. The Orphanage has burned to the ground. It becomes apparent that Engstrand has set the fire deliberately; now he attempts to get Manders into his power by threatening to throw the guilt on him. Trapped, Manders is forced to agree to help Engstrand with his "sailors' home." Then, in an interview with Oswald, Mrs. Alving tells him the truth about his father's character and about Regina's parentage. Oswald pleads for Regina to stay on and take care of him as a sister, but she, disgusted with the situation, leaves to join Manders and Engstrand in their tavern venture. Now that Oswald is sure his disease is of hereditary origin, and now that he has been deprived of the love and care of Regina, he grows bitterly morbid; he warns his mother that the next attack of his illness will destroy his sanity. He has provided poison against this exigency, and he makes his mother promise to give it to him when the time comes. The tragedy ends as Oswald's mind snaps; he cries.

"Mother, give me the sun," and Mrs. Alving realizes with horror that it is her duty to poison her own son.

This drama is only incidentally a study in hereditary disease. Its main theme is the falseness of marriages of convenience; the primal cause of the catastrophe which ends the play was the marriage into which Mrs. Alving was forced and in which she was maintained by the hypocrisy of Manders. The title is symbolic: among the "ghosts" with which the play deals is the traditional idea that a woman's place is beside her husband no matter what he is. The ghost of her husband's vice and of her own vacillation pursues her down the years and eventually breaks out in her son and in the burning of the Orphanage.

En Folkefiende (*An Enemy of the People;* drama, 1882) was written in the burst of indignation which swept over Ibsen following public attacks on *Ghosts.* The theme is the hypocrisy of middle-class "vested interests" who turn savagely on the exponent of truth who menaces their property. Dr. Stockmann, physician in a small country town, has helped to develop the mineral baths which are to attract tourists to the place. Now that the baths are completed he is rewarded by the city with a well-paying job as inspector. He discovers, however, that the baths are contaminated by nearby tanneries and contain dangerous typhoid germs. When, in a burst of scientific integrity, he proposes to publish this truth in spite of the damage to his own interests, he brings the wrath of the whole town down upon his head. The Mayor, Stockmann's brother, discovers that alterations to the bath will cost twenty thousand pounds; he demands that Stockmann withdraw his charges. When the doctor refuses, his brother removes him from his position as inspector. The local editor Hovstad, who at first supports Stockmann, withdraws his aid when he learns of the expense of the alterations. Stockmann angrily plans to bring the issue before the people, but can find no hall in which to hold a meeting. The gathering finally takes place in the home of a friend, Captain Horster. But hecklers and enemies pack the meeting; the explanation degenerates into a riot. Before Stockmann is through with his ordeal he is manhandled by the people and his daughter loses her position as a schoolteacher. Through his honesty he has only succeeded in making himself into "an enemy of the people," a hated pariah. But Stockmann doggedly determines to fight on for the truth even though the whole community is against him. Thus the message implied in *An Enemy of the People* is that the majority is not always right.

Vilanden (*The Wild Duck;* tragedy, 1884) is a half-realistic, half-symbolic drama in which Ibsen argues for illusory happiness and against fanatic idealism; the soul-sick reformer Gregers, through his obsession to bare the truth to those about him, only causes misery through removing their consolatory illusions.

The drama opens at a dinner party at the home of Werle, a wealthy industrialist; the party is given in honor of the homecoming of Werle's son Gregers. One of the guests is Hjalmar Ekdal, a boyhood friend of Gregers but now far below the Werles in social status. In a conversation between the two young men some past events are revealed: Hjalmar's father, "Old Ekdal," had been in a lumber partnership with Werle; the two were accused of a swindle, with the result that Old Ekdal was ruined and publicly disgraced and Werle got off unscathed. Since that time Werle, out of bad conscience, has assisted Ekdal's family financially. Hjalmar's wife Gina is a former housekeeper of Werle's. Through Werle's generosity the young couple have been set up in a photography business; they have a fourteen-year-old daughter, Hedvig, and are reasonably happy in spite of their poverty. During the dinner an embarrassing incident takes place: Old Ekdal, who does petty copying work for the Werle firm, calls at the place by coincidence to pick up some work. His son, ashamed, turns his back and pretends not to recognize him. Later in the act Gregers accuses his own father of having acted shabbily toward the Ekdals—specifically of having failed to assume his share of blame in the fraud case and of marrying off his old mistress Gina to the naive Hjalmar.

The rest of the drama takes place in Hjalmar's studio. Old Ekdal and then Hjalmar come home from the Werles, and Hjalmar gives his daughter, who has been expecting a pastry or a sweet from the dinner, a menu instead (i.e. symbolically, he cannot distinguish between illusion and reality). Then Gregers, fleeing in disgust from his father, shortly arrives to ask for the spare room the Ekdals are trying to let. Gregers is also shown Old Ekdal's "forest"—a sliding door reveals an indoor garden with trees and shrubs and containing various wild creatures in cages. Here old Ekdal, in his youth a mighty hunter and woodsman, retreats from the world to live in a realm of illusion. The "forest" also contains a wild duck belonging to Hedvig; it was wounded by Werle on a hunting trip, and is now the girl's precious possession. To her it symbolizes her aspirations; it represents to her whatever is wild and free, and she finds in the bird escape from her own sordid reality. Hjalmar too has his illusion; in a conversation with Gregers he reveals he is working on a marvelous invention which is soon to make the family rich. He also expresses his fears, however, that Hedvig will in time become totally blind.

In Act III it becomes apparent that Gregers is determined to tell the Ekdals the truth about their situation: that Hjalmar's invention is a chimera, that Gina has been the mistress of Werle, and that Hedvig and Old Ekdal are living lives of delusion and fantasy. Both Werle and Gina sense his purpose and try to dissuade him, but in Act IV he goes forward with his plans. Troubled by Greger's revelations Hjalmar accuses his wife of misbehavior with Werle. She confesses he tried to seduce her, but says she was discharged because she refused. Later Werle followed her and menaced her until he got his way; then he arranged for her marriage to Hjalmar.

At the crisis of the drama a message comes from Werle offering to pay Old Ekdal a pension for the rest of his life, the money to revert to Hedvig after he dies. But Hjalmar, who suspects this as evidence that Hedvig is actually Werle's child, rejects the offer indignantly. As Act IV ends Gregers suggests to Hedvig that perhaps if she sacrifices her most precious possession, the wild duck (symbolically her illusions) to her father, he will forgive her and love her again.

But in Act V occurs the catastrophe: Hedvig, instead of killing the wild duck, takes her own life in the "forest." Hjalmar's life is ruined: his daughter is dead, he has alienated his wife, and he has rejected the income which would have assured comfort to himself and his family. Yet as the drama ends he begins trying to rationalize the death of his daughter through a sort of maudlin sentimentality.

The raisonneur or spokesman of Ibsen's ideas in this play is the sarcastic boarder Relling. He knows that Hjalmar is an incompetent humbug, but he argues to Gregers that what every human being needs to make his life bearable is a private illusion, a fantasy into which he can retreat when adversity overcomes him. When Gregers, foolishly pursuing the truth, removes this veil of illusion, Hjalmar and his family are destroyed, and no useful purpose has been served.

Hedda Gabler (drama, 1890) is less didactic than most of the dramas of Ibsen's middle period, and is often considered his best work from the standpoint of theatrical technique. The challenging role of the heroine has attracted leading actresses throughout the years since the drama was first performed.

Hedda is a "superior woman" of upper middle-class origin (her father is of the military class) whose temperament and intelligence little fit her for the passive role of a housewife. Her husband, George Tesman, is a pedantic and none too brilliant scholar; he is content to spend his life studying and collating the creative work of others. Hedda soon comes to despise him, and regrets she did not accept another suitor, the brilliant but unstable young author Eilert Lövborg; indeed he is her natural mate. Hedda has married George because she expected him to go far in a professorial career. As the drama opens George and Hedda are returning from their honeymoon, and Hedda is beginning to realize her mistake. She confides to her middle-aged friend Judge Brack that she was horribly bored on the European trip, and the sly Brack sees a chance to indulge in an extramarital romance. Hedda's frustration is increased when she hears that Eilert has reformed under the inspiration of a devoted companion, Mrs. Thea Elvsted, and has written a book which shows unmistakable evidence of genius. When Thea comes to visit and confesses she has abandoned her husband to become Eilert's mistress, Hedda, enraged, determines to break her influence over Eilert. She taunts Eilert into taking a drink, and he rapidly begins to slip back into his old profligate ways. The men, George included, depart for a party together and end up in a wild orgy during which Eilert loses the precious manuscript of his book. By chance the manuscript comes into the possession of Hedda. It seems to her like a "child" produced by the love of Eilert and Thea, and she burns it gloatingly in her fireplace. When she tells George of this he is horrified; but when she points out to him that this brilliant work, if published, would get Eilert the professorship that George himself covets, he reluctantly agrees to keep silent about the matter.

When Eilert discovers the loss of the manuscript he comes in despair to Hedda to confess to her that he feels he has lost his only child; he hints he is contemplating suicide. Hedda maliciously lends him one of her two pistols, thus forcing him to take the step he had not really considered seriously. She imagines that Eilert will take his life in some dramatic manner which will make it seem he died for

her love. But instead he shoots himself, apparently by accident, in a
sordid house of ill fame; Hedda is denied her morbid triumph. Then
Judge Brack, who guesses the whole story, threatens to reveal the
origin of the gun that killed Lövborg unless Hedda accepts his affections. But he misjudges her, proudly refusing to accept this ignominy,
Hedda goes into the next room and shoots herself. Brack, as the
corpse is discovered, says in horror, "People don't do such things."

The character of Hedda is often misinterpreted. She is not a naturally malicious person, neither is she pathologically neurotic at the
time the play opens. Her personal tragedy is that the stolid and dull
middle-class life to which she has committed herself by her marriage
allows her no outlet for her natural talent and individuality. She and
Eilert are by far the finest minds in the drama; both are destroyed by
a society which refuses to allow their talents free expression. *Hedda
Gabler* is the pendant to *A Doll's House;* it demonstrates the social
censure the "superior woman" must bear if she tries to flaunt convention and live according to the urges of her inner being. Hedda is
especially resentful to be denied intellectual companionship with the
men; the males of the drama go off to their evening of drinking and
heavy conversation to leave her to talk trivialities with Thea. It is true
that Thea, steady and devoted, has been an ideal support and inspiration for Eilert, but she provides him with little true intellectual companionship. Hedda is not entirely right, nor is Eilert; yet the lives of
both might have been happy had they not been warped and frustrated
by bourgeois taboos.

Gerhart Hauptmann (German, 1862-1946)

Hauptmann began his literary career in the eighteen-eighties as a
naturalist, and in this rôle eventually became the central figure in the
nineteenth-century German naturalistic movement. His literary development, however, kept pace with the times; around 1893 he turned
to a mystical style influenced by the Symbolists, and this gradually
evolved from 1908 to 1917 into a sort of Neo-romanticism. He remained in Germany under the Third Reich, although he was not
entirely on good terms with the government, and in the atmosphere
of Nazism continued his excursions into romantic paganism. The
works of this period are generally inferior; Hauptmann, it has long
been thought, will be remembered chiefly for the great naturalistic

dramas of his youth. But there are those who prefer his fiction and the symbolistic plays.

Like many naturalists, Hauptmann demonstrated a strong mystical element from the beginning of his literary career. He was by temperament and inclination a romantic. Accidentally born into an era of scientific naturalism, he was versatile enough to be able to adjust his talents to the *Zeitgeist*. The sensitive element in his nature, however, made him highly conscious of style; his works differ from the classic naturalism of the French school chiefly in their refined and subtle artistic perfection. Even in such ultra-naturalistic dramas as *Before Dawn* and *The Weavers* Hauptmann clothes his characters in a sort of mystic poetic veil; they seem like personages from a Symbolist drama who have accidentally strayed into a naturalistic setting. Hauptmann also lacks the clumsiness of language which mars the work of some naturalists. He is a poet by inclination, and constructs well-ordered and vivid sentences through that sort of poetic instinct common only to the greatest artists.

In the naturalistic plays of the eighties and nineties Hauptmann endeavors to present the scientific determinism and the dogma of heredity of the naturalistic school. His temperament, however, found little sympathy with this stark doctrine, and his personal ideas are expressed more sincerely in the plays of his middle period. In such dramas as *The Assumption of Hannele* and *The Sunken Bell* and in novels like *The Fool in Christ, Emanuel Quint* Hauptmann expresses a mystical adulation of nature and the life-forces of the universe combined with a vague humanitarian socialism. These ideas, although modified during the "pagan" period following the First World War, dominated the entire latter half of his career. Like Tolstoy, Hauptmann found the answer to all political problems in the essential brotherhood of man; and like Bernard Shaw, he believed the secret of metaphysics to lie in the forces which continually regenerate life in man and animal.

LIFE: Hauptmann was born in Silesia in 1862. His youth was strongly influenced by Lutheran doctrine as well as by the Moravian pietism which also had its due impact on Goethe's youth. He had the advantages of a Gymnasium and University education, although he was a poor student and made scant use of his formal learning. In his twenties Hauptmann still had only a vague concept of his own capabilities; he dreamed variously of becoming a sculptor, a painter, or a musician. An early marriage to a well-to-do German heiress gained him financial security, but proved otherwise unrewarding; after a divorce he remarried in 1904. This marriage was reasonably successful, and produced a single son.

Hauptmann began writing as early as 1887, but his real beginning as an author dates from the time of his meeting with Arno Holz toward the end of the decade. Holz, the father of German naturalism and at that time the leading naturalistic dramatist in Germany, encouraged Hauptmann to write for the Freie Bühne, the theatre which served as the focus of the movement. Hauptmann responded with *Vor Sonnenaufgang* (*Before Dawn;* 1889), one of the most powerful plays to emerge from the German naturalistic movement. The drama created a tremendous popular controversy, and when the dust had settled Hauptmann was a famous man. He followed with *The Weavers* (1892) and *The Beaver Coat* (1893), and before long was hailed as the leader of the new German drama. His neo-romantic or symbolistic period began with *The Assumption of Hannele* (1893), although several subsequent works showed naturalistic elements. In 1912 he was awarded the Nobel Prize for Literature. He was highly honored by the German Republic (1920-1933) but was attacked by Nazi critics during this period. With the inception of the Third Reich in 1933, however, he was one of the few major German authors to remain in Germany, and managed to remain on amicable terms with the Nazis. During the latter years of his life he lived at Agnetendorf, in Silesia, where he surrounded himself with a corps of disciples and basked in the comfort of his success. He continued to produce through the period of the Second World War, the first two of the *Atrides* plays appearing in 1941 and 1944 respectively and the remaining two posthumously in 1948. He died in what had become Polish territory in 1946.

CHIEF WORKS: *Vor Sonnenaufgang* (*Before Dawn;* drama, 1889) is a brutal study in naturalistic determinism somewhat resembling Ibsen's *Ghosts.* The action takes place in the house of a *nouveaux-*

riche peasant family who have been entirely corrupted by their success. Torn by alcoholism, disease, and spiritual disillusionment, the family seems destined for imminent extinction. Helene, a daughter, however, retains some vestiges of decency; and when Alfred, an idealistic young man of socialist tendencies, falls in love with her, a chance for the regeneration of the family becomes apparent. But Alfred, weak and impractical, lacks the strength to drag Helene from the mire. He is appalled by her hereditary background, and flees in horror when he learns what he believes to be her true character. Alfred is intended as a personification of the intellectual socialist movement of the nineteenth century, earnest and humanitarian but lacking any true conception of lower-class problems.

Die Weber (*The Weavers;* drama, 1892) is based on an historical uprising of the Silesian weavers in 1844. The only two characters of any individuality are Moritz Jaeger, an ex-soldier and part-time professional agitator, and the wealthy manufacturer Dreissiger. The actual strike comes to nothing, although the workers, enraged by the police murder of an inoffensive old weaver who has not even taken part in the insurrection, destroy the looms and machinery which are the sole support of their own existence. With the exception of Jaeger and Dreissiger the characters are treated entirely as masses rather than as men; their individual personality is submerged in their identification with the group. This technique foreshadows not only Hauptmann's own Symbolist period but the *Massendrama* experiments of the expressionistic school in the period around 1910.

The social message of *Die Weber* is nothing less than an attack on the industrial revolution. The machines are the true villains of the drama; the workers recognize their essential enemy and seek to smash the machines in their desperate rebellion. Their gesture is hopeless, since there is no possibility of a return to the handcraft by which their ancestors made their living; and Hauptmann offers no hope that the weavers or anyone else will be able to establish a social order in which the machines bring about the prosperity of the workers who operate them. The latent possibility of amelioration through social action or socialism is always present; yet at the end of the drama the plight of the weavers, and by implication the entire European proletariat, looks bleak indeed.

Hanneles Himmelfahrt (The Assumption of Hannele; drama, 1893) is a transitional work bridging the gap from naturalism to symbolism. Hannele is a child of mystic sensibilities who is cruelly brutalized by her stepfather Mattern. In despair she flings herself into an icy pond; she is rescued and brought to the almshouse, where her delirium is presented to the audience in an imaginative dream scene. In her dream Hannele sees her dead mother come from heaven to console her, and the village schoolmaster, her only living friend, appears at last in the guise of Christ. Hannele is assumed into heaven, and only her body remains in the bleak almshouse at the end of the play.

This drama is in one sense a socialistic treatise as well as a study in symbolic mysticism; Hannele, an exploited proletarian child, is murdered by society as much as she is by her stupid and brutalized father.

Die Versunkene Glocke (The Sunken Bell; drama, 1896) is Hauptmann's best-known Symbolist drama. The theme is the struggle of the creative artist in a materialistic world, and especially the conflict in his own mind between the demands of his calling and the duties and obligations he owes to his family. The hero, Heinrich, is a bell-founder obsessed with the idea of creating an artistically perfect object. Rautendelein, a nymph, is a symbol of the perfection of nature, and therefore the goal of Heinrich's aesthetic aspirations. But Heinrich, torn by pity and loyalty toward his family, cannot follow the nymph, and he dies without achieving his ambition. An artist must choose between fulfillment of his creative urge and a normal and serene family life; he cannot hope to achieve both. The idea of personifying the opposing emotions in Heinrich's mind in two women is typical of Symbolistic technique.

Der Ketzer von Soana (The Heretic of Soana; novella, 1918) is the story of an especially devout young priest, Francesco Vela, who, in attempting to save the souls of a scandalous incestuous family, the Scarabotas, and particularly of the fifteen-year-old beautiful daughter, Agata, is converted in reverse to paganism and the worship of Eros. The lapse is not without battle, but it is spring—March through May —and the restrictive fetters of Christianity and an ascetic clerical celibacy are met and overmatched by the forces of nature and an unconstrained world symbolized by figures from Greek antiquity: Pan, Apollo, Eros—"older than Cronus," Bacchus or Dionysus, Priapus, and sarcophagi with dancing maenads and satyrs.

This is a story within a story. The exterior narrator is apparently a tourist, then a visitor (perhaps Hauptmann himself), traveling near Lugano in the Italian part of Switzerland and climbing via Soana toward the summit of Monte Generoso where he gradually becomes acquainted with a bespectacled goatherd, "the heretic of Soana," who liked to be called Ludovico. This recluse, obviously well-educated, relates some things about Argentina, Seneca, Swiss politics. After some time he states his heresy, "I had rather worship a live he-goat or a live bull than a hanged man on a gallows. I do not live in an age that does that. I hate, I abhor it." He later speaks about writing the story of his conversion. Then one day Ludovico reads to his guest a narrative he has written, the story of Francesco Vela.

"Once upon a time" the young priest had been approached in his new parish of Soana by the disreputable Scarabota who lives, according to the civil head of the village with his sister-wife and brood of children up on the mountain away from the village. With his bishop's approval the priest resolves to visit these sinners because the compassion and consolation of the church must be held out to all. His first trip to the Scarabota's squalid hut at the end of March near Easter is marked by two unusual responses, to the fecundity of nature in spring and to the surprising beauty of the daughter, Agata, and by two incidents, the discovery of a phallic fetish in the house of the Scarabotas and an attack on the way home by a he-goat and a she-goat who eats his breviary which he was trying to read, saved on this occasion by Agata, the shepherdess. A good deal is made of the double shepherd image, Christian but pre-Christian too. However, there seem to be no sheep, only goats.

Sercret services, again with the bishop's approval, are arranged in the abandoned mountain chapel of Saint Agata for the outlawed family who would not be tolerated by the Soana villagers; Francesco finds that Agata's presence interferes with his thoughts during Mass and enters his dreams which become increasingly erotic. Disturbed and worried, he seeks out neighboring priests to confess to them and receive absolution. Agata's absence for the second service is even

worse, although on his homeward journey he encounters her carried
on the back of the he-goat followed by children in a kind of bacchan-
alian procession. He orders her to come to him in Soana for school-
ing. When she arrives she is stoned by the villagers, the priest takes
her in, and, excited emotionally by these incidents, Agata and Francesco declare their love for each other, shortly thereafter consum-
mating their love on an Eden-like island near the waterfall of a mountain stream. Francesco celebrated early mass next morning, torn by
the conflct between his Adam-fall and his saint-like reputation in
Soana.

Ludovico's story breaks off with unanswered questions: What became of Agata and Francesco? Did the story remain a secret? Did the
lovers find lasting or temporary pleasure? Ludovico does not satisfy
his listener, but implications lead the reader to infer the identity of
Ludovico and the defrocked priest—the eyeglasses, the rumored death
of the Scarabota parents of yellow fever in Rio, and the final appearance of a woman with a girl-child seen as an Agata-goddess figure.
The comparative evaluations of a restrictive Christianity and a vital
paganism, quietly lyrical without linguistic offense or apparent blasphemy, suggest a similarity of approach to that of D. H. Lawrence
in *The Man Who Died*. The images of blood-impulse and Isis rein-
force the congruence. As priests in Holland and elsewhere begin to
oppose the pope in the principle of celibacy for the priesthood, the
heresy in Soana seems less and less isolated.

Die Atriden-Tetralogie (The Tetralogy of the Atrides; tragic cycle,
1941-48) is a vast dramatic epic covering the Agamemnon-Electra
story from beginning to end, although Hauptmann wrote the end first.
Iphigenie in Aulis (1944), the second of the four dramas, covers the
first part of the story, the material in Euripides' drama of the same
name: the sacrifice of Iphigenia by her father Agamemnon to the
goddess Artemis to obtain success for the Trojan expedition. *Agam-
emnons Tod (The Death of Agamemnon,* 1948) follows the plot of
Aeschylus' *Agamemnon;* it consists chiefly of the murder of Agamemnon by Clytemnestra and Aegisthus. The fourth unit, *Elektra* (also
published posthumously in 1948), follows the plot as contained in
Aeschylus' *Choephoroe* or Sophocles' *Electra:* Orestes arrives from
his bandishment, joins Electra, and avenges his father by slaying

Clytemnestra and Aegisthus. *Iphigenie in Delphi* (written first and published 1941) contrives to draw the threads together and complete the cycle in an orderly manner. Iphigenia and Orestes are reunited, and in a mystical union of Apollo and Artemis the curse of the Atrides is removed at last. The *Atrides* tetralogy differs from its various classical models chiefly in its preoccupation with abnormal psychological states and in the curious veil of German medievalism which Hauptmann lays over his classic material. The cycle must be classed as Neo-romantic rather than as Symbolistic or Neo-classical.

Maxim Gorky (Russian, 1868-1936)

Gorky is the only major Russian writer of the pre-revolutionary period to remain *persona grata* under the Soviet regime. His works, although not primarily political in character, are widely read and praised in Russia today. Gorky is a naturalist, but a naturalist with a Russian temperament. He is not impressed with pseudo-scientific doctrine or with doctrine of any sort; neither does he strive to treat his material with the total and sterile objectivity of the sociologist. In fact in his treatment of character he is not even realistic. He is deeply interested in the lower classes, especially the most degraded and twisted products of the slums, but he is not a muckraker in the manner of Zola. He poetizes everything he touches, whether it is a flophouse inhabited by loose women and criminals or a band of bitter exploited workers in a bakery. All of his characters exhibit the "Russian soul," the brooding, expressive, and spiritualized temperament of Dostoyevsky's students or Turgenev's peasants. Gorky, however, was the first to attribute these qualities to the city proletariat, the first to find philosophers and poets in the factory and the boarding house. In the manner of the great nineteenth-century Russian novelists, he is filled with sympathy for the characters he creates, even the most wretched and dejected of them. They are all lovable in the end, even when they shoot themselves or each other, commit acts of cunning cruelty, or wallow in the filth of their own making. Gorky makes us feel the essential kinship of all humanity, and the callousness of the moral superiority of the fortunate. Without expounding the point specifically, he makes us realize that it is after all an evil society which turns honest men into perverts and failures. In this sense, and no other, his work is socialistic;

he is as far removed from political polemic as he is from any literary dogma.

Gorky also follows the Russian tradition in his lack of interest in plot. Not only do his stories lack a conventional beginning, middle, and end, but they often seem to lack any thread of continuity whatever; they are no more than disconnected snatches of characterization, dialogue, and action. Even in the drama, where a tightly-woven plot is usually considered essential, Gorky relies on atmosphere and dissociated dialogue to achieve his ends. Apart from characterization, his chief interest lies in the creation of ambience or mood; his plays and stories leave behind them a typical bittersweet taste, half poignant and half ridiculous. There is none of the cleansing catharsis of the classic tragedy, and little of the feeling of bleak degradation left by the French naturalists; the reader of Gorky lays down his book saddened but imbued with a warm feeling of kinship with humanity. The story *The Clown,* which illustrates this mood very well, has a quality of comic sadness about it which evokes the early films of Chaplin. There are no heroes in Gorky's tragedy, only mountebanks and scoundrels, and this tends to reduce the tragedy more to the level of the reader's sympathy.

LIFE: "Maxim Gorky" is a pseudonym meaning "bitter maxim"; his real name was A. M. Peshkov. Gorky was born in 1868 in Nizhny-Novgorod, later renamed Gorky in his honor. Although his father was an upholsterer and therefore of the artisan class, the family had come down in the world and Gorky's early years were made miserable with poverty. His mother and father both died before he was grown, and his grandfather sent him out in the world to make his own living. Unlettered and declassed, he worked at a variety of menial jobs: bootmaker's apprentice, helper in a bakery, handyman in a draftsman's office, and pantry-boy on a Volga steamer, where a friendly but alcoholic cook named Smury taught him the rudiments of letters and introduced him to the world of literature. On one occasion he sought to be admitted to the University of Kazan, but found it "wasn't the fashion" to educate illiterate ragamuffins with no money. In 1889 he became a lawyer's clerk, and his employer, A. I. Lanin, encouraged and assisted him with the task of self-education; soon he began to write. His first story was published in 1892. With the publication of the story *Chelkash* in 1895 he became a famous author overnight, and in 1898 his stories were published in volume form. He was barely thirty years old. With *The Lower Depths* (1902) he became a world literary figure; the drama played for over five hundred consecutive performances in the 1903-04 season in Berlin alone.

In the early years of the century Gorky had become a sympathetic socialist, and after a while began to take an active part in the revolutionary movement. When he was elected to the Imperial Academy in 1902 the selection was countermanded by the government on the grounds that Gorky was "under the supervision of the police." In protest against this step the famous academicians Chekhov and Korolenko renounced their memberships. Gorky, by now a fervent revolutionist, took an active part in the abortive 1905 revolution and was confined for a short time in jail. The following year he made a trip to America to raise revolutionary funds. He was at first greeted warmly by a committee including Mark Twain, William Dean Howells, Jane Addams, and Edwin Markham; but when the Russian embassy disclosed that Gorky was not actually married to the woman who accompanied him as his wife, the newspapers began a campaign of denunciation. The committee abandoned him, he was turned out of several hotels in succession, and a projected White House reception was cancelled. Gorky's reply was to write an essay entitled *The City of the Yellow Devil* in which New York, and America generally, was portrayed as an inferno full of lost souls driven mad by their lust for gold.

At the time of the 1917 Revolution Gorky, although still a political independent, was greeted warmly by the Bolsheviks and encouraged to found a bureau to aid authors and intellectuals impoverished by the war. He did little important writing after 1917; his most important post-Revolutionary book was *Recollections of Tolstoy* (1919). From 1921 to 1928 he lived abroad, mostly in Germany and Italy. After his permanent return to the U. S. S. R. in 1929 he became a sort of official Soviet spokesman on literary matters. When he died in 1936 he was considered so important that the government attempted to blame his decease on a Trotskyite plot.

CHIEF WORKS: *The Lower Depths* (Russian *Na dne,* sometimes translated as *The Night's Lodging;* drama, 1902) is the work by which Gorky is chiefly known in Western Europe and America. In structure, especially in the ending, the play lies under the influence of Chekhov; it is really a sort of proletarian *Cherry Orchard.* The scene is laid in

a flophouse or inn in an unnamed Russian city. The place consists
of a cavernous basement with a single window, presided over by
Kostylev, a part-time buyer of stolen goods. The chief tenants in this
extraordinary hostel are The Actor, an alcoholic and voluble failure;
Vassilissa, Kostylev's young wife; Pepel, a petty criminal; Natasha, a
sister of Vassilissa; The Baron, a conceited and spurious young gentleman; and Bubnov, a capmaker. Except at the very end there is no
action whatsoever. The characters rant and declaim to each other;
Pepel makes overtures to Natasha, and Vassilissa, perceiving this,
offers to aid him in his suit if he will help her to escape from her
husband. Meanwhile a mysterious old pilgrim, Luka, has entered the
basement and is influencing the characters almost without their notic-
ing it. His intent is apparently to stimulate them from their lethargy,
or to encourage them to become themselves; after he is gone one
character remarks, "He worked on me like acid on a dirty old coin."
Toward the end of the play a squabble breaks out. Natasha is burned
by an overturned samovar, and Pepel, in a rage, kills Kostylev.
Natasha, hysterical, tells the police that Vassilissa and Pepel have
killed the manager, and The Actor, filled with a Chekhovian melancholy, wanders offstage and hangs himself. A bare recital cannot
convey the poignant and strangely poetic atmosphere of this play.

   Twenty-Six Men and a Girl (story, 1899) is Gorky's most famous
short story, and typical of the style of the others. Twenty-six workers
slave all day long in a sweltering and ill-ventilated basement bakery,
as Gorky himself did in his youth. Their sole consolation, and the one
bright event in their daily routine, is the appearance of a young girl
who comes every day to buy bread. But a soldier who works in the
courtyard outside jeers at their idealism; he wagers he can seduce
the girl. When their idol of purity falls, the workers feel degraded and
angry; and when the girl comes again for her bread they greet her with
hoots and insults. Like *The Lower Depths,* this story has a poetic
mood which raises it above gutter realism; in addition its basic theme,
the alleviation of misery through vicarious purity, is an idealistic one.

Alexander Kuprin (Russian, 1870-1938)

Kuprin resembles both Bunin and Gorky in the content of his novels.
Although he is educated and cosmopolitan in outlook as Bunin is, he
is closer to Gorky in style. His two chief novels, *The Duel* and *Yama,*

are biting satires on two aspects of pre-Revolutionary Russian life. Like Gorky, he often sentimentalizes his material, but he overcomes this failing with a vigorous and accurate command of style. His structure is erratic, and he tends to wander through his story with little seeming plan or goal; here he is in the tradition of Goncharov and Chekhov, who left their mark on every major Russian author of the fin-de-siècle period. But unlike these authors he is concerned largely with physical action; there is an impetuous and vigorous element in his work which derives from the western adventure story rather than from any Russian source. "Perhaps the greatest of living Russian novelists is Kuprin—exalted, hysterical, sentimental, Rabelaisian Kuprin!" said Stephen Graham in 1916.

LIFE: Kuprin was born in the Russian province of Penza in 1870 of wealthy middle-class parents. He was educated at the Cadet School and later at the Military School of Moscow, where, to judge by certain stories he later wrote about cadet life, he was terribly unhappy. Upon his graduation he was commissioned in the army, but he was little fitted for a military career. He attempted to write in his spare time, but found that this only earned him the scorn of his fellow officers and the persecution of his commanders. He resigned after four years of misery, and like Gorky wandered about Russia taking one menial job after another and writing in his hours off. His first story was actually published while he was still in the army. From 1900 to 1906 he was active in journalistic and publishing circles in Petersburg; he worked for a time in Gorky's *Znanie* publishing house, and was loosely associated with the socialist movement. In 1905 his novel *The Duel* won him widespread fame, at least in Russia. During the First World War he served in the army; upon the outbreak of the October Revolution he joined the White forces under General Yudenitch. and took part in an attack on Petersburg. With the breakup of the White forces he escaped to Finland, then to France, where he lived for almost seventeen years. In 1937 he returned to the Soviet Union and was warmly greeted. He died shortly afterward, in 1938, of cancer.

CHIEF WORKS: Kuprin's best-known novel is *The Duel* (Russ. *Poyedinok;* novel, 1905), a bitter satire of the Russian army, clergy, and conservative element generally. The army as exposed by Kuprin is a completely senseless and degenerate bureaucracy, dominated by bestiality and riddled with incompetence. This novel had the good luck to appear in the bookstores early in 1906, when the Russian public was thoroughly disgusted with the army as a result of the disastrous war with Japan; the book enjoyed an enormous success.

Yama (sometimes translated *Yama: the Pit;* novel, 1908-15) is labelled a trilogy but is actually a novel in three sections. It consists of an exposure of life in an Odessa brothel, including the conditions which cause prostitution and the evils which result from its practice. Following in the wake of Zola's *Nana* (1880), this book enjoyed an enormous *succès de scandale*. Although its characterizations are sometimes vividly drawn, it is not equal in quality to *The Duel*.

Of Kuprin's many short stories, probably the best is "The Bracelet of Garnets," which gave its name to a volume of stories published in Russia in 1911 and in English in 1917. It concerns the love of Zheltcov, a humble clerk, for the Princess Vera Nicolaievna; he pursues her hopelessly for seven or eight years, and kills himself when her relatives force him to stop writing her letters.

Jules Romains (French, born 1885)

Jules Romains is a novelist in the technical tradition of Balzac and Zola. The great work of his life is the novel series *Men of Good Will,* a magnificent twenty-four volume panorama of French society in the twentieth century. Romains is the chief of the modern novelists who treat humanity in terms of groups and classes rather than as individuals; *Men of Good Will* is the *roman fleuve* or collective novel brought to the summit of its perfection and increased to a size where it actually includes a definitive portion of the society it claims to represent. The series is not as huge as Balzac's *Human Comedy,* but the individual novels are more closely integrated. Romains, in fact, maintains that the work is a single novel with a single comprehensive plan. It is not, however, a tightly knit organic whole in the sense of Proust's *Remembrance of Things Past* or Martin du Gard's *Les Thibaults:* it is a novel series of which each volume contains the same characters seen at successive stages in their development.

Romains attempts a presentation technique similar to that of Dos Passos and Joyce, but he does not develop it to so radical an extent. We might say that Romains' checkerboard has larger squares than those of *Ulysses* or *U.S.A.* Where Dos Passos alternates from character to character on a single page, Romains devotes an entire chapter to an incident in the life of a single character, or set of characters, and then goes on to the next. Thus Romains' work has a more conventional appearance; each chapter reads like a chapter of a normal novel.

The great problem in writing such a pattern novel or collective novel is to make the individual details, incidents, and persons seem credible and at the same time keep the overall panorama, the gigantic movement of the work, firmly in the reader's mind. Romains has succeeded in uniting the microcosm and the macrocosm better than any of his contemporaries; his details are sharp and vivid, but the great sweep of the action is never forgotten. In this quality Romains resembles the Tolstoy of *War and Peace* more than he does any contemporary author.

Romains demonstrates two qualities of the naturalistic school: he is intensely interested in science and the scientific mehtod, especially in medicine, and he attempts to treat humanity sociologically rather than individually. He differs from the classic naturalists, however, in his latent sympathy for humanity and in his insight into psychological processes. Many of his chapters are long internal monologues, a psychological device which Zola seldom permitted himself. The weakest parts of *Men of Good Will* are the abstract analyses of social tendencies, and the best are the highly documented narrations and the impassioned intellectual dialogues.

LIFE: Romains was born Louis Farigoule in 1885; his father was a teacher, and the son was educated at a Paris lycée and at the École Normale Supérieure. His university training lay largely in the scientific field, and he carried the objective attitude of the scientist into his literary undertakings. In 1908 he published *Unanimistic Life,* a semi-lyrical work expressing a theory of "Unanism" in which humanity is studied as an organism composed entirely of groups. From 1909 to the time of the First World War Romains served as a lycée professor in various French cities including Paris; at the end of the war he began to devote his full-time attention to literature. His first novel, *Death of a Nobody,* appeared in 1911, and another novel, *Les Copains* (in translation *The Boys in the Back Room*) in 1914. Shortly after the war Romains began to work out the ideas of Pan-Europeanism which were to appear in fictional form in *Men of Good Will:* "a united, coherent Europe, surmounting frontiers and nationalities." In 1923 appeared *Knock, ou le Triomphe de la Médecine,* a comedy satirizing medical avarice. The play achieved an enormous success on the French stage. Work on *Men of Good Will* was begun in 1931 and continued through the Second World War. In 1940 Romains came to America, where he continued to write through the period of the war, the occupation, and the liberation, after which he returned to Paris and semi-retirement.

CHIEF WORK: *Les Hommes de bonne Volonté (Men of Good Will;* novel series) began appearing in French in 1932 and in English in 1933. Thus far twelve volumes have appeared in translation, corresponding to twenty-four in the French edition. Each English volume contains two "books" which have separate titles. The titles of the complete volumes of the English translation are as follows: I, *Men of Good Will,* 1933; II, *Passion's Pilgrims,* 1934; III, *The Proud and the Meek,* 1935; IV, *The World from Below,* 1935; V, *The Earth Trembles,* 1936; VI, *The Depths and the Heights,* 1937; VII, *Death of a World,* 1938; VIII, *Verdun,* 1939; IX, *Aftermath,* 1941; X, *The New Day,* 1942; XI, *Work and Play,* 1944; and XII, *The Wind is Rising,* 1945.

The action of the series describes the careers of the chief characters in the period from the turn of the century through the First World War to the brink of the Second World War. Actually there are about sixty characters whose personalities are sketched in detail, but only about a dozen of these play a major part in the work. Chief among these characters are Pierre Jallez, a poetic and introspective young student who becomes a journalist, dabbles in communism, engages in various unsatisfactory romances, and grows somewhat disillusioned in the thirties; Jean Jerphanion, his companion, an extroverted man of action who fights in the Battle of Verdun and holds long conversations with Jallez; Frédéric Haverkamp, a real-estate entrepreneur who makes a fortune promoting a health spa near Paris and later becomes a war profiteer; Quinette, an eccentric bookbinder who, like Gide's Lafcadio *(Les Caves du Vatican),* conceives the idea of committing a perfectly unmotivated, and therefore absolutely undetectable, crime; and George Allory, an opportunistic novelist who stakes everything on an effort to be admitted to the French Academy but fails in two elections. The women in *Men of Good Will* are less important; they generally serve as intellectual foils or physical adventures for the men. The dominant ideas of the series are: the essential kinship of all European peoples; the theory that human beings actually function in groups, however much they may believe in their individual wills; and the influence of social, philosophical, and psychological ideas on the actual events of political history. The best of the volumes is usually conceded to be *Verdun,* which contains some of the best battle scenes to be written in the twentieth century as well as a magnificent analysis of the motives behind the heroic French stand at Verdun. Unlike most naturalists, Romains has taken the trouble to acquire an extensive knowledge of strategy, logistics, and military diplomacy; thus his description of war has a compass lacking in the versions of Barbusse or Dos Passos.

Roger Martin du Gard (French, 1881-1958)

After Romains, Martin du Gard is the chief exponent of the quasi-scientific *roman fleuve* in the twentieth century. The great work of his career is the ten-volume novel *Les Thibaults,* which like the Rougon-Macquart series of Zola traces a middle-class French family through its evolution and eventual decline. Where Dos Passos and Romains attempt to depict a cross-section of an entire nation, Martin du Gard restricts himself to a single clan. The Thibault family, however, extends its influence into enough of French society of the twentieth century to make the novel an encompassing document of social trends.

Martin du Gard differs from both Dos Passos and Romains in his technique. He is a conservative, plodding author who writes in the manner of Flaubert and Zola and strives for precision rather than for striking effect. Although this quality makes his novel less interesting from the point of view of style, it contributes to the cold objectivity, the complete scientific detachment with which Martin du Gard views the struggles of his characters. No other naturalist in the twentieth century has managed to present his characters so dispassionately, or to apply the objectivity of the true scientist to literature with such striking success.

Martin du Gard shows the influence of modern science in two separate aspects: the above-mentioned detachment and objectivity, which saves him from the partisan bitterness of Dos Passos, and the exact knowledge of scientific principles, processes, and theories with which he outfits the minds of his characters. Martin du Gard, like Romains, is especially interested in medicine and has a sound grounding in medical principles; he succeeds in conveying medical details to the reader in a way that Lewis' *Arrowsmith* does not. He is especially adept as well in depicting children and adolescents. It is only when he abandons the bourgeoisie and attempts to describe the worlds of bohemians and aristocrats that his hand falters. He has no detectable political prejudices of any sort; he is one of the few naturalists who can draw a convincing portrait of a business-man or a priest.

LIFE: Roger Martin du Gard was born in 1881 of a Catholic and conservative bourgeois family whose traditional home was in Lorraine. He was educated in Paris lycées and at the École de Chartres, where he was trained as an archivist. This training undoubtedly influenced his literary method; he was able to apply the scholarly and scientific principles of research he acquired here to the gigantic mass of data he incorporated into *Les Thibaults*. His first novel, a mediocre one, was published in 1908; he destroyed several other early works. In 1913 he published *Jean Barois,* a novel of personal development which contains a foreshadowing of the technique of *Les Thibaults*. This novel was accepted by the publisher principally through the recommendation of André Gide, and Martin du Gard was able to maintain himself successfully as a writer thenceforth.

Martin du Gard spent the years of the First World War in the army; after the Armistice, in Germany, he began the writing of *Les Thibaults,* which he had already sketched out clearly in his mind. This task occupied him steadily from 1920 to 1937. The first volume of the work appeared in 1922, and he averaged a volume every two years thenceforth. Encouraged by Gide and Jacques Copeau, Martin du Gard also wrote for the theatre. In 1937 he was awarded the Nobel Prize for Literature in recognition of a single novel, *Les Thibaults*. He took little part in the Second World War; at the time of the fall of France he escaped with considerable hardship to Southern France, where he made no published comments on either occupation or liberation. He dislikes interviews, and is almost morbidly self-effacing. A character in *Les Thibaults* described as "ugly with an ugliness which was ridiculous and yet sympathetic" is said to be partly a self-portrait.

At his death in August, 1958, Martin du Gard was highly honored by the great writers of France. Albert Camus wrote a significant and appreciative preface to the publication of his complete works.

CHIEF WORK: *Les Thibaults* (translated as *The World of the Thibaults;* novel series, 1922-36) may be considered a single integrated novel; it is much more closely knit than Romains' *Men of Good Will.* It was, however, published in sections with separate titles: Part I, *The Grey Notebook,* and Part II, *The Penitentiary,* in 1922; Part III, *High Summer,* in 1923; Part IV, *The Consulting Day,* and Part V, *Sorellina,* in 1928; Part VI, *Death of the Father,* in 1929; and Part VII, *Summer 1914,* in 1936. Since one section contains three volumes and another two, the total work consists of ten volumes in French. In English the work appeared in two volumes: *The Thibaults* (1939) and *Summer 1914* (1940).

The action of *Les Thibaults* begins around the turn of the century as the father of the clan, Oscar Thibault, is at the height of his maturity and the two sons, Antoine and Jacques, are boys of lycée age. Oscar Thibault somewhat resembles Martin du Gard's own father; he is domineering, conservative, and Catholic, a watchful parent but a poor companion to his sons. The elder son, Antoine, is a practical scientific-minded man of action; he becomes a physician, flings himself into his profession with energy and enthusiasm, and earns some success Jacques is an introvert and a thinker; he dabbles in literature but eventually turns to socialism, in which he sees the utopian and humanitarian religion of the future. In 1914 Jacques, a fervent pacifist, is killed as he attempts to drop peace propaganda over the front lines. Antoine, less perceptive, accepts the war as necessary and throws himself into it with the enthusiasm he brings to every problem he encounters. His practical nature serves him no better than Jacques' idealism, however; he is killed in the trenches, and the Thibault line is extinct.

The best parts of *Les Thibaults* are the precise and powerfully convincing narrations: a justly famous scene in which Antoine performs an impromptu operation to save the life of a child injured in a traffic accident, the calmly related but exciting narrative of Jacques' flight over the Allied trenches to drop pacifist pamphlets, and the precisely documented description of old Oscar's decline and death. Much weaker are the sections in *Summer 1914* devoted to the diplomatic and strategic backgrounds of the war. Unlike many naturalists, Martin du Gard is at his best as a student of human nature; his Thibaults are three-dimensional flesh-and-blood figures, and are infinitely more interesting than his social groups and classes. His description of the causes of the war and of the war itself is probably the fairest and most objective analysis to appear in fiction to date. He is by no means disloyal or indifferent toward France, nor does he experience an adolescent sense of adventure in war as Hemingway does; at the same time his pacifism does not lead him into one-sided polemics in the style of Dos Passos or Remarque. Martin du Gard's interest in individual character has also enabled him to treat human passions with an insight given to few naturalists. His descriptions of the love-making between Antoine and his Jewish mistress Rachel are precise and sensual without descending into sordid sensationalism. *Les Thibaults* stands directly in the tradition of Zola, yet it is a novel that Zola, with his impassioned radicalism and his lack of interest in individual character, could never have written.

Pio Baroja y Nessi (Spanish, 1872-1956)

Baroja is the chief Spanish naturalist of the twentieth century. His personality, his interests, and his style are more complex than those of many naturalists; he blends objectivity with utopian mysticism in an intricate and ingenious manner. He was trained as a physician, and yet he draws his characters mainly from the slums and tenements of the Spanish cities. His chief work, *La Lucha por la Vida (The Struggle for Life),* is intended as a naturalistic trilogy with anarchistic content, but actually turns into a terse and stylistically pure study of character in the manner of Stendhal. Baroja, however, is neither Stendhalian nor anarchistic in his idealization of humanity, in his almost religious reverence for human life and the forces which propel it. His novels, half mystic and half savage, are the epitome of the Spanish spirit seen through the medium of the twentieth-century naturalistic novel.

LIFE: Baroja has led a life almost as colorful as that of Gorky. He is a Basque by birth; his father was a mining engineer, and Pío was born in San Sebastian in 1872. His boyhood and youth were spent in Madrid and Pamplona; in 1893 he took a medical degree at Madrid and accepted a post as a country doctor in the Basque country of Guipozcua. Baroja, like many another author in the twentieth century, brought to literature the detachment and the preoccupation with abnormality of a man trained in the medical discipline.

After a few years of practice, however, he returned to Madrid and became a baker, operating a struggling business in partnership with his brother for seven or eight years. This experience taught him something his medical practice had not: the sensation of the struggle for existence among the lower classes of a Spanish city. He began to write shortly after the turn of the century; his first major novel, *El Mayorazgo de Labraz,* appeared in 1903. It was the first novel in modern Spain to use Basque elements as a background. *La Lucha por la Vida* appeared the following year. He continued to write into the thirties, although his work was interrupted when he was forced to leave Spain at the time of the entry of Fascist troops into Pamplona. He spent the Second World War in France. His works began appearing in English in 1917, but his fame has thus far been restricted to a rather limited circle of critics, professors, and students of Spanish literature.

With the paperback publication of *The Restlessness of Shanti Andía* in 1962 (written as *Las inquietudes de Shanti Andía,* 1911), Baroja found a somewhat wider audience among those who read English. Shanti Andia, born a wanderer and a Basque, is an heroic nonconformist, in love both with the Basque country and with the sea. His adventures are sea-inspired and sea-led, following the past of his uncle, Juan de Aguirre, a dead sea captain, and his aimless, mysterious voyages. At the happy end of his life he is somewhat troubled that none of his sons, apparently, will go to sea. The subject of some doubts concerning his political beliefs, Baroja nevertheless was accorded distinction and honor in Franco's Spain while maintaining his independence and died in Madrid in October of 1956 rather than like so many of his fellow writers in 1936. Ernest Hemingway is reported to have admired Baroja as a writer (and perhaps because he had lived for some time at Pamplona) and in a conversation with him to have deplored the fact that "you have not yet received a Nobel Prize, especially when it was given to so many who deserved it less, like me." Which pretty much dates the conversation as mid-fifties.

CHIEF WORK: Most of Baroja's work can be grouped into series, trilogies, or novel clusters of various kinds. Notable among these series are: *Tierra vasca* (a set of Basque novels, 1900-03); *La vida fantástica* (fantastic novels, 1902-06); *Memorias de un Hombre de Acción* (a picaresque series centering around the hero Eugenio de Aviraneta, 1913-25); and *Agonías de nuestro Tiempo* (chiefly novels of idea and monologues, 1926-27). More famous, however, is *La Lucha por la Vida (The Struggle for Life),* a trilogy consisting of *La Busca (The Quest,* 1904), *Mala Hierba (Weeds,* 1904), and *Aurora Roja (Red Dawn,* 1904). The trilogy depicts the youth and manhood of a discontented young city drifter, Manuel Alcazar. Manuel, born of the city slums, is at first an ineffectual anarchist and loafer; he is regenerated through the love of a good woman, La Salvadora, and eventually achieves self-realization through acceptance of the doctrine of struggle and work. Although the message is ostensibly a plea for anarchism, the trilogy ends on a note of energy and optimism which rings more like the militant socialism of Saint-Simon and Fourier. The work is remarkable chiefly for the energy with which the ideas are presented, and for its colorful scenes of lower-class city life. The characters, even the hero, are not notable; they seem only half-living personifications without convincing and concrete existence.

Another important Baroja work is the novel series entitled *Las Ciudades (The Cities).* The most important unit of this group, *César o Nada (Caesar or Nothing;* novel, 1910) is also Baroja's best-known novel in English-speaking countries. The protagonist, César Moncada, is a fanatically ambitious youth somewhat resembling the Julien of Stendhal's *Le Rouge et le Noir.* He educates himself until he masters finance, politics, literatuie, and the arts; then he sets out boldly to conquer society and assume his rightful place in life. At first he plans a clerical career; rebuffed by the Church, he then turns to politics. Through the patronage of Don Calixto Garcia Guerrero, an important political figure, he manages to get himself elected as deputy on the conservative ticket. Utilizing his financial knowledge, he outwits the Minister of the Treasury, forcing him to resign, and makes himself a small fortune in the same affair. César now begins to shift toward the liberal viewpoint, still, of course, from motives of interest. This proves to be a false step. The clergy and police oppose him; the working-men themselves turn against him, and he loses an important election. After he is shot in an attempted assassination he resigns from the field of political activity, preferring to be nothing if he cannot be Caesar. This novel is a study of an ambitious but amoral "Napoleonic" personality, as well as an attack on Spanish conservatism and on the political activities of the Church.

5. REGIONALISTS AND RURAL NATURALISTS

The naturalistic movement, properly speaking, represented an attempt to create a literature for an age of science and industrialism. It thus tended to emphasize the more typically modern aspects of society: the factory, the city, the proletariat, suburban life, and the world of commerce. Its locales are generally urban or suburban, and its characters are persons in one way or another involved in the world of capitalism. In the twentieth century a wing of the naturalistic movement, however, has turned in the opposite direction: toward the land, the farm, and the peasant. This school represents in part a reaction to industrialism, and even to civilization itself. Such authors as Knut Hamsun and Jean Giono are part of a back-to-nature movement which idealizes rural life and occasionally even skirts a sort of mystical primitivism.

The movement itself takes two principal forms. REGIONALISM is a form of literature laid in rural settings and making extensive use of local customs, language, and characteristics, but in which the chief interest lies in the personality and psychological motivation of the rural characters involved. Goethe's *Hermann und Dorothea* and George Eliot's *Adam Bede* foreshadowed this genre, and its chief modern advocates are Hardy, Ramuz, Willa Cather, Giono, and Faulkner. Some of these authors, especially Giono and Faulkner, are psychological and artistic rather than regional in their approach to the novel, but their settings are strongly influenced by regional characteristics.

RURAL NATURAI ISM, or AGRARIAN literature, on the other hand, is economic and technical in its approach; it is the rural equivalent of the city novel of industrialism. The practical problems of farming are related in great detail; the rural population is shown struggling against nature and the land rather than against each other. Naturally the two tendencies sometimes overlap; Hamsun's *Growth of the Soil* treats of human conflict as well as of the struggle for life. The agrarian novel,

however, does tend to show the peasant or farmer as an economic
creature whose main problem lies in wresting a living from the land.
The development of this genre can be traced to various nineteenth-
century novels of the type of Zola's *La Terre;* its chief modern advocates are Knut Hamsun and Ole Rölvaag.

Knut Hamsun (Norwegian, 1859-1952)

Knut Hamsun is chiefly famous in America for a single book, the
magnificent *Growth of the Soil* (1917). He has produced, however,
at least a half-dozen novels deserving of a place in world literature.
At first glance Hamsun appears to be a singularly gifted but naive
writer, especially if the reader is familiar only with *Growth of the Soil.*
This, however, is an artistic illusion. He is a highly sophisticated
author, in spite of his lack of formal education. He views the peasant,
not with the first-hand intimacy of a fellow-toiler, but with the profound detachment of the philosopher. He is drawn to the soil by a
mystic affinity for its prolific properties; to him the earth is Demeter,
the life-giver, the eternally renascent source of man's body and suste-
nance. He objects to modern civilization not because it is vicious but
because it is unnatural; i.e., that it causes man to depart from his
traditional relation with the earth and to confine himself within a
purely synthetic framework of cities, factories, conventions, and pro-
hibitions. Thus *Growth of the Soil* is more akin to Thoreau's *Walden*
than it is to Zola's *La Terre* or to any other naturalistic study of
peasant life.

In style Hamsun's work, which at first seems primitive and elemental, is actually a carefully contrived and patiently worked form of
prose poetry. It is undoubtedly influenced by the Bible, especially by
the historical style of the Pentateuch. The sentences frequently begin
with "and," the diction is stark and almost bereft of adjectives, and
there is much poetic repetition and parallelism. A long passage in
Growth of the Soil describing the meeting and mating of the protagonists ends, "She did not go away at all. Inger was her name. And Isak
was his name." Here we almost feel we are in the presence of Adam
and Eve.

LIFE: Knut Hamsun, born in 1859, sprang from the well-to-do
"peasant aristocracy" of Northern Norway. He had no formal education, but at the age of nineteen he had already written a novel and a

considerable amount of verse. As a youth he worked at many jobs, both clerical positions and the hardest sort of manual labor. He tried to save enough money to enter the University of Christiania, but this proved impossible; in 1882 he therefore emigrated to America. In Wisconsin and Minnesota Hamsun worked at odd agricultural and manual jobs, but soon found that America was less a land of opportunity than he had expected. He returned to Norway in 1884 and was able to pick up some money lecturing on his experiences in the New World. He returned to America in 1886-88, this time with more success; he lectured on literature in Minneapolis, saved money as a harvest hand in North Dakota, and served as a street-car conductor in Chicago. According to local legend he was dismissed from this last position because he was generally to be found in a sort of philosophical haze reading Euripides on the back platform and ignoring the stops. Later, in 1920, Chicago newspapers were to describe him under the headline "Horse-Car Conductor Wins Nobel Prize."

Hamsun's first important work was *The Cultural Life of Modern America* (1889), a critical essay in which he found little to commend in American life. His first major novel, *Hunger,* was published in 1890; the book was an immediate success, and he was able to live the rest of his life as a professional writer. From 1889 he lived in a fishing village near Grimstad, in Northern Norway, with his wife and five children. *Growth of the Soil,* his best-known work, appeared in 1917, and for this novel specifically he was awarded the Nobel Prize for Literature in 1920. During the two World Wars he showed considerable sympathy for Germany, even at the time of the Nazi occupation of Norway in 1940. This attitude provoked considerable resentment among many Norwegians. No action was taken, however, partly on account of Hamsun's age. He died in 1952.

CHIEF WORKS: *Growth of the Soil* (Norw. *Markens gröde;* novel, 1917) is the story of the development of a rural community in a pioneer area of Northern Norway. Isak, the hero, is a personification of primitive humanity in its most favorable light: he is persevering, elemental, honest, essentially kind, but none too intelligent. He is not a brute in the Zola tradition, but rather more similar to Rousseau's noble savage.

As the novel opens Isak is to be seen tramping north, away from the towns, into the undeveloped forest land. There he halts and builds himself a hut, returning to the town occasionally to carry up tools and materials on his back. He makes it known that he is in need of a woman to help him, and presently Inger appears over the hill. She is a sturdy, taciturn woman, disfigured with a hare-lip which has so far prevented her from getting a husband. Inger stays, and she and Isak produce a thriving family of children. Gradually the land is cleared, animals are bought with the profits from timber, new buildings are constructed, and the prosperity of the farm, now named Sellanraa, attracts new settlers to the region. A single tragedy mars the idyll: Inger, frightened by the sight of a hare when she is pregnant, bears a hare-lipped child. Mindful of her own miserable youth, she strangles the child on impulse. The "crime" is discovered, and she spends eight years in a correctional institution. But at the institute she acquires city manners; she learns to sew with a machine, and brings a new vigor back into the life of the farm.

Civilization itself is the villain of this novel. One son, Eleseus, goes to town to become a clerk, but city ways corrupt him; he becomes disillusioned and unhappy. Toward the end of the novel he returns to Sellanraa and finds contentment operating a country store. Another sub-plot is the story of Geissler, a down-and-out former official who tries to make a fortune by working copper mines in the region of Sellanraa. But the profits from the mines are not "real"; they are based on the purely synthetic and arbitrary need for the metal, and Geissler is disappointed at last. At the end of the novel only old Isak, who has stuck to his rural ways and has sought doggedly to build up the value of the soil, has succeeded in life. The style of *Growth of the Soil* is Biblical and poetic, and the characters of Isak, Inger, Geissler, and the sons are powerfully drawn.

The concept of the corrupting influence of civilization also occurs in a series of Hamsun's later novels: *Wanderers* (1922), *Vagabonds* (1927), *August* (1930), and *The Road Leads On* (1933). The central figure in each of these works is a "wanderer type"—a natural man, constantly in touch with the rhythm of nature, gaining his living by his hands and loath to attach himself to the wage-bondage of city culture. Although these works present Hamsun's personal ideal even more clearly than does *Growth of the Soil,* they are not equal to the masterpiece in literary quality.

Selma Lagerlöf (Swedish, 1858-1940)

Selma Lagerlöf's work is a curious mixture of romanticism and realism. She is fascinated with Swedish folk-lore, with its strange super-
naturalism and its dark, almost Gothic gloom; her novels are filled
with wolves pursuing sleighs in which illicit lovers are fleeing, Byronic
heroes who make pacts with the Devil, and elfin adventures reminiscent of Hans Christian Andersen. At the same time she portrays the
life of the rural Swedish peasant and the gentry of the Värmland
district with a decisive and penetrating realism. Her novels turn away
from the European tradition which Swedish authors had so long imitated and seek their subject matter in the life of rural Sweden. She
rejects the naturalistic excesses of Strindberg and the imitators of
Ibsen, a group who were at the height of their prestige when she began
to write. She sought to create a literature which was thoroughly and
characteristically Swedish, and at the same time human and universal
enough to find acceptance by foreign readers. These goals she attained;
her books have been translated into a dozen languages, and *Gösta
Berling's Saga* has won its position as one of the great novels of world
literature.

LIFE: Miss (afterwards Dr.) Lagerlöf was born in Värmland, a
district of Southern Sweden, in a comfortable and traditional family.
She grew up in the family estate, Marbacka, which appears in several
novels and lends its name to one. As a young girl she was afflicted
with a paralysis, probably poliomyelitis, which confined her to bed
for a considerable time and caused her to remain a permanent semi-
invalid. During this period she became studious and thoughtful; she
began to write poems and romances. Shortly after she began practicing
as a country school-teacher at the age of twenty-five she published
Gösta Berling's Saga, her first and most famous novel. This work won
an award from the magazine *Idun* and also secured recognition from
the Danish critic Georg Brandes, who fought an enthusiastic campaign
for the book in the world of Scandinavian letters. In 1895 she abandoned teaching to become a professional writer; she travelled extensively, especially in Italy. She published *The Wonderful Adventures
of Nils* and *The Further Adventures of Nils* in 1906; these children's
tales found a wide acceptance in Scandinavia, and immediately took
their place in standard Swedish folklore. In 1909 she was awarded the

Nobel Prize for Literature, the first woman to receive this honor. As her writing became more remunerative she was able to buy back her beloved family estate, which had been sold to strangers. She remained on this estate intermittently until the end of her life. In 1940, weakened and distressed over the spread of the Second World War to Scandinavia, she died of peritonitis.

CHIEF WORK: Selma Lagerlöf is admired in non-Scandinavian countries chiefly as the author of *Gösta Berling's Saga* (novel, 1891), a half-satirical, half-romantic work portraying the career of a virile, carefree, and irresistible young roué. Gösta Berling, the protagonist, combines the engaging amorality of a Byronic hero with the deep and brooding melancholy of a Hamlet; he is irresistible to women and yet popular among men. He early decides to enter the ministry, but abandons this career when he finds himself little fitted for it. He eventually ends up as a protegé of the Mistress of Ekeby Hall, who maintains a dozen or so old warriors on her estate as pensioners out of philanthropy. The story thenceforth is disconnected and episodic: Gösta falls in love with the Countess Elizabeth, a beautiful and virtuous young noblewoman; enters into a sinister friendship with Sintram, a blacksmith who is actually a sort of personification of evil; and helps defend Ekeby Hall against a rioting mob who are incited to deviltry by Sintram's machinations. At last Gösta reforms, marries Elizabeth and plans to devote the remainder of his life to good works, following the example set for him by his worthy patroness.

Gösta Berling's Saga was considerably influenced by the author's reading in Carlyle, especially *The History of the French Revolution,* which seems to have inspired the scene of the storming of Ekeby Hall The character of Sintram owes something as well to Goethe's *Faust.*

Jean Giono (French, born 1895)

Jean Giono is a lyrical novelist of great talent, less a naturalist than a prose-poet of peasant life. His novels are laid in Southern France, in the Basses-Alps and in the valleys of the Upper Durance. In this sun-baked and rocky mountain region live a race of peasants half Italian and half French, sturdy, independent-minded, and passionately in love with their land. Giono grew up among these people; he writes about them from the inside as one of their number. His method is not the photographic external realism of the naturalists; he penetrates to the core of his characters and unfolds their inner reactions in a manner similar to the stream-of-consciousness technique of Joyce, Woolf, and Vittorini. His Durance peasants are strange and irrational creatures, yet their actions have the logic of biology; they are elemental men in the true sense of the word. They are closely attuned to the rhythm of life: the recurrence of seasons, the reproduction of life, the wresting of food from the soil, and human birth and death are constantly in their minds. Giono's work has a certain Dionysian quality; the raw life forces are laid bare of the social conventions which ordinarily hide them, and the Christian Puritanism which seeks to deny or deflect natural drives is absent entirely. Giono parallels Whitman in many respects, and he resembles Knut Hamsun more than he does any other modern author. He differs from Hamsun primarily in his artistic subtlety; his peasants, boldly drawn as they are, are still a hundred times more complex than Hamsun's Norwegian pioneers. Moreover Giono has a keen sense of humor; he portrays the ludicrous in human existence as well as the elemental.

Giono's style is so highly compressed that it occasionally falls into preciousness. His images are exaggerated but unerring; a girl's eyes blink "gently like a bird about to take flight" and in the mountain evening "the roots ease their grip on the rock." In spite of their peasant setting his books are totally subjective; his sensitivity to physical environment is reminiscent of Proust. To Giono every sensation is important. His attitude is sensual but not erotic; sexual love plays a smaller part in his work than in the work of any contemporary French novelist. He views the physical life with the mind of the peasant, and to the peasant the harvest and the wind are as important as any human passion.

Giono is not an agrarian novelist; he is little interested in the technique of agriculture. He is concerned with two things: the biological relations of man, animal, and nature, and the character of the human mind. He views both of these poetically rather than scientifically; he wastes little time on technical details or in accurate transcription of the peasant *patois*. Giono is essentially an internal novelist whose subject matter involves him with the external world.

LIFE: Giono was born in a small Provence town in 1895; his father was a Protestant shoemaker and revolutionist who was sixty when Jean was born. His mother, much younger, was a Parisian laundress. Jean spent a year in the local lycée, then dropped out to work in a bank. In 1914 he entered the army, fought at Verdun, and conceived such a fervent hatred of war that he remained an active pacifist all the rest of his life. He began to write immediately after the war, but his early poems attracted little attention. His first recognition came in 1928, when the *Nouvelle Revue Française* published a short story, "Champs." In 1929 his first novel, *Colline,* appeared, closely followed by *Un de Baumugnes* (translated as *Lovers are Never Losers*); the latter novel won the Prix Brentano for 1931. *Le Chant du Monde (The Song of the World;* 1934) was also successful. Giono's pacifistic ardor increased over the years, or rather remained firm in the face of growing nationalism and militarism; he was imprisoned for pacifist activity in 1939. Since 1930 he has lived in a modest house in the valley of the Durance with his wife and mother. At least two successful films have been made from his works: *Harvest* (1938) and *The Baker's Wife* (1939).

Among his other activities Giono made an effective translation of Melville's *Moby Dick* into French. Novels have continued to appear with great regularity: *Les âmes fortes* (1949), *Les grands chemins,* (1951), *Le hussard sur le toit* (1951), *Le bonheur fou* (1957), and *Angelo* (1958) among others. He has also written reminiscences and travel books about Provence, and in 1968 published *Ennemonde et autres caractères.* Critical works about Giono have been appearing in the fifties and sixties not only in France but in the United States as well.

CHIEF WORKS: *Regain (Harvest;* novel, 1930) is a story of the decline and regeneration of the land in a remote Provence valley. Aubignane, a village high in the mountains, is gradually reduced to poverty; one by one the inhabitants leave for larger towns in the plains. Finally only Panturle, a dogged young peasant, and Mamèche, a decrepit harridan, are left. The land dries up, the goat ceases to give milk, and it seems as though the valley can no longer support human life. Mamèche, however, vows she will go off and find a mate for Panturle to bring new life to the village; she disappears one day, and years later her corpse is found in the brush. But before she dies she manages, by popping up unexpectedly like a ghost, to frighten into the valley an itinerant knife-grinder and his servant-girl, the miserable young Arsule. Panturle, fleeing in fright from the unaccustomed visitors, falls down a waterfall; he is rescued by Arsule and the knife-grinder, and the girl stays with him as his wife. Gradually the two struggle alone to bring vitality back to the valley. They borrow seed wheat, fashion a plow, wrench the rocks from the soil, and produce a fine wheat crop in a year when the plains people's corn fails totally. Their success attracts other settlers to the valley, and soon Aubignane begins to grow into a prosperous village again. The story comes full cycle when Arsule bears a child. In structure and plot the novel greatly resembles Hamsun's *Growth of the Soil;* the style, however, is more lyrical and the characters more complex and passionate.

Jean le Bleu (translated as *Blue Boy;* novel, 1932) is a sort of poetized autobiography; its main lines are drawn from Giono's own life. The boy Jean, at the beginning of the novel six or seven years old, lives in the house of his shoemaker father. In spite of the protests of the mother, the father shelters in the attic a continual succession of political refugees, and the boy makes friends in turn with each of these eccentric and unhappy characters. He also learns music from two ragged musicians, Décidément and Madame-la-Reine, and is hugged and babied by the young girls of the town. When he is old enough to work he goes to stay with the farmer Père Massot in the country; there he learns to admire the fields, the animals, and their patient peasant masters. Still only a child, he already knows much about life, love, and death; he is far less naive than a city boy. The story ends with the outbreak of the First World War; a short closing passage tells of Jean's return from the army and his interview with his dying father. *Jean le Bleu* is structurally a set of connected lyrical episodes rather than a traditional novel.

"La Femme du Boulanger" ("The Baker's Wife"; story, 1935) is based on an episode briefly related in *Jean le Bleu.* The unnamed baker is thin and measly, his wife young and voluptuous. She flirts with all the village men, then runs off with a shepherd from nearby Les Conches. The baker is disconsolate and unable to work, and for several days the village is without bread. But life must go on; the curé and the schoolmaster form a little delegation to find the erring pair—they have taken shelter on an island in the river- -and bring the wife back to her husband. It is all very well, they argue, for love to have its way, but for the entire village to be deprived of bread is too much. When the wife returns, the village, happy to have its bread again, readily forgives her, and the baker is at last forced to do the same. This story was made into a successful film by Marcel Pagnol.

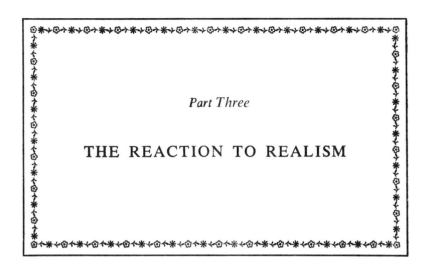

Part Three

THE REACTION TO REALISM

6. LITERATURE OF PSYCHOLOGY AND ANALYSIS

The term "psychological literature" is today used in many different senses. In the France of the seventeenth century it referred to the analysis of moral sentiments and the conflict of the ideas of right and wrong in the minds of tragic heroes. In the nineteenth century the term "psychological novel" was applied to novels of the type of Stendhal's, in which the hero's inner conflicts were laid bare for the edification of the reader. Later in the century the works of Poe, Baudelaire, and Dostoyevsky were termed "psychological" because these authors were preoccupied with unusual or abnormal states of mind. All of these elements are reproduced in the literature of the twentieth century as a part of the broader reaction against external realism. Hermann Hesse treats moral problems from the psychological point of view; Alberto Moravia concerns himself chiefly with internal analysis of the motivations of his characters; and an influential group led by Arthur Schnitzler and Hugo von Hofmannsthal in Europe concentrate their attention on the sexual or neurotic complexes popularized by the Freudian and other schools of psychoanalysis. These authors differ widely in content and technique, but they are essentially alike in their purpose: to present human motivation from the inside,

81

from the point of view of the mind concerned, rather than from the
point of view of an external observer. Some are influenced by
modern psychiatry, others react strongly against it, and still others
seem to ignore it entirely. They agree, however, that it is inside the
human brain that the significant battles of life take place, and that
mental conflicts have a subtlety, an intensity, and an importance far
beyond what might be expected from mere external examination of
a human being.

Alberto Moravia (Italian, born 1907)

Post World War II revealed to the world two exciting things about
Italy: its highly imaginative and creative film industry *(Open City,
Paisan, The Bicycle Thief,* and a long succession of Federico Fellini
films like *La Strada, La Dolce Vita, Guilietta of the Spirits, 8½,*
and the *Satyricon)* and a group of novelists who were doing equally
exciting work: Moravia, Vittorini, Pavese, Italo Calvino, and others.
Perhaps the most interesting of these to the American reader, the
Fellini of the novelists, has been Alberto Moravia.

Moravia, one of the most talented of the new generation of Italian
novelists, began as something of a prodigy; he gained a precocious
success among Italian readers at the age of twenty-two with the publication of *Gli Indifferenti (The Indifferent Ones)* in 1929. His later
works, however, far surpass this early novel in quality.

Sickly and introspective during his youth, Moravia was nevertheless
a warm anti-fascist, and was eventually forced into exile by the Musso-
lini regime. His world fame dates from the period after the Second
World War. The publication of *Woman of Rome* (1949) and *The
Conformist* (1951) have gained him wide acclaim as a master of the
psychological novel.

Moravia's technique relies strongly on the contrast of psychological
types, a contrast which is usually demonstrated through internal reaction rather than external action. His favorite situation is the crisis
in which a weak, passive, or amorphous personality conflicts with a
strong, aggressive, or even sadistic protagonist. The action of the novel
characteristically records the internal mental processes of the passive
or receptive character. In *The Woman of Rome* a prostitute is utilized
as this passive character, and each of the four aggressive men who

influence her life are utilized in succession as protagonists. In *The Conformist* the passive character is a young man who, seeking only to be like everyone else, ends as a Fascist and a thorough-going scoundrel. The passive characters in Moravia are perhaps to be pitied, but they are not always intended to be admired.

Moravia's style is conventional, even old-fashioned. He generally utilizes either the first-person narrative or the hero-centered narration—we see the thoughts and images that pass through the hero's mind in painstaking chronological succession. This simplicity, coupled with Moravia's interest in sexual experiences and adventures, has made him popular among the wide reading public; but his lubricity, when it occurs, is merely superficial. His deeper interest is in the analysis of human psychological processes.

At least two of his novels *(The Woman of Rome* and *The Conformist)* contain latent anti-fascist content. Moravia is not a political writer, however. Since he grew up in Italy under the Fascist regime he inevitably encountered individuals who were influenced by their contact with totalitarianism, and he has described these types in his novels. The Fascist police officer in *The Woman of Rome* is by no means a villain, and before we finish the novel we almost find ourselves sympathizing with him. At the same time we develop an understanding of, and repugnance for, the things fascism does to decent minds; and in this sense the novel is profoundly anti-fascist.

LIFE: Born Alberto Pincherle in Rome in 1907 of Jewish parents who were in comfortable circumstances, and stricken with bone tuberculosis at nine, the young man began writing fiction as an invalid and had already published his first novel before he recovered his health in his mid-twenties. In choosing to write under a pseudonym, Moravia had several reasons: the family might be shocked by his themes; his own name was obviously Jewish; a professor of religious history already published under the name Alberto Pincherle; and fascist censorship was a potential threat (a real one, as it turned out). Additionally, as in the case of Stendhal, there may have been an unconscious rejection of his own identity, the substitution of a second personality, a kind of "masked voyeur."

In 1941, after a second novel *(Le ambizioni sbagliate,* 1935, translated both as *The Wheel of Fortune* and *Mistaken Ambitions)* and a third *(La mascherata,* 1941; *The Masquerade,* 1952), Moravia was forbidden by the Fascist censorship to publish anything. In the same year he married Elsa Morante, another novelist; they were subsequently separated. In the fall of 1943 with the Nazi occupation of Rome Moravia had to hide out in the mountains south of the city to avoid arrest. After the liberation he returned to Rome and to writing with a series of successes. Besides the novels already mentioned *(La romana,* 1947 and *Il conformista,* 1951) there appeared the novellas, *Agostino* (1945) and *La disubbidienza* (1948, translated together as *Two Adolescents,* 1950), *L'amore coniugale* (1949, translated as *Conjugal Love,* 1951), *Il disprezza* (1954, translated as *A Ghost at Noon,* 1956), *La ciociara* (1957, translated as *Two Women,* 1958), *La noia* (1960, translated as *The Empty Canvas,* 1961), *L'attenzione* (1965, translated as *The Lie,* 1966), several volumes of short stories, a book of essays, and writing for the cinema. His politics in the post war period were leftist but independent and made very little impact on his fiction. He did assist in the founding in 1953 of a political-literary review, *Nuovi Argamenti.* Except for occasional travel and the period of wartime exile, he has remained fixed in Rome. The novels of the sixties have extended Moravia's range and concerns into areas of epistemology and metaphysics.

CHIEF NOVELS: *La Romana (Woman of Rome;* novel, 1949) is the life story of a prostitute ostensibly related by herself. Adriana, the heroine, is a none too intelligent but affectionate and basically decent girl. She is betrayed first by her shrewd and grasping mother and then by her own sense of pity; she cannot help feeling affection for the men she meets. For this reason, of course, she is an incompetent prostitute, and brings only trouble to the men in her life. These are Gino, a young chauffeur; Astarita, a Fascist police official; Giacinti, a callous and wealthy business-man who buys her affections as though they were groceries; Sonzogno, a brutal "strong man," professional thief, and murderer; and Giacomo, a young liberal and revolutionist. Adriana first experiences love with Gino, but soon outgrows him. Her friend Gisella, a hardened woman of the streets, introduces her to Astarita, and she finds him as faltering and self-conscious in love as he is thorough and ruthless in his profession. The great passion of her life is Giacomo, the young radical she hides in her apartment, caresses, and aids with money. Adriana is an unconscious agent of evil; unwittingly she brings about the downfall of each of these men. Gino is fired for stealing from his employer a compact actually taken by Adriana; Sonzogno comes into the possession of this compact, tries to sell it, and becomes involved in a quarrel in which he kills a jeweler. Astarita, seeking both Sonzogno and Giacomo, is through a coincidence murdered by the former, who is then shot by the police; and Giacomo, who has turned informer for Astarita, kills himself out of remorse.

Il Conformista (*The Conformist;* novel, 1951) is a study of a young man without political convictions who is impelled by the spirit of the times to become a Fascist. Marcello Clerici, the hero, is dominated by a single desire: to be like everyone else. Inwardly, however, he feels himself a horrible monster. He has sadistic and homosexual tendencies which certain shocking experiences in his boyhood bring to the surface and intensify. In his desire to forget these anomalies by conforming to the society about him, he becomes a Fascist spy and is sent on a mission to Paris to aid in the murder of Professor Quadri, a teacher of his college days who is now a political refugee. Marcello, who was about to get married anyhow, combines this mission with his honeymoon. In Paris he carries out his instructions, keeping them secret from his bride Giulia; she gains some knowledge of them, however, and is horribly shocked. After Quadri is killed in an ambush through Marcello's tip, the couple return to Rome. By this time Marcello, shaken by his experiences in Paris, begins to recognize that his nature is far from a normal one; he fails only to recognize that a norm is an artificial concept and that no one is entirely normal. With the outbreak of the war he settles down in the country with his wife and baby. In 1944 the imminent fall of the Fascist regime fills him with dread; he realizes now that he cannot hope to conform to the new change of events. The matter is solved for him in a way he did not expect; he is killed in an air-raid as he attempts to flee from anti-Fascist mobs.

Il disprezzo (A Ghost at Noon; novel, 1954) begins Moravia's study of the relation of art to sexuality. Genuine art and genuine love must be to a large degree spontaneous. If either becomes excessively self-analytical, it loses impetus, becomes passive in watching itself in action. The passive artist-lover of this novel is a would-be dramatist, Riccardo Molteni, who makes his living as a film critic and later a scriptwriter for bad movies, taking this job to "make money" which he thinks will please his wife Emilia, with whom he is very much in love.

Molteni tells his story in his own person. The first script paid a first installment on a luxury apartment. For the next he is on contract to collaborate with a German film writer named Rheingold on a version of the *Odyssey*. Rheingold wants to make of it a psychoanalytic drama, whereas the producer Battista wants a spectacular extravaganza along American film-epic lines. Molteni in the middle does not know what he wants, but the marriage with Emilia is beginning to break up. The four characters leave Rome for Capri where the film is to be written in two cars. Battista, bold, brassy, egocentric, and fancying himself a Don Juan, suggests that Emilia ride with him, leaving the other two colloborators to discuss the script on the journey. Molteni agrees over Emilia's objections, which increases her scorn for her husband and his failure to understand her real needs. His efforts to "please" his wife serve to alienate her further.

The film script progresses on parallel lines. A scriptwriter can hardly be an honest artist; the business is necessarily a kind of prostitution, a betrayal of masculinity, which is the real reason for Emilia's contempt and rejection. Molteni is not an artist because he is not a man, and he is not a man because he is not an artist. Rheingold wants to do the hidden Freudian drama in Homer—Ulysses wanders because he is afraid to go home to his wife, but Penelope is alienated because he fails to come home. This may not be good Homer, as Molteni sees, but it allows Moravia to manipulate Rheingold's interpretation to illuminate the Molteni-Emilia situation. And Molteni understands: Ulysses is a civilized man, Penelope a "primitive" woman. But he is too intelligent; he thinks too much; he is a Hamlet-Prufrock. The problem is insoluble. One can only wait for catastrophe. In a final argument Emilia tells her husband he is not a man, that she is leaving for Rome with Battista; Molteni dreams a reconciliation, but the vision of Emilia fades like the ghost of Creusa in the arms of Aeneas. She is killed later that afternoon in an auto accident on the way to Rome.

The problem is that of the creative mind turning inward upon itself, and Moravia will return to it in the painter of *The Empty Canvas* and in *The Lie,* a novel about a novelist writing a novel. This is similar to what Gide was doing in *The Counterfeiters,* but Moravia adds the sexual dimension to the metaphysical probing.

La ciociara (Two Women; novel, 1957) is the story which grew out of Moravia's winter in the mountains in 1943-44 to escape the Nazi occupation of Rome and to wait for the liberation. The main character-narrator is this time a woman (compare *La Romana),* Cesira, petty bourgeois, lower class shopkeeper in the Trastevere section of Rome. She is shrewd, turns to black-marketing without scruple, and makes money. The second most important character is her opposite in many ways, Michele, a bookish intellectual and idealist, who is regarded by the peasants and workers as an idiot, somewhat like Dostoevsky's Prince Myshkin.

Cesira tells her story and that of her dauhter Rosetta in a kind of Joycean natural stream of association because that is her character and that is the way Moravia hears her talk. She is prudent, systematic, frugal, tends to business even after the bombs start falling on Naples (after all they will not come to Rome, "because in Rome there's the Pope"), rejects overtures from men although she is a widow because promiscuity is bad for business. After the prologue in Rome, action shifts to the mountain refuge preceding the Liberation. There they meet Michele, oddly pure, who reads the story of Lazarus to the baffled people and tries to explain that the Italians have no right to complain of the war since they supported or passively accepted the fascism that brought it about. They must lose everything and suffer in order to understand. He offers himself as hostage to retreating German troops who eventually shoot him. But later his example and words will be remembered. Cesira remembers and learns.

After the liberation which does not bring much happiness although plenty of excitement, Cesira and Rosetta are attacked and violated by Moroccan soldiers in a church. The worst of it is Rosetta's reaction; she becomes hard, bitter, cynical, promiscuous for money. After a long time Cesira remembers Michele's words, "I understood that Michele had been right, that for a time we too had been dead, Rosetta and I, dead to the compassion we owed to others and to ourselves. But our suffering had saved us at the last moment." She is eloquent, complex, an authentic character.

La noia (The Empty Canvas; novel, 1960) has as its artist figure a

would-be painter, Dino; but the problem of artistic creativity is related here not only to the *libido* but to metaphysical and ontological
problems of the artist's relation to reality in the concrete. Dino nar-
rates; born into wealth he has become a dilletante: trying to create
an identity for himself as poor, artistic, and in revolt against his
mother (a father is lacking), he can only become a rich man pretending to be poor—living in a studio in the Via Margutta with
canvases, paints, and brushes. His neighbor Balestrieri is an untal-
ented yet genuine artist. Dino has trouble believing in the reality of
objects around him, a sort of sensory impotence or *noia*. The failure
of cognition is also the failure of communication. Moravia has almost
no sympathy for ultra-modern art. Dino, who starts out as a nonrep-
resentational painter, becomes no painter at all. As Kandinsky says,
"Marvelous is the empty canvas."

Balestrieri paints portraits, female nudes by preference (his real
reason for painting is sexual conquest); although anatomically and
aesthetically imperfect, they point to the artist as sexually well adjusted. Dino doesn't like girls; although his mother tries to get him
involved, the fault is largely hers with her domineering, assertive
masculinity. Balestrieri dies of sexual excesses with the last of his
mistresses, Cecilia, and Dino tries to take over. Death is at least
better than boredom, or an empty canvas. Dino's hope of using Cecilia
as a link with the real world doesn't work out. She is indifferent to
his money; for her sex is important. Dino's mother is the opposite.
Money is her sex, her prudery; she keeps the household cash in the
bathroom. Money is at the root of alienation. When Cecilia leaves
Dino for her lover Luciani, he tries to end it all by driving his car
into a tree. But he survives, although he can't be said to live.

L'attenzione (The Lie; novel, 1965) is a novel about authenticity,
thus inviting comparison with the existential ideas of Pirandello and
Jean-Paul Sartre. Here the artist-protagonist is a would-be novelist,
Francesco Merighi, a journalist with ambitions. He abandons his first
attempt to write a novel because it seems to him inauthentic. Instead
he keeps a diary of the most banal events of his daily life to gather
material for an authentic novel. By observing life around him closely
he discovers two things: his wife Cora is engaged in a secret career
as a procuress under cover of a dress shop and he himself is in love

with his stepdaughter Gabriella or "Baba." His life has the same kind of artificial and fictional sensationalism of which inauthentic novels are made. In this crisis his diary no longer seems true, and he begins to "novelize" it as he goes along.

Therefore the novel is about the writing of a novel, or rather a diary, which brings it in some relationship to Gide's *The Counterfeiters* and Proust's *Remembrance of Things Past*. But like Pirandello not only does art imitate life, but life begins to imitate art, and the possible (often inevitable) inauthenticity of one's living means no existence at all. Francesco sees the people around him playing roles: Consolo plays at being editor-in-chief of his paper; Cora pretends to be a housewife and a mother (but attempted to prostitute her own daughter at fourteen—and succeeded, it appears later). By temperament Francesco is a genuine artist, but journalism has corrupted him. He and Baba would like to be lovers, but the convention of incest (legal, not biological) keeps them apart—although perhaps that is the reason for his desire.

The inauthentic life consists of automatic, puppet-like words and gestures. Francesco begins inventing scenes for his diary—a chapter of love-making with Baba. Soon he finds it difficult to distinguish fiction and truth. There are scenes partly invented and partly real (the invented parts seem somewhat more "real") with the country parents of Cora (a fine scene with the drunken father-in-law rejecting all his "identities" and insisting "I am what I am!"); with Francesco's brother, a rather vulgar, libertine stockbroker; and the "confessions" of Baba. Francesco will never know the truth. As for what really happened, this does not exist (Pirandello's shadows); but what remains is a diary, or a novel, or is it? Omniscience in a novel is no longer possible. The novelist must depend upon a single point of view, limited by character, place, time, life, astigmatism, and the current philosophy of relativism and despair.

Jean Anouilh (French, born 1910)

The work of Anouilh, perhaps the most brilliant French dramatist of the mid-twentieth century, once relatively little known in America, although *Antigone* had been staged several times in this country in the early fifties and *Ring Around the Moon,* Christopher Fry's adaptation of *L'Invitation au chateau,* had attracted considerable attention by the middle fifties, has since that time become familiar chiefly through the televised version of *The Lark* and the filmed *Becket* starring Richard Burton and Peter O'Toole. Anouilh is a psychological dramatist, although not in the modern pseudo-scientific sense; his attitudes are often those of the neoclassic drama of the seventeenth century transposed into modern dress. His most interesting dramas are his tragedies; they are simultaneously a modern expression of the classic tragic principle and a sensitive approach to the portrayal of human mental processes.

Anouilh's theatre falls into two relatively distinct sections: prose tragedies in modern dress collected under the titles *Pièces noires* ("black plays") and *Nouvelles Pièces noires;* and whimsical comedies with serious undertones published as *Pièces roses* ("rose-colored plays") and *Pièces brillantes* ("sparkling plays"). All these plays are practical and effective stage drama written for actual production; Anouilh is a man of the theatre who is intimately familiar with professional stage techniques.

Anouilh's chief contribution to modern drama is his part in the revival of the tragic principle in the theatre, especially his concept of the tragic hero. In his view humanity is made up of two kinds of people: the anonymous mass of normal nonentities who accept the banality of daily life, and the heroes. The first group is motivated chiefly by a desire for a complacent happiness; the second group is satisfied only with martyrdom. Thus his modernizations of Greek myths—*Antigone* (1944), *Eurydice* (1942), and *Medée* (1946)— show us human beings who come to destruction because they will not compromise, just as the classic hero came to his downfall through an inherent tragic flaw in his own personality.

In Anouilh's comedies a common theme is the contrast between artificial, snobbish, or conventional behavior and real or natural behavior. His heroes and heroines are usually young people in love who achieve happiness through defying conventions. Anouilh has a natural gift for whimsy; he is a master of dialogue, and is skilled at creating a characteristic poetic mood in the drama. A possible weakness is his diffuse approach to characterization; his characters are too often symbols or dramatic pawns rather than warm and living human beings.

In his plays of the nineteen fifties and sixties Anouilh reveals increasing concerns with the relationships of reality and illusion and with art and theatre in Pirandellian terms, even directly suggesting in *The Cavern* (1961) that Pirandello has done this before (in *Six Characters in Search of an Author*). One of his characters in *The Rehearsal* says that "naturalness and truth, in the theatre, are the least natural things in the world. . . . Life is very pretty, but it has no form. Art has an object precisely to give it form." The theatricalism of this playwright assumes that any art is more effective and honest when its medium is exposed rather than when it is concealed.

As a man of the theatre, directing as well as writing plays, Jean Anouilh has recognized and applauded such new talent as Samual Beckett and Eugène Ionesco. He himself has been a prolific dramatist for over forty years. During the 1972-73 season Anouilh's latest play, *Le Directeur de l'Opéra* (one expects at least one new play from him each year), has been brilliantly staged by the author and Roland Piétri at the Comédie des Champs-Elysées.

CHIEF DRAMAS: *Antigone* (tragedy, 1944) is the best known of Anouilh's *Pièces noires*. The plot is based on Sophocles' *Antigone*, although Anouilh adds a modern setting, a good deal of Parisian argot, a set of modern soldier guards, and other anachronisms. Creon's position is made as defensible as Antigone's, perhaps even more so. Creon realizes that Antigone is theoretically right in her desire to bury Polynices; he opposes the ceremony merely on grounds of political expediency. He wishes to make an edifying example of Polynices' fate, and also hopes the matter will be forgotten as soon as possible. "Thebes has a right now to a Prince without a history," he says. But Antigone, the fanatic child of the blood of Oedipus, prefers to see the city destroyed if necessary to carry out her ideal, and Creon is finally forced to execute her.

It has been suggested that this play, published under the German occupation, is an allegory of France's predicament in 1942. Creon is the voice of reason and compromise; he has "collaborated" or surrendered to reality in the interests of public order. Antigone, the consecrated, has "resisted" against this collaboration even though she realizes this resistance may do the city more immediate harm than good.

L'Invitation au château (*The Invitation to the Chateau*, adapted by

Christopher Fry as *Ring Around the Moon;* comedy, 1947) is an amusing parody of a country-house imbroglio in the English manner. Horace and Frederic, twins, live in a vast chateau with their aunt Mme. Desmermortes. Although the brothers are externally identical (they are played by a single actor), Frederic is virtuous and Horace extremely cynical. Horace plans to help his brother win the love of Diana, a rich heiress, by stimulating her jealousy; he introduces Isabelle, a young dancer, into the château as a niece of one of his friends. Isabelle plays her part so well that she eventually falls genuinely in love with Frederic. She also completely upsets the life of the château; her sincerity and virtue contrast strongly with the artificiality of the other guests. Diana's wealthy father Messerchmann, despairing after futile efforts to buy Isabelle off, at last ruins himself deliberately in order to remove the riches which have up to now thwarted his daughter's chance of happiness. Horace forthwith declares his love for the Diana whose money has formerly excited only his contempt; and Isabelle, at first attracted to Horace, later realizes she loves Frederic, Horace's virtuous alter-ego. Other characters are Lady Dorothée India, a naive and pompous cousin; Patrice Bombelles, a priggish young secretary; Isabelle's garrulous mother, a piano teacher; and Mlle. Capulat, companion to Mme. Desmermortes and an incorrigible romantic who begins to spout alexandrines whenever the action approaches a climax. This fantastic and farcical comedy somewhat resembles Wilde's *The Importance of Being Ernest,* although its technique is more complex and refined and its theme—the artificiality of polite society—is more effectively developed.

L'Alouette (drama translated by Christopher Fry as *The Lark,* 1955) is Anouilh's treatment of Joan of Arc. We see more of the peasant yet middle-class girl of Domrémy than we do in Shaw's play; the roots in Lorraine include the sheep and the larks and the family as well as the visions. This Joan acts in love for the common man. The Inquisitor is Joan's sworn and perfect enemy because he is frightened by those who are worthy of themselves, people who will never submit to domination by an Idea which is a safeguard for mediocre man. Like Antigone, Joan claims, 'I don't want to live your time." She refuses finally to make the compromise that remaining alive would require of her; in dying she captures control of time and its dependents, appearance and reality.

Becket, or The Honor of God (drama, 1960) is a play written by chance, according to Anouilh, its source an old book, Augustin Thierry's *The Conquest of England by the Normans,* picked up from a stall along the Seine for its pretty green binding. The springs of the drama depend on an outmoded historical concept—that Becket was a Saxon—which makes part of the conflict between him and the Norman King Henry. The drama is in the friendship between these two men, companions in pleasure and in work—pleasure for the first act, work as chancellor and the appointment as archbishop for the second. Anouilh, who admired Eliot's treatment of the murder in the cathedral, avoided that emphasis, placing it earlier. Henry II, as he is being flagellated for his responsibility in the murder, remembers the whole play in good memory play fashion (like Tennessee Williams' *Glass Menagerie),* at least as far as the middle of the third act, by which point an audience forgets the original memory-device launching.

This act includes a very amusing family scene with Henry, Queen Eleanor of Aquitaine, the Queen Mother, and two of the sons. Henry is bored with them all: "No one on this earth has ever loved me except Becket!" Then we are shifted to Thomas Becket's exile in France—the honor of God is now more important to him than the honor of the King and he won't be manipulated—and to a view of a rather decadent and time-serving political papal court. Act four concentrates on the last meeting between Henry and Thomas on the windy channel shore at La Ferté-Bernard. Thomas knows the trouble: "We loved each other and I think he cannot forgive me for preferring God to him." The death at Canterbury is given short shrift—only as the end of an impossible yet compelling personal relationship.

La Grotte (drama, *The Cavern,* 1961) starts out as a murder mystery with a corpse and a superintendent of police but quickly becomes a parallel to *Six Characters in Search of an Author* while it examines simultaneously the relationships of the classes, the rich upstairs aristocrats and the poor working people of the kitchen basement, or the cavern. Here the characters assume life and impose their story on the Author; the situations in *The Cavern* have been arranged, visibly manipulated, to give emotional meaning to the characters, not to tell a story. This play as a *tour de force* satirizes many playwrights including Pirandello, Giraudoux, Wilde, Rostand and even Shakespeare, with a good deal of self-parody as well. Anouilh winks in the mirror when he has the Author declare, "Useless! I can't believe that life is as ugly as that. Good lord, there are decent people everywhere! It's our duty to say so and to write plays with good kind people in them and good wholesome sentiments. And to the devil with literature." In the end the Author reveals himself as a character in his own play.

Arthur Schnitzler (Austrian, 1862-1931)

Schnitzler, a contemporary of Freud, was one of the first authors in Europe to apply the new psychological concepts of the twentieth century to literature. A physician by training, he viewed the human being primarily as an animal subject to disease; and among the diseases of the animal he included love, or the sexual urge in its manifold forms. It is inaccurate to say that Schnitzler was influenced by the Vienna school of psychoanalysis; actually he developed his ideas simultaneously and along parallel lines, but independently of this group. He uses little of the vocabulary of the Freudians and even manifests a hostility to formal psychiatry; his approach is nevertheless that of a cultured and cynical psychiatrist who was turned from medical practice toward literature.

In another sense Schnitzler is part of the fin-de-siècle decadent movement; he was associated with Hofmannsthal in the romantic reaction of the *Jungwien* ("Young Vienna") group, and there is much of the conscious perversity of Rimbaud or Wilde in his work. "There are many Sicknesses, and only one Health," remarks his favorite character Anatol. Yet Schnitzler wisely avoids making a dogma out of this decadence; he is too sophisticated, in fact, to believe anything wholeheartedly. At the bottom he is a skeptic. To him nothing is true and yet everything can be argued. He takes pleasure in demonstrating that all his characters, even those who contradict each other, are right. This again betrays Schnitzler's medical background; the true scientist contemplates and observes all but commits himself to nothing.

Schnitzler is particularly adept at dialogue, and this quality makes him a dramatist *par excellence.* Among his non-dramatic works the most effective are those composed almost entirely of dialogue, or, as in the case of *Leutnant Gustl,* of monologue. In addition his skill at creating mood is great. He is naturally somewhat circumscribed in this respect; his talent inclines toward moods of disease and melancholy. But Schnitzler is not without a sense of humor; he mixes a bitter irony into the most poignant of his studies of degeneracy, and occasionally divagates into pure and uninhibited satire.

LIFE: Schnitzler was born in Vienna in 1862, the son of a prominent Jewish medical specialist. His literary talent was precocious; he is said to have written a five-act tragedy at the age of nine. In 1879 he was admitted to the medical school of the University of Vienna, at that time beginning to come under the influence of Charcot and the concept of "nervous diseases." After his graduation Schnitzler practiced medicine under the tutelage of his father for some time, then served briefly as the editor of a medical journal. He began writing as early as 1880, and beginning in 1891 a number of his shorter plays were produced in Vienna. The *Anatol* cycle (1893) brought him success overnight, and *Liebelei* (1895) confirmed his reputation as one of Austria's leading young dramatists. In 1894 Schnitzler definitely abandoned medicine for literature.

In 1896 or 1897 the play, *Reigen* (translated as *La Ronde),* was produced; it is light in spirit although somewhat cynical on the subject of love: in ten scenes we move merry-go-round fashion from The Prostitute and The Soldier through the Soldier and the Parlor Maid, the Parlor Maid and the Young Gentleman, the Young Gentleman and the Young Wife, the Young Wife and the Husband (legitimacy just seemed to creep in), the Husband and the Sweet Young Thing, the Sweet Young Thing and the Poet, the Poet and the Actress, the Actress and the Count, and finally the Count and the Prostitute to bring us full circle. The French film of this play is a classic and a delight, a tribute both to Schnitzler and Vienna.

After the turn of the century the quasi-Freudian element in his work became increasingly prominent; he also began to develop a certain consciousness of his Jewish ancestry. *Professor Bernhardi* (1912) was a bitter analysis of anti-semitism in Vienna as well as a plea for the individual's right to a delusory happiness. After the First World War he became even more embittered. Although his success by this time was assured and he was able to live in a luxurious Viennese villa which remained his home until his death, the air of melancholy in his work constantly increased. Schnitzler died in Vienna as the Nazi movement began to loom large in nearby Germany, and only months before the celebration of his seventieth birthday.

CHIEF WORKS: *Anatol* (one-act drama cycle; played 1893) consists of seven one-act dramas centering around the characters of Anatol, a sort of professional Casanova, and his friend Max. In each playlet other characters, usually women, are added, but Max and Anatol remain. Anatol himself, gay but cynical, adept in seduction yet incorrigibly romantic, is one of the most engaging creatures of modern literature. His attitude toward women is totally Machiavellian, but at the same time he feels a genuine affection for them; he has simply learned by experience that chastity, loyalty, and understanding among persons of the opposite sex are illusory and that to pursue them as ideals is fatal. Most of the seven plays end with the woman abandoned, heartbroken, or dead by suicide.

Der einsame Weg (*The Lonely Way;* drama, 1903) is a study of a young boy's disillusionment with his mother and his idealized image of his father. Felix Wegrath learns that his mother has for years betrayed his recently deceased father, and that his real father is actually Julian Fichtner, an old painter he knows only as a friend of his mother's. When the truth comes out the artist, touched at the boy's loneliness, attempts to claim him as a son. But Felix remains loyal to his presumptive father, the man who has reared and educated him and provided a home for his mother; he bitterly resents the way Fichtner and his mother have cheated this dead man who on the surface seemed soulless and insipid. The moral is that "biological" fatherhood is less important than the actual affection between the boy and the man he thought his father.

In *Professor Bernhardi* (drama, 1912) Bernhardi, a Jewish physician, attempts fruitlessly to save the life of a girl dying of an inept abortion. In her delirium the girl is happy, even exultant, and momentarily expects the arrival of the lover who has caused her predicament. A nurse secretly sends for a priest to administer the last sacrament. Professor Bernhardi, however, refuses to allow the priest admittance to the girl; he knows she is soon to die, and that the appearance of the priest will only fill her with a terrible dread. After the death of the girl this action causes a terrible *cause célèbre;* Bernhardi is attacked by a shocked Catholic majority, and eventually sent to prison for his "crime."

Among Schnitzler's tales *Sterben* ("Dying" or "To die," 1895) is probably best known, Felix, the hero, is at the beginning of the action ill of consumption; he is nursed by his faithful and healthy wife Marie. Gradually the couple despair, and realize that Felix must inevitably die. As this realization grows in Felix's mind he comes to mistrust, then to hate the woman he has loved and who has devoted her life to him. The couple flee to Italy, and there, as Felix begins to hemorrhage and enters his final torments, he seizes at his wife insanely and attempts to drag her after him into death. The theme is the triumph of death—or of the fear of death—over love.

Hugo von Hofmannsthal (Austrian, 1874-1929)

Hofmannsthal, along with Schnitzler the leader of the psychological wing of the Austrian Neo-romantic movement, is known in America chiefly as the author of librettos for the operas of Richard Strauss. He is, however, primarily a lyric poet; his best dramas are highly poetic in mood, and his approach to literature is that of the decadent poet rather than the man of the theatre. Like Schnitzler, Hofmannsthal is interested in human nature primarily in its abnormal manifestations. He disregards the happy marriage, the normal sexual passion, the economic struggle for life, and the political and social problems of his day; his heroes are the neurotic, the libertine, and the artist. Many of his dramas are in verse; it is a verse heavily loaded with association, misty and melancholy, frankly aristocratic and decadent in character. In one period of his career he was greatly impressed with the Greek tragedy and sought to adapt and imitate it for the modern stage, but his Greeks are less classical heroes than moody and suicidal Viennese of the fin-de-siècle. In another aspect Hofmannsthal is the poet of Freudianism, but the scientific doctrines of Freud become in his hands a chaos of violence, incest, and repressed desires, a sort of psychiatric metaphysics.

Hofmannsthal, a versatile artist, adapted the whimsical and poignant Viennese melancholy of his time to his literary purposes, but always retained a certain detachment from it. *Ariadne auf Naxos* (1913), a comic libretto written for Strauss, is light and bantering, indicating that Hofmannsthal's usual *Weltschmerz* was at least partly contrived. Several of his Renaissance plays, especially *Der Tod des Tizian,* are marked by an optimistic eulogy of the life-force. Hofmannsthal was a conscious and deliberate decadent in the manner of Oscar Wilde rather than a poetic human derelict like Baudelaire or Rimbaud.

LIFE: Hugo von Hofmannsthal was born in Vienna in 1874 of Spanish-Jewish parents. His youth was comfortable; he was well educated at the University of Vienna, and began to write poetry and drama at an early age. It was the critic Hermann Bahr who discovered the young poet and persuaded him to turn his attentions entirely to literature. *Der Tod des Tizian* and *Der Tor und der Tod,* two of his best dramas, appeared before he was twenty. His youthful dramas were typical of the fin-de-siècle movement which also included Mallarmé, Maeterlinck, and Wilde. Shortly after the turn of the century, however, he began to work out an original style under the influence of two important elements: he was impressed with the psychological theories of the new Viennese school, especially those of Freud, and he formed a partnership with the composer Richard Strauss. Actually he collaborated with Strauss rather than wrote librettos for him; the result was close to the ideal of "integrated art" as conceived by Richard Wagner. *Elektra* (1903) served more than any other work of literature to bring the concept of the "Electra complex" to the attention of the general public, just as *Ödipus una die Sphinx* (1906) succeeded in popularizing the Oedipus complex. In 1911 Hofmannsthal wrote *Jedermann,* a German version of the English morality play *Everyman,* which emphasized the richness and luxury of the life of the young man called by Death. Life is considerably more lush and seemingly harder to leave than in the medieval play. This version has become a frequent vehicle for university theatre productions.

In the period after 1910 Hofmannsthal turned from classic and medieval themes to an increasing preoccupation with Austrian folk material. *Der Rosenkavalier* (1911), again an opera libretto, was followed by the comedy *Der Schwierige* (1921) and the drama *Das Salzburger Grosse Welttheater* (1922). Hofmannsthal's later dramas and novels are psychological in approach and usually Austro-German in setting. As a part of his personal rediscovery of Austrian nationalism he was converted to Catholicism in middle age. He was married and had three children; of these he was particularly fond of the eldest son, Franz. When this young man took his own life in 1929 Hofmannsthal, heartbroken, died of a heart attack the following day.

CHIEF DRAMAS: *Der Tor und der Tod* (*Death and the Fool;* drama,

1893) is a short symbolist play typical of Viennese poetry of the period. Claudio, the dreamy young hero, sits by an open window in his luxurious home wondering lazily about the meaning of existence. A servant enters and informs him that strange and ominous beings are wandering in the garden. Shortly thereafter enters Death himself, a sophisticated gentleman impeccably clad and playing a violin. Seeking to demonstrate to Claudio the futility of his life, Death produces for him the images of his mother, his sweetheart, and his best friend; Claudio realizes he has failed to make the most of his relations with all three. Now, too late, he realizes that the ivory-tower existence of the aesthete is not enough, that since death ends all one must plunge into life and live it to the utmost.

Der Abenteuer und die Sängerin (The Adventurer and the Singer; drama, 1899) analyses the career of a Casanova-like roué, the Baron Weidenstamm. Returning to Vienna after an absence of many years, the Baron attends the theatre and sees on the stage Vittoria, a former mistress, now a prima donna. She recognizes him as well; and after the performance they meet. She is now married, and her life is centered around her beautiful son Cesarino. Vittoria's husband suspects that Cesarino is actually the Baron's son. This is true, as the Baron admits; in fact he is inspired to relate to his son the story of his career—the many lands he has visited and the women he has known. But at the end the victory is Vittoria's, as her name hints. The Baron has learned nothing from his philandering, and has remained a shallow creature; but she has used the great love of her youth as a continual source of inspiration in her career. The experience has not only helped her to success on the stage but has provided her with Cesarino, the focus of her life.

Elektra (tragedy, 1904) is ostensibly based on the *Electra* of Sophocles but owes much as well to Oscar Wilde's *Salome,* which it resembles in tone. The plot follows the Sophoclean original with one exception: at the end of the play Electra, overcome with elation, breaks into a "nameless dance" at the end of which she falls down dead. The tone of the tragedy, however, is thoroughly un-Sophoclean. Electra is a raving neurotic, obsessed with the image of her dead father whose ghost has "ravished" her symbolically. She no longer feels the emotions of normal women, and can think only of blood and revenge.

She is dramatically contrasted with her more stable sister Chrysothe-
mis, who longs for a mate but in a normal human way. The connection
between Electra's love for her dead father and the abnormality of
her sexual character is a model literary presentation of the Electra
complex.

Julien Green (American-French, born 1900)

Julien Green's world is an inferno of strange, unhappy, and vicious
creatures who exist only through virtue of their obsessions; it is the
world of Edgar Allan Poe seen through modern eyes. His interest is
not primarily psychiatric in the medical sense, yet his most typical
characters are persons whose mentality is unmistakably warped. Stylistically his novels are dominated by an intense simplicity; the line is
direct, the presentation is bare of documentation, and there are no
sub-plots or secondary characters to divert us from the primary action.
Even though his content often resembles that of the eighteenth-century
Gothic novel, his style is that of the *roman pur* of the French tradition.

Green's concentration and intensity sometimes lead him into stark-
ness, or even into oversimplification. *Mont-Cinère (Avarice House)*
superficially resembles Balzac's *Eugenie Grandet* in plot: a tender and
sensitive child is brutalized by a miserly parent. The copious detail
and documentation of Balzac is missing, however, and the young girl
does not "come alive" as Balzac's Eugenie does. Green has a powerful
talent for inventing Gothic situations and even for conceiving characters, but he lacks the necessary creative power to make his characters
seem real. For this reason his stories—short, intense, and economical—
are often better than his novels. His masters are Gide, Poe, Melville,
the French symbolists, Blake, and the Brontës; he rejects the modern
realistic movement in the novel.

LIFE: Julien Green was born in   Paris of American parents in
1900: both his parents were Southerners. He was schooled in a
French lycée, and was virtually bilingual from early childhood. Although he came to America at nineteen to attend the University of
Virginia, he was never entirely at ease writing in English, and America
has remained throughout his life a strange and exotic land for him.

Shortly after his return to France from Virginia Green wrote *Mont-
Cinère* (1926), his first important novel; he thenceforth devoted him-

self entirely to fiction-writing. A second novel, *Adrienne Mesurat,* won him the Prix Femina in 1927. His chief novels appeared almost simultaneously in France and in America, and his popularity in the two countries has been approximately equal. His memoirs, published in English under the title *Personal Record* (1938-39), were well received; they contain portraits of Gide, Dali, Malraux, Cocteau, and Gertrude Stein, as well as an evaluation of Green's own personality and philosophy. Green spent the years from 1940 to 1945 in America, during which time he wrote a novel, *Varouna,* published in English as *Then Shall the Dust Return.* In the nineteen fifties and sixties Julien Green has continued to publish widely, doing some plays for the theatre, including *L'Ombre* and *Sud,* preparing further memoirs (an English translation of *Diary 1928-1957* appeared in 1964), and writing such new novels as *Le Malfaiteur* (1955) and *Minuit* (1967) among others. He has identified himself with an anti-catholic position in France.

CHIEF NOVELS: *Mont-Cinère* (translated as *Avarice House;* novel, 1926) is set in a Virginia mansion, evidently inspired by a house belonging to one of Green's relatives. (The translator of the English edition conveys the connotations of the name Mont-Cinère by renaming the house "Ashley House.") In this gloomy residence live the widowed Mrs. Fletcher, a miserly and bitter tyrant; her daughter Emily; and her ailing mother Mrs. Elliot. Mrs. Fletcher refuses to touch the savings-account her husband has left her; she rigidly economizes, even to the point of forbidding the servants to light a fire in the middle of winter. Her enemies are her daughter, filled with a natural and unspoiled charm, and her mother, a wise and tolerant old invalid. Mrs. Fletcher isolates Emily completely from the outside world and seeks to deny her any sort of natural life. The girl nevertheless manages to gain some contact with the external world through church social work. The grandmother dies, and Emily, desperately seeking to escape from her mother, marries the indigent Frank Stevens, a nearby farmer. But by this time Emily herself has begun to develop the intense possessiveness of her mother, and increasingly resents Frank's intrusion into the life of the house. When she realizes that the house will legally belong to Frank upon her mother's death, she sets fire to it and dies in the flames. The theme of this novel is the gradual growth of a vicious avarice in the innocent heroine through the influence of her mother.

Adrienne Mesurat (translated as *The Closed Garden;* novel, 1927) is similar in theme; this time the tyrant is M. Mesurat, a crotchety and selfish old father. He virtually imprisons his invalid elder daughter Germaine, even refusing to admit she is ill; he also isolates his younger daughter Adrienne to prevent her from finding a husband and leaving him alone. When Adrienne secretly falls in love with Dr. Denis Maurecourt, her father, suspecting something from her attitude, confines her to the house and even sets her sister to spy on her. Presently, however, Germaine, whose illness becomes more grave, escapes from the house in desperation to seek medical treatment. Her father, furious, tyrannizes Adrienne even more; and she, desperate, puts herself into the power of Mme. Le Gras, a woman of evil reputation who she hopes will help her escape. At one point it appears Adrienne may achieve a union with Dr. Maurecourt through the mediation of another woman, the Doctor's sister; but the sister balks when she hears of Adrienne's relations with the immoral Mme. Le Gras. When Dr. Maurecourt visits her professionally she confesses her love, but he discreetly rejects her. Immediately after, Mme. Le Gras visits her, finds her in a despondent semi-coma, and robs her of her entire savings. Adrienne, on the brink of insanity, is once again rejected by the Doctor and his sister, and at last wanders away from the house in a state of amnesia. Although the subject of this novel is essentially a study of an environmentally induced neurosis, the treatment is literary rather than pseudo-scientific in the manner of the naturalistic school.

Léviathan (translated as *The Dark Journey;* novel, 1929) is the story of the moral deterioration of Paul Guéret, a poor young tutor. Married to the unpalatable Marie, he falls in love with Angèle, a laundress and, unknown to Paul, a part-time harlot managed by the restaurant-owner Mme. Londe. Helpless, Paul falls totally under the spell of Angèle and Mme. Londe. When he learns of his sweetheart's true character he is dejected, then enraged; he seeks her out, attacks and violates her. Fleeing from justice, he kills an old man he mistakenly imagines has recognized him; actually Angèle, her face mutilated, has refused to name her attacker. The mother of Paul's pupil, the neurotic Mme. Grosgeorge, attempts to intervene in his life to save him, but only becomes hopelessly involved herself. She commits sui-

cide; Angèle dies of a fever, and Paul is arrested for Mme. Grosgeorge's murder because of ambiguous statements she makes before
her death. *Léviathan* is probably Green's most complex novel. It does
not center around any single character: Paul, Angèle, Mme. Londe,
and Mme. Grosgeorge are equally important and the reactions of each
to the basic situation are described in detail.

Hermann Hesse (German-Swiss, 1877-1962)

The work of Hermann Hesse oscillates between two extremes: the
novel of psychoanalysis on the one hand, and the intricate "idea
novel" or intellectual allegory on the other. In either case Hesse is
definitely in the camp of those who react against nineteenth-century
naturalism.

Time, place, and milieu are only vaguely established in his novels,
and often the entire action seems to unroll on a totally unrealistic and
nebulous plane. It is not that Hesse lived in an ivory tower—he was
an avowed anti-fascist and his work not devoid of social content—but
merely that he believes reality to consist of something more subtle
than the mere cataloguing of physical detail. He is the artist of the
mind, whether this mind struggles consciously with ideas or whether it
allows itself to be swept along by the vague and cryptic tide of the
subconscious.

The heroes of Hesse's novels are "superior creatures"—intellectuals, men of letters, ascetics, sensitive youths, or artists. German
critics apply the term *Künstlerroman* to the novel in which an artist
struggles against an uncomprehending and materialistic society to
achieve his aesthetic ideal, and most of Hesse's work might be included in this category. Sometimes the artist is merely a sensitive
adolescent, and sometimes he achieves the stature of a great social
leader, but the pattern remains the same.

Another problem which often concerns Hesse is the conflict between the ivory-tower existence and the life of struggle in the world:
must the artist engage himself in the social battles of his time, or
should he withdraw into a contemplative and artificial existence in
order to preserve himself from contamination? Hesse is usually for
engagement, although not always on the political level. His heroes

stand with the men of good will, but retain their individuality and remain aloof from party animosities. In other words Hesse believes in social action but not in political action, at least not on the partisan level.

Hesse's work is not intended to curry the favor of the millions. His reputation was considerable in 1950, especially among German-speaking readers, yet he did not achieve the wide early fame of a Mann or a Gide. The awarding of the Nobel Prize to Hesse in 1946 confirmed his position in world literature, and by the time of his death in 1962 his reputation had begun to soar. His work has been taken up with particular enthusiasm by young American students of the uneasy and protesting generation who find in themselves a strong attraction to such characters as Demian and the Steppenwolf, whose psychedelic adventures they see as a "trip," the world of hallucination with or without the aid of drugs. Hesse's idealism, criticism of the bourgeois establishment, and view into the chaotic abyss of twentieth century life they find particularly appealing. Practically all his works by 1970 were being newly translated and issued in paperbacks including the early poetry, *Peter Camenzind, The Prodigy (Unterm Rad), Gertrud, Rosshalde* (1914), the stories "Klein and Wagner" and "Klingsor's Last Summer" (a little gem), and *Narcissus and Goldmund* (1930), as well as the better known and perhaps more artistically secure works. *The Journey to the East,* for example, in its new 1968 translation had actually reached its twenty-second printing as a paperback by 1970. The Hesse boom is nothing short of phenomenal and could hardly have been predicted fifteen years ago.

Although Hesse is not primarily concerned with stylistic perfection, he is a competent master of German prose. His earlier works, especially those written under the influence of psychoanalysis, have a certain dreamy quality about them which greatly adds to their effectiveness. In his later works the intricacy and nebulosity of his ideas often make his style turgid, even tedious, but his novels are worth the effort required to read them.

LIFE: Hesse was born in 1877 in the Swabian town of Calw; his family were Protestants of the professional class. On his mother's side the ancestry was Franco-Swiss, and after extensive travels Hesse himself settled permanently in Switzerland in 1912. He later applied for and was granted Swiss citizenship. Since 1919 he has lived in the village of Montagnola, near Lugano.

Hesse's literary career began with a pair of novels in the tradition of the *Künstlerroman: Hinterlassene Schriften und Gedichte Hermann Lauschers* (*Posthumous writings and poetry of Hermann Lauscher,* 1901), and *Peter Camenzind* (1904). Both these works treated the problem of the artist with a gentle and sympathetic irony. In 1916-17 Hesse came under the influence of Jungian psychoanalysis in a sanitarium near Lucerne. His analyst was Joseph B. Lang, who became his personal friend and served as model for the character of Pistorius in *Demian* (1919), one of his finest novels and permeated with the symbols and attitudes of psychoanalytic method. After the war Hesse's attitude became more philosophical. He became especially interested in Eastern mysticism; *Siddharta* (1923) is laid in an Indian milieu. With *Narziss und Goldmund* (1930) Hesse gained popularity with the elite of the German reading public, and his reputation has continued to grow ever since.

Hesse has consistently voiced pacifistic and liberal ideas in his work. As early as 1914 he published a courageous essay, *O Freunde, nicht diese Töne,* deploring the chauvinism which had broken out in Germany with the beginning of the war. After his voluntary and permanent exile from Germany he consistently maintained an anti-Nazi stand, and was attacked by German critics as a weak mind depraved by "Jewish" psychoanalysis.

Hesse had carried on extensive correspondence with his friend, Romain Rolland, a Frenchman similarly self-exiled in Switzerland, which was published in 1954. He maintained at least a cordial relationship, including letters, with two other great writers of his era, Thomas Mann and André Gide. The latter visited Hesse in Montagnola in 1947, in his isolated home, the Casa Rossa, a carmine-red house with a mountain view and garden where he had installed himself in 1931, the house having been placed at his disposal for life by a prosperous friend. His longest major novel, *Das Glasperlenspiel* (translated as *Magister Ludi),* appeared in 1943 and contributed to the award of the Nobel Prize in 1946. Becoming more of a recluse in his later years (with a sign on the garden gate: NO VISITS PLEASE) Hesse is reported to have tacked on his door the words of an old Chinese sage, Meng Hsieh:

When one has grown old and his work is done, it is his right in stillness to make friends with death.

He does not need men. He knows them; he has seen enough of them. What he needs is quiet.

It is not becoming to seek out such a man, to accost him, to plague him with chatter.

The seemly thing is to pass by the gate of his dwelling, as if no one lived there.

Hermann Hesse died quietly in 1962.

CHIEF NOVELS: *Demian* (novel, 1919) is a novel of personal development describing the efforts of a sensitive and tormented young boy to find himself. Written in Berne, the novel is strongly influenced by psychoanalysis; certain Nietzschean elements are also detectable. The hero, Sinclair, is at the opening of the novel about sixteen. He is greatly troubled by the contrast between the normal, good, decent and serene life of his family and the dark and brutal other world he senses all about him—the world of violence, lust, and the Devil. Various symbols appear in his life to help him resolve this disparity in his own mind. The first of these is Frank Kromer, a bully who blackmails Sinclair by threatening to reveal his secret vices; Kromer is a symbol of the evil or bestial element in Sinclair himself. Next is Max Demian, a handsome and self-assured boy somewhat older than Sinclair who lives with his mysterious mother and is reputed to be a free-thinker. Demian, who awakens Sinclair to an understanding of his own dreams and secret aspirations, is a symbol of the free-thinking intellect. Next appears Pistorius, a young musician and former theological student. He talks to Sinclair of the minor Greek god Abraxas, a divinity who united the divine and diabolic elements in the universe. Although he does not realize it, this synthesis is Sinclair's own goal. Later, when he goes to the University, he achieves this goal through contact with Demian's mysterious mother, "Mother Eve," and the other mystics and seekers who frequent her household. The novel closes with the outbreak of the First World War; Sinclair, wounded, at last realizes that the lustful and diabolical elements in man's soul are as essential to his nature as the divine elements.

Steppenwolf (novel, 1927) is one of Hesse's best-known works in Europe; it did not appear in English, however, until 1947. The hero,

Harry Haller, is an artist who thinks of himself as a "wolf of the steppes"—the barren wastes to which the artist is banished by a Philistine society. Shut out from all normal human enjoyment, he becomes a wild creature exulting in his isolation. After a time he becomes fascinated with the dualism of human existence—the struggle between form and spirit, mind and flesh. He encounters two women, Hermine and Maria, who symbolize this dichotomy for him, but fails to achieve any sort of synthesis. The novel ends in the fantastic interlude of the "Magic Theatre," a dreamlike sequence resembling parts of Joyce's *Ulysses*. Consoled and edified by the images of this spectacle, Haller decides not to take his own life.

Die Morgenlandfahrt (novella, 1932, translated as *The Journey to the East,* 1957, 1968) is the first person narrative of a man in quest, the musician H. H., and recounts the apparent failure of a pilgrimage through Space and Time to the East undertaken by the League shortly after the World War (the First, that is). The League made up of idealists is led by an unknown President who turns out to be the lowest servant of them all, Leo. Klingsor and Paul Klee and Pablo (of the *Steppenwolf)* are in the group and their idealism is mixed up with Don Quixote and Siddhartha among others. Great hopes are dashed when they come to the gorge of Morbio Inferiore, where Despair breaks up the journey (reminiscent of *The Faerie Queene* and *Pilgrim's Progress).* The servant Leo disappears. But much later H. H. discovers an Andreas Leo who lives in the town where he has been staying since the journey was abandoned. He turns out to be the same Leo, who calls H. H. to account for his individual failure of faith and vision which created the despair. The Journey to the East is an ongoing quest; men are always joining it even as others become dropouts. The final vision is of the participation of losers in the success of the victors as candle images melt into each other. The individual loses his self-importance.

Das Glasperlenspiel (1943), translated as *Magister Ludi,* (1949) was specifically commended by the Swedish Academy in Hesse's Nobel Prize citation. The novel is an intricate fantasy of life in some future age, when our twentieth century is referred to as the "Age of Digests." Within this vague and mysterious future civilization exists a semi-secret society, the Castalians, who live a monastic existence and concern themselves with preserving the cultural and intellectual heritage of the past. Their most secred task is the performance of the Glass Bead Game *("das Glasperlenspiel"),* an intricate mathematical contest involving music, art, philosophy, grammar, and architecture. The Game is never specifically described, but apparently its purpose is to unite all these intellectual activities into a higher synthesis. Joseph Knecht, the protagonist, is educated at Waldzell, the monastery headquarters of the society, and is at last chosen *Magister Ludi* or Master of the Games. He has many conversations with his friends, Fritz Tegularius, an individualist and non-conformist who chafes against the discipline of the society, and Plinio Designori, an outsider who represents the normal and active intellectual life. At last Knecht, impatient with the ivory-tower detachment of Castalian life, resigns his office and resolves to devote himself to the education of Designori's son Tito. He follows Tito on a vacation into the mountains, and there drowns in a lake while attempting to emulate the younger man's swimming feats. The usual interpretation of this allegory is as follows: Knecht, weary of an artificial, celibate, and cloistered existence, attempts to engage himself in life as it actually is and to devote himself to the improvement of a single human being. His cloistered life has weakened him, however, and when he attempts to follow Tito into the world of the physical struggle against nature (the basic struggle of mankind) he is killed.

The novel consists mainly of conversations and exposition; with the exception of the ending there is little plot or dramatic incident.

7. THE NEO-ROMANTIC MOVEMENT

Literary history is marked by periodic recurrences of romanticism, the most important of which occurred about 1800 in England and continental Europe. A revival of this movement began at the turn of the twentieth century, when it formed a part of the wider literary reaction against the realism and naturalism of the nineteenth century.

The authors who participated in this romantic movement shared an interest in the exotic or unusual as opposed to the prosaic or ordinary, a certain flamboyance or ingenuity of language, a liking for fantastic, heroic, or superhuman characters, and an inclination toward fantastic plot material. Some, like Maeterlinck, sought frankly to escape into an irrational world of dream; others were attracted to exotic geographical settings. Although Neo-romanticism tends toward the irrational and fantastic, not all of these writers were superficial; the content of such authors as Cocteau, Maeterlinck, and Saint-Exupéry is far from trivial.

The aesthetic element is strong in this romantic revival. Romantic authors tend to be more interested in sheer beauty of language than realists do; some, like Edmond Rostand, make a virtual cult of verbal preciosity. Strong visual and other images also characterize these authors, especially Saint-Exupéry. Stefan George abandons the didactic and informative element in literature entirely and frankly champions the doctrine of art-for-art's-sake, and all the authors in this section are more or less tinged with this tendency. A minority, including Andreyev, lapse frankly into a decadent escapism; their cult is that of Poe, Baudelaire, and the late nineteenth-century Joris-Karl Huysmans. This negativism, however, is not typical; the majority of Neo-romantic authors are idealistic in attitude. The ideals of twentieth-century romanticism are the beautiful, the exotic, the strange, the heroic, and the mysterious—essentially the aspirations of Keats, Schiller, or Chateaubriand.

Edmond Rostand (French, 1868-1918)

Rostand is chiefly famous in English-speaking countries as the author of a single play, *Cyrano de Bergerac.* Several other plays, including *L'Aiglon* and *Chantecler,* however, are still considered standard dramas in France. Along with his lesser contemporaries Jean Moréas and Emile Verhaeran, Rostand revolted against the triumphant naturalism of the fin-de-siècle stage and sought to revive the poetic drama of the French Golden Age; but Rostand, more romantic by nature, created a more virile and more original drama than the other two. Although he laid his chief play in the time of Corneille, Rostand is not precisely a Neoclassic poet; he is closer to the preciosity of the Renaissance in style and his concepts and situations are often those of nineteenth-century romanticism. His chief Neoclassic quality is his rigid adherence to the Alexandrine line and to the five-act classic structure; his romantic qualities are his preoccupation with elegant language, his love of dramatic theatrical devices, and his exaggerated characterization.

Rostand is especially adept in handling words in a fresh and fanciful manner; in this respect he almost resembles the English Elizabethans. He is fond of puns, double-entendres, complex catalogues, fanciful metaphors, and elaborate conceits, and he has at his command a wide stock of unusual, archaic, and bizarre words. No French poet since Rabelais has achieved such a sheer exuberance of language, and no poet since Racine has exceeded him in producing such perfectly constructed plays.

LIFE: Rostand was born in Marseilles in 1868 of an old Provençal family. Educated in Paris, he began to publish poetry in 1884 and produced his first play in 1888. After a marriage to the poetess Rosemonde Gérard his work improved markedly; he achieved his first wide success with *Les Romanesques* in 1894. *Cyrano de Bergerac* appeared in 1897 and *L'Aiglon* in 1900; the following year Rostand was elected to the French Academy. His later works were somewhat less successful, *Chantecler* (1910) probably because it was too advanced for its time. His reputation, however, remained enormous up to the time of his death in 1918, and his influence on younger dramatists continued into the twenties.

CHIEF WORK: *Cyrano de Bergerac* (verse tragedy, 1897) is laid in the Paris of 1640; the action opens in the theatre of the Hôtel de Bourgogne. Cyrano, a fiery Gascon poet with an extraordinarily long nose, is insulted by one Valvert and conducts a duel with him while simultaneously composing an impromptu ballade. On the last line of the envoi he strikes down his opponent as he has threatened. Roxane, a beautiful lady, witnesses this performance and sends for him; Cyrano, who has been long in love with her, is elated. But at the interview Roxane confesses she is actually enamoured of Christian, a young cadet in Cyrano's company. True to his gallant nature, Cyrano takes Christian in hand and sponsors his affair with the woman he himself loves; he even substitutes for Christian in a balcony serenade. Later Christian is killed in a battle. After fifteen years Cyrano visits Roxane in a convent; he reads her some letters of Christian and she recognizes the voice as that of the lover who sang to her from beneath the balcony. Cyrano dies content in the knowledge that Roxane is now aware of his love, although she cannot accept it.

Stefan George (German, 1868-1933)

George is the central figure of the early twentieth-century art-for-art's-sake movement in German poetry. Around him formed the George Circle ("der Kreis um Stefan George"), a set of young poets and writers who edited the review *Blätter für die Kunst* and spread the doctrine of *Artistenkunst* among the prewar generation. George himself was enormously influential; his volumes, especially *The Seventh Ring,* were read avidly by the youth of the 1914 era, and his popularity in time grew into something like a cult.

Like most other aesthetic poets of the fin-de-siècle, George began in reaction against nineteenth-century realism and naturalism. In his case he also rebelled against the romanticism which had been the curse of German poetry for the better part of the century. He was influenced by Mallarmé and the French Symbolists, but he also owes much to the ideals of classic Hellenism: restraint, symmetry, and simplicity. Many of his poems are addressed to, or inspired by, a youth called Maximin, but this boy was to him merely what Beatrice was to Dante: an ideal focus for his aesthetic, moral, and spiritual aspirations. In this sense the Maximin-figure in George's poetry is a symbol of Hellenism, suggesting the Greek culture which set up images of beautiful boys and worshipped them as gods.

George's poetry seems esoteric upon first examination. He is extremely preoccupied with typography, with the general appearance of the poetry on the page; his books are printed in Roman type instead of the traditional German Gothic, he commonly ignores the standard German capitalization of nouns, and many of his poems utilize geometric arrangement of the lines in the manner later to be associated with E. E. Cummings and the American imagists. Structurally George is conventional; his poems often have a severe classical structure and rhyme pattern. His originality lies especially in his diction: he uses words of the common German vocabulary, but seldom utilizes them in the ordinary manner. The reader is made conscious of the original etymology of the words, or of their less obvious associations. Thus his poetry, which may seem banal on first examination, often gains power and depth upon subsequent readings.

LIFE: Stefan Anton George was born in 1868 in the Rhenish village of Büdesheim, near Bingen. His background was middle-class and Catholic; his family originally came from Lorraine and probably included French blood. Stefan, an eager student, attended the Darmstadt Gymnasium and later studied at the Universities of Berlin, Munich, and Paris. He travelled widely during his youth; he was fascinated with languages and soon mastered all the modern Latin tongues. He learned Norwegian specifically in order to read Ibsen in the original. In 1889, during an important sojourn in Paris, he became an intimate of the Mallarmé circle which also included Heredia, Régnier, Vielé-Griffin, Gide, and Pierre Louys; his early poems were written under the influence of this Symbolist cénacle. In 1892 he helped to found and edit the *Blätter für die Kunst,* the influential review which became the center of the aesthetic movement in Germany. His first important volume, *Hymnen (Hymns),* appeared in 1890; thenceforth his poetic production continued at a moderate but steady rate.

Some time before 1907 occurred the pivotal incident in George's artistic career: the meeting with "Maximin" which inspired *The Seventh Ring* and much of his later poetry. The identity of this youth is unrevealed, but it appears George's actual meetings with him may have been as infrequent as those of Dante with "Beatrice." *The Seventh Ring,* his best-known volume of poetry, appeared in 1907 as George approached forty. At this period, the climax of his career, George was a picturesque character; he wore his hair long, affected aesthetic manners, and commanded his disciples with absolute authority. After 1914 he left Germany only for infrequent trips to Switzerland, whose mountains he dearly loved. He was awarded the Goethe Prize in 1927. The Nazi movement sought to claim him as its own during the early thirties, and at the time of the Nazi assumption of power Dr. Goebbels invited him to become a member of the German Academy. George declined coldly, and shortly after departed for Switzerland never to return. He died at Locarno on the Lago Maggiore in 1933.

CHIEF WORKS: *Hymnen (Hymns;* poems, 1880) spring from Pindar rather than from the Hebrew psalms or Christian hymns. The work covers a yearly calendar, thus suggesting the theme of the cyclical recurrence of life. Most poems in this volume are descriptive. "Ein Angelico" is an interesting description and personal interpretation of a Renaissance painting.

Die Bücher der Hirten und Preisgedichte (Books of Eclogues and Eulogies; poems, 1895) is again deceptively titled; the poems involve an adulation of a transcendental nature-spirit not to be found in the superficial pastoralism of Theocritus and his Roman imitators. Most poems treat descriptions, although some are vague and nebulous sketches of persons. "Der Tag des Hirten" ("The Shepherd's Day") is one of the simplest poems in the volume, and one of the most successful. It suggests both Hesiod's *Works and Days* and Virgil's *Georgics.*

Das Jahr der Seele (The Year of the Soul; poems, 1897), like *Hymnen,* follows the calendar in its construction. The theme is the poet's ceaseless search for companionship.

Der siebente Ring (The Seventh Ring; poems, 1907) is George's most important volume. The title is inspired by the construction of a tree, with successive rings which are nevertheless all centered around a single focus. The theme is similar to that of Dante's *Vita Nuova:* a spiritual description of the author's career, climaxed by a passion for a beloved one. The fourth "Ring" or section contains eulogies to Maximin and the other "Rings" anticipate and recollect the Maximin experience.

Maurice Maeterlinck (Belgian, 1862-1949)

Maeterlinck, the chief Belgian poet of the twentieth century, is a poet and mystic who is at the same time a successful popular dramatist. a Gallic mind whose works contain something of the transcendental melancholy of the German forests. At least two or three of his plays must be ranked among the greatest Symbolistic works of modern times. In addition he has served more than any other Symbolist to make the principles of his school known among the non-literary public. If he is not precisely a popularizer he is at least a poet of fantasy who is neither difficult nor esoteric, and who has been widely appreciated by the general public.

Not all of Maeterlinck's dramas can be considered Symbolistic; in fact of his major works only *L'Oiseau bleu* and *Les Aveugles* accurately fit this term. *Pelléas et Mélisande* is a sort of Gothic fairy-tale, and *Monna Vanna* is a Renaissance costume piece built around a Corneillian conflict of emotions. Maeterlinck's dramas are, how-

ever, marked by consistently recurring themes: (a) the essential
mystery of life, the irrational and inexplicable pattern of destiny;
(b) the transitory and fragile nature of human happiness; (c) the
unfailing sureness of the heart contrasted to the artificiality and corruption of organized society, i.e., a sort of romantic anarchism, and
(d) the simplicity of the human soul once the artificial layers of convention are removed. The last element is particularly apparent in his
dramatic technique; his characters seem oversimplified, two-dimen-
sional, and shadowy. Maeterlinck himself declared that he wrote "for
marionettes;" he is interested not in the subtleties and inconsistencies
of the individual but in that which is universal in every human soul.
In this sense he is diametrically opposed to the naturalistic tradition.

Maeterlinck's style is highly original; he creates a sort of misty
pale-blue mood which is easily recognizable and which accounts for
much of his effectiveness. Sentences are left unfinished, mysterious
or meaningless remarks are unexplained, and symbols without reference are sprinkled throughout the action. His best dramas, e.g.,
L'Oiseau bleu, cannot be rationally explained line by line; they must
be absorbed in their totality and their message comprehended through
the emotions.

LIFE: Born in Ghent in 1862, Maeterlinck was educated by the
Jesuits in a local college and early destined by his family for the law.
He was admitted to the bar in 1886, but showed no aptitude whatsoever for the profession; he is said to have lost every case he under-
took. In 1886-87 he made a significant trip to Paris, where he moved
in literary circles and formed important attachments with several
French Symbolists including Villiers de l'Isle-Adam. He began to
write about this time, and managed to publish several poems in *La
Pleïade.* Back in Belgium, he resolved to devote himself entirely to
writing, and in 1889 produced his first volume of poems, *Serres
chaudes* (the term means "greenhouses" or "hothouses"). Languid
and imitative, the poems attracted little attention. Later in the same
year, however, he published *La Princesse Maleine,* a drama which
won him the support of the important critic Octave Mirbeau. Thenceforth his success was assured. In 1891 appeared *Les Aveugles,* and
during the successive years his chief remaining works: *Pelléas et
Mélisande* (1893), *Monna Vanna* (1902), and *L'Oiseau bleu* (1908).
La Vie des Abeilles, an important prose work, appeared in 1901; in it

Maeterlinck applied his personal experiences in bee-keeping to a quasi-mystical, quasi-scientific philosophical essay. In 1911 he was awarded the Nobel Prize for Literature. He was also offered a seat in the French Academy, but declined because he preferred not to abandon his Belgian nationality for French citizenship.

After the First World War Maeterlinck's production declined sharply. He travelled widely, lectured in America, and inexplicably broke with his companion of many years, Georgette Leblanc, and married Renée Dahon. Upon the fall of France in 1940 he came to America, where he remained throughout the war. Returning to France in 1947, he died at his villa near Nice in May of 1949.

CHIEF DRAMAS: *Les Aveugles* (*The Blind;* drama, 1891) is a Symbolist allegory of the skepticism of modern Western civilization. The characters, six men and six women, wander morosely through the world seeking they know not what and guided only by sterile and obsolete ideals. Their chief guide is a priest, a symbol of Catholicism, who is actually dead and who finally abandons his charges in a dark forest. The play was eventually listed on the Catholic *Index.*

Pelléas et Mélisande (drama, 1893) is a fantasy laid in the setting of a medieval forest. The mood throughout is that of an enigmatic and melancholy fairy-tale. The action commences as Golaud, grandson of the old king Arkel, wanders through the forest and finds the mysterious Mélisande weeping by a fountain. He takes the girl back to the castle and marries her, although her identity remains undisclosed. But the younger brother of Golaud, Pelléas, is immediately seized with love for his sister-in-law, and she returns his affection. Although the two are chaste in their love, they can scarcely conceal the nature of their emotions, and Golaud gradually grows furious with jealousy. Pelléas and Mélisande, determined to part, meet in a park to exchange a farewell kiss. Golaud surprises them at this moment, kills Pelléas, and wounds Mélisande; she dies, however, not from this wound but from a broken heart. This play is famous as the inspiration of the Debussy tone-poem of the same name.

Monna Vanna (tragedy, 1902) is a powerful costume piece, written in prose but suggesting Corneille or Racine in its portrayal of conflicting emotions. Giovanna (Monna Vanna) is the wife of Guido Colonna, commander of the garrison of Pisa, which town is besieged by a hostile Florentine army. Prinzivalle, the mercenary who com-

mands the besieging army, loves Giovanna; years before he had encountered her briefly and has followed her fortunes ever since. He
agrees to betray his Florentine employers and come over to the Pisan
side if Giovanna will render herself to him; and she agrees to this
proposal in spite of the remonstrances of her husband. But the
Florentine council learns of the plot and lays plans to arrest Prinzivalle;
he and Giovanna are forced to flee for shelter into Pisa. By this time
Giovanna loves Prinzivalle in spite of herself. When her husband,
sure she has surrendered herself to Prinzivalle, promises to spare the
mercenary if only she will confess the truth, she falsely incriminates
herself and brings shame upon her reputation to save her lover.

L'Oiseau bleu (The Blue Bird; drama, 1908) is Maeterlinck's best-
known play. Tyltyl and Mytyl, children of a poor wood-cutter, are
unhappy until a fairy, Berylune, appears and sends them in search of
the Blue Bird of happiness. They set off, accompanied by the Dog,
a faithful defender, and the Cat, a treacherous enemy. Other allegorical
figures also accompany them: Light, Milk, Bread, and Fire. They
visit the Land of Memory and the Palace of Night, but find no Blue
Bird there able to survive the light of day. Likewise the Kingdom of
the Future produces no happiness. Disconsolate, they return home
and find that the Blue Bird has been safely locked in its cage all
the time. Tyltyl gives the bird to a neighboring girl who is ill; the bird
escapes and flies away. The key to the allegory is that happiness must
be searched for close to home, and that once achieved it cannot be
held in a selfish grasp but must be shared.

Gabriele D'Annunzio (Italian, 1863-1938)

D'Annunzio is a typical poet of the fin-de-siècle romantic revival.
Unfortunately for his reputation he lived on into the twentieth century,
and had to make the most of this bad timing on the part of fate. He
succeeded well enough to make himself one of the chief Italian poets
of the century, but he became after a while a sort of anachronism;
his spirit is that of the nineties, and his ideas those of Nietzsche,
Baudelaire, and Oscar Wilde.

The dominant note in D'Annunzio's work is the triumph of the
ego; and the ego in his case is chiefly a creature of the senses. He
speaks frequently of the mind and the soul, but his concept of these
entities is banal; essentially his works are studies in refined sensualism.

Since the search for sensation is never complete, since each sensation must be climaxed by an even more intense experience, D'Annunzio's life somewhat resembled a flight after the horizon; he searched constantly, experienced deeply, but never achieved serenity or satiety. The heroes of his novels and plays are reflections of himself, and thus they too are driven by an urge for constantly heightened sensation. The search can never achieve fulfillment, and it usually ends in tragedy or death. For this reason D'Annunzio, like most decadents, constantly links together passion and death as though they were merely two sides of the same medal.

LIFE: D'Annunzio's life was as fascinating as that of any of the characters he created. He was born in a small town of the Abruzzi in 1863. His father, a landowner with pretensions to aristocracy, added the name D'Annunzio to the family name of Rapagnetta. Gabriele was educated at the University of Rome. He was a precocious poet; he began writing as a child and published his first volume of verses in 1879. In 1894 *The Triumph of Death* made him, at thirty-one, Italy's most famous author. His amatory career was no less remarkable; a short, small man, prematurely bald and almost frail in appearance, he nevertheless commanded the affections of a startling number of grand ladies including the actress Eleonora Duse. His literary output was great; his works comprise forty-nine volumes in Italian, not including private correspondence published separately. In addition to all this D'Annunzio led an active public life. Dashing off to France in 1912, he became a violent French patriot and offered to serve France in the First World War; instead the French government sent him home to propagandize for Italian intervention. Once Italy had joined the war D'Annunzio threw himself into the fray with fervor. He served in the cavalry, infantry, and navy; his exploits included a dangerous raid on an Austrian seaport in a small motorboat. Next he turned to the air; he piloted a plane in several missions over Vienna and was wounded twice, the second time with the loss of an eye. In September, 1919, indignant over the internationalization of the port of Fiume on the Adriatic, he led an impetuous band of 12,000 "Arditi" who raided and captured the town; he held it and governed it as virtual dictator until 1921.

D'Annunzio was a living incarnation of youth, and it was a bitter ignominy for him to grow old. He postponed the process for as long as possible, but senility was inexorable. He was unhappy under the Fascists, who honored him officially but failed to accord him the position of national idol he felt he deserved. In 1937 he was stricken with the illness which was to end his life. Luisa Baccara, a talented and well-known pianist, gave up her career to nurse this petulant and wasted man of seventy-four. He died in 1938 at Vittoriale, his private estate on the Lago di Garda in the Alps.

CHIEF WORKS: D'Annunzio's fame in Italy rests chiefly on his lyric verse; in English-speaking countries he is better known for his novels. The most important of these is *Il Trionfo della Morte* (*The Triumph of Death,* 1894), a work reflecting the ideas of Nietzsche and Schopenhauer as well as the attitudes of Baudelaire. The novel relates the tumultuous and passionate affair of George, a poet somewhat resembling the author, and Hippolyte, a married woman who follows him all over Italy. Hippolyte loves as a normal woman, passionately but gently, and asks only to be with George as much as possible. He, however, is dominated by darker lusts. He wishes to possess his mistress completely, to allow her no private life or secret moment. In addition he fears the fate of his father, who has settled down to a grubby existence with his mistress and brought misery to his legal wife and children. George finds the prospect of such banality horrifying. He entices Hippolyte to a dangerous sea-cliff, clasps her in his embrace and leaps with her into the sea as she, realizing his intention, cries out in horror.

Il Fuoco (*The Flame;* novel, 1900) is similar in tone. Again the subject is a passionate love affair; the details in this instance are drawn from the author's relations with the actress Eleonora Duse.

Francesca (drama, 1902; translated as *Francesca da Rimini*) is D'Annunzio's best-known play. The heroine is the famous medieval lover who appears in Dante's *Inferno.*

D'Annunzio's most important volumes of verse are *Primo Vere* (1880) and *Canto novo* (1882).

Ferenc Molnár (Hungarian, 1878-1952)

Molnár is a facile and competent author whose content often fails to meet the level of his technique. The sentimentality which mars his lesser works, however, is controlled in his best-known drama, *Liliom.* The play is a masterpiece of psychological fantasy, and has become a standard repertory piece in the modern theatre.

Molnár was born in Budapest in 1878; his family was well-to-do and he had the advantages of a good education. From his earliest youth he was certain of his vocation as an author. As a young man he held various positions in the field of journalism, but turned to writing seriously around 1907. An important incident in his career was his 1907 marriage, which collapsed after a short time. This experience lent him the skepticism toward human relationships which forms the main theme of *Liliom* and other subsequent works. He had little talent for domestic felicity; in all he was married three times. Of Jewish birth, Molnár fled Hungary in 1940 and came to America; he became a U. S. citizen, and died in New York in 1952.

Molnár's plays, novels, and stories are invariably well-constructed. He has a flair for smoothly-flowing dialogue, and his characterizations are often appealing. He has no pretences to profundity; his writing is chiefly intended for entertainment, and it generally fulfills this mission splendidly. Where ideas or messages occur, as in *Liliom,* they are generally unremarkable and never interfere with the flow of the plot.

CHIEF WORK: *Liliom* (drama, 1909) is a character study of a gay and irresponsible circus barker. Liliom, the hero, is fundamentally vulgar, yet there is no evil in him; he is simply an engaging and amoral ne'er-do-well. He loses his circus job through neglect, and in order to avoid going to work he marries Julie, a poor servant girl. Although he mistreats Julie unfeelingly, even beating her on occasion, she is steadfast in her love for him. The play consists chiefly of a series of incidents in Liliom's career subsequent to his marriage. The most important of these is a robbery in which Liliom and a ruffian friend attempt to hold up a bank messenger, Linzman, but are easily over-powered. Liliom, faced with capture, commits suicide. He is shortly brought before a fantastic heavenly tribunal, which gives him a chance to return to earth sixteen years later for a single day to expiate his sin through good deeds. Liliom, disguised, visits his wife and his young daughter, and finds that the still-faithful Julie has made a virtual cult of her departed husband for the sake of the girl. Liliom unfeelingly destroys this illusion and tells the girl the truth about himself; he ends by slapping her. Yet even in cruelty Liliom is irresistible to women; the daughter declares the slap felt "like a caress," and Julie sadly agrees that such things are possible.

Leonid Andreyev (Russian, 1871-1919)

Andreyev is a writer of great talent whose work was marred and distorted by a lifetime pessimistic neurosis. In style he derives from Tolstoy and the Russian realists, but his content is consistently morbid; he represents fin-de-siècle decadence in its most acute form. To Andreyev all human ideals are chimerical and death is the only certainty; death, in fact, plays such a large part in his work that it may be considered his favorite protagonist. His cynicism is especially apparent in his attitude toward sex; Andreyev views love only as a bestial passion which obliterates the last traces of human decency and self-respect. In the tale *The Abyss* (1902) a decent young man, driven berserk by the bestiality of a pair of itinerant vagabonds, violates his own fiancée in the woods, and this act may be taken as symbolic of the degradation which pervades Andreyev's entire work.

Occasionally, as in *The Seven Who Were Hanged,* Andreyev attempts to show human decency and idealism struggling against the corruption to which all life is bound. In this narrative the heroic purity of the terrorists has a sort of religious quality, the sole religion to be found anywhere in his work. But for such martyrs there is no hope in Andreyev's universe; their idealism serves only as an ineffectual protest against the overwhelming wrongness of their environment.

It is undeniable that Andreyev is a skilled artist, although his skill lies mainly in an ability to create scenes of tension and horror. *The Red Laugh* (1904) is one of the most shocking—and most convincing—tracts against war ever written. Its opening words, "Madness and horror," sufficiently convey its tone. Andreyev also has a knack for characterization, especially in the case of frustrated or unhappy characters. This is most apparent in *He Who Gets Slapped* (1914), a tragicomedy in which the characterization of the persecuted circus clown is a genuine masterpiece.

LIFE: Andreyev was born in Orel, in central Russia, in 1871. He studied law at St. Petersburg and later took a law degree at Moscow, but his youth was a miserable fiasco; he attempted suicide on three occasions, engaged in all sorts of debauchery, and according to legend once lay down on the railway tracks to test the sensation of the train passing over him. He earned a dubious living for several years as a journalist, then turned to free-lance writing; encouraged by Gorky, he published his first stories in 1901. The following year *In the Fog* earned him wide recognition, but a storm of abuse and criticism soon followed it. Andreyev was widely accused of viciousness and immorality, mostly because of the sexual scenes in his tales *In the Fog* and *The Abyss;* at last, angry and depressed at this reaction, he withdrew to Kuokkala, in Finland, where he remained the rest of his life.

Andreyev lacked any profound political convictions. In his youth he warmly espoused the liberal cause, although mainly for emotional reasons. He spent a brief period in prison after the abortive revolution of 1905. *The Seven Who Were Hanged* was intended as a tribute to the radical martyrs of the Czarist regime. In 1917, however, Andreyev supported the Kerensky government, and thereafter was *persona non grata* with the Bolsheviks. In the final years of his life he violently attacked the Soviet regime and wrote impassioned propaganda for the White forces. He died of a cerebral hemorrhage in Finland in 1919.

CHIEF WORKS: *The Red Laugh* (Russ. *Krasny smekh;* novella, 1904) is a ghastly portrayal of the consequences of modern warfare. The narrative is divided into two parts, each written in something like the stream-of-consciousness technique of Joyce's *Ulysses.* Part I follows the consciousness of a soldier who loses his legs in the Russo-Japanese war. After horrible experiences he returns to his native town, broken in body and mind. He is unable to make the adjustment to civilian life, and shortly dies insane. Part II continues the narrative through the mind of the soldier's brother; here the degeneration of the civilian population is shown. Andreyev portrays war as an overwhelming madness from which come only destruction and horror.

The Seven That Were Hanged (Russ. *Rasskaz o semi poveshennykh;* novella, 1908) is a careful psychological study of the knowledge of imminent death of various mentalities. The book is also a tribute to the martyrs of the revolutionary cause. Eight persons are concerned: a minister of state who is informed he is to be assassinated at one o'clock in the afternoon; five terrorists arrested for the attempted crime, three of them men and two women; and two common criminals, a bandit and a murderer. The minister spends a night of terror, although the assassination is averted. The bandit is flamboyant and makes a great play of bravado; the murderer is whining and abject. The five terrorists await their death with a calm and serene courage resembling a sort of religious conviction. Technically the work is an interesting experiment in intertwining eight streams of thought while keeping each strand separate up to the end.

He Who Gets Slapped (drama, 1916) opens as a troupe of madcap players prepare for a circus performance. Into this group comes the man known only as "He," who demands to be taken on as a clown. Apparently "He" is a person of importance, but whether he has abandoned his former life through disgrace or failure or through choice is never revealed. The clowns immediately dub him "He who gets slapped" and assign him a rôle as a sort of punching-bag in their performance. "He" soon falls in love with Consuelo, a beautiful bareback rider. She, the illegitimate daughter of the gambler "Count" Mancini, is about to be married off to the Baron Regnard, an elderly roué. "He," in order to save her from this fate, poisons her on the eve of her engagement, then drinks poison himself. The Baron, heartbroken, shoots himself.

Antoine de Saint-Exupéry (French, 1900-1944)

Saint-Exupéry, supremely of the twentieth century, seeks to do for the air what Conrad earlier did for the sea. His purpose is not merely to recount his personal aviation experiences, although these enter intimately into his literary works, but to report the impressions of flight on a sensitive and highly poetic mind. A professional aviator, he does not over-romanticize flying, yet his touch transforms the sensation of mechanical flight into a magical and exhilarating spiritual experience.

Although he is not primarily interested in literary technique his style is highly original. The inner thoughts of characters are reported in impressionistic form, and the sights and sounds of flight in something like imagism. The narrative line, however, is clear and lucid; Saint-Exupéry is never "difficult" in the manner of Joyce or Proust. His best-known books are all drawn from personal experience; they lie somewhere along the line between pure fiction and autobiography. Along this line *Night Flight* most closely approaches the pole of pure fiction, and *Flight to Arras* the pole of straight autobiography.

LIFE: Born in Lyons in 1900, Saint-Exupéry was drawn to airplanes when he first saw them as a boy during the First World War. He decided then to become a pilot, and he never abandoned this ambition. He learned to fly at a military aviation school at Strasbourg, but after he was commissioned he left the service to become a commercial pilot. He flew extensively in Africa, and on one occasion almost lost his life when he was forced down in the Libyan desert. He was then sent to South America, where he helped to establish an airmail route from Brazil to Patagonia. Meanwhile he began a second career as an author; his first book, *Courrier Sud (Southern Mail),* appeared in 1929. *Vol de Nuit (Night Flight,* 1931) was a much better-written work, and earned immediate acclaim. His work has subsequently received numerous formal awards, including the Grand Prix of the French Academy in 1939.

With the outbreak of the Second World War Saint-Exupéry re-entered military service; he experienced several narrow escapes in the air during the harrowing days of May, 1940 and eventually escaped to join the Free French forces in exile. In the summer of 1944 his plane was reported missing on a mission over Southern France.

CHIEF WORKS: *Vol de Nuit (Night Flight;* novel, 1931) is based on the author's experiences in South America. Rivière, supervisor in charge of the Patagonian airmail service, has begun scheduling night flights in defiance of the common opinion that they are unsafe; he is driven by an intense determination to compete with rail and sea transport. Fabien, a pilot, is killed in the night service, and Rivière almost abandons his project. His sense of duty wins over his despair over the loss of his friend, however, and the night flights continue.

Terre des Hommes (translated as *Wind, Sand, and Stars;* narrative essays, 1939) is a work without a comprehensive plot; it consists of a set of disconnected sketches drawn from the author's flying career. Within the general framework are several narrative vignettes: an experience in Spain during the Civil War; a forced landing in the Libyan desert; the story of the slave Bark, redeemed from servitude and restored to his former self Mohammed ben Llaoussin; and Guillaumet, a flyer downed in the Andes who struggles through the snow for a week until he is finally rescued.

Pilote de Guerre (translated as *Flight to Arras;* narrative essay, 1942) relates the author's experiences during the Fall of France. Although the French general staff is thrown into utter chaos and no intelligence could be of the slightest use to it, the narrator is forced to take up a reconnaissance flight to scout the advancing German forces. Seventeen of twenty-three remaining French aircraft have been lost on such flights, but the narrator and his gunner miraculously escape. From this experience the narrator learns of the superiority of Man over individual men, and conversely of the strength of the individual confronted by an anonymous collective force.

The three works described above have been collected in English under the title *An Airman's Odyssey* (New York, 1942).

Pierre Louys (French, 1870-1925)

Pierre Louys is an escapist, an aesthete, and a decadent, and at the same time a highly cultured scholar with an extensive classical background. His chief theme is that of erotic love, yet his work, mildly aphrodisiac, never deteriorates into sensationalism. He has a typical French gift of restraint, which enables him to skirt the most perilous subjects without violating the canons of decorum.

Louys is an impassioned devotee of Hellenism. He admires the sensual paganism of the Greeks, especially their adulation of the beautiful, and he is profoundly opposed to the Puritan element in modern European culture. Naturally, with this bias he tends to romanticize Greek culture; he shows us only its Dionysian side and ignores its Apollonian elements of reason, restraint, and symmetry. Nevertheless his background in classicism is sound. His imitations of Greek lyrics, published under the title *Les Chansons de Bilitis,* are authentic in tone and were actually mistaken for translations of antique poetry by some scholars.

Although Louys is ostensibly a modern-day Hellenist, his attitude toward love often resembles that of the medieval troubadour. He makes a cult of dominating passion, of devotion to the object of one's love, even of the chastity which preserves love in its pristine purity; this last especially is hardly a pagan concept. His work is basically authentic but highly romanticized, the product of careful scholarship plus a delicate and refined aesthetic imagination.

LIFE: Louys was born Pierre Louis in 1870. As a schoolboy at the École Alsacienne in Paris he met André Gide, who remained his lifetime friend even when the literary interests of the two authors later diverged. He was also associated from the time of his youth with the poets Henry de Régnier and Paul Valéry; he was for several years a disciple of the Parnassian poet Heredia, whose daughter he married in 1899. Louys' first literary publication was a translation of Meleager in 1893. *Les Chansons de Bilitis,* the Greek imitations which won him his first fame, appeared in 1894. *Aphrodite,* his masterpiece, was published in 1896; it was ideally suited to the spirit of the fin-de-siècle and received immediate acclaim. The novel was, however, denounced on moral grounds by several self-appointed censors, and narrowly escaped suppression.

Louys is also important in French literature as an editor. As a young man he published the poetry review *La Conque* (1891 ff), which contained poems by many authors later to be famous. In 1896 he founded *Le Centaure,* an even more important review. A recluse in his later years, he died in 1925 in Paris.

CHIEF WORK: *Aphrodite* (novel, 1896) is laid in Alexandria in the year 58 B.C. The central figure is the handsome Greek sculptor Demetrios, who like Pygmalion becomes enamoured of his own statue, in this case a figure of Aphrodite. Queen Berenike falls in love with Demetrios, but he, devoted to his art, spurns her. Later he meets the beautiful courtesan Chrysis and becomes madly enamoured of her. She demands of him three gifts: the mirror of Rhodopis, a possession of her enemy Bacchys; the comb of Tounis, bride of a high priest; and a pearl necklace draped around Aphrodite's hands in the Temple of Love. Demetrios carries out these tasks, but is afterwards filled with remorse; he refuses the favors of Chrysis which his deeds have won. When the city arises in indignation over the crimes, Chrysis, to expiate her part in the affair, comes unclothed to the great beacon of Alexandria carrying the three stolen objects. Her beauty convinces Demetrios she is actually an incarnation of Aphrodite, the inspiration of his statue; he realizes she is a symbol of the aesthetic perfection he has worshipped. He reaches out for her but it is too late; she has taken poison and presently dies.

Jean Cocteau (French, 1889-1963)

As a poet and dramatist Cocteau owes much to the surrealists who were his contemporaries, and even more to the symbolatry of literary Freudianism. His world is a bizarre and dreamy one, cluttered with the machinery of the fairy-tale and thick with the peculiar air of poetic mystery which has become a Cocteau trade-mark. His preoccupation with this mood has led his detractors to dismiss him as a sort of literary sleight-of-hand artist intent on mystifying his audience at any cost, even that of meaning. Cocteau is more properly treated as a man of the theatre than as a serious poet; in the theatre his sleight-of-hand tricks find their proper place, and the mood he achieves becomes an effective dramatic device.

Cocteau's content is frequently that of the nineteenth-century Gothic school: enchanted knights, sleeping beauties, the unearthly and unerring operation of fate, the magic which pervades the prosaic objects of everyday life, and the ubiquity of death in all human experience. Anachronism is a favorite Cocteau device; he is fond of staging a fairy-tale in modern dress or of adding modern soldiers to an Oedipus tragedy. In his drama on Orpheus the hero is unable to enter a poetry contest because he has mislaid his birth certificate.

To Cocteau the paragon of humanity, in fact the only useful member of society, is the artist. He expresses all the folklore of the traditional artist-cult: the artist is misunderstood and persecuted by society, the artist's ways are inscrutable, and the artist, integrated with the universe, has in him a spark of the divine lacking in ordinary men. Cocteau stands squarely for art-for-art's-sake and ignores any form of social content; thus he illustrates to perfection one form romanticism may take in the twentieth century.

LIFE: Cocteau was born at Maisons-Laffitte, ten miles from Paris, on July 5, 1889 (although until his death it was generally thought he had been born in 1891); his family were traditionally Parisian lawyers. His first volume of poetry, *La Lampe d'Aladin* appeared in 1909. After a friendship with the young André Gide he produced his first serious work, the novel *Le Potomak* (1919). His real fame, and his major literary activity, dates from the post-war period. He has experimented in every artistic medium: painting, music, sculpture, poetry, prose, the cinema, the stage, and even the circus. His motion pictures (e.g. *Le Sang d'un Poète, L'Eternel Retour, Orphée*) were especially important in introducing surrealism into the French cinema. His intimate friends have included such artists as Stravinsky, Picasso, Diaghilev, and Gide, and a host of society leaders including the Comtesse de Noailles, as well as Edith Piaf, street singer and ultimately café chanteuse.

During the Occupation of 1940-45 Cocteau was accused by his enemies of excessive intimacy with the Germans, but after the war his prestige returned almost to its former heights. In 1955 he surprised friends and enemies alike by becoming a member of the French Academy. (Surprise has always been one of his favorite literary techniques.) Cocteau in poor health during his last years suffered a stroke early in 1963. On October 11, at the age of seventy-four years and at his home in Milly-la Foret thirty miles from Paris, he died seven hours after the death of Edith Piaf. He told reporters on that day, "I had a fever since this morning, and I must say the death of Edith Piaf has caused renewed sadness and discomfort." Later he said, "The boat is going down," and died of a heart attack.

CHIEF WORKS: *Orphée* (play, 1927; film, 1950) is one of the more original adaptations of the Greek myth in modern literature; when compared with Anouilh's *Eurydice,* Williams' *Orpheus Descending,* and the film, *Black Orpheus,* it is seen as the first attempt at combining surrealism with this classic story symbolizing the poet or artist in the world, a very modern world in each case. Cocteau adds to the basic story of Orpheus and Eurydice, who pass to and from the realm of the dead through a mirror, and the murdering Bacchantes, or critics, the characters of Heurtebise, a glazier, who understand, manipulates, and comments on the action; a horse, who acts as inspiring muse; and Death, a very beautiful young woman stylishly dressed with her assistants who make up a surgical operating team complete with rubber gloves. (In the film Death and her assistants ride into the city on motorcycles.) The breaking of glass and the rolling in of the head of Orpheus represents his murder by the public, and Cocteau identifies himself with Orphée. The movie directed by Cocteau from his adaptation of his own play remains, along with *Red Shoes,* one of the most significant and exciting uses of surrealistic techniques in the cinema as an art form.

Les Enfants terribles (novel, 1929) is a bizarre novel of a childhood "club" which continues to bind its members into adulthood. Paul, a young lycée student, is injured in a snow-fight and is taken

home in a taxi by his friend Gérard. Forced to abandon school,
Paul remains in his room for several months attended by his sister
Elizabeth; their mother is ailing and soon dies. Gérard, a frequent
visitor at the flat, becomes almost a member of the family; soon the
three form an intimate cénacle with a secret language, eccentric habits,
and a fierce mistrust of outsiders. Another girl, Agathe, is reluctantly
admitted to the circle and is tentatively paired off with Paul. Elizabeth,
subconsciously jealous of her brother, marries a rich American youth,
Michael, but he is killed in an auto accident on his wedding-night; the
marriage serves only to provide the "club" with Michael's magnificent
house to live in. Elizabeth gradually becomes more openly drawn to
her brother; she tampers with the mail in such a way as to break up
his affair with Agathe. Paul, in love with Agathe, takes poison in
despair. As Elizabeth's full perfidy is unveiled she shoots herself, certain now that her beloved brother will belong to her alone. This novel
was made into an effective motion-picture released in America under
the title *The Strange Ones.*

  La Machine infernale (*The Infernal Machine;* tragic cycle, 1934)
is one of several Cocteau adaptations of classic myths. The theme is
the Oedipus myth, beginning with the arrival of Oedipus in Thebes
and ending with the catastrophe of Sophocles' *Oedipus the King.* The
cycle consists of four "acts," actually separate one-act plays. In the
first act Jocasta, an aging nymphomaniac who collects young men, is
warned by the ghost of her husband Laius that a young conqueror
is soon to arrive. In Act II Oedipus confronts the Sphinx; the monster,
bowing to the fate which hangs over Oedipus' head, readily tells him
the answer to the riddle in order that he may repeat it back to her. In
Act III we witness the wedding-night of Oedipus and Jocasta. The act
is heavy with Freudian irony; Oedipus accidentally falls asleep with
his head across the cradle which contained him as a child. In the final
act, seventeen years later, we see the dénouement as it is to be found
in Sophocles. Cocteau's version ignores most of the moral and religious content of the Sophoclean tragedy. The "infernal machine" of
the title is the vast mechanism of fate, "one of the most perfect
machines constructed by the infernal gods for the mathematical annihilation of a mortal man."

Michel de Ghelderode (Belgian, 1898-1962)

Ghelderode, although known in his native land through the Flemish Popular Theatre productions of his plays, *Saint Francis of Assisi, Barabbas,* and *Pantagleize,* some twenty years earlier, was "discovered" by the world in Paris through the staging of his plays at the Théâtre Marigny by Jean-Louis Barrault and his company in the late 1940s and early 1950s. *The Chronicles of Hell* in 1949, for example, had the kind of *succès de scandale* that goes back to Stravinsky's *Rites of Spring* and Victor Hugo's *Hernani* for comparable uproar; and the charges included indecency and blasphemy, which probably contributed to dramatic impact. By the 1960s his plays were being produced often in experimental theatres from Sweden and Poland to the United States and Mexico.

What makes Ghelderode chiefly neo-romantic (but he's slippery, being also realistic, naturalistic, expressionistic, even absurd) is his medievalism, the recurrent settings in Flanders in the olden days with its coarseness and brutality, its street fairs, puppet shows, old churches, and funeral processions. He really believes in the existence of the Devil, much like the devils of medieval miracle and morality plays, and, of course, black magic. As a somewhat Joycean Catholic, Ghelderode declared himself neither anti-clerical nor pro-clerical, neither condoning nor condemning, his originality in seeing everything from the people's point of view like Breugel or, as he said himself, from beneath. His religious dramas have a peculiar shock value in such devices as the pantomimed miracles and angels swinging on trapezes in *Saint Francis* as performed in 1927.

Ghelderode remains a subject of controversy. This became evident in the Fall 1963 issue of the Tulane *Drama Review.* Eric Bentley seems to be among the yea-sayers, pointing out that Brecht and Ghelderode share two things: both were born in 1898 and both are still formative forces.

LIFE: Born in Brussels in 1898, Michel de Ghelderode, the youngest of several brothers and a sister, spent an uneventful but sensitive childhood according to his own account, influenced chiefly on the imaginative side by a mother rich in proverbs, songs, and haunted stories, who claimed to have seen the Devil many times since her convent training at Louvain. His father was principal clerk at the *Archives Générales,* and Michel followed him eventually in this kind of work for some twenty years, reveling in the relics of a bygone Flanders during the times of Maria Theresa, Philip II, Charles V. He found his own masters of literature among whom he speaks principally of Shakespeare, Charles de Coster, Cervantes, and then of Kyd, Marlowe, Ben Johnson, Hoffmann, Edgar Allen Poe (he once wrote a play, *Death Looks In at the Window,* in the manner of Poe or in what would have been his manner had he written plays), Monk Lewis, and Victor Hugo. He speaks also of music and particularly of painting, the very Flemish masters, Hieronymus Bosch, Pieter Breugel, Jordaens, who led him toward the art of the theatre. Although apparently very much the Fleming in his spirit and sympathies Ghelderode wrote in French and his plays were then translated into Flemish.

He began as a short story writer and there are references to some fifty of his stories. His plays, some very long and some very short but none cut or lengthened to fit traditional three or five act theatre, also number about fifty. Ghelderode is supposed to have started writing following a serious illness at the age of sixteen, but his most productive period as a playwright began in 1927 when the Flemish Popular Theatre commissioned the Saint Francis play. With this group he learned the resources of actors, the possibilities of staging, up-to-date equipment, the practical and economic life of the theatre. Within ten years he had written most of his best plays.

A solitary and almost a recluse by choice, the dramatist was pulled into the bright light of publicity by the success of his plays in Paris. In August 1951 he recorded the Ostend Interviews which were broadcast by French television in 1951-52. His plays are full of misshapen buffoons, torturers, degenerates, lascivious monks, and lecherous old men; they are also full of the presence of Death. Death came for Michel de Ghelderode in Brussels in April 1962.

CHIEF DRAMAS: *Christopher Columbus* (drama, 1927) is described as a dramatic fairy tale in three scenes, with the author's note for the director: Dances, lights, music, some acrobatics, pathos, absurdity, tragedy, a message for those who like messages. This play is spectacle and enchantment, and plays swiftly, without pause, in the perspective of dream. Time shifts or slides into the future from 1492 with casual references to Lindbergh or Buffalo Bill. For the dramatist Columbus became a synthesis of all travelers, all wanderers, all the "erratics" of his age and of all ages. Columbus was the man who escapes, and isn't this the worry of all men today; isn't it our daily worry? Columbus returns from America to prison and to death and therefore to liberation.

Pantagleize (drama, 1929), a farce to make you sad, is unique Ghelderode in having a contemporary setting: a city of Europe between one war and the next. It is a fantasy about a political revolution put together by a grotesque group of malcontents, led by sheer accident by a modern innocent, an old fool, a Charlie Chaplin clown who is completely non-political, but who says the key words, as in a bad spy picture, to trigger the uprising: "What a lovely day!" Innocents are always ripe for slaughter. Dreamers who remain true to the promptings of their instincts are dangerous to this dehumanized society of the modern world which prizes intelligence first and leads to the fragmentation of mankind. Pantagleize is Ghelderode's Everyman who faces the problem of commitment in life. At the beginning of the play and the day he has no real identity in his society, forty years old, growing old, unfit for anything except love, friendship, ardor—a failure, therefore, in our utilitarian age. But in the one day which pulls him into the revolution and leads to his death Pantagleize falls in love, enjoys prestige and power as a leader of men, is elated in the desperate adventures he never sought, and faces confusion in final judgment and death. Modern man does not choose his destiny: it is thrust upon him. But in one day Pantagleize reveals the richness, joy, pain, sadness, and absurdity of every man's destiny, reaffirming our essential humanity.

Fastes d'Enfer (Chronicles of Hell; drama, 1929) has been called a Tragedy *Bouffe* in One Act. It is somewhat like an *Opera Bouffe,* but the comedy is mephitic and not at all funny; and the subject, religion and church turned inside out into a kind of black mass, although rooted in Flemish reality, is nevertheless blown up to grotesque proportions.

The setting is a decaying Episcopal palace in old-time Flanders, Gothic with a bay window looking out on a summer storm and a crowd in the public square no less stormy; along the walls a clutter of

baroque objects, idols, witches' masks, devils, totems, instruments
of torture; in the foreground a table banquet-laden. Jan in Eremo,
Bishop of Lapideopolis, is dead. During the wake he rises from death,
casts terror on all present, and dies again when the host of the extreme unction has been removed from his throat (he was too evil
to swallow it). Many of the characters are grotesquely satirical: the
chaplain, Carnibos, who is the complete glutton and frequently flatu-
lent; the nuncio's secretary, Sodomati, who seems appropriately
named; and Krakenbus, the envious and spiteful. Simon Laquedeem,
auxiliary bishop, presents a brief history of Jan in Eremo as the
Anti-Christ. At the end bells ring, censers are swung, and bedlam
is general. This is the stage play that shocked Paris, but it is clearly
theatrical.

Miss Jairus (drama, 1934), a mystery in four tableaux, vies with
Pantagleize for the position of greatest play. This is somewhat like
Molière's *Misanthrope,* a hard nut to crack, the play that Ghelderode
himself hoped he would grow to apprehend even if he could never
hope to comprehend it. *Miss Jairus* is the Bible story of a resurrection
(reluctant?, mistaken?) transposed to Bruges, the Flemish city of
Death in a vanished age (which makes it omnipresent). The Mystery
(which reinforces the Christ analogy) develops within three seasons,
from autumn to spring, from the first death of Blandine Jairus to the
second release and a reenactment of the Easter week crucifixion.
Blandine and Lazarus, more than a little decayed, have more in common in their understanding of death, and life, than the daughter has
with her parents or betrothed who selfishly want her to live. The
attitudes of the church, of business men, of medical science are ax-
amined and thrust through with satirical stilettos. As Ghelderode said
by way of explanation, the important thing is that there should be no
outbreak of scandal. As to the tears that the lock-gates are publicly
opened for, as to the masks that are worn in the funeral procession,
everyone knows that this too is theatre! Here then the Hamlet "trap-
pings and the suits of woe" are dramatized once more. Like *Hamlet*
and *The Misanthrope, Miss Jairus* is a play whose metaphysical
dimensions cannot be ignored.

Hop, Signor! (drama, 1935), a play in one act set in Flanders in
olden times, is based on two pieces of history: one, blanket-tossing,

once very popular in Brabant, tossing either a doll or a person, as a game or a punishment (in which case it might be contrived that he fell badly and ended up broken in the street); and two, the burning alive near Antwerp of Margaret Harstein in 1555, a beautiful courtesan who had committed some unaccountable crime. The main character, Signor Jureal, is a sculptor of the old Gothic school, decorating cathedrals with gargoyles, thoroughly medieval; but a new age is coming into fashion, the renaissance, represented by two courtiers, Adorno from Italy and Helgar from England. Adorno says, "Your art, Jureal, bears witness to an age that has passed away. One must please and you displease. The artists of today turn toward antiquity. Their works no longer express the Christian's hope or despair, but the joy of living. . . ." Jureal is married to the beauty, Margaret Harstein, who wants to be rid of him. His only sympathetic companions are two dwarfs, Tallow and Wick, ugly as gargoyles. Margaret is courted by Adorno and Helgar, while the lascivious monk, Dom Pilar, spies on them. The executioner, Larose, a handsome, blonde athlete with a rose in his mouth, seems to be attractive to Margaret; but all the characters without exception are impotent. And most are guilty, little matter of what, Margaret perhaps of witchcraft. Jureal is killed by blanket tossing at a festival in the streets; the affair has been manipulated by Adorno and Helgar, competing for Margaret's favor. Adorno then kills Helgar and flees, leaving his dagger. Margaret is taken off by the Magistrate, leaving the dwarfs to comment, "It is all played." "Hop, little Signor! You were noble!" as they pantomime the blanket tossing with a disjointed marionette.

8. IMPRESSIONISM
AND STREAM-OF-CONSCIOUSNESS

As a part of the broader reaction against realism a number of authors in the twentieth century began to doubt the essential validity of "reality" as the term is understood by the realists and naturalists. To this new group the "real" was not so much the external incident in the life of a character as the internal mental processes which developed in reaction to this incident. Among the devices invented by twentieth-century authors to depict this internal life were the techniques known as impressionism, stream-of-consciousness, and internal monologue. These techniques came into predominance in the period immediately after the First World War; by 1925 they had been practiced by four or five major authors and by a host of mediocre imitators.

Various authors utilized these devices differently; Joyce is far from Proust in his basic approach to the novel. Nevertheless these authors shared certain basic premises: (1) that the true existence of an individual lies in his mental processes, not in the external incidents of his life; (2) that the mental life of the ordinary person is disjointed, intuitive, and associative rather than sharply logical; and (3) that psychological association—i.e., the mental linking of objects which have been encountered in juxtaposition—is one of the chief processes forming our emotional attitudes toward things. Thus a loved one's glove reminds us of the beloved person herself, and participation in a railway accident will cause us forever to associate train whistles with fear.

To portray this interior ilfe on the printed page, these authors were obliged to invent new and radical narrative techniques. Proust is the most traditional of them and the most significant European of them all; he achieves his stylistic subtlety merely through endless ramification and examination of the problem from all sides. Joyce, on the other hand, is the most radical, following and outdistancing Edouard Dujardin's interior monologue of *Les Lauriers Sont Coupés* (1888); he departs completely from the syntax and grammar of ordinary fiction and creates, not only a new literature, but virtually a new language. Both Joyce and Proust carry their new techniques to their logical climaxes; thus they are difficult to surpass in their genre. Nevertheless their would-be imitators are to be numbered by the hundreds, and countless other authors show their influence in one form or another.

Impressionistic authors, being chiefly concerened with the mental life of the individual, are generally somewhat detached from social, political, or ethical problems. Proust is the most intellectual of these authors, yet even he is curiously passive toward the problems of modern social evolution. Some of these authors have pretenses of metaphysics, but even this is not their chief interest. They are concerned with the way the human brain reacts to its external stimulations, even the most trivial. To them a cup of tea or a handclasp may be as important as the fall of an empire; their attitude is entirely an individual and subjective one.

Marcel Proust (French, 1871-1922)

Proust's masterpiece *A la Recherche du Temps perdu* was published as a series of seven novels; actually it is a single integrated work in which every part is linked to the whole. The entire work must be read before the reader can gain a full comprehension of the author's purpose, and even then the reader will find it necessary to check back occasionally on characters and circumstances in the earlier sections. The work fills sixteen volumes in the original French, and Proust devoted to it the labor of seventeen years; it demands a corresponding thoroughness in reading.

Proust's chief interest is in epistomology; i.e., the study of the means by which the mind acquires, processes, and assimilates information from the outside world. He approaches this study, however, as a novelist and not as a philosopher; his work is far from being a novel of ideas. To Proust human experience, whether pleasure or pain, is meaningless at the moment of its actual occurrence. Its real existence lies in two other realms: the realm of anticipation and the realm of recollection. We may savor coming delights in our minds before they occur, and thus enjoy a pleasure quite lacking in the actual incident where pleasure is marred and confused by a host of irrelevancies. Likewise the mind can achieve its highest pleasures in seeking to recover the savor of experiences hidden out of memory. This search is facilitated through conversation, through revery, and especially through chance association of objects and sensations: a pair of slightly uneven paving blocks underfoot suggest to the narrator of the novel a similar sensation in Venice years before, and thus aid him to reconstruct the entire Venice experience. It is not so much that the incident is relived by this means, but that it is actually lived for the first time. Thus psychological association, particularly what is known as the *dèjà-vu* experience ("already seen" literally, but already tasted, heard, smelled, or felt—like the uneven paving blocks—as well), lies at the base of Proust's method.

This preoccupation involves Proust in a study of time as a flowing substance; here he was greatly influenced by the philosopher Henri Bergson (1859-1941). To Bergson time is an elastic substance whose duration and very existence can be altered by subjective factors, and to Proust time is an erratic sensation which can be halted, speeded up, or even reversed in the inner mind where real experience takes place.

Proust's subject matter is diverse, but he is more preoccupied with various forms of decadence than are most authors. His novel involves degeneration and death, homosexuality in both sexes, sadistic cruelty, and a host of psychological aberrations such as the Oedipus complex. These matters are presented, however, with utter decorum. Proust even bowdlerized the incidents of his own life before incorporating them in the novel where he felt decorum would be violated. Much of his content is drawn from actual French society of the 1870-1914 period, yet names and places are invariably changed where individuals would be shown in an unfavorable light. It is a mistake to assume that Proust is writing the story of his own life in his novel. Everything is transformed, altered, twisted and inverted until the original experience becomes merely the suggestion for the fictional incident.

Proust's style is difficult in English and even more so in French. He makes little effort to achieve concision or to recommend himself in any way to the popular reader. His sentences are long and convoluted, often covering a page or more; his thought seems to wander aimlessly (although it does not), and he seldom leaves a subject until he has examined it from all sides. He is capable of devoting twenty pages to an analysis following upon the sensation of eating a small cake soaked in tea, along with the memories and associations evoked by this apparently trivial gustatory stimulus.

Saint-Simon and Mme. de Sévigné were important influences on Proust. From them he learned the art of characterization as it was known in the French classic age, a method very different from the Dickensian English method but also very effective. He is fond of presenting character obliquely—through the comments of another person, through an apparently unimportant gesture, or through a subjective reaction in the mind of the narrator. One of the marks of greatness his novel bears is that it includes a dozen or so characters who remain fixed in the reader's memory. The most important of these are the narrator's grandmother, the Baron de Charlus, Mme. Verdurin, M. Swann, Odette, Françoise, Robert de Saint-Loup, Aunt Leonie, and the narrator's mistress, Albertine.

Most of these characters are drawn from persons Proust actually knew, but the details are broadly transformed; in the case of Albertine the sex is apparently changed. Some of these characters, e.g., Swann, occupy major portions of the work; others, like Aunt Léonie, appear only in a few pages and are characterized with a minimum of strokes. In either case the characterization is powerful, well-rounded, and faultlessly finished.

Proust's chief literary weaknesses are his inability or unwillingness to present his ideas with concision and his failure to sustain interest paragraph by paragraph. This is as much as to say that he is not a facile magazine-story writer. To those who wish to make the requisite effort, his novel is an exciting and deeply rewarding experience.

LIFE: Proust was the son of Dr. Adrien Proust, a prominent Parisian physician. His mother, born Jeanne Weil, was a cultured and extremely beautiful Jewess. Marcel was born in Auteuil in 1871 immediately after the bloody events of the Commune and the German occupation, and his mother's experiences undoubtedly influenced the child's health. He remained a hypochondriac and partial invalid throughout his life. His early childhood, however, was happy; he played in the Bois de Boulogne and was frequently taken to the fashionable Normandy sea-side resorts of Trouville and Cabourg. The family vacations were spent in Illiers, a town near Chartres where the ancestral home of the Prousts was to be found and where Marcel's aunt, Mme. Amiot, still resided. All these experiences found their way into the novel: the Norman resorts became Balbec, Illiers became Combray, and Mme. Amiot became Aunt Léonie.

Proust was schooled at the Lycée Condorcet in Paris and later attended both the Law School of the University of Paris and the Sorbonne; he received his *licencié* from the latter in 1892. Provided with a modest income by his family, he was not obliged to take steady employment. He dabbled in literature, wrote for *Figaro,* and began to move in aristocratic circles, where he achieved remarkable success considering his Jewish parentage. He was introduced to such social leaders as Mme. Halévy-Straus and Mme. Arman de Caillavet; his ingratiating manners conquered the snobbish Robert de Montesquiou and even won a preface from Anatole France for Proust's *Les Plaisirs et les Jours* (1896). This volume gained Proust a certain acclaim in society circles and determined him to follow a career as a novelist.

After the death of his mother in 1905 he began to work out the plan of his novel. Gradually he withdrew from the world; he moved through a series of lodgings and finally settled in a large apartment at 102 Boulevard Haussmann. Here he caused his room to be lined with cork to exclude outside noises and ordered the windows permanently shut; his asthmatic attacks had increased by this time to the point where he could work only at night and was sent into spasms by the odor of trees or foliage. In 1911 *Du côté de chez Swann,* the first "novel" of his work, was finished. He offered it to various publishers of his acquaintance, but no one would take it. Finally he was forced to have it published by Grasset at his own expense. It appeared in 1913 and was received almost without comment. During the period of the war Proust, sensing that death would cut the book short before it was finished, wrote at an increasing rate. The second section of the work, which appeared in 1918, won the Prix Goncourt the following year; and the publication of *Le côté de Guermantes* in 1920 brought him a world-wide fame. In 1922, still feverishly correcting proof, he died of asthma complicated by pneumonia.

CHIEF WORK: *A la Recherche du Temps perdu* is an integrated novel cycle consisting of seven separately-published sections and filling sixteen volumes in the original French. The title, translated by C. K. Scott-Moncrieff as *Remembrance of Things Past,* is literally "In Search of Lost Time"; this phrase more accurately defines the spirit of the work.

Although the structure of the novel is complex and involves an extremely diffuse presentation of time, the general outline of the work is chronological. The content of the seven novel-sections can be summarized as follows:

In *Du Côté de chez Swann* (translated as *Swann's Way;* 1913) the boyhood of the narrator Marcel is described and the symphonic themes of the work are introduced. Marcel begins by recollecting his childhood sojourns in the country town of Combray, where his parents used to take him in the summer. Fiercely affectionate toward his mother, the boy is grief-stricken when he is made to go upstairs to bed early because of the arrival of a guest, M. Swann. He cannot go to sleep until his mother comes upstairs to bid him goodnight; and she, distracted by the conversation of the guest, is unable to do this until very late. Thus the theme of tormented love, specifically the person who loves more than he is loved in return, is introduced. Each of Marcel's future experiences of love is to follow the same pattern.

The walks Marcel takes with his family through the environs of Combray, the walks which give their names to two sections of the novel, are also described. The first of the two routes commonly taken by the family on their promenades is "Swann's way," leading past the estate of the wealthy and somewhat mysterious Swann. As he learns more of Swann, Marcel grows to associate this route with the aggressive rising culture of the bourgeoisie and with sensual love. The other route is the "Guermantes way," leading toward the ancestral home of the Guermantes, the feudal suzerains of the region. Marcel associates this "way" with the proud and now decadent aristocracy of the *ancien régime*, with medieval art and architecture, and with the traditions of medieval Catholicism.

Lingering behind his parents on one of these walks, Marcel peers through a hawthorn hedge into the Swann grounds and catches his first glimpse of Gilberte, daughter of Swann and his wife Odette. The sight of the little girl seen through the hawthorn blossoms is Marcel's introduction to love; althougl. he goes on to more serious affairs, he is always to connect sexual love with the anticipatory emotions of this moment. Later, as a young boy, he plays with Gilberte in the Tuileries in Paris; before the novel ends he is to see her marry his friend Saint-Loup, age, and gradually become stout and complacent.

In another important passage Marcel tells how, in later years, he happened to taste a small cake *(madeleine)* which had been dipped in tea, and felt an exquisite and quite inexplicable pleasure. Through a chain of associations he was able to establish that this sensation had subconsciously reminded him of the *madeleines* his Aunt Léonie used to give him when he was a child in Combray, and this had suggested to him the whole pattern of his happy childhood. Thus another theme is established: the connection of memory to apparently trivial physical sensations, and the manner in which chains of association may lead our minds down the path of memory to the past. It is this particular chain of association which impels Marcel to begin recounting the events of the novel.

Marcel's wise and affectionate old grandmother also occupies a place of importance in *Swann's Way*. She is Marcel's confidante in all his thoughts; she takes him on expeditions to the seaside resort of

Balbec, and she contributes to his education by talking to him of Racine, Mme. de Sévigné, and other classic authors. Two other important characters in this section are Léonie, Marcel's flighty and hypochondriacal aunt whose remarks become family traditions, and the servant Francoise a garrulous and ludicrously ungrammatical peasant woman who stays on to care for Marcel long after his parents are dead.

The reader is presently introduced to the circle of Mme. Verdurin, a vulgar bourgeois social climber who struggles to establish a fashionable salon and eventually succeeds. Mme. Verdurin's literary *gaffes*, her hypocritical ecstasies over music and art, and her exaggerated manner of speaking make her one of the most notable characters of the novel. Then, in a long flashback, the history of Swann's relations with Odette is revealed. Swann is one of the chief characters of the work. Jewish by birth, wealthy, restrained and diffident in manner, kind and affectionate but continually unhappy in love, he is not without resemblance to Proust himself. It has been argued that "Marcel," the narrator, represents Proust's youth and Swann the Proust of his mature years. Swann's experiences in love are much like those of Marcel. Odette de Crécy is an obviously vulgar and superficial young woman; when Swann first meets her he sees her for what she is, yet in his imagination he rationalizes her into an incarnation of abstract beauty. She accepts his advances for mercenary reasons, but soon shows herself to be shamelessly cynical. Swann is helpless under the spell of his fixation; he knows her faults, yet to him she is woman personified. She becomes his mistress and bears him a child, Gilberte; when they go to live on the estate in Combray the neighbors, sympathizing with Swann, nevertheless refuse to receive Odette. When Swann marries her he has long since escaped from the spell she casts over him; he performs the marriage only to assure the legitimacy of his daughter.

In *A l'Ombre des jeunes Filles en Fleurs* (translated as *Within a Budding Grove;* 1918) the relations of Swann and Odette are followed after their marriage. Aspects of the Dreyfus affair, especially its reception in polite society, are also described. Marcel, Jewish through his mother, instinctively sides with the liberal Dreyfusards, yet many of his friends, especially the aristocrats he most admires, are anti-Dreyfusards. The intricate nuances of snobbery which proceed from this affair are delineated with great delicacy and precision.

The dominant event of the section is the entrance of Albertine, a young girl Marcel first encounters at the seaside resort of Balbec. At first he sees her only as an anonymous member of a mysteriously attractive group of young girls on the beach. Gradually he distinguishes her from the others and falls in love with her, never imagining his love is capable of consummation. At this time Albertine symbolizes for him all the freshness, chastity, and vitality of youth; he idealizes her as he has done before with Gilberte and as Swann has done with Odette.

Le Côté de Guermantes (translated as *The Guermantes Way;* 1920) chiefly concerns the aristocratic circle of Mme. de Guermantes, the dazzling duchess Marcel first sees in the church at Combray. Later he is introduced to her salon and conceives a profound admiration for the genuine noble and aristocratic ideals she symbolizes. He also becomes friendly with Robert de Saint-Loup, a young officer whose amatory experiences form a secondary plot. The section parenthetically relates the death of Marcel's grandmother, a crushing blow from which he recovers only gradually. It then proceeds to an analysis of the Baron de Charlus, one of the principal characters of the novel. Charlus is the epitome of perversion; in addition to being a snob, he is simultaneously a homosexual, a masochist, and a sadist. Proud of his noble ancestry, he refuses to be introduced to any but the highest of society; yet he openly consorts with waiters and bellboys and humbles himself before low persons whose affection he desires. He is not without a certain wit, but uses it mainly to heap sarcasm and insolence upon his social inferiors. He is especially rude to Mme. Verdurin, whom he considers a vulgar and classless person of no importance.

Sodome et Gomorrhe (translated as *Cities of the Plain;* 1920-23) is mainly devoted to a comparison and analysis of various forms of perversion. M. de Charlus' experiments in immorality are described, especially his affair with the conceited and fickle young musician Morel. His relations with this young man form a contrast to the loves of Marcel and Swann respectively; the Charlus-Morel affair substitutes depravity for true passion, yet the same principles of human relation seem to operate. In all three cases the objects of passion are unworthy ones, and love is shown as a disease which the lover is helpless to combat and from which he recovers only gradually. Two other characters are analysed in detail in this section: M. Vinteuil, a composer whose sonata sends Mme. Verdurin into simulated ecstasies and serves as a *Leitmotif* for the love of Swann and Odette, and M. Cottard, an apparently stupid doctor who is later revealed as a famous scientist.

La Prisonnière (*The Captive;* 1923) is almost entirely devoted to the climax of Marcel's infatuation with Albertine. The girl is enticed to live in his apartment, which she leaves only to go on mysterious expeditions with her friend Andrée. A strange life begins for Marcel, in which he becomes the virtual slave of the "prisoner" Albertine. Ill, he is unable to leave the house and now feels himself the passive party of the relationship; he is tormented with vague feelings of jealousy and resentment. Marcel's old servant Françoise disapproves of Albertine; the three occupants of the house engage in a complex and hectic intrigue of mingled love and suspicion. Marcel, however, discovers that the consummation of his love for Albertine is less rewarding than its anticipation has been: he also begins to suspect his mistress of Lesbian tendencies. At the end of the section Albertine goes away, leaving him forlorn but somehow relieved.

Albertine disparue (translated as *The Sweet Cheat Gone;* 1925) describes Marcel's sensations after the departure of his mistress. He is fascinated to observe the gradual transition from grief to indifference; soon he finds that he derives more pleasure from the memory of Albertine than he ever found in her presence. Not long afterward she is killed in a riding accident. He is again stricken with grief, but consoles himself by reliving their happy moments in recollection. As he recalls the past, however, he begins to remember incidents which now assume an ominous significance; Albertine's immorality appears to him increasingly certain. In an interlude Gilberte Swann, Marcel's first love, marries his friend Saint-Loup; society is scandalized at the match but gradually comes to accept it.

Le Temps retrouvé (translated as *The Past Recaptured;* 1927) chiefly recounts events which transpire after the First World War; this final section contrives to draw all the threads of the novel together. Marcel is at last provided with definite proof of Albertine's perversion. He visits Saint-Loup, who now occupies Swann's old estate at Combray, and is astonished to think it is the same place he first spied on Gilberte. M. de Charlus degenerates completely and is repudiated by all respectable society. As the novel ends every aspect of Marcel's world is changed into something new. The Princesse de Guermantes has died and the Prince has been forced to marry the vulgar Mme.

Verdurin for money; the lady has more than fulfilled her audacious social ambitions. Swann has passed away as well, and Odette has become a fashionable society leader. Marcel realizes at last that there is no stability in persons, places, or things; only in the world of the mind are true permanence and true wealth to be found.

Into this narrative structure is woven the thematic pattern of the novel, its real essence. Several distinct themes are introduced in the opening volumes, restated as the story proceeds, and drawn together at the end in a symphonic climax. The most important of these themes are as follows:

(1) True pleasure and satisfaction are to be found, not in actual experience, but in two other realms: anticipation and recollection. Of these the most rewarding is recollection, which is best approached through some trivial physical sensation which will set into motion a complex train of mental associations.

(2) Applying this principle to sexual relations, the narrator concludes that the consummation of passion is seldom equal to its anticipation. Love can never be equal between two human beings; there must be one who loves and one who is loved. Even if the object of love is unworthy, the passion is no less genuine; for the point of passion is not union and understanding with the loved one but the ephemeral pursuit of the image of love which the mind forms in anticipation.

(3) Human personality is subjective, depending solely on the observer's point of view. We see in other human beings only that side which is presented to us, or which we wish to see. An individual may appear in an entirely different light to different acquaintances. Often we approach the same personality from two or more points of view— e.g. we have scant respect for a person we know intimately, then we learn he is considered an eminent authority in his field or is loved by someone we respect—and we are astonished to discover that two such diverse personalities are actually one.

(4) Human society is formed of a pattern of circles arranged one above the other; snobbery is among the most universal of human qualities. Each circle rejects members of the class below it and professes a democratic scorn for the standards of the circle above. Acceptance into any circle is based, not on merit or on quality of character, but on the principle of *fait accompli;* once an individual has forced acceptance into a group by marriage or through social machinations

he is immediately and unquestioningly accepted. Mme. Verdurin, by marrying a Guermantes, becomes the most aristocratic of the aristocrats.

It is important to note that this stratification extends, not only through the realm of aristocratic society, but into the lowest and most vulgar elements of society. Servants, even thieves, perverts, and ruffians differ little in their basic social attitudes from aristocrats.

(5) Permanence is not to be found in the realm of physical substance, since the chief characteristic of the phenomenal world is constant flux or change. It is only in the region of thought that stability, permanence, and true satisfaction are found.

(6) The five senses, and the arts based on these senses, are intimately interconnected and have only been falsely separated by human convention. Music may provoke a visual or tactual image in the mind, and accidental vision stimuli may suggest a theme from classical music. The methods of painting, literature, and music are essentially one; an appreciation of one is transferable to the others. This concept resembles the aesthetic theory of the Symbolist school of poetry, with which Proust has many affinities; it is also related to the theory of the integration of the arts as promulgated by Wagner and others.

9. EXPRESSIONISTS AND EXPERIMENTERS

The triumph of science and industry in the twentieth century caused many modern authors to conclude that literature had been left in a backwater, that it was hopelessly anachronistic in the age of the airplane and the radio. One of the chief manifestations of the urge to create a literature worthy of the machine age was the emergence of the expressionistic school, which sprang up in the German theatre around the turn of the century. The tendency soon spread through continental Europe, and by 1920 expressionism was the dominant school in experimental European drama.

Three chief influences, in addition to modern civilization itself, went to make up expressionism. The first of these was the work of August Strindberg (1849-1912), a brilliant but erratic Swedish dramatist and novelist who actually wrote expressionistic works a generation before the formation of the school. His fantastic and oddly perverted dramas, especially *The Dream Play* (1902), were widely played in Germany and caused a sensation almost equal to that created by Ibsen a generation before.

The second influence was that of psychiatry, especially the work of Sacher-Masoch, Freud, and Jung. The universal presence of perversion in the minds of even normal persons and the existence of subconscious and unperceived emotions provided the expressionists with fertile material for a fantastic literature. Last, Marxism, which viewed social strife not in terms of the individual but in terms of amorphous and homogeneous masses, had its due influence on the expressionists. Only a few became outright Marxists, but most of them used the concept of class solidarity to create a literature in which masses, not individuals, were the protagonists. Thus expressionistic literature tends to deemphasize the individual and to obliterate individual character; the protagonists are often given such labels as "Father," "Bank Clerk," or "Billionaire," rather than specific names. Likewise individual identity often disappears entirely in an amorphous mass of humanity. Toller's *Masse Mensch* has only one distinguishable individual character, and even she is submerged by the mass before the drama ends.

In Italy an important stimulus to the expressionistic movement was provided by Filippo Marinetti (1876-1944). Marinetti, an unimportant author in his own right, was the founder of Futurism, of which the avowed aim was to revolutionize literature to make it worthy of the mechanical age. The Futurists abandoned the sex theme, which they felt had been monstrously overemphasized in all previous literature, and sought literary material in the beauty of the airplane, the dirigible, and the machine gun. The message of Futurism is often a sort of activism in which action of any kind, even destructive action, is the goal.

In practice the most striking characteristic of expressionistic literature, whether in the drama or the novel, is its weird, fantastic, or unreal atmosphere; the action seems to move forward in a nightmare. Everything is distorted or oversimplified; the elements of conflict are presented in their bare essence rather than encumbered with detail. The stage settings of expressionism often carry out this tendency; they are stark, fantastic, and anti-naturalistic, consisting of oddly inclined planes and surfaces. In style as well expressionism abandons the conventions of previous literature; the dialogue is often spoken in a sort of telegram-style, staccato and devoid of unnecessary speech parts.

Expressionism is found in it purest form in the drama of Wedekind, Kaiser, Capek, and Toller. Its influence, however, was great; its mark is obvious in the work of Eugene O'Neill, Pirandello, and Werfel, and it was deliberately imitated by a score of lesser dramatists. Some authors in this section, e.g., Lorca and Kafka, are not specifically members of the expressionistic movement; the expressionistic qualities in their work developed independently of, but parallel to, the main body of the school in Germany. They are included in this section because of their intrinsic kinship to the expressionistic movement.

Although expressionism is most typically a movement of the theatre, Kafka confied himself entirely to the story and the novel. The dream sequence in Joyce's *Ulysses* should also be cited as an example of expressionism in the novel.

A Predecessor: August Strindberg (Swedish, 1849-1912)

Strindberg began as a naturalist, and turned from this technique toward an embryonic form of expressionism in mid-career. His novel *The Red Room* (1879) was hailed as the first naturalistic novel in Scandinavian literature, and his early dramas *The Father* (1887), *Comrades* (1888), and *Miss Julia* (1888) have become classics of the naturalistic theatre. Strindberg, however, is probably more important as a predecessor of the symbolistic and expressionistic drama of the early twentieth century. Here the influence proceeds chiefly from two fantasies of his later period: *The Dance of Death* (1901) and *The Dream Play* (1902). These two dramas, of which the second is the more important, are not often performed today, but they mark the beginning of the expressionistic technique later to be utilized by Wedekind, Kaiser, O'Neill, and others.

The chief quality of Strindberg's work upon first examination is its brooding pessimism and its revelation of hitherto unremarked and sinister forces of nature. This Mephistophelian quality struck a sympathetic note among audiences of the fin-de-siècle, newly interested in the dark powers of the unconscious mind. Strindberg's work is dominated by emotion, instinct, and passion. Sexual themes are predominant, but Strindberg's view of sexuality is hardly an ordinary one. He presents love as a cruel battle in which each party seeks to overwhelm and dominate the other; its twin poles are a blind and bestial desire and a hatred toward the object which inspires such an enslaving passion. Much of this attitude proceeds from Strindberg's own experience of love, which was in the main chaotic. His attitude toward woman is virtually the antithesis of Ibsen's feminism; he views woman as a Dionysian power of nature which attempts to stifle the freedom-loving intellectualism and spirituality of the Apollonian male.

Strindberg derived the style of his naturalistic works from the literary movements of his time, but his later expressionistic fantasies are totally original. In the prologue to *The Dream Play* he explains that his purpose is to imitate the disconnected but seemingly logical form of the dream. The background is ostensibly that of reality; but on this surface the author's subconscious embroiders an intricate pattern of memory, experience, free fancy, absurdities, and improvisations. Not only is the action diffuse but the characters themselves take on a certain dreamlike quality. They lose the complexity we are accustomed to find in living people and become mere embodiments of traits: i.e. they are reduced to two dimensions. The characters thus become, not what they "actually" are, but what they seem to a central observer, who may be thought of as either the author or the audience. Instances of this technique are clearly seen, not only in the German expressionists of the 1900-14 period, but in Joyce, Kafka, and O'Neill.

LIFE: Born in Stockholm in 1849, Strindberg was the son of a housemaid and an impoverished would-be aristocrat. One of many children in a crowded household, half-starved and frightened by his father, he becaume morbidly nervous and subject to uncontrollable fits of rage. At first he planned to become a Lutheran minister; he attended the University of Uppsala to prepare himself for a religious vocation. When he lost his faith, however, he turned to a study of medicine; but he soon found himself equally unsuited for a scientific career.

There followed a period of chaotic uncertainty, during which he tried his hand at tutoring, teaching, telegraphy, journalism, and acting. A position in the Royal Library at Stockholm, which he held from 1874 to 1882, provided him a minimum of security. In 1877, after a tumultuous courtship, he married the aristocratic but neurotic Siri von Essen. During the early years of their stormy marriage Strindberg won renown through the publication of *The Red Room*. A series of cheer-ful historical plays was followed in 1882 by *The New Kingdom,* an attack on modern Sweden. In 1883 he travelled to Switzerland, where he associated with Russian revolutionaries and acquired a growing social consciousness. He became a Deist, a pacifist, and a believer in the social philosophy of Utilitarianism. His novelettes of this period are generally optimistic, at least compared to his later works, but reflect the quarrels of his domestic life in their attacks on women and opposition to feminism. A series of stories, *Married I* (1884) and *Married II* (1886) describe his view of love as the "battle of the sexes."

Divorced in 1887, Strindberg then married the Viennese journalist Frida Uhl; but a single year of domestic wrangling, which made it clear that his attitude toward marriage was pathological, resulted in another divorce. In *By the Open Sea* (novel, 1890) he repudiated socialism as a degenerate form of Christianity and turned to an absolute indi-vidualism. After a nervous breakdown he took as his third wife a young actress, Harriet Bosse. In the eighteen-nineties Strindberg underwent a violent mental and philosophical metamorphosis. He was recon-verted to Christianity through the inspiration of Swedenborg, and transmuted his intense personal suffering into the dramatic trilogy *To Damascus* (1898-1904), a sort of autobiographical allegory which also marks the inception of his expressionistic period in technique. During the later years of his life his writings display a curious revival of the motifs of his previous work. He died of cancer in 1912, and was accorded an international funeral.

CHIEF DRAMAS: *Fadren* (*The Father;* drama, 1887) is Strindberg's most notable contribution to the literature of the "battle of the sexes"; technically it belongs to his naturalistic period. The "father" in this play is a distinguished mineralogist who is thwarted in his studies and continually harassed by his wife Laura. Their antagonism comes to a head in a conflict over the education of their daughter Bertha. The father wants her removed from the influence of the women who sur-round her, while Laura insists that the child be kept at home. In order to make certain of having her own way, Laura tells the doctor her husband is mad, and all but succeeds in making him so by suggestions concerning the paternity of Bertha. When, in a stormy scene, he is provoked into throwing a lamp at his wife, the doctor declares him insane, the nurse tricks him into a straitjacket, and even the pastor who knows Laura to be wrong ultimately sides with her, overwhelmed by her feminine power. Strindberg here portrays sexual relations as an "embattled opposition of two spirits destined to destroy each other in the ineffectual endeavor to be one."

Fröken Julie (Miss Julia; drama, 1888) is a naturalistic study of the triumph of the "natural man," rising from non-moral peasant and proletarian stock, over the effete and anemic aristocracy. The heroine, Miss Julia, is the victim of the same kind of rearing to which Bertha in *The Father* is subjected. Inheriting her mother's passionate nature and antagonism toward men, she has been brought up by her father as if she were a man. Jilted by her fiancé when she attempts to dominate him, she drifts into the kitchen of the Manor House (the single set of the drama) during the earthy festivities of May Eve. Deliberately she arouses the passions of the valet Jean (the natural man); she dances with him, forces him to lose his self-control, and finally seduces him. Then, attempting to face the question of her honor and afraid to confront her father, she suggests to Jean that they flee together. Jean, cold-blooded and practical, conceives a plan of setting up a hotel on Julia's capital. When she confesses she has no money in her own right, he first persuades her to rob her father's money-box, then, when she loses her nerve, urges her to suicide. When she finally kills herself she demonstrates the naturalistic doctrine of the weakness of the aristocracy in contrast to the rugged thought and direct action of the lower classes.

Dödsdansen (The Dance of Death; drama, 1901) is a two-part drama with expressionistic elements presenting the theme of the battle of the sexes as in *The Father.* The technique of this drama, however, is more original than that of the earlier play. Part I presents the dominant male figure of the Captain who is the proud and hated commander of a Coast Artillery group on an island. His wife Alice, a former actress, is embittered by her isolation and by memories of her earlier triumphs. They have a mutual friend in Curt, master of the quarantine, who had originally introduced them to each other. The Captain has separated their daughter Judith from her mother by sending her to a city whence he receives secret messages by telegraph. When Alice discovers his use of the telegraph, their basic mutual antagonism flares higher; both appeal to Curt to act as their arbitrator. Lured by passion for Alice, Curt becomes dominated by her will. But when her behavior sends the Captain into an uncontrollable paroxysm of anger, Curt nurses and soothes him in sympathy.

After a trip to the city for medical attention, the Captain returns with Curt's son whom, against Curt's will, he intends to train as a cadet. He has procured custody of the boy from his mother. When he announces to Alice that he has also filed papers for divorce, she threatens to reveal his defalcations with military funds. The doctor alleges that the Captain is lying about instituting divorce proceedings and that he is actually on the point of death. A bitter quarrel breaks out, at the end of which the Captain threatens Alice with a saber and then falls into a swoon.

Alice turns to Curt, but is repulsed. The Captain begs Curt not to leave him. Husband and wife are temporarily reconciled when Alice confesses that she did not reveal the Captain's financial misbehavior after all. Asking only for peace, the Captain finds Alice willing to continue with him as a nurse. On this hopeful note the first part of the drama ends.

Part II of *The Dance of Death* is a repetition and intensification of the same pattern. Judith has returned home and is being courted by Curt's son Allan. Quarreling has broken out again between Alice and the Captain, who has now retired. Out of a virulent hatred of Curt, the Captain does everything in his power to destroy him personally, socially, professionally, and financially. He meanwhile plans a marriage for Judith with an elderly colonel. When he learns through a vicious telegram from Judith that her love for Allan has triumphed over his schemes, he falls into his final paroxysm and dies. In an epilogue Alice says that she is inclined to think well of him because all of life seemed a hoax to him. She sums up by revealing that she had both loved and hated him, and gives him her final benediction.

In the figure of the Captain we see Strindberg's concept of the paternal tyrant determined to be superior to the natural forces of life, represented by Alice. Curt is the "average man," drawn toward both at once and thus doomed to be an eternal victim. The sea is the source of life, an all-encompassing natural force. The island symbolizes momentary human life thrown up by this eternal force; it is full of seaweed, monstrosities, and corruption. The price of individuality is too high, and the individual finally finds peace in the all-encompassing serenity of death.

Ett drömspel (*The Dream Play;* drama, 1902) is the most purely expressionistic of Strindberg's theatre; it is similar in technique to *Spöksonaten* (*The Ghost Sonata,* 1907) but superior in quality. *The Dream Play* is based on the disconnected but apparently logical form of the dream; it thus anticipates later attempts to incorporate the Freudian concept of the dream into literature. In a prologue the daughter of the Hindu god Indra asks her father to explain the world to her. She says that she sees beauty in life but hears in it a constant undercurrent of wailing. She is told to observe the world for herself and report her findings to her father.

In the variegated tapestry of life which is then unfolded, there are several prominent threads. An Officer waits eternally for Victoria to come out of the opera, while the Portress at the opera knits the fabric of life. There is a Lawyer mired in man's misery and meanness, and the Lawyer's Wife (The Daughter) who lives with her children in poverty and squalor. There is also a Door which the Daughter wishes to open. The savants quarrel about their beliefs in what the opened door will reveal. When the Door (symbol of the meaning of the universe or of religious truth) is finally opened it reveals nothing. Finally, there is a Poet who gives meaning to life by translating what the Daughter tells him.

At the end, after the Door has been opened, Strindberg's judgments are revealed through the speech of the Daughter of Indra, who believes that all are to be pitied, especially the rightminded. When the rightminded demand that she be stoned, she predicts her death and ascension. Creation proceeds out of the meeting of the Divine with earthly matter; the fall into sin was caused by the spirit's mingling with earthly corruption. The world is a dream, an image of this impure commingling. Man craves to suffer as Divinity suffered, but he also craves pleasure. From this conflict within man arise suffering, injustice, and universal misery.

Frank Wedekind (German, 1864-1918)

Wedekind is the first of the German expressionists; his *Frühlings Erwachen* established the character of the movement as early as 1891. In his later period he was greatly influenced by Strindberg. Another influence in his work was his early training in biology, which led him into a quasi-scientific preoccupation with sex. Wedekind remained

throughout his life a violent foe of nineteenth-century sexual mores;
he felt the sexual urge to be a normal and natural one, and sought to
epitomize it as a sort of primitive life-force ("Erdgeist") in his drama.
This force is represented in two of Wedekind's dramas, *Der Erdgeist*
(1895) and *Die Büchse der Pandora* (1903), by the fantastic character Lulu, a vampire-like woman who destroys men through her
sexual wiles.

Wedekind's work is marked by a mingling of hallucination and
reality similar to that found in the later dramas of Gerhart Hauptmann.
His plays are generally wild and unrestrained; he makes little use of the
impersonal mass techniques common in later expressionistic drama.

CHIEF WORK: *Frühlings Erwachen* (*The Awakening of Spring;*
tragedy, 1891) bitterly demonstrates the evils of Puritanical repression
on adolescent sexuality. The heroine, Wendla Bergman, a perfectly
normal girl of fourteen, is insulated from reality by her sex-inhibited
mother, who leads her to believe that conception results from the mere
emotion of falling in love. As a result Wendla is helpless when confronted with reality, and allows herself to be seduced by a schoolmate,
Melchior Gabor. Melchior himself is expelled from school because he
circulates a handwritten document purporting to explain sexual matters among his schoolfellows. When Wendla becomes pregnant her
mother's ignorance and prudishness again are brought into play; an
abortion is attempted and Wendla dies. Learning of these events,
Melchior is driven insane by his conscience. Thus the play demonstrates how two healthy and normal children can be destroyed by a
hypocritical and unnatural sexual code.

Der Erdgeist (The Earth Spirit, drama, 1895) is the first of the
Lulu plays. Lulu is the opposite in at least one important way of
Goethe's Margaret or Gretchen in *Faust:* she is the eternal-womanly
that draws us downward, the female principle of sexual attraction but
herself indifferent and therefore innocent. Many men (and even one
lesbian woman, the Countess Geschwitz) are pulled toward her and
toward their own destruction as moths to a flame. Perhaps Lulu's
father is Schigolch, but no one knows for sure (and he least of all,
probably); she is different things under different names for different
men: for Doctor Goll, her first husband, she is Nelly, and he dies of
a heart seizure in a jealous rage; for the artist Schwartz, her second
husband, she is Eve, and he cuts his throat with a razor because she

cannot reciprocate his love; for an editor-in-chief, Doctor Schoen, her third husband, she is Mignon, and Lulu fires five shots from a revolver into him when he threatens her in the hidden presence of two others madly in love with her, his own son Alva and the schoolboy Hugenberg. Rodrigo, an acrobat, is also drawn into the circle.

The most expressionistic device in the play, in addition to the mythic symbol of Lulu, is the Prologue with an Animal Trainer in a menagerie tent that represents the world. Carrying his whip and firing his revolver, he calls to an assistant, "Bring the snake this way!" and Lulu in a Pierrot costume is carried in with the introduction, "She was created to stir up great disaster, to lure, seduce, and poison, to be the master of murder . . . , woman's primal form." She is carried out, as the Animal Trainer announces that he will put his head between the jaws of a beast of prey, and the play begins.

Georg Kaiser (German, 1878-1945)

The dramas of Georg Kaiser are complex experiments which have been called everything from "allegorical" to "cubistic." Kaiser himself applies the term *Denkspiele* ("thought-plays") to his dramas, contrasting them with *Schauspiele,* or mere spectacles. Yet his plays are not intellectual drama in the manner of Bernard Shaw. Kaiser, greatly influenced by Strindberg and Wedekind, writes in the tradition of expressionism and is considered one of the leading exponents of this technique in the twentieth century. His favorite devices are the impersonal allegorical character labelled only with a profession, the formless masses who chant their racial emotions in a sort of chorus, and the animizing of machinery and power.

For Kaiser the basic element of the universe is energy. Energy appears as a protagonist, in one way or another, in many of his plays— in the *Gas* trilogy as the artificial energy of the gas, and in such plays as *Europa* as the abundant reproductive energies of the human race. At the same time Kaiser is suspicious, even antagonistic, toward modern industrialism. The modern factory or office to him is a vast mechanism contrived to grind down human beings into senseless and obedient robots. Like Toller, Kaiser sees the factory worker as a man reduced to a leg, an arm, or an eye; the factory is not interested in his organs of pleasure or in his intellect. Thus, although Kaiser is in one sense a dramatist of the age of machinery, from the point of view of attitude he is bitterly opposed to the spirit of the century. In this respect, as a matter of fact, he typifies the attitude of the expressionistic movement as a whole.

LIFE: Kaiser was born in 1878, the son of a Magdeburg merchant. After a Gymnasium education he entered business, and at twenty-one went to Argentina as an executive of an electrical firm. The climate disagreed with him and he soon returned to Germany; his health remained poor for the rest of his life. In 1921 Kaiser was indicted for the theft of some furniture from a rented house; he defended himself with the extraordinary plea that such acts were to be permitted to men of genius, especially when dogged by poverty. He was convicted, however, and served a jail term.

His first literary work, the drama *Rektor Kleist,* was written in 1902, but success came only with *Die jüdische Witwe* in 1911. During the dozen or so years that followed Kaiser was the acknowledged leader of the expressionistic school in Germany. He wrote over forty expressionistic plays, most of which were produced. American audiences were introduced to his work through the Theatre Guild production of *From Morn to Midnight* in 1922. This production was one of the landmarks of the expressionistic movement in America, and undoubtedly had a due influence on Eugene O'Neill.

Kaiser's reputation diminished with the passing of expressionism as a movement in the thirties. He wrote two novels in his later years, but they attracted little attention. He died almost unnoticed in 1945.

CHIEF DRAMAS: *Von Morgens bis Mitternacht (From Morn to Midnight;* drama, 1916) is a fantasy describing the breakdown of a bank employee in a brief twelve-hour period. The hero, labelled only "Bank Cashier," is a man who has been crushed down by the bureaucratic system until he is only an automaton. One day, however, he waits on an Italian lady he mistakenly imagines to be a gay and sinful creature; she makes certain overtures of friendship to him which he misinterprets as coquetry, and he impulsively embezzles a large sum of money in order to run off with her. When she indignantly rejects his proposal he is stupified; he cannot return to the bank and he has no idea how to turn his stolen fortune to some good. He squanders it on frivolity, including monstrous prizes to bicycle riders in a fantastic race, and is eventually betrayed to the police by a callous Salvation Army lass. He dies with a "gasp like an Ecce and a sigh like a Homo."

The play demonstrates the impossibility of escaping from the bureau-cratic monotony which characterizes modern business.

The masterwork of Kaiser's career is the radically expressionistic *Gas* trilogy, consisting of three integrated but separately playable dramas. The first of these, *Die Koralle* (*The Coral;* drama, 1917) takes place in a huge gas factory where the Billionaire, a self-made man, rules a whole race of workers through a sort of benevolent tyranny. He is aided by his Secretary, who is physically identical to him; the two can be told apart only because the Secretary wears a bit of coral on his watch-chain. Although the Billionaire is sympathetic toward the workers from whose ranks he has risen, he does not under-stand them and they hate him violently. The Billionaire is further dis-illusioned when his own son and daughter turn against him and side with the workers. He becomes filled with envy and hatred toward the Secretary, who is happily free from responsibility and remorse. At last he murders his double, pocketing the coral so that he is executed for his crime as the Secretary rather than as himself. In escaping into the identity of the Secretary he at last achieves a sort of peace.

Gas I (drama, 1918) continues the story of the Billionaire's Son, an idealistic young man who converts the factory into a cooperative enterprise and so increases its efficiency that the organization is soon supplying energy for all the industry of the world. A terrible explosion takes place; many workers are killed, and the Billionaire's Son, horri-fied, proposes to level the ruins and establish green farms for the workers in their place. But the workers, who have at first shouted their hatred of the factory, turn coat and put their fate in the hands of the Engineer, who wants to rebuild the factory and go on manufac-turing gas.

In *Gas II* (drama, 1920) the grandson of the protagonist of *Gas I*—i.e. the great-grandson of the original Billionaire—is now in command of the factory. The play is a fantastic nightmare of warfare and tech-nology in a scientific age. Workers are now struggling to produce gas for the extermination of the enemy; the pace is so terrible that workers drop at the machinery like flies. At last they rebel and smash the con-trol apparatus; the production of gas stops. As in *Gas I* the protagonist, this time the "Billionaire Worker," sides with the workers and urges that hatred give way to brotherhood. Figures dressed in yellow and blue, mere soulless automata, order the reconstruction of the control apparatus. The Billionaire Worker appeals to his worker comrades, but at the last moment the Chief Engineer (symbol of the technician in modern society) offers the workers a new and violently deadly gas to be used against the enemy. When the workers accept, the Billionaire Worker seizes the container of gas and smashes it, destroying factory and workers. It can be seen that the *Gas* trilogy is a powerful, if somewhat exaggerated, foreshadowing of industrial and military developments which have actually come to take place in our own time.

Ernst Toller (German, 1893-1939)

Toller is the most impassioned and forceful of the German dramatic expressionists; he often seems the most obscure as well. His drama *Masse Mensch* (1920) carries the technique of mass dramatic action to its absolute ultimate; the characters are devoid of any individual personality at all, and seem to act like a swarm of ants in an ant-hill. Toller is not only a violent champion of expressionism but a violent social revolutionist as well. He is too individualistic to integrate himself with any party or to accept the stereotyped dialectic of Marxism; his doctrine is a wide and mystical human brotherhood, cutting across racial and national lines and uniting all mankind in a struggle against poverty. This is a highly emotional credo, and Toller expounds it in a highly emotional form of drama. His plays are seldom coherent or well organized; their merit lies in the impassioned arguments of the protagonists and in the effective portrayal of mass action.

LIFE: Toller, born the son of a Jewish merchant in German Poland in 1893, was twenty-one when the First World War broke out. His first experience of life was encountered in warfare; he was horrified and disgusted, and as soon as he was discharged for medical reasons he became an active pacifist. He was thrown into jail, released at the time of the 1918 revolution, and imprisoned again in 1919. This time the ordeal was longer; he remained in prison until 1924, and emerged broken in health and bitter in spirit. His first serious writing was done during this prison term. He continued to write steadily up to 1939; his plays were remarkably well received considering their radical technique and content. In 1932, fleeing Nazism, he came to America, where he continued writing; an interesting autobiography, *Eine Jugend in Deutschland,* appeared the following year. In 1939, depressed by the war and by personal domestic troubles, he committed suicide in a

New York hotel room.

CHIEF DRAMAS: *Masse Mensch* (translated as *Man and Masses;* drama, 1920) is a bitter study of revolution and its inability to solve the basic problems of the masses. From a dramatic point of view it is an experiment in the use of mass humanity as the protagonist of a drama. The workers in an imaginary state rebel against an imperialistic war being waged by the regime. They are led by an idealistic female social worker, who attempts to moderate their fanaticism with reason. But as soon as the workers learn the taste of power the irrational violence of the herd is unloosed. They demand a total destruction of the extant state, and set about to destroy with the utmost bestiality. The woman leader abandons them, is arrested by the state and flung into prison, and is eventually—ironically—executed for inciting the mob to violence. In the end the revolution is crushed.

Die Maschinenstürmer (*The Machine Wreckers;* drama, 1922) is laid in England during the Weavers' Rebellion of 1812. A prologue contains a free translation of Lord Byron's maiden speech before the House of Lords defending the weavers. As the play begins the weavers in Nottingham are determined to smash the newly-introduced looms, which they regard as monsters about to destroy their very livelihood. Jimmy Cobbett, an educated idealist of working-class origin, tries to persuade the weavers that the fault lies in the grasping and callous bosses, and that the machines themselves could serve to benefit the workers under a different system. But the weavers are suspicious of him because his brother Henry is a minion of the owners and because they resent his superior culture. When he attempts to oppose their attack on the machines they ruthlessly murder him. This play forms an interesting contrast to Gerhart Hauptmann's famous *Die Weber,* in which the author implicitly commends the workers' action in overturning the machines.

Karel Capek (Czech, 1890-1938)

Capek among his own people is admired not only as a dramatist and novelist but as an important literary and political symbol of the Czechoslovakian Republic. In English-speaking countries, however, he is known chiefly as the author of a single play, *R.U.R.* Not only did this play give to the English language a new word, "robot," but it was the first of a whole series of nightmarish fantasies of the future; the genre later included such important works as Huxley's *Brave New World* and Orwell's *Nineteen Eighty Four.*

Capek, born in Prague in 1890, is thoroughly Czech in attitude and spirit. His optimism and his whimsy are the very antithesis of the German temperament, and his loyalty to his people was one of the dominant influences of his life. He was a lifetime friend of the great Czech statesman Jan Masaryk, and his life was dominated by a fervent consecration to the cause of Czech freedom.

Capek's literary career began shortly after the war with a collection, *Money and Other Stories,* and the drama *R.U.R.,* both published in 1921. Less well-known but equally interesting are the plays *The Makropolus Story* (1922) and *Power and Glory* (1938). His work also includes a half-dozen novels of high quality. Several of Capek's minor works were written in collaboration with his brother Josef, an author and painter.

After the 1938 Munich Conference Capek, sick at heart over the betrayal of his country, began to fail in health. His death from pneumonia in December of that year may be considered in a sense one of the casualties of the fall of Czechoslovakia.

CHIEF WORK: *R.U.R.* (drama, 1921) is properly considered Capek's masterpiece. The initials of the title stand for "Rossum's Universal Robots." A firm incorporated under this name has found the secret of constructing mechanical automatons which can replace human beings for all occupations; eventually the robots are to assume the entire labor of the world. Identical to humans externally, the robots are nevertheless essentially different; they have no higher nervous system and no ego and are therefore impervious to sentiments of any kind. Thus they are indefatigable and absolutely loyal to their masters.

The factory technicians, however, make the mistake of constructing a superior form of robot with a faculty something like human reason. These super-robots lead their rudimentary fellows in a revolt against the humans and exterminate them totally with the exception of one man, Alquist, an architect. In the confusion it is discovered that the formula for making robots has been destroyed; thus it appears that both humans and robots are doomed to extinction. At the last moment Alquist discovers that certain of the robots manifest pity and altruism and are therefore the equivalent of human beings. He gives his blessing to two of the creatures, Helena and Primus, to begin the foundation of a new race of humans.

The argument of this play is that machines of any kind are in danger of mastering the human race if their aims are not kept firmly under control. With his typical optimism, however, Capek chooses to give the drama a happy ending.

Franz Werfel (Austro-Czech, 1890-1945)

Franz Werfel is sometimes considered an expressionist, although he wrote expressionistic works *per se* only during a brief era from 1915 to 1920. His works, in fact, fall into three clear periods: the lyric poems, most of them mystical and humanistic in tone, written from 1908 to 1914; the expressionistic dramas and poems dating from the period of the First World War; and the novels and realistic dramas written in the period from 1920 to 1945. During this last period Werfel, while retaining some vestiges of expressionistic technique, became more conventional in style; *Das Lied der Bernadette* (1941) had no difficulty in reaching the best-seller lists in American translation.

Although his style has varied widely, Werfel's ideas have remained consistent. His dominant theme is that of human brotherhood, which sometimes takes the form of pacifism and at other times expresses itself in a quasi-Catholic mysticism. He is antagonistic toward nationalism and a violent foe of fascism, yet his emotional nature finds little in common with the cold and logical doctrine of socialism. Neither is he impressed by Zionism, the chief form of Jewish nationalism. He feels simply that all men, whatever their nationality or ancestry, must recognize their common brotherhood and attempt as individuals to reconcile their differences through friendship and understanding.

LIFE: Werfel, of Jewish ancestry, was born in 1890 in Prague, then part of the Austrian Empire. His father, a wealthy manufacturer, provided him with an excellent education. His first contact with militarism came in 1911-12 when he was called up for military training; he subsequently served in the Austrian army during the war. He began to write poetry as early as 1908, but his first success came in 1915 with the production of his violently pacifistic, and violently expressionistic, drama *Die Troerinnen,* an adaptation of Euripides. His prestige grew constantly during the twenties and thirties.

In 1940, with the fall of France, Werfel was at first reported killed. In reality he managed to escape to America. Two important works came out of his World War II experiences: the novel *Das Lied der*

Bernadette, a devout work highly sympathetic to Catholicism, and *Jacobowsky und der Oberst,* a witty tragicomedy describing the reactions of German, French, Polish, and British minds to the war. Werfel died in America in 1945.

CHIEF WORKS: *Die vierzig Tage des Musa Dagh (The Forty Days of Musa Dagh;* novel, 1933) is an epic novel describing the struggle of the Armenian people against the Turks during the First World War. Gabriel Bagradian, a Paris-born Armenian, has come home to the land of his people and now assumes command of the village of Yoghonoluk in its stand against the enemy. Outnumbered, the Armenians retreat to the nearby mountain of Musa Dagh, where they fortify themselves and hold out for forty days until they are finally rescued by the French navy. The heroic Bagradian, however, falls asleep and is forgotten in the evacuation; he is killed by a Turkish bullet.

Jacobowsky und der Oberst (Jacobowsky and the Colonel; drama, 1944) is a farcical comedy with a serious message. Jacobowsky, a shrewd and witty Polish Jew who has fled Hitler the length and breadth of Europe, is caught by the 1940 débacle in Paris. There he joins forces with the Polish Colonel Tadeusz Boleslav Stjerbinsky and the Colonel's servant Szabuniewicz. Jacobowsky miraculously acquires a limousine and the three flee toward the Allied lines, first stopping to pick up the Colonel's French mistress Marianne. Throughout the play Jacobowsky is a symbol of resourceful Jewish optimism, while the Colonel and Marianne serve as personifications of Polish decadence and French apathy respectively. A comic Gestapo officer serves to incarnate both German efficiency and German stupidity. At the end of the play a cool British officer (symbol of English courage and nonchalance) offers a passage on a naval vessel to any two of the four refugees, but after discussion it is decided that only Jacobowsky, optimistic and enterprising. deserves to escape and begin a new life.

Franz Kafka (German-Czech, 1883-1924)

The world of Kafka is a vague and uncanny one, permeated with a characteristic atmosphere which Kafka has made uniquely his own. The locale is always uncertain, the details of economic and social environment are lacking, and the very characters seem like wraiths. Yet Kafka's works have a convincing reality, one which proceeds from a contact with certain universals rather than from documentary accuracy. It is the reality we encounter in Dante rather than the reality of the naturalists of our time.

Kafka has left us only three novels, all unfinished at his death and published posthumously, a number of short stories and sketches and parables, and one novella, *The Metamorphosis.* His prestige and influence since his death have nevertheless become enormous. Such authors as Gide and Werfel and Camus have freely acknowledged the impression Kafka's writing made on them; his works have been translated into all modern languages and tons of criticism have been written about them. Much of this interest is due to Kafka's peculiar quality of uniqueness; his work is so different from anything previously written that the reader cannot help being moved and influenced by its mere originality.

Essentially Kafka writes a form of allegory, although it is far from the unwieldy and obvious allegory of the middle ages. Allegory is a form of literature in which persons and incidents stand as symbols of forces of a less concrete nature, but in Kafka the forces symbolized are intangible, equivocal, and elusive. In *Das Schloss* we are never sure whether Kafka is portraying man in his search for God or man enmeshed in a bureaucracy; it is possible that Kafka himself did not know. Perhaps he felt that divinity itself is a sort of bureaucracy similar to the insurance office in which he worked. Kafka was an intuitive writer; it is easy to extract meanings from his allegory, but no one explanation has more validity than another. The meanings are there for the reader to find, and he is welcome to find as many as he pleases.

Kafka's heroes are usually men inflicted with an overwhelming sense of guilt. This is not a moral or theological sense of sin, neither is it in any way connected with the legal concept of crime. Man is guilty merely because he is born; he finds himself in the grip of forces over which he has no control and he is made to answer for acts committed under the influence of this force. He may search for some meaning in this situation. but the meaning is unknowable; all he can do is grope feebly in what he hopes is the right direction. A Jew by birth, Kafka is unable to achieve the Christian concept of Grace, by which God reaches out to withdraw the individual from his ignorance. In Kafka's work God remains wrapped in isolation, and it is doubtful whether He even wishes man to aspire to Him.

In technique, if not in mood, Kafka is close to the German expressionists of his generation. His heroes are unnamed ("Joseph K." or merely "K.") and it is sometimes difficult to tell which biological species they belong to (e.g., the tale "The Burrow"). His highly abstracted and conventionalized décors are likewise expressionistic.

Der Prozess, adapted by Gide and Jean-Louis Barrault for the stage became a fantasy not unlike other expressionistic dramas of the period. In style, however, Kafka is far from the expressionists. He relates the most fantastic incidents in the most restrained and precise of prose. Part of his daily work included writing technical accident reports, and he brought to his literary work the same precision, the same objectivity, and the same air of rational plausibility he used in his official writing.

A minor theme in Kafka is his preoccupation with the similarities between man and the animals. Several of his tales are related by animals, and in other cases the reader is never sure whether the protagonist is an animal or a human. Another characteristic is his skill in portraying large and incredibly intricate systems—bureaucracies, governments, or organizations—without losing his way in the profusion of detail. Here again his civil service training aided him. A third characteristic which might be cited is his utter lack of interest in physical love, the staple material of most modern novelists. Kafka's heroes are interested in sex only as a means to the attainment of other ends, and if they do fall in love it is in an abstract, uncanny, and quite disembodied way.

There have been three major directions or modes of attack in the vast critical literature that has grown up in the interpretation of Kafka, each of which is illuminating but if followed to the exclusion of the other two becomes too limiting and even absurd in the analysis of particular passages. One is the school of Freudian critics, best represented (and most absurdly) perhaps by Charles Neider in his book, *The Frozen Sea,* who uses Oedipal complexes, father fixation, and latent homosexuality in a sexual interpretation of everything Kafka wrote. The "arrest" in *The Trial* becomes sexual arrest, and indeed the young man of thirty does seem to have some problems. This approach can clarify some of Kafka's writings ("A Country Doctor," for instance), suggests additional meaning in others, and can obscure meaning for still others. The second school of critics is made up of the religious interpreters, like Max Brod and the Chicago critics, who may emphasize either Jewish or Christian exigesis of the Kafka texts. The "arrest" of *The Trial* becomes the recognition, however clouded, of original sin and Joseph K. is guilty as all mankind is guilty. Certain pieces of Kafka's writing seem to demand this kind of approach, "An Imperial Message," "The Married Couple," and the parable of the Law from the cathedral chapter of *The Trial*. It provides ancillary understanding for other fictions but as an exclusive interpretation is misleading, an *ignis fatuus,* for a large portion of Kafka. The third school of critics is less clearly defined, but the approach could be called sociological, if that is interpreted to mean the political, vocational, institutional and bureaucratic automatism of our daily twentieth century lives. The "arrest" of *The Trial* becomes more literal, a Nazi-type house arrest not followed by due process of law but leading to execution, with a totalitarian suppression of human rights and individual liberties. *The Castle* benefits particularly from this broader social view, and so does "The Hunger Artist." There is no good reason, except for critical "blinders," why all three modes of looking at Kafka cannot be used, often simultaneously.

The absurdities of Kafka's existential world have become the commonplaces of our everyday existence. The inexplicable and the unexpected are what you had better be prepared for. Philip Rahv has called attention to Kafka's preoccupation with "the experience of human loss, estrangement, guilt, and anxiety," but points out that "Kafka is something more than a neurotic artist; he is also an artist of neurosis."

LIFE: Kafka was born in Prague in 1883 of Jewish parentage. His father, a physically robust and dominating person, was very important in the author's development. Franz was terribly resentful of his father's tyranny and of his intolerance to any opinions other than his own, but at the same time he was obsessed with a paradoxical desire to win his father's approval. Since in turning to literature Franz was choosing a path his father had specifically disapproved, his family relations were almost unavoidably tragic.

Kafka, a good student. attended a Prague Gymnasium and went on to the German University of Prague, where he studied law out of despair of finding any more suitable subject. His private reading was wide; he knew French, Czech, Latin, and Greek well, and studied

Hebrew during his later years. The young Kafka participated in student literary affairs and formed a fast friendship with Max Brod, at that time a promising young author.

In 1908 Kafka, now a doctor of jurisprudence, obtained a position with the Prague office of the government accident insurance bureau. Here he continued to work until his health failed shortly after the war; he was a capable and cheerful civil servant, well liked by his colleagues and commended by his superiors. Some time around 1912, encouraged by Brod, he began to write; his first work, a prose collection entitled *Betrachtung (Observations)* appeared in 1913. In 1915 a story, "Der Heizer" ("The Stoker," published in 1913), was awarded the Fontane prize; this story later formed the beginning chapter of the novel *Amerika*. The following year he began work on *Der Prozess;* fragments of his three novels were written between this time and 1923. Kafka destroyed more than half of what he wrote during his lifetime, and himself published none of his major works, except *The Metamorphosis* in 1915, published in Leipzig as *Der Verwandlung.*

In 1912 Kafka met a German girl, "F.B.," who influenced and obsessed him greatly over a period of five years. Sincere love apparently existed on both sides, and Kafka passionately desired to live a normal life and raise children. He could not bring himself to marry "F.B.," however, because he feared losing his independence, because he was tormented by feelings of inadequacy, and because of his failing health. The affair ended in a tragic parting in 1917.

Kafka's health began to deteriorate before the war, and by 1916 he was definitely tubercular. He refused to enter a sanatorium, but compromised on a restful stay in the country. In 1923 he met Dora Diamant, a young Polish Jewess who provided him with something like domestic happiness. The couple lived in Berlin during the worst of the inflationary period; Kafka's health received a severe blow from this experience. Later they settled happily in Prague, where Kafka wrote some of his best stories. In 1924 he was removed to a sanatorium with a high fever, and on June 3rd of that year he died.

We owe to Max Brod, Kafka's lifetime friend and literary executor, much of what we know of the author and his work. Kafka himself ordered his writings destroyed at his death, and it was only after a severe moral struggle that Brod decided to publish them. Brod also wrote the standard biography of Kafka, a valuable and irreplaceable document. On the other hand there were strong temperamental differences between Brod and Kafka; the two often quarreled, and Brod's basic interpretation of Kafka's work has been brought into question.

The Diaries of Franz Kafka 1910-1923 were edited by Max Brod and published in English in 1948-49.

CHIEF WORKS: The stories and parables and other short pieces of fiction are perhaps Kafka's major contribution to form and his main influence on the subsequent work of such writers as Borges, Lagerkvist, and Welty, a kind of reinstatement of parable as a viable form in the twentieth century. Fantasy is treated as fact, and vice versa. Explanation is left to the reader who is not coerced by the writer to arrive anywhere, only to set out. "An Imperial Message" is a message for you alone: its significance is of the utmost importance but it can never arrive and you can never stop hoping for its arrival as you look out the window. We are all "In the Penal Colony"; and we all work at building "The Great Wall of China," without seeing how our work fits into a master plan or even knowing if there is one. "A Report to an Academy" gives us an evolutionary view of what it means to be human and civilized which is not at all reassuring; the speaker is a former ape. And "A Hunger Artist" shows what the artist or saint or merely sensitive man can expect in a world which is no longer interested in what they have to offer, preferring the violence and vitality of the panther. There is no "negligible" piece of Kafka's writing. The scraps turn up loaded with insights into the post-Kafkan world. "The Burrow" is the best view of the futility of building shelters from atomic attack, of seeking security instead of living, that we have.

Der Verwandlung (*The Metamorphosis; novella,* 1915) is perhaps Kafka's "greatest story"; it is certainly the only relatively long piece of fiction that he ever finished. The author had written to a friend, "the books we need are of the kind that act upon us like a misfortune, that make us suffer like the death of someone we love more than ourselves, that make us feel as though we were on the verge of suicide, or lost in a forest remote from all human habitation —a book should serve as the ax for the frozen sea within us." The main character in this novella is Gregor Samsa (if not an anagram for, then a parallel to, Kafka), a commercial traveler, which is the equivalent for the American traveling salesman; and he lives when home in a central European city (probably in Czechoslovakia) with father, mother, and a sister, Grete, in a family that he supports by what has become an unsupportable way of life. The first sentence reads: "As Gregor Samsa awoke one morning from a troubled dream, he found himself changed in his bed to some monstrous kind of vermin." He has become a gigantic bug (something like a cockroach) which will plague his "decent" family and become progressively smaller and less human throughout the story until in death he is swept up and disposed of by a charwoman with a broom.

If you grant the first sentence, everything that follows is completely logical and realistically presented. Gregor tries to get ready for work; he is afraid of losing his job; he feels a little stiff from not having slept well. The family, which has been parasitical, now has to readjust to take care of themselves and Gregor. They keep him locked up in his room. After all he *is* family, but you can't let a son or brother who is so afflicted out in society. Gregor had been too good a son after his father's failure in business and had devoted himself to earning money for his family with no life of his own. This can be very dehumanizing and an explanation for what has occurred.

The whole story is told from the point of view of Gregor's perceptions until the coda at the end. The longer he's a bug the more difficult it is to communicate with anyone, although apparently the chief clerk of his company and even his parents and sister could not understand his words when he first tried to explain things to them. Their reaction is seen chiefly in the clerk's response to Gregor, "Ugh!" as he flies down the staircase. The father is brutal and repressive. Gregor learns how to manipulate his new body, to find food that he can eat, rotten, repulsive food. Weeks pass and months pass. Grete understands him best of all and tries to make him comfortable, removing excess furniture from his room. Once, when Gregor had broken loose outside the room, his father had thrown an apple at him which caused a serious injury. He fails rapidly now. The family has gotten along by getting jobs and taking in three lodgers. When Gregor is discovered dead, the lodgers are expelled; mother, father, and sister decide to take a day off from work; and the family is regenerated by their sudden release. At the end Grete springs to her feet and stretches her young body.

This story (one thinks of Miller's *Death of a Salesman* and, hopefully, of Ovid's *Metamorphoses)* is compelling and provocative to the imagination. One student has successfully choreographed the action. The symbol of the bug is extreme and has shock value. It's not even a dog's life that Gregor leads. He doesn't know at first whether to recognize his transformation or not. The most shocking thing to the reader is how little surprised Gregor is by what has happened. The "job" theme, the pervading "presence" of the employer, is a feature of paternalistic, despotic social organization which limits human development. The family is both a potential for emotional satisfactions and a millstone grinding to powder the dutiful son. Gregor never had a chance to live.

Der Prozess (The Trial; novel, 1925) is the story of a man condemned and executed for a sin or a crime he never understands. Joseph K., arrested in his room by mysterious and non-committal guards, is later released and allowed to go to work, but is left with a feeling he has been accused of something. A few days later he receives an order to report to the court for questioning. He goes to a large building not unlike a warehouse, where he is confronted with a preposterous tribunal of old men who badger him ruthlessly. He defends himself with heat and wins the applause of the audience. A week later, anxious as to the verdict, he returns to the court but finds it empty. He hires an Advocate, but finds this person knows as little as he. After dallying aimlessly with the Advocate's housemaid for some time, Joseph abandons this line; he visits a painter, Titorelli (symbol of the artistic life), who is said to have some influence. But the painter, who speaks in vague and ambiguous terms, is of little assistance. Neither is a chaplain (symbol of organized religion) at the cathedral he visits next. Still ignorant of the charge against him, Joseph is visited one evening by two in frock coats and top hats. They seize him courteously and firmly and drag him off to a quarry, where they coolly stab him in the heart.

Joseph K.'s crime is usually interpreted as the universal sense of guilt and helplessness brought on by consciousness of human frailty, and the court as the omniscient divine power which condemns men to unhappiness (or damnation) without apprising them of the nature of their transgression.

In *Das Schloss* (*The Castle;* novel, 1926) a man called K. arrives on foot at a town dominated by a mysterious and immense castle; he has been engaged in advance as land surveyor to the Count. When he presents himself, however, no one seems to have heard of him, and the Castle appears to be inscrutable and impregnable. He goes to' an inn, where he is treated rather brusquely but given accommodation; later a telephone call to the Castle establishes that his arrival is expected.

The rest of the novel concerns K.'s efforts to be admitted to the Castle or to speak to someone of authority. He never learns exactly who is in charge of the Castle, nor why he has been hired if his services are not required. The Count remains an awesome and nebulous figure; his name is scarcely ever mentioned. K. acquires two frisky young assistants, Arthur and Jeremiah, but later begins to suspect they are spies. He establishes communication with a man called Klamm who is said to have authority, but Klamm is unable or unwilling to assist him. He seduces a barmaid, Frieda, who is alleged to be Klamm's mistress, in the hope of gaining information, but this avenue too proves unrewarding. As the unfinished novel closes K. has not yet set foot inside the Castle, nor has he gained any understanding of the mysterious persons who inhabit Castle and village. The novel is usually interpreted as an allegory of man's efforts to seek out and know divinity, but can be interpreted equally well in purely social and vocational terms.

Amerika (novel, 1927) is written in a lighter style than either of the other two novels; it also contains relatively more action and incident. The hero, Karl Rossman, emigrates to America, which Kafka never visited and of which he had only a nebulous concept. There he goes to live with his Uncle Jacob, a millionaire who arranges for his education. He is introduced to Mr. Pollunder, a wealthy American who owns a sinister country-house; at this house Karl falls in love with a girl known as Miss Clara. As the house becomes more ominous Karl decides to flee; he sets out on his own and soon meets Robinson and Delamarch, two eccentric vagabonds who drag him off on their wanderings. The three obtain jobs in a hotel, but Karl is tricked by a conspiracy of jealous employees and fired. Robinson and Delamarch prove false friends, and Karl escapes from them after a brief affair with a female friend of theirs called Brunelda. At the end of the unfinished novel he departs to join a vast enterprise known as the Nature Theatre of Oklahoma, which seems to promise unlimited opportunities for happiness and wealth.

Amerika contains more vivid characterizations than any of Kafka's other works. It also includes incidents of considerable excitement: e.g., the quarrel with Brunelda and the two vagabonds in their apartment. The Nature Theatre of Oklahoma presents the most optimistic picture in all of Kafka's nightmare world. A story by E. B. White called "The Door" conveys the typical Kafka anxiety transported to the American scene by an American in what is probably New York City.

Federico García Lorca (Spanish, 1899-1936)

García Lorca (or merely Lorca, as he is generally called in English-speaking countries,) is a poet by temperament who turned to the stage to secure a wider audience. He was so successful in this strategy that he is usually thought of primarily as a dramatist, although his lyric verse is of a very high quality.

Lorca's style demonstrates two principal influences which are in a sense the diametric poles of his work: the Spanish peasant temperament as manifested in folk literature, and the highly artificial preciosity *(Gongorismo)* of the Spanish golden age. These two antitheses merge imperceptibly in his best works and lend a certain tension to the result.

Judged by his poetry alone Lorca resembles the French surrealists and the more radical of the Anglo-American imagists. His early popular ballads are folk literature related in surrealistic style: "My heart of silk is filled with lights of lost bells, of lilies and leaves." His drama, however, tends toward the characteristics of continental expressionism. The characters are seldom rounded or complex; they are drawn with bold, even stylized lines. The action is formless and unlocated in time, even in the tragedies which have highly climactic plots. Lorca's themes are those common to the greatest Spanish literature: blood and pain, passionate and sensual love, fertility and barrenness, and the cruel satirizing of pomp and hypocrisy. Lorca is not a "gentlemanly" author; he resembles Dostoyevsky and Baudelaire in his preoccupation with sin, cruelty, and passion. His style itself is highly sensual; his images are drawn from the most vivid phenomena of nature, and he has a horror of empty abstraction. Because of this interest in concrete imagery Lorca must be considered a poet who writes drama rather than a dramatist who utilizes a poetic technique. Lorca's work is still today chiefly appreciated in avant-garde circles, but critical opinion of his work is growing constantly more favorable. It is likely that he will in time grow into a sort of Spanish Whitman: a deeply rooted native poet whose work was too elemental for its time. Among his other great poetry he wrote an "Ode to Walt Whitman," "The King of Harlem," and "Lament for Ignacio Sanchez Mejias." The "Lament" for the death of a bullfighter "at five o'clock in the afternoon" has been choreographed and filmed.

LIFE: Lorca was born in Granada in 1899; his father was a well-to-do farmer and his mother a schoolteacher. He studied law at the University of Granada, then moved on to Madrid in 1919 to join the Residencia, a liberal college at the University of Madrid dominated by young modernists and revolutionaries. He published his first play in 1920 and his first poetry volume, *Libro de Poemas,* in 1921. He continued to write profusely throughout his lifetime.

In 1929 Lorca came to America, took up residence in a Columbia University dormitory, and wrote a book of bizarre poems, *Poeta en Nueva York,* to commemorate his visit. He returned to Spain in 1930 for the staging of his most popular work up to that time, *La Zapatera prodigiosa.* In 1931, under the new Republic, Lorca was put in charge of a government-sponsored travelling theatre, La Barraca, which brought modern and classical drama to every city in Spain. Several of Lorca's own tragedies were premiered by this group. In 1933 he went to Latin America to produce his own and other plays; he was received with great enthusiasm and proclaimed "the ambassador of Spanish letters."

In 1936, as the Fascist revolt in Morocco spread to Granada, Lorca was unexpectedly arrested and shot by the Falangists. No explanation of this act was ever proffered by the government; Lorca had never engaged in politics and seldom ventured any public expression of political opinion. His murder was apparently motivated solely by his tenuous connection with the Republican government.

CHIEF DRAMAS: Lorca's plays may be arranged roughly into two groups: the tragedies and the lyrical farces. Of the first, *Bodas de Sangre (Blood Wedding,* 1933) is the best-known. As is common in expressionistic drama, the chief characters are unnamed; they are types rather than fully rounded persons. The Bride, a young girl, is about to marry the Bridegroom, although the latter's mother disapproves of the match. Leonardo, a former suitor of the Bride but now married to the Wife, threatens to prevent the marriage by force. On the day of the wedding Leonardo confronts the Bride openly, and she unwillingly confesses her passion for him. Immediately after the ceremony they flee together. The Bridegroom pursues them in a fiery rage, and he and Leonardo kill each other with knives. The Bride and the Mother, united in their grief, are left alone to contemplate the knife which "slides in clean through the astonished flesh and stops there, at the place where trembles enmeshed the dark root of a scream." *Blood Wedding,* a highly poetic work, is written partly in free verse with spaced ballad-like songs representing a lullaby; an epithalamial, or marriage, song; and an elegiac lament.

Yerma (tragedy, 1934) is a study of a barren woman and the mental torments which proceed from her childlessness. Yerma is a woman with an overpowering maternal instinct; she handles the children of other mothers with an instinctive grace and longs even for the troubles and vexations that come with motherhood. She is faithful to her husband Juan, although Victor, a former suitor, lurks about her ominously. She consults Dolores, a sorceress, and begins to suspect that the blame for her childlessness lies with her husband; but in spite of the temptation she preserves her honor intact. In the final act her husband guesses her suspicion and orders her to abandon her futile and senseless longing for children; Yerma now realizes that he loves her only in a sensual and superficial manner. "You want me as you sometimes want a pigeon to eat," she tells him. Then, seized by an insane compulsion, she strangles Juan and realizes that she has lost her last chance of motherhood.

La Casa de Bernarda Alba (The House of Bernarda Alba; tragedy, 1936) was published after Lorca's death; it is a study of a powerful woman and her tyranny over her mother and daughters. The drama opens with the death of Bernarda's husband, who has previously taken the side of the daughters; now Bernarda's authority is supreme. Only one of the daughters, Adela, is still of marriageable age, and Bernarda isolates her totally from possible suitors. On the other hand she seeks to marry off another daughter, the aging Angustias, to Pepe el Romano by promising a large dowry to the young man. La Poncia, a quick-tongued servant in the household, opposes this scheme and takes the part of Adela. Inevitably Adela herself falls in love with Pepe el

Romano, who returns her affection at the very time he is supposed to be courting Angustias. At last Bernarda discovers this illicit affair; Pepe is driven off with rifle shots, and Adela retreats into her chamber and kills herself. Bernarda, still indomitable, orders that the word shall be spread her daughter died a virgin.

La Zapatera prodigiosa (*The Shoemaker's Prodigious Wife;* "violent farce in two acts," 1930) is a highly original comedy of marital love. As in *Blood Wedding,* the characters are not named but merely designated by their relationships. The Shoemaker, a worthy but querulous old man, is married to the Shoemaker's Wife, a pretty and passionate young woman who regrets the dashing suitors she rejected. Although she is faithful to the Shoemaker, he imagines she is flirting with all his customers; and finally he runs off disconsolately to roam about the world, leaving his wife to realize for the first time how much she loves him.

In the second act the Shoemaker's Wife is desperately unhappy. She is untactfully courted by Don Blackbird, the Sashmaker's Apprentice, the Hatmaker's Apprentice, and most of the remainder of the town loafers; and the gossips are beginning to whisper of her promiscuity. Even the Mayor, attracted by her dubious reputation, begins rolling his eyes at her. At the critical moment the Shoemaker returns disguised as a wandering puppeteer with a scroll and a trumpet. He offers various shows, including "The Art of Closing the Mouths of Gossipy and Impudent Women," and secretly observes his wife's behavior. When she innocently confesses to him her love for her absent husband, he reveals his identity; the wife welcomes him in tearful joy. In her closing lines the wife recommences her spiteful complaining to the old man, but serves notice that their quarrel is purely a domestic one and that they will stand together in the future against the rest of the world. A chorus of women painted in various bright hues lends an expressionistic and stylized quality to this comedy.

Pär Lagerkvist (Swedish, born 1891)

For almost fifty years in Sweden Pär Lagerkvist has been their most important man of letters. Beyond Scandinavia his reputation spread more slowly, and it is only since he received the Nobel Prize for Literature in 1951 that many of his works have been translated and made generally available. His earliest writing was in poetry; a volume published in 1913 was called *Angest (Anguish)*, to be followed by other volumes at approximately five year intervals. Baudelaire and Rimbaud were important influences on his verse. But it is in other areas that he has finally made his chief impact abroad. As a dramatist he regarded himself as a follower of the expressionistic Strindberg; he was the first man in Sweden to recognize the real importance of Strindberg's later plays from *To Damascus* (1898) on, especially the Chamber Plays, on the development of subsequent modern drama. His own work for theatre begins with *Sista mänskan (The Last Man,* 1917) and three one-act plays in 1918 *The difficult Hour (Den svära stunden),* while probably his best known play remain *Bödeln (The Hangman,* 1933). Throughout a long writing career Lagerkvist has maintained the view that naturalism in literature is thoroughly inadequate to portray the reality of modern experience. Many of his plays were written as novellas as well, and it is sometimes difficult to know which medium came first. The most significant novellas (often referred to as novels by his critics and publishers) begin with *The Eternal Smile (Det eviga leendet,* 1920), which carries an E. M. Forster type of fantasy, characteristic of the shorter fiction of both authors ("The Celestial Omnibus," for instance) into a longer form, and *Dvärgen (The Dwarf,* 1945), and continue with *Barabbas* (1950) which has been available in English since 1951 and in paperback since 1962. This genre would include much of Lagerkvist's work in the sixties like the connected novellas *Pilgrim pä havet* (1962) *(Pilgrim at Sea,* 1964) and *Det heliga landet* (1964) *(The Holy Land,* 1966).

The Swedish author seems to be coming closer to an existential view, what is sometimes referred to as existential humanism, in his later writing. One other genre of major impact is what would be referred to casually as the short story but might more accurately be called "short fictions"; neither story, nor sketch, nor parable (but partaking of each) these rather fantastic fictions, most Kafkaesque, are the kind of prose piece done by Borges and a few others. The best collection by Lagerkvist is the *Onde Sagor (Evil Tales,* 1924). He deals with many oppositions: good and evil, light and darkness, success and failure, life and death, the cosmic and the familiar, comfort and despair. Often there is no resolution. Often life is seen as grotesque, even absurd; but he carries affirmation in the same cup with negation. André Gide, who helped introduce his work into France, remarked, "It is the measure of Lagerkvist's success that he has managed so admirably to maintain his balance on a tightrope which stretches between the world of reality and the world of faith."

LIFE: Pär Fabian Lagerkvist was born at Växjö in the southern part of Sweden, the son of an old peasant family, in 1891. "Nourished on Strindberg" and educated on Bible reading (his parents are described as "pietists"), at the *gymnasium* where he learned to accept evolution and political radicalism, and for one term in 1911 at the University of Uppsala, he began writing and studying independently at that time. In the spring of 1913 the young man made a trip to Paris where he was fascinated by cubist and expressionistic art, hoping to apply theories of painting to writing. During the first World War, Lagerkvist lived in Denmark, studying drama and theatre history in Copenhagen. In 1919 he worked as a theatre and art critic for a daily newspaper in Stockholm. During the twenties he spent much time in France and Italy. From 1930 on he has lived in a suburb of Stockholm called Lidingö but has traveled frequently in Europe and the Near East. In 1940-41 he was elected to the Swedish Academy and ten years later was given a Nobel Prize. His private life has remained private, a difficult feat in this century but perhaps easier in Sweden that it would be elsewhere; he has repeatedly told interviewers that what he has to say is to be found in his published works. In Scandinavia Pär Lagerkvist's plays have a long record of successful production; but one of them, *The Hangman,* directed by Per Lindberg was much more of a success in Norway at the National Theatre in Bergen than in Stockholm itself. His début on the Swedish stage came in 1921 with a production of *The Secret of Heaven* with Harriet Bosse (who, it will be remembered, was Strindberg's third wife) in the principal role and an Yngve Berg décor using a spherical acting area representing a small planet isolated in space. In an essay of 1918 called *Modern Theatre: Points of View and Attack,* Lagerkvist had written that Naturalism ignores the fact that the world has changed. He rejected the psychological realism of Ibsen's plays, the literal, drab, middle-cl ss interiors as "no longer adequate as a means of expression . . . for the violent and abrupt contrasts in modern life."

CHIEF WORKS: *Det eviga leendet (The Eternal Smile;* novella, 1920) is a fantasy of eternity where the unnamed dead discuss their confusion about life; some were happy and some unhappy but they decide to seek out God to find out why. Eventually they find him, an old man sawing wood who tells them, "I meant nothing. I have done the best I could. I only intended that you need never be content." The children like being with God, but he tells them to go with their parents and trust them. The dead finally feel that it is mankind's duty to be happy and to concern themselves with living. There is something of the nebulous here with characters not quite sure of their conclusions, and the device of spaced repetition (sometimes of whole paragraphs) gives the effect of only halting forward movement; but at least oversimplification is avoided.

Onde Sagor (Evil Tales, fictions, 1924) is a collection of eleven prose pieces, some of which have been separately anthologized as short stories, and some of which are less than half a page in length and are more like the Kafka parables than anything else. The first piece seems like a quiet, lyrical, realistic, conventional story, "Father and I," and recounts the Sunday afternoon walk into the woods of a boy "getting on toward ten" and his father. Father worked on the railway, so they walk along the sleepers and from the embankment Father greets the engineer when a train goes by. In the woods as it gets dark the boy is afraid. His father says the dark is not horrible "when we know there is a God." But the boy is not reassured, and as they return home an unscheduled train hurtles through the night bearing down on them along the tracks and disappears. There is no explanation; Father doesn't recognize the driver. "That was how this world, this life, would be for me; not like Father's where everything was secure and certain. . . . It just hurtled, blazing, into the darkness that had no end." The understatement is magnificent.

"The Adventure" is a one-page parable of a ship with black sails that takes a young man aboard and they sail for years with no sign of land, through a storm and darkness that last for years, the ship finally broken against a rocky island with one storm tossed tree and no other vegetation. "We laid our cheeks to the ground and wept for joy. It was the world beginning to rise up out of the depths again." This is like the desolation of a world waiting for Godot and perhaps a picture of post-atomic devastation.

The third story, "Hero's Death," is equally appalling in its brief, quiet picture of modern society, the human unfeeling thirst for spectacle. A "committee" or a "syndicate" engages a young man to balance on his head on a church spire, then fall down and kill himself for 500,000 of whatever unit of money you choose; they sell tickets. Interviewers ask the young man, who is spirited, vigorous, willing and sound, if he doesn't find it unpleasant. He agrees and adds, "But one does anything for money." He follows the agreement to the letter, but the "people" feel a certain dissappointment. Not all the pieces are this good; many are. One, "The Lift that Went Down into Hell," has been anthologized and suggests Sartre's *No Exit*. "The Basement" presents an engaging story of a cripple named Lindgren who is better adjusted to life than the narrator who both befriends and patronizes him.

Bödeln (The Hangman; drama, 1933) shows Lagerkvist's modifications of expressionistic drama at its best. The characters are generic and unnamed: hangman, shoemaker, butcher's helper, carpenter, and others. The setting is a medieval tavern which slips into a modern nightclub with a Negro jazz band with the greatest of ease. Topical association with the violence of Hitler's Germany is not restricted to that era. The created symbol of the Human Butcher as man's constant companion is vivid and strong. Medieval hate, violence, and superstition have their counterparts in the modern nightclub, and the Hangman, ever present, underlines the constant savagery in the human condition. Various tableaux are introduced into this play without acts as individuals tell their particular stories. There is a terrifying view of a potential Negro lynching, and finally the Hangman, who has been silently present, rises to tell his story, which includes his presence at Christ's execution and the hangman's mark of Cain on his forehead.

Dvärgen (The Dwarf; novella, 1945) is quite possibly the author's most impressive single work, although the English translation has occasional awkwardnesses which seem not to be related to original intentions. *The Dwarf* made a relatively early incursion into both French and English versions and has impressed many critics as an allegorical account of man's divided nature. It suggests Dostoevsky's *Notes from Underground* and other "double" stories. The dwarf him-

self as narrator, "I am twenty-six inches tall, shapely and well pro-
portioned, my head perhaps a trifle too large," clearly represents
man's *id,* that pool of instinctual and often evil drives which normally
is repressed by the censorship of the ego and superego. But the
symbol has some complications, revulsions that one would not expect,
and this view of man from underneath is both terrifying and revealing. The action takes place vaguely in the renaissance and vaguely
in an Italian city state, governed by a Prince who seems to be man's
more rational nature, the ego who tries to remain in control. With
poisonings there is a suggestion of the Borgias; but there are no
proper names which pin down the story to historical place and time
—only Maestro Bernardo (who recalls Leonardo da Vinci in his
artistic and scientific interests, although he is more ineffectual),
Francesco, the Prince as Leone, Boccarossa, Don Riccardo, Mon-
tanza, Angelica, Giovanni, Fiammetta. There is plenty of action, an
adulterous liaison between the Princess and Don Riccardo, a war
of aggression (which delights the dwarf), a defensive war and a
siege, an orgy and wholesale poisoning, murder, suicide, the plague,
and the eventual imprisonment of the dwarf by the Prince. From his
dungeon the dwarf admits, "I was a viper and the evil genius of his
Most Princely Grace, and it was his expressed wish that I should
be rendered harmless for all time." That was the sentence. But the
dwarf knows that he still belongs to the castle, welded to it, "We
cannot escape from each other, my master and I! If I am imprisoned,
then he is imprisoned too!" The evil side of man's nature is a constant, and the good is nonexistent without it.

Barabbas (novella, 1950) is again a narrative of man's ambiguous
and dual nature, but here revealed in one individual, the murderer
in whose place Christ most specifically died. Barabbas has intrigued
other writers, notably Michel de Ghelderode who wrote a compelling
play on him for Passion Week performance in 1928 and which has
since been given as a folk play as if the author were unknown—much
to Ghelderode's satisfaction. But the Belgian concentrates on the
trial and crucifixion, with Barabbas murdered shortly after Christ's
death. Lagerkvist begins his story with the crucifixion and follows
Barabbas through many years of puzzlement, brigandage, slavery
in the mines, and a kind of inverted Saul-Paul journey to Rome,

his involvement with early Christians, and his death by crucifixion
in Rome with, but not "with" as one of, the Christian martyrs who
recognize him as "he was acquitted in the Master's stead." André
Gide, who admired the ambiguity of the closing sentence, "When he
felt death approaching, that which he had always been so afraid of,
he said out into the darkness, as though he were speaking to it: —
To thee I deliver up my soul," wonders if the Galilean, without
Barabbas' realizing it, did "get him" in the end. Gide saw Lagerkvist
as showing "the mysterious springs of an emerging conscience secretly tormented by the problem of Christ at a time when the
Christian doctrine was still in the process of formation, . . . had not
yet bridged the gap between superstition and faith." It is possible
that, as Kafka too saw, we have come back to a similar period of
uncertainty.

Friedrich Durrenmatt (German-Swiss, born 1921)

Although Dürrenmatt has been variously associated with different
movements in the modern theatre, the Theatre of the Absurd, existential drama, Neo-Romanticism, Theatre of Cruelty, surrealism, and
Epic Theatre, he seems to belong most clearly with the expressionists, even if he is a creatively eclectic one. His own plays frequently
employ bits and gambits out of Nestroy, Wedekind, Brecht, and
Wilder. His ideas, with a generous accession of his own original
impulses, stem from his Protestant background with its focus on sin,
suffering, and the search for redemption, and his reading in Kierkegaard and Kafka. If he is aware of the absurdity of the world, he is
equally aware of the possibility of responsible choice. Both as novelist and dramatist he has made his mark on mid-century European
literature, although together with Max Frisch, another somewhat older
Swiss-German dramatist *(Biedermann and the Firebugs),* his greatest
impact seems to be in the theatre.

LIFE: Born in January of 1921 at Konolfingen in Switzerland the
son of a Protestant minister, Friedrich Dürrenmatt was educated at
the universities of Berne and Zurich. His grandfather Ulrich had been
active as a satiric poet and political figure in nineteenth century
Swiss affairs, having once spent ten days in jail because of a poem.
Friedrich first wanted to be a painter and worked in the style of

Bosch, Rouault, and the German expressionists, who may have led him into his dramatic style. In the early 1940's he began writing fictional sketches which were later published as *Die Stadt* (1952). His first play, *Es steht geschrieben (Thus Is It Written)* was performed in Zurich in 1947, followed by *Der Blinde (The Blind Man)* in 1948. Both show a concern with history and the world in ruins.

Dürrenmatt started writing novels while he continued to produce plays. *Der Richter und sein Henker (The Judge and his Executioner,* 1950), followed by *Der Verdacht* (1951), established his success in this area of endeavor as well. His greatest theatrical success came with *Der Besuch der alten Dame* (1955), known in England and America as *The Visit* although it really means "The Visit of the Old Lady." The novel *Das Versprechen* and the novella *Die Panne,* translated as *The Pledge* (1957) and *The Trap* (1956) increased his reputation both at home and abroad. One additional play, *Die Physiker (The Physicists,* 1961) was highly successful in the theatre and treated a timely subject, the role of scientists in a world rushing toward destruction, within the framework of a private mad house. The American production of *The Visit* with Alfred Lunt and Lynn Fontanne is a classic of the modern stage. In the late sixties Dürrenmatt was living at Neuchâtel in Switzerland and presumably writing.

CHIEF PLAY: *Der Besuch der alten Dame (The Visit; drama,* 1955) brings together expressionistic devices with lively effects of the shocking and macabre. The setting is the town of Guellen, somewhere in central Europe, completely impoverished and run down, somewhat like Thornton Wilder's *Our Town* but the time is now and the characters less human and realistic. The express trains that used to stop now go roaring through. Everyone is waiting for the announced visit of multimillionairess Claire Zachanassian, who once lived in Guellen as Claire or Clara Wascher. Her former boyfriend, Alfred Ill, now married with two children, has remained in the town as a shopkeeper. Nameless characters appear as in earlier expressionistic drama: Mayor, Schoolmaster. Doctor, Man One through Man Four. Claire arrives, pulling the emergency brake on the express, overdressed with jewelry and red hair, followed by her party: Boby, Toby, Roby, Koby, Loby, and Husband VII. Reunion with her former lover Alfred is touching and grotesque; Claire, indestructible, seems to be put together of spare parts, an artificial leg, an artificial hand. She asks strange questions and has a coffin sent to her rooms at The Golden Apostle.

There she offers the community one million marks to buy justice. As Clara Wascher she had been in court with an illegitimate child; Alfred, the father, had denied paternity and bribed witnesses. With her wealth left by her first husband, the old Armenian Zachanassian who had found her in a brothel and married her, she tracked down the lying witnesses and had them castrated and blinded; now they're Koby and Loby. The child had died after one year. Now if someone will kill Alfred she'll give Guellen a million.

In Act II Alfred experiences fear. The town is begining to look prosperous; everyone is buying on credit. Claire is waiting. The Schoolmaster and Doctor appeal to Claire to invest in the town without conditions; but as she says, she owns the dump anyway and has brought it to its present state. Ill comes to accept his guilt, achieving tragic enlightenment, but the Schoolmaster is concerned about the fall of the community (like Mark Twain's Hadleyburg) priding itself on incorruptibility and planning community murder quietly. The Schoolmaster himself falls into the conspiracy in a speech to the assembled Guelleners, telling them that we all have connived at injustice and though our poverty is extreme we are not moved by the money but by justice and "by all those ideals, for which our forbears lived and fought, and for which they died; and which constitute the values of our Western World." At this point he might as well defend the Vietnam war. Alfred is killed, and Claire carries off the body. The audience and the Guelleners are left to be uneasy in their own minds and consciences. Money buys anything—even "justice."

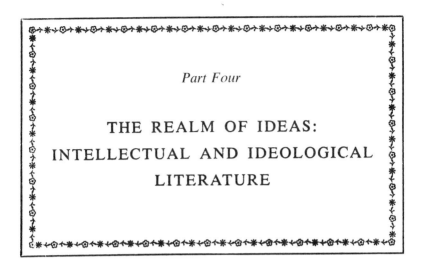

Part Four

THE REALM OF IDEAS:
INTELLECTUAL AND IDEOLOGICAL
LITERATURE

10. THE RETURN TO TRADITION AND FAITH

As a part of the general reaction against materialism which took place around 1900 there occurred a small but important revival of mysticism and religious idealism in literature. The general disillusionment with regard to science and democracy contributed to this movement, as did a reaction against the late nineteenth-century fads of evolution, agnosticism, and socialism. In England the movement was heralded by the Pre-Raphaelites, the chief of whom were Dante Gabriel Rossetti (1828-1882) and John Ruskin (1819-1900). In France there were two important predecessors: the conservative and traditionalist novelist Paul Bourget (1852-1935), whose novel *Le Disciple* (1889) attacked the skepticism of the naturalistic school; and the violently Germanophobic Maurice Barrès (1862-1923), who in *Les Déracinés* (1897) called for a return to the patriotism and Catholicism of France's classic age. Although three of these four authors lived into the twentieth century, their influence was exerted chiefly on the generation which reached maturity before 1914. In their wake appeared a school of novelists and poets who formed around 1914 what is known as the Catholic Revival movement. Much of the work of this group is mediocre, but it did include at least four important authors: Chesterton and Waugh in England; Mauriac and Claudel in France. Apart from the continent the return to tradition and faith often took non-Catholic directions: Eliot and Anglicanism, Huxley and Eastern mysticism, William Styron and traditional protestantism, Bernard Malamud and Judaism.

The authors in this group tend to be conservative in politics, although usually not in a partisan sense. Mauriac and Claudel are "conservative humanitarians" who often find themselves on the liberal side when questions of human welfare are at stake. Their attitudes toward morals vary. Claudel, however, is free from any form of Puritanism. His respect for sainthood is heartfelt and genuine, but he affirms the comforts of marriage and materialism just as heartily for those whose vocation lies in that direction. Where Claudel's Catholicism is typically French, Mauriac's takes a Jansenist, almost a Protestant, hue. In literary technique these authors tend toward romanticism and fantasy.

François Mauriac (French, born 1885)

Although Mauriac is often considered the greatest contemporary Catholic novelist, Catholic critics have pointed out that there is a touch of heresy in his work; his novels often show a powerful pre-occupation with sin more closely resembling Jansenism or Calvinism than Catholicism proper. There are many other paradoxes in Mauriac's work. He is a skillful writer, sensitive to every nuance of situation and language, but he seems half-ashamed of his literary talent and dis-parages it even in the process of writing. He is a regionalist whose principal novels are laid in his native region of southwest France, a region he ardently loves, yet even this innocent patriotism resembles too much the lust of the world for him; he invariably presents his beloved Bordeaux as a spiritual wasteland, a stark desert sprinkled with pines and populated with lost souls. A poet whose every instinct urges him toward enjoyment of the senses, he is nevertheless filled with repugnance toward the human body, physical love, and indeed the world itself. In another age Mauriac might have become a Simeon Stylites, chaining himself to a pillar to scourge the flesh; in the twen-tieth century he became the novelist of sin in the human soul.

Mauriac's novels, as diversified as they are, center around a single basic situation. The hero, "normal" in Mauriac's sense, i.e., sensual, even sensitive, but afflicted with hypertrophied conscience, is tempted in a manner which excites his physical, intellectual, and spiritual organs simultaneously. In the typical case he is attracted to a person of the opposite sex who represents his only chance for happiness and self-fulfillment. This fulfillment, however, is frustrated because it involves a capitulation to the senses, a "surrender to the flesh," and the hero's overdeveloped sense of sin makes it impossible. A titanic struggle ensues, at the end of which the hero either (a) renounces the flesh and seeks refuge in asceticism, or (b) is torn to pieces by his torments. With suitable variations this theme can be found in most of his novels.

Although built around this basic core, Mauriac's work covers a surprising area of human experience. He analyses the quest for material comfort in *Le Noeud des vipères* (*The Vipers' Knot,* 1932); social ambition in *Préséances* (*Ranks of Society,* 1921); marriage in several novels, of which the most famous is *Le Baiser au Lépreux* (*The Kiss to the Leper,* 1922); and illegitimate passion in *Le Désert d'Amour* (*The Desert of Love,* 1925), *Le Fleuve de Feu* (*The River of Fire,* 1923), and several other works. He has also written literary criticism on Pascal and Racine, various religious essays, and a life of Jesus (1937); yet these projects have not diverted him from his essential preoccupation with human sin.

Many critics have suggested that Mauriac's point of view is almost identical with that of the Jansenists, a seventeenth-century Catholic ascetic movement opposed by the Jesuits and eventually declared heretical. Although Mauriac denies this imputation, he has written four volumes on figures connected with Jansenism: one on Racine and three on aspects of Pascal. An early Mauriac essay entitled *The Suffering of the Christian* and later published along with its repudiation by Mauriac as *The Suffering and Joy of the Christian* (1929) might be mistaken for a Jansenist tract. Thus there is this final contradiction in Mauriac's career: the struggle between the doctrine he inclines toward by nature and the formal dogma of Catholicism he professes to accept.

LIFE: Mauriac was born in Bordeaux in 1885. His family were prosperous farmers and bourgeois of the Landes region, conservative and strongly Catholic. When François was still an infant his father died; he was raised entirely by his sensitive and devout mother. He was educated in Catholic schools and in the Bordeaux lycée, where he proved himself an exceptional student; in 1906 he briefly attended the École de Chartres in Paris. From the publication of his first poems, *Les Mains jointes (Joined Hands)* in 1911, he determined upon his vocation as a professional author, and continued to write steadily for the remainder of his career.

Mauriac's early novels, especially *L'Enfant chargé de Chaînes (The Child in Chains,* 1913), were over-sentimental and immature; but with *Le Baiser au Lepreux* in 1922 he created one of his finest works and won widespread acclaim. In 1925 the French Academy awarded him the Grand Prix du Roman, and in 1933 he was elected an Academician. During the Second World War Mauriac, whose Catholicism never became tainted with anything resembling Fascism, published tributes to such liberal authors as Malraux and Gide and even to the Jewish Bergson and Proust. "Let us not," he wrote, "become accomplices of the impotent creatures who are convinced, in the great silence after the cyclone, that their turn has come at last." In 1952, after the major part of his writing career, he was awarded the Nobel Prize for literature. He has published since that time a novel, *L'Agneau* (1954), *Bloc-notes, 1952-1957* in 1958, other memoirs and letters, *Cain, Where Is Your Brother;* (1962), and a book on *De Gaulle* (1964). He has been living quietly in Paris with frequent trips to an estate belonging to his wife some twenty miles outside the city.

CHIEF NOVELS: *Le Baiser au Lépreux (The Kiss to the Leper;* novel, 1922) is a study of marriage, or rather of the struggle between marriage and asceticism in the human conscience. Jean Péloueyre, an ugly but sensitive youth whose mother has died, is raised by his father in a small town of the Landes. Since he is sickly and withdrawn, he is treated with scorn by his aunt, Félicité Cazenave, who is entirely consecrated to the cult of her successful son Fernand. An early attempt to educate Jean comes to nothing; and as for marriage, his aunt gives it as her opinion that he is "unmarriageable." At last, however, his father decides to marry him to Noémi d'Artiailh, a quiet, beautiful, and saintly girl Jean has long admired.

The consummation of the marriage is a hideous fiasco, and Jean, disgusted, resolves to go to Paris to collect material for a history of his home region. He finds Paris a bleak and hostile Babylon, blighted with sin and skepticism; moreover his love for Noémi grows with his separation. For her part she "loves" him as a fellow-Christian; her affection is deep and sincere, but it proceeds purely out of her sense of duty. She implores him to return, and after a few months he does so. As soon as their love is resumed on a physical basis both parties are again repelled by it, and soon Noémi and Jean are sleeping in separate rooms. Jean, who has contracted a lung ailment in Paris, dies after a lingering illness, and as his body wastes away he begins to experience a perfect communion of souls with his wife. After his death Noémi consecrates herself to his memory.

A subsequent novel, *Genitrix* (1923), continues the history of Mme. Cazenave and her son Fernand; the latter also experiments with marriage, but at the age of fifty finds the only pure love in the arms of his mother. These two novels have been published together in English as *The Family* (1930).

Le Fleuve de Feu (*The River of Fire;* novel, 1925) treats of a similar situation, although this time the passions involved are extramarital. Daniel Trassis, a sophisticated young pleasure-seeker, has fled to a small provincial town to escape from an unwanted mistress. Weary of shabby passion, he longs for the love of a virgin, and presently discovers Gisèle de Plailly, a fellow-guest who seems to meet his requirements. Although Daniel hopes to purify himself through Gisèle's love, she is afraid the affair will degrade her; she is finally dissuaded from the act by her older companion and confidante Lucille de Villeron. Tormented by her own passions, Gisèle does momentarily give herself to Daniel, then flees to Northern France to consecrate herself to a life of asceticism. Again the "spirit"—i.e., the human conscience—has triumphed over the flesh.

Le Désert de l'Amour (*The Desert of Love;* novel, 1925) utilizes a somewhat more complex plot: a father and son who strive for the affections of the same woman. The scene is laid in Bordeaux. Raymond Courrèges, an adolescent student, and Dr. Courrèges, his father, are both in love with Maria Cross, a mysterious figure who is actually the mistress of a local merchant. The Doctor, who attends the unhappy and attractive young Maria, makes ineffectual and incomprehensible declarations of love to her; when her small son dies he defends her against the slander of the town gossips. Raymond meets Maria accidentally on a tram and soon calls on her regularly in her suburban villa. For her part Maria is interested in the youth only because of his enthusiasm and sensitivity; at the bottom she is not a sensual person. To Raymond, however, Maria is Evil: loathsome and yet irresistibly attractive. Neither father nor son learns of the other's passion. Before the novel ends both have been humiliated and degraded by their illicit lust. "Always between me and those I have longed to possess," says the father, "there has stretched this fetid region of swamp and mud." He goes on with his life of provincial boredom, family squabbles, and frustration, and Raymond vows to revenge his humiliation on the women he encounters in the future. The novel, one of Mauriac's best, includes a picture of adolescence tormented by sex very similar to that in Joyce's *A Portrait of the Artist as a Young Man*. The character of Maria is also well done; she is far from the conventional "other woman" of romantic tradition, and is motivated more by her sense of pity than by lust or avarice. The combination of love and misunderstanding which exists between father and son is also well portrayed.

Paul Claudel (French, 1868-1955)

Claudel, a diplomat by profession, might have been content to remain a talented literary dilettante; instead he found time from his diplomatic duties to make himself one of the leading poets of France. He belongs to the generation which matured in the era of Symbolism, the generation of authors which turned from naturalism and sought a deeper expression in the realm of fantasy and symbol. The spirit for which Claudel has the greatest affinity is the Gothic; he feels for the material symbolism of medieval architecture the same kinship he feels toward the fervor of the medieval saint. Claudel is a Catholic convert, and converts are traditionally fervent. Yet his Catholicism lacks any political conservatism—or did so until the era of the 1940-44 Occupation. For Claudel religion is almost entirely an emotional and aesthetic matter. On the other hand he feels that the emotions of the poet are a deeply religious matter; all artistic inspiration is an aspect of divine Grace, an instrument which the artist must cherish and utilize as though it were a veritable sacrament.

There is little Puritanism in Claudel. The mystery of creation, of the recurrence of the seasons and the fertility of animal and man, is inherent in all his work. His sense of sin is strongly developed, but the sins he portrays are not the physical vices which so fascinate Mauriac.

For Claudel the greatest sin is merely to deny one's vocation. For some this vocation may be sainthood, but for others it must necessarily be love, marriage, and productive labor.

Claudel's talent is essentially a lyrical one. The works in which he expresses himself most fully are his odes and eulogies, most of them semi-devotional in content but rich and sensual in tone. *Cinq Grandes Odes* (1910) and *Cette Heure qui est entre le printemps et l'été* (1913) contain the best of these. He is best-known in English-speaking countries for his drama, especially *The Tidings Brought to Mary* (1910). Yet even in his drama his lyrical gift is apparent; he is weak at characterization and unoriginal in plot, but skillful at creating moving and poetically effective dialogue.

LIFE: Claudel was born in 1868 in a little village in the Tardenois, the son of a provincial bank-agent. His family was traditionally Catholic, but Paul himself took no more than an ordinary interest in religion as a boy. He studied at a Paris lycée and then at the École des Sciences Politiques; in 1890 he passed the examination for the French diplomatic service. Meanwhile he had undergone an important religious experience: moved by a reading of Rimbaud, he was totally converted at a single 1886 Christmas mass at the Notre-Dame de Paris.

During his active career Claudel held many important diplomatic posts; among other offices he served as Ambassador to Japan, to Belgium, and to the United States, the last from 1926 to 1933. His first writing was published in 1890; his most important works appeared in the period 1910-30. For many years he was an intimate friend of André Gide, whom he tried unsuccessfully to convert to Catholicism. Claudel held an important post in the French propaganda service in 1939-40, but after the fall of France he was moved to collaborate to some extent with the German occupation. This decision, of course, caused him to be widely criticized after the 1944 liberation.

He was nevertheless elected to the French Academy in 1946. Having written more than twenty plays he had to wait until almost mid-century for the production of some of them. *Partage du Midi (Break of Noon),* written in 1906, was performed in 1948. *The Satin Slipper (Le Soulier de Satin,* 1929) also finally arrived at production. Two of his plays became libretti: *Christophe Colombe* (1930) for Darius Milhaud and *Jeanne d'Arc au Bucher* (1939) for Arthur Honegger. The latter became a spectacular operatic treatment of Saint Joan "at the Stake." Claudel had always felt himself inspired by Aeschylus and wrote about him. In February of 1955 Paul Louis Charles Marie Claudel died in Paris, having recently supervised a revival of *The Tidings Brought to Mary* at the Comédie Francaise.

CHIEF DRAMA: *L'Annonce Faite à Marie* (*The Tidings Brought to Mary;* drama, 1910) is laid in the fifteenth century at the time of Joan of Arc and the Great Schism. The farmer Anne Vercors, about to leave on a pilgrimage to Jerusalem, bids farewell to his wife Elizabeth and gives over the hand of his daughter Violaine to an honest young peasant, Jacques Hury. But Violaine's sister Mara also loves Jacques, and the saintly and self-effacing Violaine allows herself to be accused of misconduct in order that Jacques may choose her sister instead of herself. Through a kiss of pity for a leper, the stonemason Pierre de Craon, Violaine contracts the dread disease; Pierre seems to be cured by her gesture, while she becomes horribly disfigured and is sent to live in a lonely hut in the woods. Eight years later the child of Mara and Jacques is stricken dead. Mara, hysterical, takes the child to her leprous sister, whom she has not visited in years, and begs her tearfully to restore it. Humbly unconvinced of her ability to work miracles, Violaine takes the child; it is restored to life, but its eyes are changed from black to blue to match those of Violaine. Mara is full of gratitude. Later, however, when she suspects her husband still loves Violaine, she murders her sister by causing a heavily laden cart of sand to fall on her. As the village prepares for Violaine's funeral, her father returns from his pilgrimage. Another miracle takes place at the moment of her entombment: the long-silent bells in a deserted convent begin to peal, and the reconciled family, even the contrite Mara, recognize at last the power of sanctity that lived in Violaine.

11. LIBERALS AND HUMANITARIANS

In contrast to the religious and conservative authors treated in the preceding section, a more typical body of authors in the twentieth century are secular, humanitarian, liberal, and iconoclastic in attitude. The liberal movement among European intellectuals, which began to gain momentum in the middle of the nineteenth century, was still the most powerful force in the European battle of ideas a hundred years later. Many of its characteristics had altered in this time, but its basic principles were the same.

There are two chief sources of this liberal-socialistic ideology. The first is the classic liberalism of Locke and Jefferson and of the American and French revolutions: the concept of the brotherhood of man, of the "certain inalienable rights" of the American constitution, and the principles of freedom and justice contained in the American Bill of Rights. The second source is the proletarian movement, which began with the Chartist and socialist movements of the early nineteenth century and found its culmination in the writings of Karl Marx. Some modern authors, like Anatole France, lie chiefly under the influence of the earlier doctrines, and others, like Malraux, write in the proletarian-Marxist tradition.

A minority, of which Bernard Shaw and Jean Giraudoux are the best examples, disclaim affiliation with any doctrine or ideology, and claim to speak from original impulse. In some cases these authors assume attitudes incompatible with what is ordinarily considered liberalism; Shaw's antipathy toward vaccination and inoculation is an example. In the main, however, these authors are in one camp: they attack the capitalistic state as it is presently constituted, they demand greater rights, benefits, and privileges for the common man, they are vigorously pacifistic, and they insist upon more or less drastic revision of the economy and political structure of the modern state.

The group also shows certain resemblances from a literary point of view. They tend to lie under the influence of Ibsen, Tolstoy, Zola, and the naturalists in general, and they are often as iconoclastic in style and technique as they are in content.

Anatole France (French, 1844-1924)

Fifty years ago Anatole France was the best-known French man of letters of his time; since then his stock has considerably diminished. The reason for this is that his prestige, at least outside of France, was based chiefly on non-literary achievements: his participation in the Dreyfus affair, his colorful socialist polemics, and his personal position as a sort of nineteenth-century Voltaire scourging the manners of his time. As a literary figure his work spreads over an enormous period in time, from the early poems of the sixties to the plays of the period after the First World War. The early part of this work, culminating in the novels of the *Histoire contemporaine* series (1897-1901), are nine-teenth-century in treatment and style. The work of the period 1900-1914 is most likely to hold its own with the passing of time; it includes the satirical allegory *Penguin Island* (1908), the work of France's most frequently read in America in the twentieth century.

France entered the literary arena in the period of the Parnassian movement and the later Symbolist school. His early lyrics are sensitive, even precious, strongly influenced by classic and Parnassian models. He retained all through his career a love of scholarship and erudition and a fancy for oriental exoticism; his typical novel hero is a scholarly gentleman made vaguely unhappy by visions of sensuality (e.g. the M. Bergeret of the *Histoire contemporaine*). France's great antipathy is the same as that of Flaubert: the bourgeoisie. He was the deter-mined foe of "middle-class morality," of the hypocrisy of the respect-able, and of the reactionary chauvinism of Church and army circles during the Dreyfus affair. At the same time he deplored the excesses of radicalism; he wrote a novel, *Les Dieux ont Soif* (*The Gods are Athirst,* 1912) which presented the fanatic heroes of the Revolution in an unfavorable light and drew sharp criticism from Republican sources. As a stylist his chief merits are his tender treatment of emo-tions, especially those inspired by nature; his biting polemic, modelled on that of Voltaire and Renan; and his mild but salty irony, which he applies not only to his enemies but also to the well-beloved protagonists of his novels.

LIFE: The name Anatole France is a pseudonym; the author was born Jacques Anatole Thibault in Paris in 1844. His father, a Catholic and Royalist bookseller, sent him to the Collège Stanislas, where he received an excellent classic education from the Jesuits but developed a deep antipathy toward the Church. He became a radical poet; in 1867 he got into serious trouble when two poems were suppressed by the authorities. His early poems were technically dominated by the influence of Leconte de Lisle, leader of the Parnassian group. In 1881 *Le Crime de Sylvestre Bonnard* was awarded an Academy prize, and France became a well-known author. He turned out an enormous mass of writing during the next few years, including some of his best-known novels. In 1897 he was elected to the French Academy. The following year he interrupted his literary work to plunge into the Dreyfus con-troversy; along with Zola he did much to swing intellectual opinion to Dreyfus' defense.

An important influence in France's life was his long attachment to Madame de Caillavet, a companion who provided him with much inspiration. After her death in 1910 his work tapered off and failed to maintain its former quality. In 1921 he was awarded the Nobel Prize for Literature, and the following year his complete works were placed on the Catholic Index; it is difficult to say which distinction he considered the greater honor. Upon his death in 1924 his funeral was attended by the largest crowd to be present at such a ceremony since the funeral of Victor Hugo.

CHIEF WORKS: *Le Crime de Sylvestre Bonnard (The Crime of Sylvestre Bonnard;* novel, 1881) shows France's irony and his love of learning at their best. The hero, Sylvestre Bonnard, is a kindly old scholar totally wrapped up in his specialty but yearning for some human contact. He endeavors to come to the aid of Jeanne, an unprotected girl in impoverished circumstances, and discovers that she is the daughter of a woman he loved long ago—his sole amatory affair. To save her from a cruel and incompetent guardian he decides to abduct her; this is the sole "crime" he commits. The attempt succeeds through luck; the guardian seizes the same moment to abscond with money belonging to his clients. To provide a dowry for Jeanne, Bonnard sells his beloved library—i.e., he decides that human affection is more important than scholarly erudition. As a reward his final years are blessed by Jeanne's happiness; she marries and bears a child in which the old scholar feels an almost paternal kinship.

L'Île des Pinguoins (Penguin Island; novel, 1908) is a sort of beast fable in novel form; technically it bears comparison with Orwell's *Animal Farm.* The action takes place on an island inhabited entirely by penguins. The events allegorized are those of French history from the Napoleonic period to the Third Republic and beyond. After Trinco (Napoleon) conquers half the world and loses it again, the penguins straggle through a succession of sordid political squabbles including the Pyrot (Dreyfus) affair. Eventually they discover an explosive which destroys civilization entirely—an uncanny prediction for a 1908 novel. This novel, France's best-known work in America and England, is not typical of his writing as a whole; its tone is bitter and it lacks the gently humorous irony of the earlier novels.

Romain Rolland (French, 1866-1944)

Rolland's liberalism is of an emotional, idealistic type. In his early career a disciple of Tolstoy, he was deeply impressed with the Russian author's ethic, a form of primitive Christianity combined with an aversion to large-scale landowning and other forms of individual exploitation. He disagreed with Tolstoy, however, in his attitude toward aesthetic matters. Tolstoy toward the end of his career developed an increasing suspicion of the aesthetic impulse and judged artistic works purely on their moral content, whereas Rolland made a virtual cult of the work of art and of the artist who creates it.

The most obvious outward manifestation of Rolland's Tolstoyism is his pacifism, which he clung to doggedly through two world wars and in spite of virulent opposition. He narrowly escaped trial as a traitor during the First World War, and a large section of the public viewed him as pro-German for years afterward. This was unfair; Rolland was a sincere Frenchman in the same way that Goethe was a sincere German. He loved his native land for its people, for its traditions, and for its artists, but he rejected the chauvinism which demanded that he view Germans with hatred. At another point in his career he dabbled in communism and made a visit to Russia, but for some reason the public viewed this action with more complacency.

The typical hero of a Rolland story is an artist, divinely inspired with a genius which he himself only half comprehends and driven by a fierce compulsion to create no matter what unhappiness he brings on himself or others. Usually society refuses to accept the artist's offering, or even tries deliberately to suppress and destroy his creativity; but this only goads the artist into magnificent rages of creation. When love intervenes, the artist loves on a gargantuan scale, but in the end his physical passions are not allowed to interfere with his primary artistic mission. Rolland's style somewhat resembles that of Thomas Wolfe, although he is the more adept of the two; he is splendid at portraying large and inspiring states of emotion, but weak in cohesion and polish. He is not addicted to understatement or to stylistic subtleties, nor is he particularly concerned with ingenious symmetrical plots. He does, however, write a very poetic, lyrical prose, particularly in *L'Aube,* the beginning of *Jean-Christophe.*

LIFE: Rolland was born at Clamecy, in central France, in 1866 of an old and honorable family. He early showed an inclination toward music and the arts, and studied at both the École Normale Supérieure in Paris and the French School in Rome. In Rome he wrote his first plays, and formed an influential friendship with Malwida von Meysenbug, an aged lady who had been the intimate of Nietzsche and Wagner; his Pan-European ideas began to take form at this time. Returning to Paris in 1891, he married and continued to write drama. After the turn of the century he gained considerable fame when his great novel *Jean-Christophe* was serialized in Péguy's *Cahiers de la Quinzaine* (1904-12). In the following period he turned increasingly to the novel; his most characteristic works belong in this period. In 1913 his work was awarded an Academy prize, and his fame seemed assured.

The following year, however, the war broke out; Rolland, who was in Switzerland, remained there and began to write pacifist literature for Swiss journals and newspapers. Although he himself worked in the Red Cross to aid victims of the war, his writing brought down a veritable torrent of abuse. Most of the criticism centered around a 1915 article entitled "Au-dessus de la Melée" ("Above the Struggle"). At one point Rolland was threatened with imprisonment by the French government. In 1915, however, the Swedish Academy, at the instigation of Anatole France, awarded him the Nobel Prize for literature. He tried his hand at biography (with notable success in popularizing *Beethoven, Michelangelo, Tolstoy* among others) and at drama (one play, *Le Jeu de l'Amour et de la Mort,* 1925, about the French Revolution is very fine). During the thirties in Switzerland he carried on an extensive correspondence, even replying to the American French of at least one student admirer; the correspondence with Hermann Hesse and Richard Strauss has been published.

After the war Rolland became sympathetic toward communism; he made a trip to the Soviet Union at the invitation of Maxim Gorky, but offered no published comment when he returned. Although he opposed Nazism, he clung to his pacifism as World War II approached. He died toward the end of the war, in 1944.

CHIEF WORK: *Jean-Christophe* (novel series, 1905-13) is a vast fictional biography of two thousand pages, occupying ten volumes in the original and three volumes in the American edition. The hero is a German musician, Jean-Christophe Krafft. (Each part of this name is significant: "Jean" is the commonest of names in many languages; the hero is the embodiment of the common man. "Christophe" ("Christ-bearer") signifies his function as a bearer of light and spiritual life. "Krafft," suggesting the German *Kraft,* "strength," symbolizes Jean-Christophe's tremendous creative force, the energy which sets him apart from other men.) Although Jean-Christophe is born in the late nineteenth century, his character is modelled partly on that of Beethoven, whose biography Rolland had written in 1903.

In the first volume of the American edition, titled simply *Jean-Christophe,* the hero's childhood and youth are described. Born in a small German town, he is acclaimed as a prodigy from infancy. His mother, Louisa, is a woman of the lower classes; she loves her son with an unflagging devotion and seeks only to insure his happiness. His grandfather is a musical virtuoso and his father, Jean Michel, a conductor; they are more selfish and materialistic in their attitude toward the boy. Recognizing his talent, they sponsor his introduction into the musical world. Soon he is patronized by the local Grand Duke, and as he reaches his teens he is installed in the court orchestra. When his grandfather commits suicide and his father dies, Jean-Christophe finds himself supporting the whole family. Hard times follow, and the family is forced to live in squalid conditions. Jean-Christophe, by now a young man, becomes involved in several love affairs which only add to his confusion; he is unable to take any emotional experience lightly. All during his life his artistic instincts and his sexual passion battle inside his soul; he is continually diverted from his creative work by affairs of the heart.

During this epoque Jean-Christophe begins to realize the stifling provincialism of the small German duchy. The local burghers, stolid and hypocritical, are suspicious of anyone with artistic talent; they are hopelessly stuffy, materialistic, and vulgar. The officials of the duchy and the Grand Duke himself are arbitrary and arrogant; several times Jean-Christophe finds himself in trouble with the officials. As he begins to arrive at an understanding of his own character he realizes he must leave Germany if he is ever to amount to anything; he sadly tells his mother he must go away to study. The grief-stricken Louisa protests, but soon an event occurs which inexorably settles the mat-ter. Jean-Christophe intervenes in a sordid tavern brawl to protect a peasant girl, Lorchen; in the fight a soldier is killed. The peasants, frightened, turn against the young musician and accuse him of the crime, and he is forced to flee. He goes to Paris, the center of the artistic world, where a new epoque of his life begins.

In *Jean-Christophe in Paris* the hero's long fight for musical recognition is described. Arriving in Paris, he is accepted into musical circles, but finds music a not very lucrative profession; he is forced to take a position as a tutor. His pupils are two young girls, Colette and Grazia (the latter name signifying "grace"). He becomes affectionate with Colette, not realizing that Grazia is deeply in love with him. Soon he makes another attachment: a friendship with Olivier, an idealistic young writer. The two remain friends until Olivier's death many years later. (Symbolically the friendship represents the union of spontaneous genius and intellectual intelligence; Rolland is probably influenced by Schiller's theory of the two types of artists, the "naive" or spontaneous creator and the "sentimental," or consciously artistic craftsman.)

Jean-Christophe's destiny is also crossed by that of Antoinette, Olivier's sister. Before he comes to France he meets her briefly in Germany, where she is a governess. He takes her to an opera performance and unwittingly causes her employers to discharge her out of pique. She returns to France and Jean-Christophe loses sight of her; she slaves for years to put Olivier through the École Normale, but before Jean-Christophe comes to Paris she dies of consumption. Antoinette would have been an ideal mate for Jean-Christophe, but fate has planned otherwise. Meanwhile he returns to his affairs with other women, each of them at first an inspiration but eventually a bitter disappointment.

Grazia, who has not forgotten Jean-Christophe, marries a diplomat and secretly uses her influence to make Jean-Christophe's name known among music critics. Soon Jean-Christophe finds that an anonymous benefactor has made him famous overnight; he is disconcerted to find that influence as well as talent is necessary for success in the musical world. A romantic composer of the stamp of Berlioz, Jean-Christophe astounds the musical world with the originality of his work. Soon he is acclaimed as the musical genius of the century.

Jean-Christophe: Journey's End, the third volume of the American edition, begins as Olivier marries the shallow and materialistic Jacqueline. The two friends begin to drift apart. Saddened by this, Jean-Christophe is made even more unhappy by the Dreyfus affair, which reveals an unexpectedly bigoted and snobbish side of the French character. He begins to conclude that the rulers, aristocrats, and bosses of all nations are hopelessly corrupt, and that the only hope of mankind lies in the common people. Jacqueline soon abandons Olivier, and the two friends, reunited, discuss their liberal and humanitarian political ideas. Putting them into action, they take part in a tumultuous May Day riot. But Jean-Christophe learns that violence is no way to achieve humanitarian ideals; Olivier is killed and he himself is obliged to flee to Switzerland.

In exile he has another highly emotional love affair, this time with Anna, a married woman. His sense of guilt and the depletion of his energies interrupt his creative stream for some time. But in Switzerland he reencounters Grazia, now widowed; and with her he learns the joys of friendship between man and woman. On the whole his ten years in exile are fruitful ones.

At the end of his life he returns to France and is surprised to find he has become an "old master" without knowing it. Now the critics who scorned him proclaim themselves his discoverers. His success is complete. He never marries Grazia, although they remain close friends. She dies in Egypt, and he himself passes away not long after in Paris, a venerable and universally respected composer.

This plot actually forms only the backbone of *Jean-Christophe;* the major part of the work is devoted to conversations, soliloquies, and analyses of personal and philosophical problems. Some of the ideas contained in the work are as follows:

(1) PACIFISM and ANTI-NATIONALISM play a large part in *Jean-Christophe*. The common people of the world form a spiritual brotherhood; their shared humanity transcends national boundaries. Nationalism is a fiction, the tool of the powerful who seek to provoke hatreds for their own gain; it is these powers who promulgate the mystique of German superiority and the doctrine of French racial purity (the latter manifested by the anti-Dreyfusards). Much of this attitude, along with the concept of non-violence and non-resistance to evil, Rolland shares with Tolstoy. He resembles Tolstoy too in his admiration for the common people; the peasants, workers, and simple folk in *Jean-Christophe* are sharply contrasted to the decadent and perverted powerful of the world. The concept proceeds more from emotional Christianity than it does from socialism or any other political doctrine.

(2) The novel attacks MATERIALISM and SENSUALISM, especially that of the German burgher class with its beer and its sausages and that of French boulevard life. Jean-Christophe himself is occasionally diverted into brawls and affairs of passion, but his higher nature invariably triumphs and he returns to his music.

A connected concept is the superiority of friendship to love. Jean-Christophe's friendship with Olivier is one of the great spiritual forces in his life, whereas his affairs with women serve only to degrade and demoralize him. The one exception is his lifetime connection with Grazia. Even in this case he has little in common with her in his youth, when the affair is complicated by sexual awareness. In his maturity Grazia shows him that friendship is possible between a man and a woman, and this relationship brings him an even greater satisfaction than his friendship with Olivier.

(3) The work also involves a THEORY OF ART and an analysis of the position of the artist in society. Jean-Christophe is driven by a conviction that art should convey a moral truth, that it should inspire men to the highest and purest of visions and bring them together through breaking down the differences between them. Rolland is opposed to the doctrine of art-for-art's-sake, which holds that art is merely an exquisite form of pleasure. Jean-Christophe as an artist is chosen by destiny to convey a message to humanity; he is a consecrated soul, almost a prophet, whose life is not his own. He has a mission, and when he is momentarily deflected from it by love or politics he feels an ineffable shame.

The work also demonstrates the materialism and cynicism of critics, publishers, impresarios, and others who make money from the artist's talent. This is part of the wider theme of idealism which dominates the novel: the great ideals of friendship, art, and humanitarianism are contrasted to the avarice, fanaticism, and lust of the world.

Eugène Brieux (French, 1858-1932)

The dramas of Eugène Brieux are problem plays written to attack specific and transitory social evils; thus some of them have become anachronistic even in our own time. Brieux, a socialist and pacifist like Bernard Shaw, lacks anything corresponding to Shaw's positive ideology, e.g., the Life Force concept. His work is purely iconoclastic and negative, whatever positive ideas he may have held in private.

Nevertheless his plays have probably been as effective in achieving social reform in France as Shaw's have in England; and *Damaged Goods* is said to have had a considerable influence in opening the subject of venereal disease to free discussion in America.

In dramaturgy Brieux is in the tradition of Ibsen, Hauptmann, and Dumas *fils,* the great founding triumvirate of the problem play. His thesis plays often lack dramatic interest, and some of them achieved success on the stage only through their sensational content. Others, especially *La Robe rouge,* have considerable dramatic merit. Shaw, who prefaced the first English edition of Brieux's plays, called him the greatest French playwright since Molière.

LIFE: Brieux, born the son of a Parisian carpenter in 1858, was totally self-educated. During his adolescence he worked as a clerk; his first play, *Bernard Palissy,* appeared when he was twenty-one. His first successful drama was *Blanchette* (1892). The height of his fame, however, came with *Les Avariés* (*Damaged Goods,* 1902), which created a tremendous controversy and made its author a world figure overnight.

For many years Brieux was associated with the Théâtre Libre, a Parisian group devoted to naturalistic and socialistic dramas. Brieux avoided radical political groups, however, and considered himself a loyal French citizen; he was a Commander of the Legion of Honor and an Academician. He died of pleurisy in Nice in 1932.

CHIEF DRAMAS: *Les Avariés* (translated as *Damaged Coods;* drama, 1902) is Brieux's best-known play, although its dramatic merit is slight. George Dupont, a carefree young playboy, contracts syphilis. He consults a specialist, who tells him he must indefinitely postpone his marriage with his cousin Henriette. Instead the cocky and impatient George turns to a charlatan who produces a facile disappearance of the symptoms; George marries Henriette six months later. The next act shows the birth of their child, hopelessly marked by the disease. A discussion by the specialist warns against the dangers of ignorance of social diseases and argues for better education of young people in such subjects. *Damaged Goods* was played several times in America in spite of attempted censorship; a special performance was presented for members of Congress when public staging was suppressed.

La Robe rouge (*The Red Robe;* staged in America as *The Letter of the Law;* drama, 1900) is an exposé of certain evils in the French legal system. An old man is murdered in the Basque town of Mauléon; the town prosecutor, Vagret, hopes to use the case to advance his own fortunes. The local panel of judges as well are hopelessly subverted by ambition, since their advancement seems to depend on the number of spectacular convictions they can perform. The one unbiassed judge is La Bouzule, an old man of seventy who is due to retire and thus devoid of ambition. Mouzon, the examining magistrate, fastens onto one Etchepare as the most likely suspect. He browbeats the man and his wife, virtually ruins the family, but is unable to elicit a confession. At the trial Vagret heatedly demands the head of Etchepare, although he begins to doubt the man's guilt himself. Etchepare is freed by the court, but is demoralized by certain revelations the prosecution makes about his wife's past. When he repudiates his wife Yanetta, she, in despair, kills Mouzon. The law, motivated solely by the ambition of its officers, has not found the guilty party to the crime, and has only succeeded in forcing a desperate woman into another and equally heinous crime. The judges are ironically cheated of their promotions, since Mouzon, the only one to win advancement, is murdered before he can take office.

Jean Giraudoux (French, 1882-1944)

Giraudoux, a lifetime pacifist and impassioned foe of nationalism, is in another sense a devoted and patriotic Frenchman. He admires French culture without wishing to impose it upon others, and he approves what is good in the German temperament while vigorously opposing German chauvinism and Prussianism. His pacifism is of a curiously sentimental and poetic type; yet this did not prevent him from giving his life to his country during the Second World War. If Giraudoux had been born in the seventeenth century he might have been another La Fontaine; as it was circumstances forced him to become a pacifist and political propagandist.

In his personal philosophy Giraudoux is a sort of Epicurean; he asks nothing better than to be allowed to enjoy the French national pleasures of good food, good wine, conversation, and love. The heroes of his novels and plays are those who seek humbly to enjoy the modest pleasures within their reach; the villains are the bigots and fanatics who are driven to cruelty by their "ideals." Giraudoux feels that few ideals are worth a war and that crusades generally cause more misery than happiness; he would find it a better world if each of us kept to his personal pleasures and left his neighbors alone.

As a writer Giraudoux is fanciful, imaginative, diffuse, and witty; his style is a sort of intellectual impressionism in which he constantly intrudes to make whimsical personal comments. Even in Giraudoux's drama the characters speak the ideas of the author; his best characters are something like himself, and those who differ from him are mere cardboard effigies. The chief fault of Giraudoux's novels is their lack of cohesion, their discursive and whimsical gait. His admirers, however, may find this quality the most charming part of his work.

LIFE: Giraudoux, born in Bellac, a small town of Limousin, in 1882, received an excellent classical education in a Châteauroux lycée and later attended the École Normale Supérieure in Paris. He at first planned a diplomatic career, but abandoned this to wander about Europe and North America for five years (1905-10). In 1910 he won a post in the French foreign service, and travelled to Russia and the Orient. His literary career began about this time; his earliest publication was a set of stories, *Provinciales,* in 1909. During the First World War he served in the infantry, was wounded, and received the Cross of the Legion of Honor. He resumed his diplomatic career after the war, but soon turned back to writing in earnest. *Siegfried et le Limousin* (novel, 1922) won him wide fame, especially when it was adapted for the stage in 1928. His major works were written in the period between the two wars.

In 1939-40 Giraudoux served in the French government as chief of propaganda and censorship. With the fall of France in 1940 he went to Vichy to occupy the same post in the puppet government. The circumstances of his death are rather obscure, but it appears he was killed by the Germans in 1944 when he refused to compromise his principles beyond a certain point.

CHIEF WORKS: *Siegfried et le Limousin* (translated as *My Friend from Limousin;* novel, 1922) is a whimsical study of the contrast between French and German temperaments. Forestier, a French soldier, is stricken with amnesia in battle and taken by the Germans as one of their own wounded. After the war German doctors and officials try to rebuild his memory by exposing him to a typical German environment. He is re-taught to eat and talk, christened Siegfried von Kleist, given a thoroughly German education, and thrown together with Eva, a blond young lady thought to personify the German feminine virtues. Soon he becomes a perfect facsimile of a typical German. But a French friend, Jean, reads Siegfried's prose and recognizes it as that of his "dead" friend Forestier. Jean journeys to Munich and attempts to expose the mistake in identity, but since Siegfried has become an important official, this causes governmental embarrassment. Working through Eva, Jean finally succeeds in overcoming her antipathy toward him, although not her general Francophobia. When Eva becomes aware of the Machiavellian tactics of her own government, she retires with Siegfried to her Oberammergau estate. There, after long conversations, Jean succeeds in enticing Siegfried back to France, where he plans to reintroduce him to his heritage as a Frenchman.

The thesis of the novel is that most national characteristics are environmental. But Siegfried is unable to integrate himself totally into German culture; it appears that Giraudoux believes some essential racial differences exist. From a literary point of view the best parts of the novel are the satires on the outwardly systematic but essentially romantic German mentality.

Amphitryon 38 (drama, 1929) is, as its title indicates, one of a long list of modern plays on the Amphitryon theme from Greek mythology. Jupiter, enamored of the moral Alcmene, contrives to start a war to remove her husband Amphitryon, then attempts to seduce Alcmene by assuming the guise of her husband. He is successful upon his first attempt; the news leaks, and soon the entire town is rejoicing over the honor which has come to it. But Alcmene is an honorable wife; she stands alone in viewing the seduction with horror. When Leda, another favorite of the god, visits her to exchange opinions, she persuades Leda to accept the embrace of Jupiter in her stead. Thus out-tricking the god, she plays for time until her husband returns. In the final act Jupiter and Amphitryon conduct a debate in which the prize is to be Alcmene herself. At length Alcmene saves her honor by promising Jupiter something no god has ever experienced, and which is a thousand times more valuable than love: human friendship. The play ends in a tribute to conjugal bliss.

La Guerre de Troie n'aura pas lieu (The Trojan War Will Not Take Place; drama, 1935; also translated by Christopher Fry as *Tiger at the Gates),* again based on a Greek myth, is a study of the causes of modern warfare. The action opens as the Trojan War is

about to begin. Hector, Andromache, Cassandra, and Hecuba are the
advocates of peace, but others serve to gain by the war: Priam sees it
as a means of enhancing the royal prestige and reducing the grumbling
of the plebeians; the poet Demokos sees in it an opportunity to write
stirring patriotic verses; and Helen, selfishly infatuated with Paris, is
willing to permit the extinction of the entire Trojan nation as long as
her personal pleasure is not interfered with. Although Hector, in an act
more brave than any military deed, permits himself to be slapped by
the Greek envoys, the war party eventually wins out, and the "men of
good will" look sadly on as the destruction begins.

La Folle de Chaillot (The Madwoman of Chaillot; drama, 1945),
left in manuscript at the time of his death and given brilliant production by Louis Jouvet with *mise-en-scène* by Christian Bérard
in 1945-46, later in New York with Martita Hunt as the Madwoman
and filmed with Katherine Hepburn in the role, has become Giraudoux's best known play in the theatre world. It is light and gay, a
poetic fantasy rather than a realistic picture. The play opposes good
and evil in a clear-cut way; financiers with their stock manipula-
tions are bad, while the dispossessed, peddler, ragpicker, juggler,
street singer, are good. But the poor are not really wretched. Like
the eccentrics, they live a complete individualism and are relatively
carefree. The Countess Aurelia, the madwoman of Chaillot (there
are three others: of Passy, of St. Sulpice, of La Concorde—who are
rather wacky friends), traps the entrepreneurs who are looking for
oil in Paris, who would destroy the city for gain. The Countess
simply gets rid of them through a trap door down in her cellar,
explaining that "Wickedness evaporates." And that makes a charming entertaining fantasy.

Andre Malraux (French, born 1901)

Although Malraux has been associated with various political groups
both left and right during his long career, he is essentially a Marxist
writer when he is at his literary best. He views human conflicts
chiefly as struggles between social classes, and he considers the
individual important only in his relation to these class struggles.
His novels often show internal conflicts taking place in the minds
of his characters, but in such cases the characters are generally

trying to work out some phase of their relationship to the masses —questions of duty, questions of action or non-action, or conflicts of individual and group morality. The dominant theme of Malraux's writing is that the group is vastly more important, and more powerful, than the sum of its members. In *Le Temps du mépris* (1935) a communist terrorist is jailed by the Nazis and is later released when a fellow-communist, whose name he does not even know, surrenders in his place; the terrorist has been rescued by the heroism of the group. This situation is typical of many in Malraux's fiction.

Malraux's style is characterized by intensity. His characters are always shown at a crucial period in their lives; they are usually depicted in moments of great danger, struggle, or moral crisis. Consequently his novels tend to cover relatively small periods of time; the action of *La Condition humaine,* his best-known work, occupies only a few days.

LIFE: Malraux, born of wealthy Parisian parents in 1901, was educated at the Lycée Condorcet and later studied languages and archeology at the Paris School of Oriental Languages. In 1923 he travelled to Indo-China to put his archeological knowledge to use. After excavating a number of rare and valuable objects, he began to find local politics more interesting than archeology; he joined the Young Annam League and became an active political agitator. 1925 found him in China as Associate Secretary-General of the Kuomintang party; in this office he participated in the National Liberation movement of that year. By 1927 he was a member of the "Twelve" who headed the Chinese popular front coalition. Shortly afterward he abandoned the Kuomintang when Chiang severed his connections with the Third International and veered to the right. From his Chinese experiences came his first novels: *Les Conquérants* (1928), *La Voie royale* (1930), and *La Condition humaine* (1933). the last of these won Malraux a Goncourt Prize and was justifiably lauded by critics as one of the greatest modern revolutionary novels.

In 1936 Malraux, who had meanwhile learned to fly, went to Spain to form a Loyalist air group. Out of his Spanish service came *L'Espoir (Man's Hope),* one of the best novels to proceed from the Civil War. In 1939 he served in the French tank corps, was captured in the retreat of 1940 but escaped, and continued to fight in the F.F.I. for the duration of the war. After the war Malraux became associated with Charles deGaulle's R.P.F. party, a right-wing republican movement sharply opposed to liberalism and socialism; he continued, however, to maintain a liberal attitude in his published writings while serving as a sort of intellectual mentor for the R.P.F. Considered a propagandist for de Gaulle, he survived attempted assassination in 1947.

In 1951 he published in its most accessible form *Les Voix de Silence* (*The Voices of Art,* 1953), on which he had worked for more than fifteen years. It views the world as a museum of all art and artifacts. It is very exciting to read, but his art "history" is apocryphal according to Francis Henry Taylor of the Metropolitan Museum. In the sixties Malraux turned to autobiographical writing, characteristically publishing *Anti-mémoires* in 1967, which, after anti-plays and anti-novels, was only to be expected sooner or later. He has been living in Versailles, which is a pleasant surburban ride from Paris.

CHIEF WORK: *La Condition humaine* (translated variously as *Man's Fate* or *Storm Over Shanghai;* novel, 1933) is Malraux's masterpiece. The action takes place during the 1927 uprising in Shanghai. Ch'en, a Chinese terrorist, commits a murder which enables his group to seize a load of arms to precipitate the uprising. The plans work out smoothly; the Reds, acting in concert with the "Blues" or Nationalists of Chiang Kai-Shek, seize police stations and soon hold command of the city. But the coalition with the Nationalists is short-lived; the Kuomintang forces usurp the victory earned with the blood of the Reds, and the Red International inexplicably fails to support its loyal adherents. Ch'en rebels against this betrayal and resolves to murder Chiang. He flings himself under Chiang's car and explodes a bomb; he dies, but Chiang is not in the car and escapes injury. The police soon learn Ch'en's identity and round up his group. The family of Hemmelrich, a German music-store owner and active member of the group, are killed; Katov, a Russian, and Kyo, a half-breed, are captured. Kyo poisons himself in jail and Katov and his comrades are executed. Although their heroism has been betrayed, their action has not been in vain. The Party, for obscure reasons of its own, has chosen to sacrifice them, and their heroism is the greater since they accept their death unquestioningly. The individualistic Ch'en, who rebels against authority and takes matters into his own hands, is the cause of the subsequent destruction of the group.

Erich Maria Remarque (German, 1898-1970)

Remarque's *All Quiet on the Western Front* appeared in 1929 at the height of the pacifistic reaction to the First World War, and probably exerted more influence than any book of its kind ever written. It sold over a million copies in Germany alone, in spite of the violent attacks of right-wing forces, and was widely read in every civilized country. In addition it was filmed several times in Europe and America, thus reaching an audience which would not ordinarily be likely to read a novel. Remarque would be an important author were it only for this single book; the success of *The Arch of Triumph* adds to that importance.

Nevertheless Remarque is not a great novelist. He writes in the tradition of naturalism; his novels consist of gripping plot incidents interspersed with lyrical passages of a certain beauty. His insight into character is sound; he views his characters from the inside rather than from the outside as most naturalists do. His concept of the structure of the novel is hackneyed; *All Quiet on the Western Front* is built around the construction contrived by Barbusse and imitated by count-less other war authors. *The Arch of Triumph* is likewise unoriginal in structure. Remarque is essentially a forceful and capable, but not brilliant, author who writes popular novels of an unusual power and effect. It is the content of his books, and the author's obvious sincerity and conviction, which lend Remarque's work its vitality.

LIFE: Erich Maria Remarque was born in Osnabrück, Westphalia, in 1898, the son of a bookbinder. There is nothing literary or cloistered about his history. He was educated in the Osnabrück Gymnasium, fought in the World War and was wounded five times, tried to make a living after the war as a school-teacher but gave it up, then wandered through a variety of odd jobs. Always interested in automobiles, he eventually became a writer of automotive advertisements, then editor of *Sportbild,* a general sports magazine. He had been brooding over his war experiences for a number of years, and in 1929 he wrote *All Quiet on the Western Front.* The timing was perfect; the book, the first of its kind in Germany, was an astounding publisher's success. In 1932 Remarque bought a house on the Lago Maggiore in Switzer-land with his earnings. The Nazi *coup* the following year made his exile permanent, and in 1939 he came to America. He has since applied for American citizenship. *The Arch of Triumph* (1946) sold widely, and was made into a successful motion picture.

He continued to publish novels in the fifties and sixties: *Spark of Life* (1951), *A Time to Live and a Time to Die* (1954), *The Black Obelisk* (1957), *Heaven Has No Favourites* (1961), and *The Night in Lisbon* (1964). Although reasonably interesting they have produced relatively little stir. As an American citizen Mr. Remarque, still writing in German, had been living the post-war years in Ticino, Switzerland, until his death in September of 1970 of heart collapse with his wife, Paulette Goddard, at his bedside.

CHIEF WORKS: *Im Westen nichts Neues* (translated as *All Quiet on the Western Front;* novel, 1929) is related in the first person by Paul Baümer, a young German soldier. His squad is a heterogeneous one, intended to symbolize various elements in the German nation: the hardened opportunist Katczinsky, the stolid farmer Detering, the vociferous Müller, the idealistic Kemmerich, and a half-dozen others. The soldiers, virtually boys by age, soon become hard and cynical; they learn that a loaf of bread is more important than the capture of a province and that a dry place to sleep is the most precious of all possessions. Many scenes are brutally naturalistic. On the other hand an especially touching scene is Paul's interview with his mother, a naive old lady who understands nothing of the war and warns Paul to "be careful" at the front. At the end of the novel only Paul and his friend Albert Kropp are still alive of the group. Paul returns home to find his mother dying of cancer—a symbol of the diseased society awaiting the returning soldiers at the end of the war.

In *Der Triumphbogen (The Arch of Triumph;* novel, 1946) Remarque abandons his pacifism for an active anti-Nazism. The novel is laid in Paris in the months leading up to the German invasion of France in 1939-40; the hero, at first apathetic toward politics, at length changes heart and performs a heroic and dangerous assassination of a Nazi agent.

Ignazio Silone (Italian, born 1900)

Silone is an important author for two reasons: he is one of the most effective anti-Fascist propagandists of the thirties and forties, and he is an observant regionalist in the tradition of Giovanni Verga (1840-1922). His chief works, the novels which center around the character of Pietro Spina, are basically adventure stories. To the framework of the adventure plot, however, are added the other elements which give Silone's work its high quality: the impassioned and active character of Spina himself, the detailed pictures of peasant life, and especially the sympathetic but devastating irony with which Silone views the Italian peasant.

Silone, a socialist and humanitarian, treats the Italian lower classes with great objectivity; his peasants are never falsely heroic, and at their worst they occasionally resemble animals. The peasant in Silone's novel is an illiterate and exploited drudge whose entire life is plagued with poverty, disease, and the tyranny of his masters. He is politically naive; he opposes Fascism only when his personal interest in interfered with. He is superstitious rather than religious, and stubborn rather than courageous. Nevertheless Silone shows him to be superior to the middle-class landowners who suppress him, the officials who harass him with taxes and punishment, and even the priests who help to maintain him in his degraded station. Silone wishes his reader to sympathize with the peasant not because he is noble and freedom-loving, but because he may some day become so.

Silone's chief character, the revolutionist Pietro Spina, is perhaps the least successful of his characters from a literary point of view. Essentially a satirist, Silone is at his best in caricature. The pompous provincial official, the hypocritical priest, the superstitious old peasant woman, and the bellicose local patriot are his specialties; he sketches them with a sure hand. It is only natural that Spina, Silone's ideal political man, should not come through as well; he is a personification of the forces which are eventually to free Italy rather than a rounded human personality. At the same time there is something of the saint about Spina which makes him impressive even when he is not entirely believable. Silone's novels will no doubt be read when the issue of Fascism is long forgotten. Unfortunately for their literary effectiveness, Silone revised and rewrote his pre-war novels after he turned from left to right, at least toward the right, in the manner of Dos Passos and Malraux. *Bread and Wine* and *Fontamara* are much better, even great, works in their original versions. He did try to indicate the difference in the Italian versions of *Bread and Wine* by reversing the title from *Pane e vino* to *Vino e pane*.

LIFE: Silone (his real name is Secondo Tranquilli) was born on May Day in 1900 in Peschina, a small town of the Abruzzi; he later

utilized this town as the model for the fictional towns Fontamara and
Pietrasecca. He was politically active from his earliest youth. After
writing for several leftist publications and editing a young people's
paper, *Avanguardia,* he visited Russia (1921) and returned to continue working as a journalist. When the Fascist police raided the *La-
voratore,* a labor paper, Silone narrowly escaped capture; his brother
was jailed by the police and died in custody. Silone now went underground; aided and sheltered by peasants in his native Abruzzi, he
continued his anti-Fascist activities. In 1930 he abandoned the Italian
Communist party, which up to then he had accorded a sporadic loyalty;
henceforth he remained as firmly anti-Communist as he was anti-
Fascist. He left Italy in 1931 and eventually settled in Switzerland,
where he edited the anti-Fascist paper *Avanti.* His major literary
works were written during his Swiss exile. *Fontamara* appeared in
1933, and *Bread and Wine* and *The Seed Beneath the Snow* in 1936
and 1942 respectively. The latter two works were published first in
English, since Silone was naturally denied access to Italian publishers.
Parts of both novels were also incorporated into a drama, *Egli si
nascose (And He Hid Himself),* which was performed in Zurich and
in New York City.

In 1944, at the height of the war, Silone made his way back into
Italy disguised as a priest. He has continued to write, and has also
been active in post-war Italian political circles, particularly as
a spokesman for the Socialist party. He married an Irish writer,
Darina Laracy, in 1944; she worked on translating his books into
several languages. Silone published his first new post-war novel in
1953, *A Handful of Blackberries,* which already shows his shift in
political sympathies. A later novel, *The Fox and the Camelias,*
appeared in 1961; but his best work seems to remain that of his
period of exile.

CHIEF WORKS: *Fontamara* (novel, 1933), an embryonic novel not
typical of Silone's later work, involves a group of peasants in the small
village of Fontamara who vigorously oppose efforts of Fascists and
landowners to take their land rights away from them. They attempt a
revolt, but it comes to nothing because the peasants quarrel among
themselves and cannot agree on a coordinated plan of action. The
emphasis on group cooperation marks this as the most Marxist of
Silone's novels, although it was written after his break with official

Communism.

Pane e vino (*Bread and Wine;* novel, 1936) relates the Odyssey of Pietro Spina, a young peasant of the Abruzzi who acquires a certain amount of education, becomes a socialist, and attempts to aid the peasants of his native region. Spina, returning to Italy after a period of exile, makes contact with a liberal priest, Don Benedetto. Through the aid of the priest Spina obtains clerical garments; he assumes the name Don Paolo Spada and begins to make his way south through the mountains. When he reaches the Abruzzi he settles down and begins work among the *contadini;* he soon acquires a reputation as a courageous and generous friend of the common man. Christina Cola-martini, an intensely religious young girl, is especially attracted to "Don Paolo," but cannot accept his liberal political ideas.

On a visit to Rome Spina meets Pompeo, an Abruzzi youth with revolutionary principles. For a time he sees Pompeo as a possible disciple and assistant. When the Ethiopian War begins, however, Pompeo is seized with a patriotic fever and plans to betray Spina to the police; Spina barely escapes. Returning to Don Benedetto, he has a long conversation with him; both men deplore the absence of true religion in the world, and agree that religion as it presently operates in Italy is a force of evil.

As the novel ends Don Benedetto, whose ideas have made him suspect, is killed when he partakes of poisoned sacramental wine. Spina escapes over the mountains, and Christina, attempting to follow him, is killed by wolves.

Some of the symbols of this novel are as follows: the title suggests that some sort of sacrament or sacrifice is necessary for Italy's redemption. Spina upon his return to Italy stains his face with iodine to appear twenty years older; his contact with foreign society has given him a maturity lacking in the adolescent Italian youth who support Fascism. Spina, in clerical dress, represents the true saintly force in Italy. Don Benedetto is poisoned by sacramental wine; i.e., the very founts of holiness of the Church have become poisoned from within.

The Seed Beneath the Snow (novel, 1942) relates further adventures of Pietro Spina. Spina himself does not play as important a part in this novel, which is chiefly devoted to caricatures of the Abruzzi officialdom. No Italian version of this work has yet appeared.

The School for Dictators (dialogue, 1938) is likewise published only in English. Written in the form of a philosophical dialogue, this political tract attacks Fascism by pretending to defend and explain its methods. Irony is the chief rhetorical device.

Arthur Koestler (Austro-Hungarian, born 1905)

The American reading public tends to regard Koestler chiefly as an anti-totalitarian writer, and certainly he is one of the most capable of the modern authors who have turned their talents in this direction. There is, however, another facet to his work often ignored or slighted: he is a psychological novelist in the modern neo-Freudian tradition, highly sensitive to the subconscious side of mental activity and greatly interested in abnormal, perverted, or neurotic states of mind. He is not particularly concerned with the mental processes of the "normal" Nazi or communist. His interest generally falls on one of two other types: the totalitarian official or spy who begins to doubt the validity of his position, and the refugee, usually Jewish, whose mind is filled with dread of the machinery bent upon his destruction. These two situations produce many forms of reaction in the human mind, and it is with their mental manifestations that Koestler is concerned.

In style and content Koestler is conventional, at least for the mid-twentieth century. He makes great use of internal monologue in the style of most psychological novelists; sometimes, as in the delirium sequence in *Arrival and Departure,* he becomes involved in intricate Freudian dream-allegories. Occasionally vestiges of his journalistic training are visible in his style; he tries for sensational or shocking effects almost in the manner of the Sunday supplement. At the same time he is aware of this tendency toward journalistic superficiality, and in his better works surmounts it to achieve a convincing sincerity.

LIFE: Koestler was born in Budapest in 1905 of Jewish parentage. His father was Hungarian and his mother Viennese, and as a boy Koestler spoke German at home and Hungarian at school. Although, as his literary temperament formed, be began to "think in German," in 1940, at the age of thirty-five, he was forced to abandon this language for English. The circumstances of Koestler's life obliged him to become a fluent linguist; he is familiar with all the chief modern languages but entirely at home with none of them. Since 1940 he has written directly in English.

As a Viennese student Koestler became interested in Zionism; in 1926 he travelled to Palestine to work on a collective farm. This life little suited his temperament, and he returned to Europe to become a journalist. This career took him to the Near East, to Paris, and finally to Berlin, where he arrived on the day of the Reichstag Election in 1930. Gradually he became a fervent Marxist; the following year he took out Communist Party membership. In 1931 he was the only correspondent on the history-making expedition of the dirigible Graf Zeppelin to the polar regions, and on his return he embarked on a lecturing tour in Germany. In 1932-33 he visited Soviet Russia. During his absence the Nazis assumed power in Germany, and he was unable to return; instead he resumed his journalistic career in Paris. In 1936 he went to Spain as a special correspondent for the London *News Chronicle;* he was captured by the Fascists and spent four months in jail, but was eventually released through the intervention of the British government. This experience, along with his later imprisonment in France, suggested to him the prison setting of *Darkness at Noon.*

Koestler began to become disillusioned with the Communist Party around 1938, and in 1939, at the time of the Russo-German nonintervention pact, he formally denounced the U.S.S.R. His reasons for this change of heart he has well described in his essay in *The God That Failed,* a collection of statements by intellectuals who have abandoned communism. In 1939 he was imprisoned by the French as an alien; he escaped to England to join the Britsh army in 1940. He has spent a good deal of time since the war partly on the French Riviera and partly in rural New Jersey, but more recently as a naturalized British citizen has made his home base London. Among the rather varied writing of the period of the late fifties and the sixties, including essays and autobiographical material along with ficton, have appeared *The Trail of the Dinosaur* Essays, 1955, *Arrow in the Blue (Autobiography,* 1952-54) *The Sleepwalkers* (1959), *The Lotus and the Robot* (a book about Zen Buddhism, 1960), *The Act of Creation* (1964), *The Ghost in the Machine* (1967) and *Drinkers of Infinity* (Essays, 1968).

CHIEF NOVELS: *Darkness at Noon* (novel, 1941) is a study of the betrayal of the Revolution by the Soviet regime and of the moral crisis of a Soviet official accused of disloyalty. (Russia is not specifically designated as the setting, but the implication is obvious.) The novel opens as Nicholas Rubashov, a former Commissar of the People, finds himself in prison for political crime. At first confused and resentful, he at length begins to take an interest in establishing contact with his fellow-prisoners through a system of wall-tapping. By this method he keeps abreast of almost everything that goes on in the prison.

Interviewed by Ivanov, a former college friend and now a political agent, Rubashov is promised a prison term instead of execution if he will make a false confession of seditious activity. (The counter-Revolutionary action implied is the "Trotskyite conspiracy.") Returned to his cell, Rubashov spends two weeks in thoughtful contemplation during which he reviews his entire life. He remembers comrades he has betrayed and sent to their deaths in the name of Revolutionary principles, and he remembers his mistress Arlova who met her death because of him. He comes to realize that the Party is only a vast and self-perpetuating machine which has lost all contact with the ideals of the Revolution. Disillusioned, he willingly makes the required confession. But a new governmental purge follows close on the heels of the one which has entrapped him; Ivanov, his inquisitor, is arrested, and the deal Rubashov made with him is repudiated. Rubashov is led into the cellars of the prision to be shot, and at last realizes the true extent of the Machiavellian cynicism of Soviet communism.

The prision details in this novel are drawn from the experiences of Koestler's friend Eva Weissberg, who spent eighteen months in a Russian prison, as well as from Koestler's own experiences.

Arrival and Departure (novel, 1943) is laid in a seaport in "Neutralia," evidently Lisbon, Portugal. Peter Slavek, a refugee from Germany, arrives in the city hoping to find a way to join the British army to fight Nazism. Formerly a hero to the Bolsheviks because of his refusal to betray his comrades under torture, he is now an enemy of the Party because of his break with it at the time of the Russo-German pact. During the course of the novel his reasons for seeking martyrdom are uncovered by the psychoanalyst Sonia Bolgar, who takes him into her home when he is starving. His "heroism" is eventually traced to a juvenile trauma and its resultant guilt complex.

After Sonia's analysis has cured him of a psychosomatic paralysis of the leg, he feels free to flee to America in pursuit of Odette, a French girl whose fiancé has been killed in the war. Odette, however, has rather odd tastes in pleasure, and soon Peter begins to suspect she is having an affair with Sonia. This disillusions him about Sonia, whose analysis of his character he has previously accepted so totally. When he catches a glimpse, as he thinks, of a comrade of his Party days, the spirit of heroism reawakens in him; he abandons his flight to America and instead throws in his lot with the anti-Nazi forces.

The chief conflict in this novel is that in Peter's mind between the psychoanalytic explanation of his complex, which seeks only to "adjust" him to a life of personal pleasure, and the radical-liberal ideal, which reawakens in him at the end of the novel.

Bertolt Brecht (German, 1898-1956)

In a very amusing book of popular circulation in London (and, incidentally, highly informative and reliable both in factual information and generally in critical evalution, allowing for satiric exaggeration), *Bluff Your Way in the Theatre* by Michael Turner (1967), the author's note at the beginning indicates a one, two, three, four star system of evaluation of dramatists, "stingy" in the award of ratings "in the hope of stimulating competition and raising fashionable standards." One and two are "of modest pretentions" and "quite fashionable;" three, "really important, copper-bottom cult names that can be relied upon to create an ambience of confidence about the bluffer in any group of people"—including of those in this book Ibsen, Shaw, Strindberg, Anouilh, Sartre, Pirandello, Ionesco, Behan, Pinter—(Shakespeare is also placed in this category). There is only one four-star rating, Bertolt Brecht. Of course this is a British view, with rather gentle satire directed at fashionable snobbism. But there is a residue of serious evaluation.

Robert Brustein in *The Theatre of Revolt* (1964) discusses modern drama with relatively equal attention to Ibsen, Strindberg, Chekhov, Shaw, Brecht, Pirandello, O'Neill, and Genet. Brecht, whom he calls "the most enigmatic—at once both direct and hidden, at once both simple and complex," is related to Shaw, as another Marxist dramatist. "Both support a 'non-Aristotelian' theatre, characterized not by cathartic emotional effects but by preachment, protest, and persuasion." But whereas Shaw's work is modified by a genial character and a melioristic social philosophy, Brecht's revolt "is intensified by his savage indignation and his harrowing

vision of life." Two other "propagandists" for Bertolt Brecht are
Martin Esslin and Eric Bentley, both formidable and persuasive.
One can easily see some of the techniques of Brecht's Epic Theatre
and Alienation-effects in a good deal of modern drama from about
1940 on, from Thornton Wilder to Friedrich Dürrenmatt. And
Brecht plays can be given effective theatrical production, *The Threepenny Opera* and the *Rise and Fall of the City of Mahagonny* with
Kurt Weill's music, and recent productions of *Galileo* in London
and Dublin.

The cult of Brecht produces passions for and against him. His
early work (1918-1927 ca.) is viewed as primarily expressionistic
(influence of Wedekind, Toller, Kaiser), the second period until
1938 or thereabouts primarily didactic and propaganistic (Epic
Theatre) after his conversion to communism and to his own evolving dramatic theories, the third (1938-1947) a period of exile first
in Scandanavia, then in the United States, when wrote his greatest
plays, including *Mother Courage, The Good Woman of Setzuan,
The Life of Galileo,* and *The Caucasian Chalk Circle,* and the
fourth (1947-1956) of disappointing production as a playwright
(he wrote quite good lyric poetry in both the first and fourth periods)
but of significant work as a director of his own theatre in East
Germany, the Berliner Ensemble, which had extraordinary success
on tours to Paris and London and continued to do so in the sixties
under the leadership of his widow, Helene Weigel.

Brecht's basic ideas and repeated themes are three, according
to Turner as guide: "1) The poor are *basically* good in their
earthy vulgarity; the rich are inevitably corrupt and decadent;
2) Goodness in this criminal world is suicidal: to exist, man has
always to compromise and at the very least accept expedients, to
succeed he must outcheat the rest; and 3) Each person has two sides,
good and evil."

Brecht, who wanted more than anything to instruct and influence the masses, has come to have his primary appeal to the intellectuals. The Epic Theatre, or "non-dramatic drama," he advocated
(no relation to epic as traditionally interpreted, really rather
episodic), appealing to reason instead of emotions, didactic theatre,
didn't work that way; his "pupils" never came to his plays, or if

they did, they left. His principal theatrical theory, the "V-Effekt" (Verfremdungseffekt), translated as "A" or Alienation-Effect, a distancing by constant reminders that one is in a theatre to avoid the illusionism and emotionalism of realistic, naturalistic, or romantic drama (a spectator should think, analyze, be critical rather than feel), with acting that breaks up empathy, has resulted in such plays as *Mother Courage* "which involved the spectator immediately." As a communist who didn't always see or toe the party line he embarrassed the Party, but not enough to make him sympathetic to the other side. Of such are the ironies of the career of Bertolt Brecht.

LIFE: Born in Augsburg, the chief town of Bavaria in southern Germany, in 1898, the son of middle-class and prosperous parents, a Catholic father with a paper mill and a Protestant mother, Eugen Berthold Friedrich Brecht was christened in his mother's Lutheran church (Brustein says, paraphrasing Joyce, that he had "the cursed Lutheran strain in him, injected the wrong way"). Old enough to experience the stupidities of the First World War (and to protest in a pacifist school essay) Brecht left the *gymnasium* in 1916 and went to Munich to study medicine, soon drafted as a medical orderly in a military hospital: "if the doctor ordered me: 'Amputate a leg, Brecht!' I would answer: 'Yes, Your Excellency!' and cut off the leg." In November of 1918 Brecht was part of a two-day Communist Revolution in Bavaria, a member of the Augsburg Revolutionary Committee, but he escaped detection. His first play, *Baal,* written as an angry response to a play by Hanns Johst (later a leading Nazi poet) launched Brecht into a series of plays from 1918 to 1927, some worked on with the help of Lion Feuchtwanger, an already established author, including the first to be performed *Trommeln in der Nacht (Drums in the Night),* and *Im Dickicht der Städte (In the Jungle of Cities),* a play set in a Chicago that Brecht could have known only from movies and Upton Sinclair's *The Jungle.* His first collection of poetry was published in 1927 as *Bertolt Brechts Hauspostille (The Domestic Breviary),* called by one critic "the devil's prayer book" and containing in ballad forms "putrefying corpses, drowned girls, dead soldiers, and murdered infants," as in "The Ballad of Marie Farrar, Infanticide." It also included a moving autobiographical poem, "Concerning Poor B. B."

His first major success came with *Die Dreigroschenoper (The Threepenny Opera)* with music by Kurt Weill in 1928, a "steal" from John Gay's *The Beggar's Opera* of exactly two hundred years before, but with modern relevancies and a hit song. "The Ballad of Mack the Knife." Another collaboration with Kurt Weill, *Aufstieg und Fall der Stadt Mahagonny (Rise and Fall of the City of Mahagonny)* written shortly thereafter and much more original has achieved subsequent popularity (in the sixties). Together they are Brecht's best "musicals," and excellent recordings are available. In Berlin from 1924 to 1933 the playwright, as an active communist from about 1930, ran into increasing problems with the growing Hitler power and fled to Vienna on the day after the Reichstag fire, sought sanctuary elsewhere in Europe, and ended up temporarily in Denmark to continue the fight against Fascism. His writings, more propagandistic and even journalistic, were less artistic. From Denmark in 1939 he went to Sweden, to Finland, and finally to America in 1941 via the Siberian Express to Vladivostok in a last minute escape and a Swedish ship to San Pedro, California. He lived on the edge of Hollywood and continued writing the great plays, begun with *Mutter Courage und Ihre Kinder (Mother Courage and Her Children)* written in 1939 in Sweden, *Leben des Galilei (Galileo)* of the same period, *Der Gute Mensch von Sezuan (The Good Woman of Setzuan)* finished in 1940, continuing with *Die Gesichte der Simone Machard (The Visions of Simone Machard)* in collaboration with Lion Feuchtwanger, 1941-43, and *Der Kaukasische Kreidekreis (The Caucasian Chalk Circle)* in 1944-45.

Never much at home in the United States, living with a group of German émigrés, Brecht was summoned in September of 1947 to appear before the Committee on Un-American Activities and did so appear in Washington at the end of October. He completely confused the committee by adroit lying, received their thanks, and with the airline reservation in his pocket went to New York and left almost at once for Europe. By the end of 1948 Brecht arrived via Zurich and Prague in the eastern sector of Berlin, went into re-hearsals with his wife Helene Weigel to play Mother Courage under his direction. The opening in January 1949 was the real beginning of the Berliner Ensemble. Brecht went back to Zurich and took some time to make up his mind about permanent residence in East Berlin, not minimizing the problems but ultimately deciding to go ahead. As Martin Esslin has said, in the course of his life he "was deeply involved in the experience of his epoch:" two World Wars, Nazi persecution, political exile, involvement with the Soviet Union alternately warm and cold, a victim of the American anti-Communist witchhunt of the forties, and wrangling in East Berlin during his last years about films and plays and censorship, even suppression. He died of a coronary in August 1956 after fatigue from theatre rehearsals.

CHIEF PLAYS: *Die Dreigroschenoper* (*The Threepenny Opera,* 1928) is a lively redoing of John Gay's *The Beggar's Opera* (1728) with yeoman assistance from Kurt Weill's music and staging suggestions, placards, non-realistic acting—breaking character to address the audience, and screen projections. Set in late-Victorian London, the story and characters remain much the same as in Gay: Mackie Messer or Mack the Knife Macheath marries Polly Peachum, daughter of a receiver of stolen goods and gang-leader of professional "beggars," but is betrayed to the authorities by the other women he has deserted. The chief of police, Tiger Brown, a former buddy in the Indian Army, winks at his escape with the help of own daughter, Lucy Brown, another of Mack's loves. But back at the brothel he is arrested again, saved at the scaffold by the queen's pardon because this is an opera, not real life. The criminals are all good middle-class citizens with normal tastes and morality; their wickedness is nothing compared to what goes on in "respectable" society. In good cynical tone, "what is robbing a bank compared to founding a bank?"

Aufstieg und Fall der Stadt Mahagonny (Rise and Fall of the City of Mahagonny; opera with Kurt Weill, 1930) takes place in a fictional American city that seems to be either in Florida or on the California coast and at the same time near the "gold fields of the north," founded by a bunch of crooks, led by the widow Leocadia Begbick in a gambling canteen operation to get the gold from those who dig the gold, a laissez-faire business operation. Four men arrive, Paul, Heinrich, Jakob, and Joe; an approaching hurricane causes the abolition of all restrictions; the city riots itself to pieces. The glutton Jakob eats himself to death; the boxer Joe is killed in a fight. Paul, who had found love with the prostitute Jenny, spends all his money and runs up debts. He is arrested on a number of charges, acquitted on all counts save one: he is sentenced to death for the greatest crime, lack of money. Some of the songs are brilliant examples of parody and satire, the sweetest melodies covering scabrous lyrics. The hurricane music is dramatically most effective.

Mutter Courage und Ihre Kinder (*Mother Courage and Her Children;* play, 1939) is considered by three out of five Brechtians to be the master's masterpiece. "A Chronicle of the Thirty Years' War," it takes place in Sweden, Poland, and Germany in twelve scenes from 1624 to 1636, but it's about all wars and human accommodation to them, particularly in economic terms. The main character, Mother Courage, is a tough old canteen woman who trails after the mercenary armies of the war, really whichever side is winning or promises the better business. She has three children, each by a different father: Eilif who is strong and brave, Schweizerkas ("Swiss Cheese") who is slow and honest, and a daughter Katrin who has been dumb (mute, that is) and mentally retarded since childhood. She loses all her children in the course of the play but clings materialistically to her job and livelihood because it's the only life she knows. The play turns out to be deeply felt and moving.

"Swiss Cheese" is the first to go. Having become paymaster in a Protestant Swedish regiment, he is captured by the Catholics but too honest to surrender up the cashbox and while his mother haggles about selling her wagon to buy his safety, he is riddled by eleven bullets (like a Swiss Cheese) and his mother dares not even claim his body. Eilif has become a hero by requisitioning a herd of cattle during a siege; he does the same thing during a brief and uncertain armistice, only to be executed as a looter. Katrin, disfigured by the assaults of soldiers, overhears the plan to take the city of Halle; distressed by her feelings for the women and children of the town, she gives the alarm by drumming on a rooftop as soldiers shoot her down. Once again Mother Courage has been haggling, looking after profits. But with nothing left at the end she still drags her

wagon along—there'll be another war. The refrain of the march-
ing song is heard again: "Christians, awake! The winter's gone!/ The
snows depart. The dead sleep on./ And though you may not long
survive/ Get out of bed and look alive!"

Leben des Galilei (Galileo; play, 1938-39) was made into an
English version in collaboration with Charles Laughton in 1947 and
opened with Laughton in the title role in New York in December
of the same year. In 1609 the middle-aged Galileo, sensuous and not
very scrupulous, living with his daughter Virginia, his housekeeper
Mrs. Sarti, and her son Andrea, as a university lecturer in Padua,
claims to have invented the telescope which he copied from a Dutch
invention. He moves from the service of the Venetian state to
Florence. Having proved that the earth is not the center of the
universe, he is forbidden by papal authority to publish his findings.
Hoping for better things eight years later from a new enligtened
pope, Urban VIII, Galileo is disappointed when the Grand Inquisitor persuades the pope that church authority would be destroyed
by such discoveries.

In 1633 Galileo's pupils, including Andrea Sarti, are distressed
by the recantation under pressure of Galileo. Andrea cries to the
broken man of science, "Pity the country that has no heroes!"
Galileo answers, "No. Pity the country that needs heroes!" Years
later Galileo living with his nagging old-maid daughter whose fiancé
deserted her because of Galileo's views, receives a visit from Andrea
about to leave Italy for Holland. The old man gives him the completed manuscript of his Discourses to smuggle out of the country.
Andrea now sees his old teacher as a hero who recanted only to
finish his work, but Galileo sees himself as a coward setting a pattern for the future in allowing science to bow to authority. The
undercutting of the conventional picture of a hero and the presentation of intelligent, skilled, urbane churchmen in the opposition rather
than the usual villains only add to the human dimensions of a
highly effective and convincing drama. Comparison with another
play on the same subject, *Lamp at Midnight* by Barrie Stavis, which
Morris Carnovsky took on tour, shows the difference between a
reasonably good, sentimental, somewhat dull play and the power of
Brecht's vision.

Der Gute Mensch von Sezuan (*The Good Woman of Setzuan;* play, 1940) is a parable play set in modern China. (The use of parable in Brecht is comparable to its use by Lagerkvist and Kafka and Borges.) The main character, Shen Te, a warm-hearted prostitute, is the only human being to offer shelter to the disguised gods who come to earth looking for one good person so that the world can be saved. Rewarded with money to buy a tobacco shop Shen Te is deluged in her fortune by parasites, poor "relatives," debtors; she is forced to assume a disguise of her own as Shui Ta, a ruthless and imaginary male cousin, in order to survive. The young "man" brutally drives the spongers away.

Shen Te meets and falls in love with a young airman, Yang Sun; but Shui Ta finds out after she is pregnant that he was only after her money. Having lost her fiancé, Shen Te is about to lose her shop and worries about the unborn baby. Shui Ta comes back and says his cousin is away on a journey; he restores her fortunes with a tobacco factory, hiring Yang as a foreman because he is ruthless enough to exploit the workers. In Shen Te's long absence Shui Ta is arrested and accused of murdering her; the gods come down as judges. Shui Ta reveals that he is Shen Te in disguise: the good cannot live in our world by remaining good. The gods are glad that Shen Te is still alive, but foolish as they are can offer no help with her problem, floating away to heaven and leaving her to manage as best she can.

Der Kaukasische Kreidekreis (*The Cascasian Chalk Circle;* play, 1945), based on an old Chinese play, is another parable. The problem in the prologue is who has the better right to the land in a portion of a fictional socialist country (similar to the Russian area of Georgia), the goat-breeding owners or the fruit farmers who would make it productive? The answer comes by means of retelling the old story of a child claimed by its real mother and by a foster mother, in this play a kitchen maid named Grusha. Solomon's judgment had discovered that the natural mother loved the child and wanted to spare it pain; Brecht reverses the parable—it is the foster mother who loves and refuses to hurt the child, the real mother wanting to use the child to establish legal claim to some property. The answer to the problem therefore is that the land should belong to those who love it rather than to "legal" proprietors. As Brustein noted, "Instead of catigating humanity, Brecht is beginning to celebrate it; instead of illustrating his themes through ironic comparisons, he is beginning to employ moral allegories and parables."

12. RELATIVISM AND EXISTENTIALISM

There are all manners of attacking organized society. The authors in the preceding section attacked it by proposing to substitute another and better organization in its place; another group of authors, a smaller but equally significant one, attacked it by suggesting that all doctrines are equally valid, that all beliefs and opinions are subjectively formed in the mind of the individual. This attitude is essentially one of emotional independence: it is the attitude of the detached mind which comprehends every system without making itself a part of any. Thus to the relativist truth ceases to be an absolute matter; it is a fleeting relationship which exists only for the individual who conceives it, and lasts only so long as the individual's situation remains constant.

This principle of philosophical relativism found its greatest expression in twentieth-century literature in the work of André Gide, who himself was greatly influenced by Montaigne and Goethe. The Existentialist Sartre, who shares the principle with certain modifications, dedives it from another source: the phenomenology of the German philosopher Heidegger and his school. Gide and the Existentialists share another idea: the principle that life is lived to its fullest only in intense activity—activity of as many diverse kinds as possible. To engage one's self in an intellectual movement, in a process, or in an emotional situation, to come to grips with life, is to live to the utmost —provided one does not throw himself into this engagement to the point where he becomes a fanatic or doctrinaire.

Thus the heroes of Gide, Sartre, and Camus are active beings who find the meaning of their lives in struggle, whether within themselves or without; they are individualists who are wary of parties, yet men of good will who strive on the side of humanity rather than with those who seek to enslave humanity for their private ends. The heroes of Gide and Sartre occasionally engage in "immoral" or "criminal" activities, but they do so in a manner that constiutes a personal

victory. This description also fits very well the characters of Unamuno, who was "existentialist" when Sartre was a child, and
Kazantzakis.

Pirandello differs in many respects from these authors. He shares
with them, however, the principle of relativism, which he carries to an
even more extreme degree. To Pirandello not only truth and virtue,
but all realities—character, incident, and even personal identity—are
matters of individual prejudice. Thus his plays and stories are fascinating experiments in appearance and reality; what seems real is only
apparent, and what seems apparent varies from person to person.
Pirandello has become the most important single influence (with
Kafka one should hasten to add) on the formation of the Theatre
of the Absurd.

André Gide (French, 1869-1951)

If Gide appears on first examination to be a complex author, it is partly
because he deliberately fostered this complexity in his own character.
He participated during his long career in a half-dozen literary movements; he has been variously described as a Puritan, a Neo-classicist,
a Satanist, a communist, an iconoclast, and an aesthete, and justifica-
tions for each of these labels can be found in his work. He himself
said on several occasions that he considered himself primarily a creative artist, yet he wrote in his memoirs that his life revolved around
the two poles of the *Bible* and the *Thousand and One Nights*. This
latter statement is revealing. Obviously there is a strong ethical element
in his work, but opposed to it there is an equally prominent interest in
aesthetic matters: sensual experience, enjoyment of beauty, and sensitivity to literary technique. It is not, however, as a novelistic technician
that Gide will be remembered. His style and construction are sometimes conventional, at least for the twentieth century, but his thought
is invariably striking. It is for his ideas rather than for his innovations
in technique that Gide must take his place in literary history.

Many of the great thinkers of our time seem concerned to resolve
the diversity of their ideas into a single credo or attitude; their lives
are devoted to a search for the truth. Gide does not believe there is
any one truth, and has no intention of trying to resolve his personal
diversities into a banal and monolithic dogma. Like Whitman and
Goethe, he contains multitudes, and he wishes to continue containing

them. He carries his relativism even into the realm of style; some of his works (e.g., *Les Cahiers d'André Walter, Les Nourritures terrestres*) are romantic and amorphous, while others *(La Portre étroite, Les Faux-Monnayeurs)* are rigidly economical, even laconic. Both as a literary technician and as a moralist Gide is a bundle of opposites, held together by their very antagonistic forces like the planets in a solar system.

LIFE: Gide's background was Protestant, bourgeois, and cultured. His father was a Sorbonne law professor; at the time of the author's birth the family lived in Paris. His boyhood was spent in a series of Paris houses and Norman châteaux, the latter the property of his mother's family. His very parentage was a conflict; his mother, a Catholic, shared an equal part in forming his character with his Provençal and Protestant father. Years later, reviewing Maurice Barrès' *Les Déracinés,* he demanded, "Born in Paris of a Uzès father and a Norman mother, where, M. Barrès, would you have me take root?"

Gide's education was sound and classical. He attended the Ecole Alsacienne, where he formed a friendship with Pierre Louys, and the Lycée Henri Quatre; he passed his baccalaureat in 1889. Throughout his carrer he retained the attitude, the love of erudition, of a classic scholar; he could read Greek and Latin easily, and was on comfortable terms with German, Italian, and English.

For a writer who was later to become famous as a moralist, his entry into literature was something of a feint. In 1891 he published *Les Cahiers d'André Walter (The Notebooks of André Walter),* a semi-autobiographical romance based on his relations with his cousin Madeleine Rondeaux. This work, emotional and heartfelt, was nevertheless marked by a certain amorphous immaturity. It did serve, however, to admit Gide into the world of fashionable letters. He soon became the intimate of Mallarmé, Paul Valéry, Heredia, and Henri de Régnier. In 1892 he published *Les Poésies d'André Walter,* a collection of lyrics in a half-Symbolist, half-Parnassian style.

Gide, however, was wary of attaching himself to any literary movement too long. He had extracted what he needed from the Symbolists; now he moved on. In 1895 he married Madeleine Rondeaux. In the following years he produced a set of allegories or parables which included *Les Nourritures terrestres* (translated as *Fruits of the Earth,* 1897), a key book among his early works; *Le Prométhée mal enchaîné*

(*Prometheus Ill-Bound,* 1899) and *Le Roi Candaule* (*King Candaule,* 1901). The first of his major novels appeared in 1902; it was *L'Immoraliste,* based partly on the experiences of his own marriage. Gide's personality and outlook were changing rapidly at this time. On a North African trip with P. A. Laurens in 1893-94 he had discovered, not only the vigorous sensuality of the tropical climate and the Arab personality, but an innate tendency toward homosexuality. The rest of his life was to find him in revolt against conventional morality. "In the name of what God, of what ideal, do you forbid me to live according to my nature?" he demanded in his memoirs.

Yet just as he had earlier declined to commit himself totally to Symbolism, he now declined to fling himself with utter abandon into hedonism. His Protestant upbringing, his basic reserve, and his affection for his wife were still part of his character; his inner conflict had only been set into relief. He now began to work out the basic relationships between the diversities of his character and to establish some sort of harmony between them. His moral evolution, and his literary development, were climaxed in his masterpiece, *Les Faux-Monnayeurs (The Counterfeiters),* which appeared in 1926. His political nature was also evolving; a brief flirtation with communism in the period 1933-36 and a disillusioning trip to the Soviet Union produced the bitterly critical *Retour de l'U.R.S.S.* (*Return from the U.S.S.R.,* 1936).

From 1909 to 1940 Gide participated in the *Nouvelle Revue Française,* a publishing venture which included a review and a book press and which published most of his own works. He spent the years of the German occupation in Southern France and Algiers; he wrote a subtle and apparently innocuous series of *Figaro* articles criticizing totalitarianism under the title "Interviews Imaginaires," and refused to have anything to do with the now collaborationist N.R.F. In 1947 he received an honorary degree from Oxford University, and in the same year he was awarded the Nobel Prize for Literature. He died in 1951, widely acclaimed as the greatest contemporary French writer. The very American critics who had deplored his "immorality" in the thirties were now eager to point to themselves as his discoverers.

CHIEF WORKS: The most important part of Gide's work is that which shows a moral or ethical tendency; and this ethic shows a developing pattern all through his career. The dominant theme of his work is a sort of dialectic activism, a struggle to maintain incompatibles in constant harmony in his personality. This idea appears in one of Gide's earliest works, the novel *l'Immoraliste* (*The Immoralist,* 1902). In this novel Michel, a young scholar of ascetic tastes, marries a young woman he scarcely knows and sets off on a North African honeymoon. He falls ill with tuberculosis, but Marceline, his wife, nurses him back to health. At Biskra he is fascinated with the happy amorality of the Arab children; and in Italy, moved by the violence of land, climate, and people, he consummates his marriage for the first time. But he has gained his health at the expense of Marceline's; in a sense he has extracted her vitality and used it to nourish himself. When Marceline dies Michel is torn with grief, but realizes he has achieved a wider life. He has discovered his true nature, and he has made himself into a vigorous physical being. He understands that his position is immoral according to ordinary standards; not only has he in a sense caused the death of his wife, but his erotic awakening has led him to the company of the Arab boys he maintains in his North African villa. Yet at the end he reflects to himself, "I feel nothing in myself that is not noble."

In *La Porte étroite* (translated as *Strait is the Gate;* novel, 1909) we see the other side of the medal; Gide presents the apotheosis, not of the vigorous hedonist, but of the ascetic who seeks death as a climax of her search for purity. Alissa, a quiet Protestant girl, discovers the infidelity of her mother and is torn with shame and grief. She rejects her lover Jerome, whom she sincerely loves, and attempts to join him to her sister Juliette; when this fails she understands that only through death can she avoid union with Jerome and preserve the purity of her ideal. She dies in a Paris sanatorium, leaving Jerome a cryptic journal which is the key to the novel. The title is derived from the Scriptures: "Enter ye in at the strait gate, for wide is the gate that leadeth unto destruction, and many there be that go in thereat; but strait is the gate that leadeth unto life, and few there be that find it." The gate is so narrow, in fact, that two cannot enter it together; Alissa must seek her consummation alone.

In *Les Caves du Vatican* (translated as *The Vatican Swindle* and as *Lafcadio's Adventures;* novel, 1914) Gide returns to the iconoclastic and amoral hero. Lafcadio Wluiki, the protagonist, is a fascinating youth reminiscent of the heroes of Stendhal. He punishes himself for acts of weakness by driving a penknife into his thigh, and he commits no act until he has convinced himself that it is absolutely unmotivated and useless. At one point he amuses himself by pitching a chance acquaintance out a train window to his death, and on another occasion he saves a young girl from a burning building merely in order to analyse his own sensations during an act of heroism. There is a connected plot in which a gang of conspirators convince certain pious Catholics that the Masons have kidnapped the Pope and are holding him captive in the Vatican cellars. An especially naive devoté, Amédée Fleurissoire, is seized with a fit of heroism and sets off alone to Rome to right matters; he is bitten by fleas, bilked by the criminals who have manipulated the conspiracy, and seduced by a cynical and derisory prostitute who has nevertheless a good heart. He presently begins to doubt whether anyone knows who the true Pope is; and he is led from this to wonder whether, when he arrives before the Throne of the Almighty, he will be able to tell God from the facsimile installed in his place by the Forces of Evil. In despair, he enters a railway carriage just in time to be flung out of the window by Lafcadio as a practical demonstration of the unmotivated act; and so his life is destroyed along with the faith. His brothers-in-law, the novelist Julius de Baraglioul (also half-brother to Lafcadio) and the scientist Anthime Armand-Dubois, are equally well drawn and illuminated by Gidian irony.

Les Faux-Monnayeurs (*The Counterfeiters;* novel, 1926) is the most important and the most complex of Gide's works; it should be read only after several of his earlier works have been digested. At the time he wrote this novel Gide was greatly interested in what he termed the *roman pur*—the pure, symmetrical, Neo-classic, and pared-down novel which derives from the tradition of *La Princesse de Clèves* and other works of the French golden age. He contrasted this tradition with the documentary technique of modern naturalism, which he considered was bogged down in meaningless detail.

If the style of the novel is simple, however, the plot is not. There is no one central character, unless it be Edouard, the novelist who, like Gide, is writing a novel called *Les Faux-Monnayeurs*. The principal characters are young men similar to Lafcadio, obsessed with the personal problem of free will and anxious to revolt against conventional morality. It is this desire for detachment—*déracinement* or uprooting—which leads his characters to steal, to commit sexual improprieties, and even to reject their families. Bernard, the most typical of these young men, writes in his notebook, "If not you, who will do it? If not now, when?" At the end of the novel Edouard offers him an even better motto: "One must always follow one's inclination—provided it leads upward." Gide wishes us to understand that "goals" are not ends in themselves, and that any activity or goal is useful only as it leads us to something higher and better.

The chief outward events of the complex plot are: the friendship of Edouard and Bernard, who becomes his secretary and disciple; the similar relations of Edouard's nephew Olivier with a notorious roué and amateur of letters, the Comte de Passavant, which end unsatisfactorily because of Passavant's affected and depraved personality; the efforts of a gang of counterfeiters to use certain of the young men in the novel as outlets for their false coins; and the bizarre suicide of Boris, grandson of an old friend of Edouard's, who becomes involved in a secret society of his schoolfellows and shoots himself in a classroom as part of a ritual. Long excerpts from Edouard's notebook are also included, most of them remarks on the technique of the novel and the theory of the *roman pur*. The dominant ideas of *Les Faux-Monnayeurs* are (1) that a full existence is achieved only through strenuous intellectual or moral activity; (2) that it is the duty of each human to seek out his own nature and follow it, no matter how immoral his actions may seem to society; and (3) that the counterfeit is often difficult to tell from the genuine, in life as in dealing with coins, or with novels.

Thésée (*Theseus;* novella, 1946), the last of Gide's major independent works, covers the same mythological ground as Mary Renault in her novel series; but Gide's Theseus as narrator of his own story is now an old man, not garrulous like Nestor but dry, succinct, ironic, intelligent, in the cloudless evening of his life. Almost cloudless, that is; he wanted to tell the story as a lesson for his son Hippolytus, but it's too late for that—*he* had been excessive in his devotion to Artemis and had paid for it with his life. Theseus, like Gide, looks back over his career with considerable satisfaction, particularly when it is contrasted with the career of Oedipus (about whom Gide had published a play in 1931). Somewhat skeptical about the legends that have grown up around the deeds of his youth, he still sees the value of "the image" and realizes that the most important thing for him was never to rest either in glory (overcoming Procrustes) or shame (abandoning Perigone or Ariadne) but to leave the past without regret, breaking free for the future. The adventure told with the fullest detail is, of course, that of the labyrinth in Crete, which ordeal is not one of endurance but of pleasure, therefore the more dangerous. The Minotaur, a sort of flower-decked Ferdinand the Bull, is lulled into passivity by the delights of golden sensuality. As Daedalus explains the only inescapable prison is one where the prisoner has no wish to escape. Theseus can beat this rap because he can say, as Gide wrote to Paul Valéry, "*Je n' ai jamais aimé la demeure, fut-ce au sein des délices.*" ("I have never liked to rest in one place, even in the bosom of delight.") This can be restlessness in youth or in maturity a sense of duty—in Theseus' case to the city of Athens and its welfare, in Gide's case to truth and humanism. Shortly after Gide's death all his work was placed on the Index by the Catholic church, which, as one critic has pointed out, was a last pleasure denied to him by dying too soon.

Jean-Paul Sartre (French, born 1905)

In the few years after the Liberation in 1945 Sartre found himself a famous man overnight. By 1950 a limited knowledge of the principles of Existentialism and a few of the epigrams of the master were an indispensable part of the equipment of every intellectual. But the limelight centered almost entirely on Sartre's philosophical position and on his personal life, and largely ignored his talent as a literary artist. The fact is that Sartre is chiefly a philosophical novelist rather than a philosopher; his philosophical principles are second-hand, but his fiction is powerful and effective. It is through his novels and plays that Sartre is likely to exert his widest influence.

Existentialism as it appears in Sartre's literature is a system based on the philosophies of Sören Kierkegaard (1813-55), Edmund Husserl (1859-1938), and Martin Heidegger (born 1889). Sartre does for these philosophers what Rousseau did for Locke: he organizes their system into a form comprehensible by the ordinary public and presents it in interesting and skillfully written literary works. The basic premise of this philosophy is the statement that "existence precedes essence," i.e., the total relativism of all sensation, experience, and morality. Most of what we ordinarily consider absolute principles are purely subjective in nature; they have been created synthetically by the human brain, and therefore may be altered or suspended at will. Human nature is one of these principles; Sartre holds that human nature is fixed only in the sense that men have agreed to recognize certain attributes of human nature; this nature may be changed if men merely agree on different attributes, or even if one man courageously acts in contradiction to the principles as ordinarily accepted. Thus Sartrian Existentialism is by nature (a) atheistic, since God is one of the subjective and synthetic concepts which men have contrived for their own convenience; (b) pessimistic, since man cannot hope for any surcease or aid outside himself; and (c) humanistic and progressive, since the possibilities of altering society and human nature for the better are unlimited.

From a literary point of view Sartre writes in the tradition of naturalism. He has been especially influenced by modern American naturalists; the mark of such novels as Dos Passos' *Manhattan Transfer* and Faulkner's *Light In August* is clearly apparent in his technique. His style is succinct, tight, and forceful; his concept of character is "hard," i.e., his characters are tough-minded and sophisticated persons who endeavor to conceal their weaker sentiments. In *Le Sursis (The Reprieve)* he attempts a complex pattern novel in which characters, incidents, and themes are tightly interwoven; this is his most radical technical experiment to date. Sartre resembles the naturalists as well in his taste for shocking and revolting detail; this is especially apparent in the drama *Les Mouches (The Flies)* and in his novels.

LIFE: Sartre was born in Paris in 1905. After finishing his lycée training he entered the École Normale Supérieure, where he encountered the philosopher "Alain" (Emile Chartier) and was led to an interest in the German phenomenologists. Upon the completion of his studies he served for many years as a lycée professor, first in Laon and Le Havre and finally at the Lycée Condorcet in Paris. Around 1936 he began to publish articles on psychology and philosophy in journals; his first literary work, the novel *La Nausée (Nausea),* appeared in 1938. The following year he published a volume of short stories, *Le Mur (The Wall);* this book earned him considerable celebrity in literary circles.

Drafted in 1939, Sartre was taken prisoner in June, 1940 and spent nine months in a German prison camp. Returned to civilian life, he recommenced teaching in 1941. During the Occupation he took an uncompromisingly anti-Nazi stand. His drama *Les Mouches* (1943) was a thinly-veiled allegory of the Occupation which somehow managed to escape suppression by the Nazis. With the Liberation in 1945 Sartre's works were soon translated; by 1948 a great cult of Sartrism had sprung up, with its headquarters in the Paris Café Flore. Sartre himself was finally forced to publish a formal repudiation of the fervent but misguided Bohemians who flocked around what they imagined to be his standard.

Sartre's chief philosophical statement, *L'Être et le néant (Being and Not-Being),* appeared in 1943; his major literary work, the novel series *Les Chemins de la Liberté (The Roads to Freedom),* began appearing in 1945. More plays followed, *Le Diable et le Bon Dieu* (translated as *Lucifer and the Lord,* 1951, and essentially a redoing of Goethe's *Götz von Berlichingen* in existential dress), *Kean* (an adaptation of an Alexander Dumas play, 1954), *Nekrassov* (Sartre's only attempt at comedy, a satire of fashionable anti-communists, 1955), and *Les Séquestrés d'Altona (The Condemed of Altona,* 1959, a powerful play on collective and individual war guilt in a German industrial family). Other writings have included a scenario, *L'Engrenage* (1962), *The Ghost of Stalin* (1968), and perhaps most importantly Sartre's defense and advocacy of Jean Genet published in 1963 as *Saint Genet, Actor and Martyr.*

In 1964 Sartre received the Nobel Prize for literature. In 1970 Janet Flanner in a "Letter from Paris" in the *New Yorker* pictured him as somewhat sad as an old liberal lost in the crowd, not recognized in various Paris assemblies by the young protesting students of a different generation of leftists. The gap is too great. His former associate and possible "mistress," Simone de Beauvoir, has written, besides *The Second Sex* (1952), a fascinating novel about the coterie at the Café Flore flocking around Sartre, called *The Mandarins* (1956).

CHIEF WORKS: *Les Mouches (The Flies;* drama, 1943) is an adaptation of the classic Electra myth as found in Sophocles. Orestes returns to his boyhood home of Argos, where his mother murdered his father a generation before; he finds the city writhing under a sense of guilt. The air is thick with flies, symbols of the guilt which has lain over the city since the murder of Agamemnon. The day of Orestes' arrival is a holiday; once a year the stone which seals the common burial-place is rolled away, and the dead come forth to live with their terrified families for twenty-four hours. The citizens are maintained in their miserable state by their priests and by Aegisthus, who finds the general neurosis useful in preventing revolt.

At first Orestes is loath to take action against this infamy; he has been educated along intellectual lines, and his personality is contemplative rather than active. Encouraged by Electra, he comes to believe that he can change his character by a mere act of will (i.e., he becomes an Existentialist). He strikes down Aegisthus and Clytemnestra and flees with Electra to the temple of Apollo. There the Erinyes, symbols of human conscience, begin to torment the pair with gory details of the matricide. Electra weakens and seeks absolution from Jupiter (symbol of Christian expiation), but Orestes refuses to repudiate his act through contrition. He assumes all the guilt for the crime himself; he declares his independence of any divine moral jurisdiction and his loyalty to the exacting and relentless inner moral law. Then he deliberately flees the city, drawing after him the Erinyes so that they will no longer torment the citizens of Argos.

Although this drama is primarily a statement of philosophical ethics, it was commonly interpreted, and intended, at the time of its original production as an allegory of the defeat of France. The French, blaming themselves for the downfall of their nation, relapse into an orgy of self-abasement. Orestes, symbol of the French intellectual class, is at first detached and impotent; later he realizes that each citizen must seize his personal guilt and struggle against it if France is to be freed from the "flies"—the Nazis and collaborationist officials. (N.B., "*mouche*" is a slang term for "police spy.")

Huis Clos (translated as *No Exit;* drama, 1944) is a one-act play utilizing only four characters. Garcin, a Latin-American revolutionist, finds himself shown into a bare hotel room by a non-committal servant, and realizes he has died and gone to Hell. Stoically awaiting tortures, he is surprised to find he is merely required to wait in the room for the rest of eternity. He is presently joined by two women, Estelle and Ines. Gradually the three come to realize they have been committed to Hell because they tortured other people while they were alive. They realize as well that the most exquisite punishment has been designed for them: they must remain together for eternity, each knowing the debasement and perfidy of the other two. Even suicide is denied them, since they are already dead. Garcin in particular is tormented by the memory of his final hours on earth. Shot as a pacifist, he conceived of his execution as a martyr's sacrifice; now he begins to wonder whether it was not an act of cowardice committed to escape military service. He eventually realizes that the question of whether he was a coward during his lifetime must be judged solely on the basis of the actions he performed, not on his "intentions" or attitudes.

L'Age de Raison (*The Age of Reason;* novel, 1945) is the first volume of a multi-volume novel series entitled *Les Chemins de la Liberté (The Roads to Freedom)*. The action takes place in Paris at the time of the Spanish Civil War. Mathieu Delarue, a lycée professor, needs a large sum of money for an abortion for his mistress Marcelle, even though he is growing bored with her. At the same time he is attracted to Ivich, a young Russian Sorbonne student. Ivich is concerned about her coming baccalaureate examinations; she is sure she is going to flunk. Her brother Boris, like Mathieu, is growing weary of his mistress, a singer named Lola. Daniel, a young homosexual, has been unable to come to terms with his aberration; he cannot accept his abnormality, neither can he integrate himself with society as a normal individual. In short each of the major characters of the novel is bored with life and finds himself in the grip of forces over which he has no control. Mathieu goes to Daniel to borrow the needed money; Daniel refuses, but begins to feel sympathy for Marcelle.

The climax of the novel comes when the major characters get drunk together at a cabaret. Ivich cuts her hand with a knife out of sheer bravado, and Mathieu, irked at being put to shame by a person of her youth, promptly pins his own hand to the table with the same knife. Now that his Existential Rubicon has been crossed, he abandons all scruples; he steals the needed money from Lola and gives it to Marcelle. But Daniel, suddenly filled with a desire to engage himself through some overt act, determines to marry Marcelle; he returns the money to Lola. Mathieu's second gesture of revolt—the theft—has been useless, yet it has served to break the inertia in which he was trapped. He realizes he has reached the "age of reason."

Le Sursis (*The Reprieve;* novel, 1945), the second volume of the *Chemins de la Liberté* series, covers a period of eight days in September of 1938, the time of the Munich Conference. As France mobilizes for the impending war each of the characters passes through an emotional trial. Mathieu convinces himself he is helpless in the face of mobilization and allows himself to be drafted "like a sheep"; Ivich, having failed her examination, ignominiously returns to her parents at Laon, where she is desperately bored; Boris is undecided whether his first loyalty is toward his nation or toward his mistress. Other minor characters—an illiterate Midi shepherd, a bedridden invalid evacuated from eastern France, a pacifistic youth rebelling against his general father—are included to provide a wider cross-section. The technique of this novel is more radical than that of *L'Age de Raison;* the narrative skips rapidly from one character to another, and snatches of documentary material are included as in Dos Passos' *U.S.A.*

The third volume, *La Mort dans l'Âme* (translated as *Troubled Sleep;* novel, 1949) transpires at the time of the Fall of France in May, 1940. Gomez, a Spanish general and friend of Mathieu, has escaped to America; he takes a bitter satisfaction in comparing the Fall of France to the defeat of Spain in 1938, when French liberals failed to aid the Loyalist cause. Boris, wounded in action, is evacuated to the rear; he is in doubt whether to escape to England to continue the fight or to remain with Lola and take a petty job as a schoolteacher. Brunet, a communist writer, is captured by the Germans. He attempts to set up a Party cell in his prison stockade, but soon realizes that the authority and organization of the Party are no longer there to aid him. He watches in astonishment as the "men of good will" among the prisoners regroup to struggle against their captors without the aid of the Party he has hitherto considered the only effective weapon against fascism. Mathieu, a soldier in a rear-echelon group, takes no part in the battle for France. The day before the armistice is to be signed, however, he becomes infuriated at his own sense of helplessness and joins a platoon of combat troops who are about to put up a last ditch fight against the occupation of a small town. Hidden in a belfry, he fires away madly at the Germans until his post is wrecked by grenades, and with every shot his new sense of freedom increases. At last he has taken action against the forces which seek to enslave him.

Albert Camus (French, 1913-1960)

Although Camus is neither a philosopher nor an "official" member of the Existentialist cénacle, he is basically an Existentialist; he views the causation of human destiny as unknowable and probably irrational, and sees little hope that man will ever resolve the chaos which surrounds him into any permanent system of absolutes. But there is a positive optimism in Camus lacking in Sartre. He argues, not only that active struggle is the only justifiable course open to the man tormented by destiny, but that this struggle is in itself a retort of a sort—that man wins the victory merely by refusing to capitulate. In addition he stresses that cooperation in group action is a sort of salvation; the sum of mankind is greater than the sum of individual men, and the individual faced with disaster can do best by placing his loyalty at the service of the group. In some respects this last attitude somewhat resembles the Marxist line toward social action as it appears in, for example, André Malraux.

As a novelist Camus, like Sartre, writes in the style of mid-century naturalism; the influence of American naturalists is apparent. His novels are full of detail some readers will find unpleasant or even repellent. Yet the final message of his novels is usually an idealistic one; the impression carried away by the reader is a sort of Aristotelian catharsis. Camus is skillful at contriving symbolic situations or allegories—e.g., the opera performance in *La Peste* in which the tenor falls dead of the plague while singing an aria from Gluck's *Orpheus*.

LIFE: Albert Camus was born in 1913 in Algiers, and remained in French North Africa up to the time of the Fall of France in 1940. His first two novels are both laid in Algerian settings. He began writing in 1938 with *Noces (Wedding Feasts),* a book of essays and Algerian local color. In 1940 he went to France, where he was active during the rest of the war in the underground; he helped run a widely-circulated underground newspaper, *Combat,* and published several personal propaganda pieces. In 1942 appeared *L'Etranger (The Stranger),* which drew considerable notice after the liberation of France made it available to the outside world. A longer novel, *La Peste (The Plague)* appeared in 1947, after the publication of *Le Mythe de Sisyphe, Essai sur l'Absurde (The Myth of Sisyphus, Essay on the Absurd,* 1942).

Camus was also interested in the drama as a third medium of expression. Two plays, *Le Malentendu (The Misunderstanding)* and *Caligula,* were written in 1943 and 1938, produced in 1944 and 1945 respectively, and published together in 1945. Other plays, *L'Etat de Siège* (thought to be based on *La Peste*) and *Les Justes,* were produced and published in 1948 and 1950. He adapted Faulkner's *Requiem for a Nun* for the French stage in 1956. His last work before his death was a four-hour stage adaptation of Dostoevsky's *The Possessed.*

A turning point for Camus seems to be represented by the essay, *L'Homme Révolté* (1951). After a few years of relative inactivity there is a shift in technique and approach for Camus. If Kafka and Kierkegaard exercised a major influence on *The Stranger* and *The Myth of Sisyphus* with accent on the absurd and the existential, Martin du Gard (for whose complete works Camus wrote an important preface for 1955 publication) and Tolstoy seem to be new influences toward attempts to understand rather than simply protest life itself. The appearance of the novel *La Chute (The Fall)* in 1956 marked clearly new directions in Camus' thought. In 1957 he was awarded the Nobel Prize for literature and had taken the place of Gide as France's greatest living writer. The publication of *L'Exil et le Royaume (Exile and the Kingdom,* stories written between 1953 and 1957) in 1957 continued the promised fulfillment. But on January 4, 1960, Albert Camus was killed in the crash of a sports car near Sens, seventy-five miles southeast of Paris. The driver, Michel Gallimard (of the publishing family) and his wife and daughter were injured. The car, traveling at 80 miles an hour on a national highway, had blown out a left rear tire and was thoroughly demolished. The death of Camus at forty-six was viewed as existentially absurd, and lamented by such prominent people as Francois Mauriac and Jean-Paul Sartre. Camus left a wife and a son and daughter.

CHIEF WORKS: *L'Etranger (The Stranger,* or *The Outsider;* novel, 1942) is about one existential man, a stranger in the universe, named Meursault, indifferent to everything except physical sensations. News of his mother's death brings no reaction except faint annoyance at having to ask leave from work. At the funeral he feels only physical discomfort and inconvenience, no sadness or regret. The day after the funeral he goes swimming, meets a girl, takes her to a comic movie and then to bed, showing no more feeling or affection for her than for his mother. At the end of a series of accidents or incidents he finds himself with a revolver in his hand one day facing a threatening Arab with a knife. Almost unconscious in the blazing Algerian sun he shoots the Arab several times. At the trial he never thinks of pleading self-defense and expresses no feelings of remorse or guilt. What really convicts him is evidence of insensitivity at his mother's funeral. The chaplain's prayers elicit a final violent reaction from Meursault, an affirmation that this life is all there is, that he had been happy in it, and that the world is tenderly and completely indifferent. He hopes for a crowd of many people shouting cries of hatred at his execution.

La Peste (*The Plague;* novel, 1947) is a political and social allegory laid in the modern Algerian seaport of Oran. After a number of unusual deaths occur, the authorities realize that bubonic plague is attacking the city. A physician, Bernard Rieux, is one of the first to recognize the epidemic. The novel follows Rieux, his friend Tarrou, the journalist Rambert, the priest Paneloux, and several lesser friends through the ordeal, which lasts for eight months. The city, isolated, becomes a sort of microcosm of modern society. Rieux labors valiantly against the disease; when it finally dies out he realizes he knows no more about plague than when he began, but feels the struggle has been worthwhile. Rambert, a somewhat superficial young Paris reporter, is trapped in the quarantine and wants only to get back to his mistress in France. He employs some Spanish underworld characters who promise to help him escape from the city, but at the last moment he feels a courageous bond of kinship with his fellow men in Oran. He abandons his escape attempt and throws in his lot with Rieux and Tarrou, who have formed an auxiliary volunteer group. Tarrou, the spokesman of Camus' Existentialist ethic, argues throughout the novel for "beginning again from zero," i.e., that in a time of catastrophe each individual must recommence his life from the point where he stands instead of brooding over "what might have been." Tarrou dies as the plague ends, as does Paneloux. The plague may be considered a symbol of any of the present-day evils against which men of good will must band together; Nazism and other forms of fascism are usually cited as the evil which Camus had specifically in mind.

La Chute (*The Fall;* novel, 1956) is called a *récit* by Camus as is *The Stranger* (*The Plague* had been called a *Chronique*). The narrator and main character is Jean-Baptiste Clamence, who describes himself as a judge-penitent. The entire novel is a prose dramatic monologue with appropriate pauses where the listener (who may be the author, or the reader) apparently says something, as in Browning's "My Last Duchess." The setting is Amsterdam, at or below sea-level, mostly in a sailor's bar named *Mexico City* and later the narrator's room. The city with its concentric canals and mists is somewhat like Dante's Inferno, deliberately a jumping-off place on the edge of Europe; and the time is post World War II. Clamence is a compulsive story-teller and seizes upon his listener in an Ancient Mariner or Captain Marlow fashion. The guilt he worries about is like that of a Kafka character, but his mind is French and clear and analytical. In his past life in Paris a successful lawyer, courteous, humane, full of self-esteem, as naturally successful with women as Felix Krull, privately libertine but immune to judgment—a thoroughly Modern Man—he fails to respond to an inarticulate call for help when he passes late at night a woman who jumps into the Seine at the Pont Royal. From that moment on his life is increasingly troubled and goes to pieces as he hears laughter behind him. That is his fall. There is also the fall of civilization under Hitler's power and the general fall of modern man for whom the cynical narrator says history will find one sentence sufficient: "he fornicated and read the papers."

There are scriptural references throughout as a framework and they are used to point up irony in this ambiguous work: Eden and Adam's fall, the Sadducee, Jean-Baptiste, the irony of Christ's saying, "Thou art Peter, and upon this rock I will build my church," in the context of coward Peter's unrocklike triple denial, and the "Just Judges" panel from the Van Eyck altarpiece "The Adoration of the Lamb"—it is not a quetsion of "Judge not least ye be judged," but rather since you are judged you must judge others to bear you company. The listener is gradually pulled into confidence with the revelation that Clamence is harboring the stolen Van Eyck panel, and hopefully the confession of complicity, from being addressed as "Monsieur et cher compatriote" to "Mon cher" and finally "cher maitre," for who is innocent? Jean-Baptiste, that voice crying in the wilderness, ultimately confesses more, "I must be higher than you, and my thoughts lift me up. Such nights, or such mornings rather (for the fall occurs at dawn), I go out and walk briskly along the canals." He has no friends now, only accomplices. This novel in a sense quotes Eliot who quotes Baudelaire, "You! hypocrite lecteur! mon semblable, mon frere!" (You! hypocritical reader, like me, my brother!)

L'Exile et le Royaume (*Exile and the Kingdom;* short stories, 1957) is made up of six stories with a thematic thread running through them. The first four take place in North Africa, the fifth in Paris, the last in Brazil. All have the theme of exile and a character who tries to find some kind of home. The first, "The Adulterous Woman," is unique in Camus' fiction in having a woman, Janine, for a protagonist. She feels sympathy for the Arabs (her husband is a cloth merchant) who are "poverty-stricken but free lords of a strange kingdom." One night she steals from her husband's bed and alone in the desert night is "opened to the tender indifference of the world," achiving a relationship with the earth and stars that her husband could never understand, which is why she tells him, "It's nothing, dear, nothing at all." "The Renegade" is a rather horrible story of a violently devoted Christian missionary who, after torture, becomes equally devoted to a heathen idol fetish and shoots his replacement; the effect is not unlike Conrad's *Heart of Darkness*. "The Silent Men" is about the return to work of laborers in a disappearing trade, barrel making, after a strike and the impossibility of communication of sympathy with the owner when his daughter falls seriously ill. In "The Guest" we have Daru, a French schoolmaster born in Algeria—anywhere else he feels "in exile"— who is forced into handing on an Arab prisoner after extending hospitality for the night. He refuses to do so, but his gesture is misunderstood and he is made to feel guilty. The Paris story, "The Artist at Work," is about a talented painter, Gilbert Jonas, who gives hostages to fortune in the acquisition of wife, children, friends, disciples, hangers-on and, in his generosity, is forced into a corner where he can no longer paint. This, too, is "The Death of a Lion" as in the Henry James' story; but Jonas leaves a single message for mankind, somewhat ambiguous, either the word *solidaire* or *solitaire*—and so the artist must find a mean between the impossible oppositions of artistic solitude and political solidarity.

The last story, "The Growing Stone," may be the most enigmatic of them all. A French engineer, D'Arrast, arrives in the small Brazilian town of Iguape to help them build a dam. He has left the "shame and anger" of Europe but finds it hard to adjust to primitive life. He does make a strange friendship with a native who has made a vow to Christ to carry a heavy stone on his head all the way to church on a local saint's day. When the native, after dissipation in dance celebration, falls down under the weight, D'Arrast carries the stone to the family hut where, because of his gesture, he is invited to sit down with them. He has at last found a place where he can belong, even in a land of superstition and miracle.

Luigi Pirandello (Italian, 1867-1936)

Pirandello began his literary career as a Sicilian folklorist and short-story writer. His early work (1894-1915) is marked by a dry and penetrating naturalism, a strong peasant sense of humor, and a skepticism toward social conventions. Gradually he began to work out a more original technique and content, and during the period of the First World War he began to write the remarkable dramas which have earned him his main fame.

Pirandello, through his contact with the literary school of Futurism and with modern pragmatic philosophy, became by 1916 a thorough-going relativist. In his mature period he not only believes that all moral positions are equally valid and depend merely on the individual vantage point, but he questions the very existence of reality as a rational substance. To Pirandello life consists merely of a succession of illusions, which put together constitute what the ordinary person terms "the truth." Reality and appearance are forever contrasted in his drama, and under close comparison the "real" frequently vanishes and leaves only illusion in its place. Where Bernard Shaw customarily begins a play with the characters in a highly romantic or emotional state and then demonstrates their progress toward rationality, Pirandello reverses the process: When his plays begin the characters are confident of the pillars upon which they have constructed their lives, but at the end this support has been destroyed for them.

To Pirandello one of the most important manifestations of this dualism is the contrast between the illusion of the theatre and the reality of actual life. Faithful to his doctrine, he believes the illusion of the theatre to be at least as "real" as life, and probably more so. In *Six Characters in Search of an Author* the line between theatre and life disappears completely; in the end it is the "real" actors who seem intangible and the fictional characters who wander onto the set real. Thus Pirandello is an idealist to the extent that he believes creations of the mind partake of a more valid existence than palpable physical objects. Two other plays about theatre (Pirandello called them "something of a trilogy of the theatre in the theatre") which pursue such illusions futrther are *Each in His Own Way* (1924) and *Tonight We Improvise* (1930). The latter, with a production by the Living Theatre, has had a strong influence on the Happening as a development of drama in the sixties.

Pirandello's avowed aim is to create an intellectual drama. By this, however, he does not mean a mere drama of ideas in which various characters debate their respective points of view before the audience. His real intent is to create a theatre in which characters come into conflict because they hold mutually incompatible ideas; this is to be contrasted with the nineteenth-century theatre in which characters conflict through a clash of emotions or passions.

Another characteristic of Pirandello's work is the abandonment of the conventions of respectable society. In his dramas daughters do not necessarily love their mothers, the villain is not always punished, and husbands often strive to unite wives with lovers; there is little of the cult of romantic love, and no respect at all for the integrity of the family. A total skeptic, Pirandello believes there are as many moralities as there are persons. He is skillful enough to be able to make his dramatic paradoxes seem plausible; thus the reader or spectator often comes away with a confused impression that the worlo has been turned topsy-turvy, and that no convention, virtue, or truth is any longer to be relied upon. Not only is this an excellent dramatic device, but it also stimulates the audience to examine convictions which have lain, unconsidered and rusty, in their minds for a lifetime.

LIFE: Luigi Pirandello was born in the Sicilian town of Girgenti in 1867; his father was a wealthy mine owner. Luigi was educated in Sicilian schools, then sent to the University of Rome, where he quarreled with his professors and questioned everything in sight. In Rome, however, he was stimulated to take an interest in Sicilian folklore, which he had before taken for granted. In 1888 he went to Germany to work in the University of Bonn, where he wrote a doctoral dissertation on the linguistics of the Girgenti dialect. Returning to Italy, he began writing fiction around 1893; his first collection of stories, *Amori senza Amore* (roughly *Passion Without Love*) appeared the following year. His best Sicilian folk-tales appeared in the period from 1894 to 1915. In the latter year his first play, *Se non così (If Not Thus)* was published, and for the twenty years that followed he applied himself chiefly to the drama. He published, however, a number of novels, the most important of which was *I Vecchi e I Giovani* (*The Old and the Young;* 1913), a political tragedy in a Sicilian setting.

In 1904-05 Pirandello suffered a personal tragedy; his wife of ten years lost her reason and continued insane up to her death in 1918. For Pirandello these early years were marked by poverty and by the apathy of the Italian public toward his work. After the war, however, he began to enjoy increasing success, which culminated in 1934 when he was awarded the Nobel Prize for Literature. During the latter part of his career he travelled widely in Europe and America. He died of a heart attack in 1936.

CHIEF DRAMAS: *Cosi è, se vi pare* (translated variously as *It is So! (If You Think So)* or *Right You are If You Think You are;* drama, 1916) is an ingenious study in the intangibility of reality. When Signor Ponza, a civil clerk, arrives to take up a post in a provincial capital bringing his wife and his mother-in-law, Signora Frola, the town is filled with curiosity over the strangeness of the ménage. The old Signora lives in an elegant apartment by herself, and the married couple take a fifth-floor flat in a squalid tenement on the outskirts of town. Moreover the old lady is not allowed to receive her daughter, but is forced to walk to the tenement and shout five floors up to her from the air-well. The townspeople, especially Commendatore Agazzi, Ponza's boss, and his wife, determine to learn the truth about the matter, although Laudisi, Signora Agazzi's brother, cynically warns there is no such thing as truth and that their quest is doomed to failure. By dint of much

untactful questioning, the gossips learn from Ponza himself the following story: he, Ponza, actually married Signora Frola's daughter
some years before, but the daughter died and the old woman
went insane with grief. Ponza remarried, and when Signora Frola saw
him in the street with his new wife she imagined her daughter was still
alive. The curious living arrangements have therefore been devised to
spare the new wife the old woman's affection and yet placate Signora
Frola as much as possible.

Signora Frola, however, tells a different story: Ponza, a wildly passionate lover, so terrified her daughter with his importunacies during
the early years of the marriage that the girl was removed to a sanatorium. When Ponza subsequently encountered her he imagined in his
madness that his wife had died and that he had married again. Signora
Frola has therefore humored him in order to prevent a recurrence of
his rage.

The only way to decide which of the two is insane is to question the
daughter. She, however, demurs; she declares she is "the daughter of
Signora Frola and the second wife of Signor Ponza," and for herself
she is nobody, or "I am she whom you believe me to be." Thus
reality is unattainable for the Agazzis, just as the raisonneur
Laudisi said it would be.

Sei Personaggi in cerca d'Autore (*Six Characters in Search of an
Author;* drama, 1921) is Pirandello's best-known play. As the curtain rises a troupe of actors, led by the Manager, are conducting a
rehearsal. Their labors are interrupted by the intrusion of a family of
six, who claim they are fictional characters and demand to be put into
a play. The harassed manager at last agrees to listen to their story and
to endeavor to find an author for them. The situation of the family is
as follows: years before, the Father has driven the Mother from his
home when she dallied with a clerk. He keeps his Son by him,
although educated away from home, as a potential solace. The
Mother, going to live with the clerk, has three more children: the
Step-daughter, the Boy, and the Child. After some years the Mother,
after the death of her lover and stricken with poverty, sends her
daughter to work in the establishment of Madame Pace (a seventh
"character" not in search of an author). This dress-shop is actually
a house of ill fame where young girls are introduced to wealthy
middle-aged men. There the Father unknowingly encounters the

Step-daughter; a liaison almost takes place, but the Mother happens to enter, and an emotional scene of reconciliation follows. But the new ménage is horribly unsuccessful; its very core is riddled with vice and suspicion. One day the Child, playing, falls into a pond and is drowned; the Boy, witnessing this, kills himself with a revolver.

This plot, however, is not presented directly. Fragments of it are related by various members of the family, and then the actors attempt to make a play of it. As soon as they begin acting, however, the truth is distorted, the conventions of the stage intrude, and the reality of fictional characters in their hands becomes as artificial as real life role-playing.

Enrico Quarto (*Henry IV;* tragedy, 1922) takes as its theme the relative nature of what is ordinarily known as insanity. A young Italian nobleman of our own time loves Matilda Spina, a haughty young lady, but she favors the handsome and foppish Belcredi. A pageant is arranged in which the local gentry dress as historical figures; the hero chooses the figure of the eleventh-century German Emperor Henry IV. Falling from his horse during the festivities, he comes to consciousness convinced he is Henry IV and is living in the middle ages. Since he is wealthy, his friends and servants humor him, and for twenty years he lives in an illusory world in which the persons around him wear eleventh-century costumes. The play occupies only the last few days of this period, when a Doctor Genoni is introduced to effect a cure of the madman. The doctor, attempting to shock "Henry IV" into sanity, plans to confront him with Frida, Matilda's daughter; this, he hopes, will bring Henry's mind back to where it left the track twenty years before. In the meantime Henry confesses to his four servants that he has actually recovered his wits some ten years before, since then he has merely been playing the game as a bitter joke on his deceivers. When Frida is thrust upon him in a dark room he seizes her passionately; Belcredi rushes to her rescue, and Henry mortally wounds his enemy of twenty years with a sword. The dying Belcredi is borne off moaning, "You are not mad," and Henry seems to regress into the delusory world which is his last refuge. At the end of the play Henry's friends, especially Matilda, begin to doubt their own sanity.

Miguel de Unamuno (y Jugo) (Spanish, 1864-1936)

Increasingly known in America since 1950, Miguel de Unamuno

was an existentialist while Jean-Paul Sartre was still a child. It is
reported that he learned Danish in order to read Kierkegaard before
the First World War. But Unamuno's existentialism is not of the
Sartrian atheistic variety, nor is it progressive or amelioristic. It is
closer to the religious existentialism of the Kierkegaard-Gabriel
Marcel line.

Philosopher, scholar and academician at the University of Salamanca as Sartre was later in Paris, Unamuno was also able to express his existentialist ideas in an even wider variety of literary
forms, including prose fiction, the drama, and poetry. He was a
Basque who spoke for all of Spain, a Spaniard who spoke for
Europe, a European who spoke for men all over the world, but
above all an individual man, tormented by the idea of death and
nothingness, who cried out for himself alone. His name says one
world in its own *lingua franca*.

LIFE: Miguel de Unamuno was born in Bilbao in Basque country
in the north of Spain in 1864. After early education in his native
city and then in Madrid, he became a teacher and subsequently
Professor of Greek at the University of Salamanca in 1891. Ten
years later he was appointed rector of the university, relieved of his
position in 1914 for political reasons, was deported to the Canary
Islands in 1924 for political reasons (attacks on the Monarchy).
He escaped to France and spent six years first in Paris and then
in French Basque country at Hendaye, poised on the border for
reentry into Spain. In 1931 he was reelected rector at Salamanca,
was made rector-for-life three years later, and in 1936 for political
reasons was removed from this rectorship-for-life, having attacked
both the republican and falangist sides in the Spanish civil war.
Four months later in great depression, to the point of madness, he
died at the year's end in virtual house arrest in Salamanca.

Always involved in controversy Unamuno moved between the
political Left which he rejected in theory and the political Right
which he rejected in practice—the only possible impossible position he could take. Paradox was a key to his life as well as to his
writings. In his later years Unamuno was described as having
adopted a costume, a variation or parody of a priest's clothing—a
black swetaer which came up to his neck and permitted only his

shirt collar to show. The "variation or parody" expresses a central ambiguity and honesty in the author.

There is a wide difference of critical opinion about the relative significance of his works. Many who focus on Unamuno the thinker select the essays published as *Del sentimiento tragico de la vida* in 1913 (*The Tragic Sense of Life,* 1921) as his greatest work, what Walter Starkie calls the continuation of *Vida de Don Quijote y Sancho* . . . , 1905 (*The life of Don Quixote and Sancho* . . . , 1927), a long monologue on the subject of death. Critics affirm and deny that it is the author's attempt to write a systematic treatise on philosophy. In any event it turns out to be more nearly passionate autobiography. The longing for personal immortality and the rational existential anguish as formulated here spill over into the poetry, drama, and fiction.

The poetry is best represented by *Rosario de sonetos liricos,* 1911, and *El Cristo de Velasquez,* 1920 (*The Christ of Velasquez,* 1951). But one additional poem, "En un cementerio de lugar castellano," has received considerable attention as a kind of companion piece to Paul Valéry "Cimetière Marin." The country cemetery in Castile and the marine cemetery above the city of Sete awake similar yet significantly different responses in the Spanish and French poets. The plays of Unamuno beginning with *Fedra,* 1924, and including *El otro,* 1932, and *El hermano Juan,* 1934, a distinctive treatment of the Don Juan theme, are still in process of being made available in English. The last mentioned would be called in English, *Brother Juan, or The World is a Stage,* and in it Brother Juan asks, "Does Don Miguel de Unamuno exist? Is it not all a misty dream?" The major approaches to Unamuno are likely to remain, with or without *Tragic Sense of Life,* his highly original fiction, as the genre most truly alive and distinctive with him, which suggests many parallels with Pirandello and Pirandellian drama.

CHIEF WORKS: *Niebla, (Mist;* novel 1914) is about fiction and reality. If it does not seem like a real novel the writer offers a new genre, at least a new name; call it a *nivola,* a mist-novel. The main character, Augusto Perez, seems to create other characters as their need arises in his developing story, including an adopted stray dog, his confidant, Orfeo. Augusto begins to live when he follows the beautiful Eugenia and then falls in love with other women as well. With the bare bones of narrative—space and time as points of reference are minimal, descriptions virtually non-existent, plot nebulous—Augusto moves through floods of dialogue towards a marriage dramatically broken off the day before the wedding day (Eugenia runs off with a former lover, Mauricio) and, in his despair to a confrontation with his author, Unamuno. The author tells his character firmly that he doesn't exist, that he is only a part of the author's (and readers') dreams or fancies. But the character talks back: "May it not be, my dear Don Miguel, that it is you and not I who are the fictitions entity, the one that does not really exist, who is neither living nor dead?" After all, he points out, Don Quixote and Sancho are more real than Cervantes himself. After sharp exchanges the writer tells Augusto he is going to kill him. Then the character who had been at the desperate point of suicide, begs for his life, but Don Miguel is adamant: "I no longer know what to do with you. God, when he does not know what to do with us, kills us." At least four areas of creation are suggested: Augusto's creation of Eugenia and Orfeo, the author's creation, and the readers' creation, of Augusto, God's creation of all of us. Make of it what you will.

Abel Sanchez, Una historia de pasion, (Abel Sanchez; novel, 1917) is a novel whose main character, perhaps even heroic protagonist, is not Abel but Cain, called here Joaquin Monegro. The story which is even barer of place and time associations and of description than *Mist,* shuffles together a sparse third person narration, dialogue, and a first person confessional diary addressed to Joaquin's daughter. The Cain-Abel story with overtones of Jacob-Esau and a central concern with Byron's *Cain* is vaguely set in a turn-of-the-century Spain and is a probing of the passion of hatred, which Joaquin ultimately sees as envy or the original sin. The two boys grew up together as if they were brothers, Abel always the more popular, the more favored, at least in the eyes of Cain. Abel Sanchez becomes a painter, a rather scientific painter, who achieves fame and a wife, Helena, introduced to him by Joaquin who had been in love with her or thinks he had. Joaquin studied medicine when Abel turned to art but always hoped to win fame in medical research rather than devoting himself to the practice which developed. As a second best, he marries Antonia, the daughter of a patient he had attended until her death.

Cain becomes increasingly obsessed by his hatred for Helena and Abel, especially for Abel. He attends him during an illness, tormented by the possibilities for Abel's death but realizing that he must have Abel alive as the object of his hatred or risk existential annihilation of his very being. Abel and Helena have a son. Joaquin and Antonia have a daughter. Abel's fame blossoms with paintings of Helena-Virgin with child and of the Old Testament Death of Abel at the hands of Cain, for which he studied the Byron drama on the subject and discussed it with Joaquin. At a banquet honoring Abel, Joaquin makes the major speech, a brilliant critical analysis of the painter and the painting which capped and assured the painter's glory. The soul struggle in Cain deepens and hardens in ice.

Abel's son, Abelin, grows up alienated from his own father and becomes a doctor and disciple of Joaquin who thus neglects his own daughter. But when she wants to enter a convent, he arranges her marriage to Abelin. A grandson is born and the two grandfathers continue their struggle for his affection which turns away from Joaquin toward the painter who makes pictures for the child, something he had never done for his own. Abel the elder now has heart trouble. In a final confrontation with Joaquin over the grandchild's affection Abel insults his "brother" for his bad blood, Cain raises his hands to his throat and immediately draws back, but the shock produces an angina attack and Abel dies. Morally at least, the Biblical story has been finally reenacted. This is a spiritual or psychopathological case history. As foreseen, Joaquin wastes away for a year and dies in despair. This is the greatest tragedy for it tears apart the family. There is the envy of fathers and sons, but the greatest envy is between brothers. Joaquin has examined his hatred to the depths and has seen it as a possible failure in self-love.

The power of this story can be compared with more diffuse treatments of the theme in Steinbeck's *East of Eden* and Joyce's *Finnegans Wake* or in Thorton Wilder's excerpted focus of the latter in *Skin of Our Teeth*.

San Manuel Bueno, martyr (Saint Emmanuel the Good, Martyr;

novella, 1931) is an almost perfectly compressed story of faith and doubt in an apparently unbelieving priest, or one who thought he did not believe, or who said he thought this to one other unbeliever, the skeptic Lazarus who was thus converted to the way of Christian life. This is Unamuno's ultimate statement—"the tragic sense of everyday life," he said—of the profound relationships of faith and disbelief. "I believe, O Lord; help thou my unbelief." Existential ambiguities are essential to its structure and its meaning. The novella is more perfectly fleshed out than the author's other narratives. There is a fictional narrator this time, Angela Carballino, with a brief postscript by Unamuno. There is a place, a rural village near a lake, but outside the world's pressured flux, Valverde de Lucerna, where Don Manuel is the parish priest who finds salvation in works, especially with his hands. His is the active rather than contemplative role, which is too dangerous—and may even lead to suicide.

Angela wants to record her memories by way of confession now that the process of beatification is being initiated. She, her brother Lazarus who later returns to his native village from America, and the priest are the main characters. Two instances of Don Manuel's doubt are put forward: the passionate sincerity of his Good Friday cry, "My God, my God, why hast Thou forsaken me?" and his silence during the communal recital of the Creed at the words, "I believe in the resurrection of the flesh and life everlasting." But he helps everydody in the village to live and to die well. Thre are two very effective minor characters, the village idiot Blasillo, a "fool-in Christ" figure, and a traveling clown-acrobat whose wife dies in Don Manuel's care while the clown is performing. They regard each other as saints.

At confession Angela grows to feel that the roles are sometimes reversed, that the priest confesses to her. Absolution as well as confession become mutual acts. Lazarus returns to take his mother and sister away to the city, to Madrid; but they are unwilling to leave Valverde and their beloved priest. Gradually Lazarus and Don Manuel are drawn to each other. Lazarus helps the priest in his work and they take long walks together. Don Manuel points out that the Social Revolution has called religion the opium of the people and then proceeds to defend opium.

After a good life the priest dies in the church with all his people with him; Blasillo, holding his hand, dies too. Lazarus dies some time later, and Angela is left to write her memoirs. She believes that Saint Manuel and Lazarus died "believing they did not believe" but believing without belief. Often called a story where nothing happens (Unamuno says so himself), it is not quite true. There are five deaths that are led up to and consummated and daily life goes on before and after. This story says in a compact simple way what many books of modern theology struggle to say. It is a statement of faith made in an existential world built on ideas of absurdity, but here is a large amount of felt life.

Nikos Kazantzakis (Greek, 1883-1957)

Kazantzakis, he would be glad to know, is a writer difficult to categorize. Poet, dramatist, novelist, journalist, philosophical essayist, translator, he seems in many ways to be a realist and story teller like Thomas Mann who continues with a stylistic legacy of the nineteenth century to write of twentieth century matters. He suggests a kind of reincarnation of Thomas Carlyle, not only in a certain explosiveness and enthusiasm of expression, but in a dedication to heroes and hero-worship. His most persistent and central list of heroes would include Christ, Nietzsche, Lenin, Buddha, and Odysseus. These figures help define the core of Kazantzakis' concern, but the list is more expansive than that and includes at various times Dante, Shakespeare, St. Francis, El Greco, Moses, Mohammed, St. Teresa, Cervantes, Homer, and many others. Always on the edge of political involvement—as a Cretan Greek he had to support independence from whatever Turks he might see as present antagonists—he nevertheless made constant efforts to dissociate himself from group commitments, notably the Communist Party. His hopes were alternately high and low for what Communism was achieving in Russia and later in China and Japan. He came as close to commitment and as often withdrew to the integrity of individual judgment as André Malraux or André Gide were doing at the same time. A final casting-up places him among the broadly liberal and humanitarian writers with a persistent emphasis on individualism. This latter emphasis seems to be related at key points to the generally current twentieth century existentialist philosophy; although Kazantzakis does not articulate its theories, he presents us with existential heroes.

Both Thomas Mann and Albert Schweitzer, whom he admired greatly and often referred to as justifying some abstemious habit, have praised his work in glowing terms. Schweitzer, who traveled to Freiburg, Germany to visit Kazantzakis on his death bed, wrote of him, "Since I was a young boy, no author has made such a deep impression upon me as Nikos Kazantzakis. His work has depth and durable value because he has experienced much, and in the human community he has suffered much and yielded much." Sponsored repeatedly for the Nobel Prize Kazantzakis reportedly lost in 1952 by a single vote. According to Helen Kazantzakis in her biography of her husband, Nikos was the only person in the University Clinic at Freiburg who did not feel disappointment when the 1957 award went to Albert Camus. He asked his wife to help draft a congratulatory telegram, his last dictation, saying, "Juan Ramón Jimenez, Albert Camus— there are two men who well deserved the Nobel." Jimenez, who had received the prize in 1956, and Kazantzakis had been close personal friends. Camus later wrote to Helen that "the very day when I was receiving a distinction that Kazantzakis deserved a hundred times more, I got the most generous telegram from him . . . drafted a few days before his death. With him, one of our last great artists vanished."

The reputation of Kazantzakis in America has been closely related to the somewhat haphazard appearance of his published works in an order quite different from that of composition or publication in Europe. *Zorba the Greek,* written originally about 1940 as *The Golden Legend of Alexis Zorba,* apeared first in 1953 after the author and the publisher Max Schuster had met the year before in Cannes. *Zorba the Greek* has since achieved great popularity, particularly among the young, enhanced by the motion-picture version with Anthony Quinn and the Harold Prince musical, *Zorba,* on Broadway in the late sixties. Wandering American students, the uprooted generation, flocked to Crete to live Zorba-fashion in the caves. Kimon Friar (translator of Kazantzakis' *The Odyssey, A*

Modern Sequel and *The Saviors of God*) writes that in the spring
of 1970 he made a week's tour of Crete giving lectures in Greek
and "a talk in English to the hippies on the beach near their caves
in Matala." Two other novels, *The Greek Passion* (filmed under
the title, *He Who Must Die*) and *Freedom or Death* appeared in
1954 and 1956 before *The Odyssey* in 1958. The sixties have seen
an increasing flow of translations and publication from all periods
of Kazantzakis' writing, including *Report to Greco,* his autobiographical memoires; several travel books; four additional novels,
The Last Temptation of Christ, The Rock Garden, The Fratricides,
and *Toda Raba;* and three of his many plays, *Christopher Columbus,
Melissa,* and *Kouros.* American college students are giving time
to individual research in Kazantzakis, and one in the spring of 1970
admitted to his religious conversion by the human Christ of *The
Last Temptation.*

LIFE: Nikos Kazantzakis was born in Herakleion, Crete, on
February 18, 1883. His father Michael was a primitive peasant,
rather unsociable and taciturn, his mother Maria, an almost saintly,
sensitive woman. He had two sisters of whom he was fond. His
childhood in Crete was overshadowed by the Greek struggle for
independence from the Turks, including the Rising of 1897 which
forced the family to seek refuge in Naxos. Nikos was educated,
first in Herakleion, then at the French School of the Holy Cross
until the age of sixteen, learning French and Italian to go with
his native, demotic Greek which he always loved, later studied law
in Athens (1902-1906) and philosophy in Paris (1907-1909). His
earliest writings, a story, "The Serpent and the Lily" and a play,
The Master Mason, he later thought little of. The greatest influences
of these years in Paris were study with the philosopher, Henri Bergson, and his discovery of Nietzsche. As he tells the story, an unknown girl came up to him in the Saint-Geneviève Library, near
the Pantheon, holding an open book with a photograph and hiding
the name beneath it, "Look, here is a photograph of you! Is it you?"
Nikos was amazed at the resemblance. It was Nietzsche and launched
him on great study, great admiration, of the German philosopher.
This account is reported by Pandelis Prevelakis in *Nikos Kazantzakis and his Odyssey.* Prevelakis, a considerable novelist and

dramatist in his own right, was seventeen when he met Nikos, then forty-three, and they remained close friends for thirty-one years. After his return to Greece, Kazantzakis was appointed in 1919 Director General of the Ministry of Public Welfare and he participated in a national mission, the repatriation of Greeks uprooted from the Caucasus.

His career in government service later included, in 1946, a brief term as acting Minister of National Education. In 1947 he was made Director of Translations from the Classics for UNESCO but retired from the post in 1948 to devote more time to writing. In the intervening years from 1920 on he traveled widely in Europe, Asia, and Africa, stopping for extended periods of writing at Aegina, an island near Athens, at Gottesgab, in the Sudetenland of Czechoslovakia, at Antibes on the French Mediterranean, Herakleion and points between. His friendships were almost as important to him as his marriages. Among the most intimate, besides those with Prevelakis and Kimon Friar, was one with Yannis Stavridakis (who reappears in *Zorba*), one with Giorghos Zorba—the actual Zorba, not the one in the novel, and one with Panait Istrati, a Greek-Roumanian writer, whom Romain Rolland had introduced to the French literary world, and with whom Nikos traveled widely and even wildly in Russia (the companions both becoming characters in *Toda Raba*). He was married twice. His first marriage, to Galatea Alexiou in 1911, ended in divorce, after a separation of some tension. He then married Helen Samiou and lived with her, when not traveling, until his death. In 1957 the Chinese government invited him to visit their country (his first visit had been in 1935). On his flight home a smallpox vaccination he had received developed a deadly infection. He died at a clinic in Freiburg, Germany on October 26, 1957, having created along with Constantine Cavafis, George Seferis, Pandelis Prevelakis, and others what is essentially a Greek Renaissance in letters after more than two thousand years.

CHIEF WORKS: *Zorba the Greek* (novel, translated into English by Carl Wildman and published 1953) remains in many ways Kazantzakis' most satisfying work. The story is episodic and there are two protagonists, Alexis Zorba, the stranger of about sixty (who is probably older and crowding seventy), a physical, sensuous, sensual

man of action with a strongly existential point of view, full of a
dedication to life—women, food, friendship, who when he can no
longer express himself in words plays the santuri and dances, and
the narrator, identified only as the Boss, or the pen-pusher, thirty-
five years old at the Dantean *nel mezzo del cammin di nostra vita,*
an intellectual, sensitive writer who seems to withdraw from life (he's
still apparently virgin) and seeks the most spiritual ideals whether
in Dante, socialism, or Buddha. The novel begins with the meeting
of these two opposite yet complementary characters at the seaport of
Piraeus in the autumn, ready to sail for Crete, follows their companionship through the winter and the spring with passing focus
on the holidays of Christmas and Easter, through their progress and
defeat in the ostensible project of working an old lignite mine on
a lease with Zorba as manager and the pen-pusher as Boss, and
ends with their separation. Unique among Kazantzakis' characters,
Alexis Zorba, neither warrior nor saint, lives life to the fullest, seeing
everything as if for the first time. The first night after their arrival
in Crete the two men stay with Madame Hortense, an old courtesan
innkeeper who becomes the third most important character. Zorba
takes pity on her, woos her, calling her his Bouboulina, and wins
her completely, following the philosophy that any man who can
sleep with a woman and does not, commits a great sin.

Days pass. The mine is not profitable, but life is good while
the money lasts. There is only one problem to disturb the Boss-Zorba
relationship. The Boss is attracted to the village widow but is reluctant to pursue her. This is the only cause for argument between
them, although they are generally opposites. But finally with Spring
the Boss weakens and spends a night with the widow. As a result,
a boy who has loved the widow from a distance commits suicide, and
his father cuts her throat. Shortly after this, Bouboulina dies, and
the money runs out. The partners split up, the Boss off to Europe
and Zorba heading north toward Russia. They never meet again,
but there are communications. A letter informing the Boss of
Zorba's death records his last words, "I've done heaps and heaps of
things in my life, but I still did not do enough. Men like me ought
to live a thousand years. Good night!"

Zorba is a vibrant, uncomplicated man, given more to action than to thought, but he has developed a working philosophy for life which he explains to the Boss gradually in one anecdote after another from his past life, giving narrative fullness to an otherwise somewhat thin plot line. He is not, however, a selfish pleasure seeker, but is capable of genuine compassion for his old Bouboulina. The Boss, an individual who seeks to escape from the world by burying himself in books, is nevertheless able to respond eventually to Zorba's influence. He does learn to dance, to sing, to observe life with wonder. Although strongly biased toward the intellectual, abstract pursuits of his creative writing, he shows, unlike Zorba, an ability to change and adapt to circumstances, if only slightly. The Boss and Zorba exhibit the same flaw in opposite ways (each leans strongly towards one range of human experience: the intellectual, the physical), and both men are "loners," essentially without family or other ties. These points of similarity and the contrast in personality types suggest that the author may have intended them to represent two halves of the human personality, a Dostoyevskian double: manual laborer and man of letters, life and art, doer and thinker, body and soul, heart and mind. Together they make up a perfectly balanced individual.

The Greek Passion (novel, translated into English by Jonathan Griffin and published 1954) is the novel thought by the author to be his best, although most readers find the characters too easily classified as black or white, the bad guys and the good guys. The action takes place in a small Greek village under Turkish rule, Lycovrissi, and environs. Every seventh year the villagers stage a passion play at Eastertime. Since it is the sixth year after the last play, the village elders meet to decide on the actors for next year's play, making their selections to fit the part emotionally as well as physically. They select Manolios, a shepherd in the service of the village archon, Patriarcheas, to play Christ, perfect for the part according to the priest, "mild as a lamb, he can read, has been in a monastery too. He has blue eyes and short beard as yellow as honey, a real Christ like an icon. And pious into the bargain." Four disciples are also chosen: Yannakos with his donkey as Peter; Michelis, the Archon's son, as John; Kostandis, owner of the café, as James; and Panayatoros, a buffoon, as Judas. The widow Katerina (there always seems to be a beautiful one in Kazantzakis fiction) is a natural for Mary Magdalen. To consider how to lead more devout lives in the coming year the disciples meet with Manolios as leader, who urges Michelis to give some of his father's possessions to the poor—which, of course, is the beginning of struggle with the Establishment.

When a wandering priest, named Fotis, and his people come to Lycovrissi seeking new homes, the village elders turn them away, but Manolios and his friends do their best to help the refugees who settle near the village on a wild mountain slope. Meanwhile there is trouble in the village. The favorite boy, Youssoufaki, of the Agha is murdered, and the Turkish Lord of Lycovissi vows to execute the Greek citizens one by one, until the murderer is found. Hearing the news, Manolios rushes in to "confess," hoping to save others by his sacrifice. But then the real criminal, a Turk, is discovered, the Greeks are saved. Another crisis occurs on the death of the old archon when Michelis turns over his inheritance to Priest Fotis and his people. The villagers whose resentment and fears of the refugees have been increasing show force against those who would take possession. The Lycovrissian priest excommunicates Manolios who leads the refugees, accused of being communists by the elders who persuade the Agha that he should call up troops. Panayataros as Judas captures Manolios and takes him before the Agha, who releases him to the Lycovrissians who in turn, led by their priest, take him to the church where he is killed and dismembered. The "passion" events, however, take place at Chirstmas time, which puts the death of Christ into the context of his birth, much like the Yeats and Eliot poems about the magi. The refugees bury the remains of Manolios and, dispossessed once more, resume their search for a new home.

The Odyssey: A Modern Sequel (epic poem, translated into English by Kimon Friar and published 1958), always considered by the writer as the heart of his creative work, was begun by 1925, consumed the major part of twelve years, was written in seven drafts, reworked and polished into twenty-four books (like Homer) and a mystical, pre-arranged number of 33,333 lines (reminding one of Dante's canto arrangement), and was published in modern, demotic

Greek in 1938. The meter of the original poem is a seventeen syllable unrhymed verse of eight beats, condensed in English to a six-beat line. One of the major redoings of the Odysseus story in the twentieth century, it bears immediate comparison and contrast with James Joyce's *Ulysses* (but consider also Hauptmann, *The Bow of Odysseus*—which Kazantzakis knew, and Ezra Pound's use of Ulysses in *Hugh Selwyn Mauberly* and the *Cantos*). W. B. Stanford examines this in *The Ulysses Theme: A Study in the Adaptation of a Traditional Hero*. There are at least two traditions of the many-sided Odysseus, the man who always has his eye on Ithaca as home and the end of his journey, which Joyce follows, and the man who has his eye on the journey, the heroic adventurer who cannot rest in Ithaca, which is followed by Dante, Tennyson, and Kazantzakis.

The Odyssey: A Modern Sequel is remarkably compact and powerful, in spite of its length, and its descriptions are intense, lyrical and vivid: "Dark night shook loose her glaucous hair then slowly turned / and took off her old ivory comb, the crescent moon; / stars browsed for salt like white lambs on the foaming waves, / and the black rooster shook his wings though night still reigned, / for he had dreamt of suns, and rose to crow in darkness." Kazantzakis ties his work together with a repetition of symbols and images, including the sun and the number seven. The sun is the subject of invocation and prologue; the cyclic repetition of days and nights, of waking and sleeping, of working and thinking, of living and dying, of light and dark, is all important, with the ascending pattern of the evolution of the soul cutting across it. Kazantzakis begins his sequel by overlapping Homer with the slaying of the suitors in Ithaca as the subject of Book I. Odysseus leaves Ithaca forever in Book II, saying farewell to father, wife, and son and setting out on his last odyssey. He goes to Sparta, makes a second abduction of Helen and takes her to Crete. They witness the bull rituals at Knossos; and Odysseus later participates in a conspiracy for the overthrow of the city, sets up a new king in Crete and, leaving Helen and Greece behind, sails southward to the mouth of the Nile. After many episodes along the river Odysseus and his men land at the Egyptian city of Thebes where they share in a rebellion against the decadent Empire of the Pharaoh. Barbarian hordes from the North follow the Ithacan's southward journey—first in Crete, now in Egypt. Here the rebellion is put down, all the rebel chiefs captured. Odysseus escapes with his friends after frightening the Pharaoh with the carved mask of a god. They move always south through dark Africa to the source of the Nile. Here the epic hero climbs a mountain to communicate with God for seven days and nights. The chief followers of Odysseus, Granite and Kentaur, build an ideal city with the help of their leader who Moses-like leaves them his commandments. When the city is destroyed by earthquake, Odysseus becomes an ascetic given to contemplation; later he continues his journey to the southern tip of Africa. After many visions and adventures he sights the ocean, builds a boat, and sails alone toward the South Pole. After a long journey he blesses life, bids it farewell, and dies, somewhat in the fashion of grand opera with a review of his past life and with his mind's escape from its last cage, its own freedom.

Odysseus has passed through seven stages, although it is not always easy to mark the transitions. He begins in Bestiality with the slaying of the suitors, experiences Battle-Hunger and Lust in Crete. Pure Intellect, the fourth stage, is found in the mountain contemplation at the source of the Nile; Despair, with the destruction of the utopian city. Detachment comes with the role of the ascetic. As Odysseus journeys through Africa people come to discuss their philosophies with him in one of the weirdest, weightiest, most eclectic, perhaps least convincing portions of the narrative; he refutes adherents to the views of Buddha, Faust, Don Quixote, the Courtesan, the Hedonist, and Christ. The last stage, after crashing into an iceberg near the South Pole, is the leap to Pure Soul.

The poetry is magnificent, the philosophy compelling, but the narrative stretches credulity and the character of Odysseus is unbelievable. Even the many-sided Odysseus of Homer cannot encompass all these diverse stages, although W. B. Stanford takes a different position, claiming that Kazantzakis "has presented a fully-integrated portrait of the hero—as wanderer and politician, as destroyer and preserver, as spiritualist and ascetic, as soldier and philosopher, as pragmatist and mystic, as legislator and humorist." The breaking point for Odysseus' clarity as a character, and for the narration as well, comes with the creation and destruction of the city.

The philosopher-saint of the books which follow is not Odysseus; the personality has undergone too radical a shift from doer and deed to contemplation. There is no doubt about the reality of Leopold Bloom as a person; the comparison knocks over the figure of the African Odysseus. But even the failure has a magnificence of its own.

The Last Temptation of Christ (novel, translated into English by P. A. Bien and published 1969) is a forceful presentation of Christ as a completely human being, insecure, racked by doubt, vulnerable to temptation in his own historical time as we are in ours. He feels himself under God's curse as a punishment for his sinful nature. Kazantzakis relives the life of Christ, but always as supremely human rather than as divine. On the cross he dreams that he has taken a different path, the easy smooth road of man. He had married and become a father, was loved and respected. Now he had grown old and was happy that he had escaped the torture and anguish of the cross. But Christ awoke from this illusion and saw that he had not escaped, but had accomplished his God-given mission.

Christ returns to the author as hero-saint, having been followed by and preceded by Nietzsche, Buddha, Lenin, and Odysseus. The return, however, is to a Christ of human anguish and flesh—not a spirit-type son of God. This Christ is a realistic human being, but an unbelievable deity. An old woman says to him in the novel, "God is not found in monasteries, but in the homes of men." Thomas says to him, "Do me a favor and don't start up again about God . . . ; don't mix him up in our affairs. Listen to me: here we've got to deal with man—with dishonest, seven-times-shrewd man."

Kazantzakis took Christ out of the church and into the world. The spiritual and moral Christ of the church had no meaning for Kazantzakis. He demanded a living, loving man, not a moralistic martyr. As he says, "The old recognized virtues have begun to lose their authority; they are no longer able to fulfill the religious, moral, intellectual, and social demands of the contemporary soul. Man's soul seems to have grown bigger; it cannot fit any longer within the old molds." Highly controversial, this novel naturally shocks the orthodox. It invites comparison with D. H. Lawrence's

The Man Who Died and with Hauptmann's *The Fool in Christ, Emanuel Quint.*

The *Report to Greco* (memoirs, 1965) has received wide critical acclaim, but as a somewhat amorphous autobiography and source-book for his other work it will probably remain ancillary reading except for Kazantzakis enthusiasts, who have already read at least the major novels. Other heroes there are in this additional book of hero-worship, most centrally Nikos' grandfather and El Greco, another artist-exile from Crete in an earlier time.

Jorge Luis Borges (Argentine, born 1899)

Borges is being made an honorary European for purposes of inclusion in this volume. He is sufficiently a citizen of the world, a cosmopolitan in the way of Goethe, and takes such delight in irony and mystification that the trick should be to his pleasure and hopefully merit his approbation. A pan-European linguist he was educated not only in Swiss schools but formed by European literature and associated with the new poets in the Spain of 1920. Although some of his poems and stories have roots in native Argentinian soil, more characteristically they are set in geographical fantasy, Tlön or Uqbar, or in a fantastic Europe, the Prague of "The Golem," or the England of the garden of forking paths. Writing in a flexible Spanish, he still depends upon translation for the English-speaking world. In any event his true literary ancestors and associates are chiefly Soren Kierkegaard (Danish, 1813-1855), the grandfather of existentialism and the modern parable, Franz Kafka, Paul Valéry, Rainer Maria Rilke, Pär Lagerkvist, James Joyce, Samuel Beckett, and the European intellectual élite rather than regionalists and local colorists. And it is in Europe and the United States that his reputation has chiefly grown to its present size.

The devotees of Jorge Luis Borges seem to have developed a cabalistic society of their own, and sometimes they are downright silly. Ana Maria Barrenechea in a work on Borges from its Mexican publication in 1957 to its 1965 impression by the New York University Press goes pretty far into the stratosphere of abstract speculation, talking about the author in terms of the Infinite, Chaos and the

Cosmos, Pantheism and Personality, Time and Eternity, and Idealism and Other Forms of Unreality. Even Borges wrote in 1964 that this book "unearthed many secret links and affinities in my own literary output of which I had been quite unaware." And Richard Burgin who has produced an excellent and readable little book, *Conversations with Jorge Luis Borges,* based on the Argentine's appearance at Harvard University as the Charles Eliot Norton Professor of Poetry in 1967-68, gives the impression of being a hypersensitive Boswell to a new Johnson. His followers all note the modesty of Borges, his deprecation of much of his own work, but they won't have it that way (although he probably has a better sense of his limitations than they have). He is the Master. At least when compared with Nabokov the circle of admirers seem to suggest the atmosphere of a church rather than a circus.

And the importance of Borges will probably survive even his enthusiasts. His books have recently proliferated in paperbacks (with a good deal of duplication in content). A *Time* blurb says, "The greatest living writer in the Spanish language today is a little-known Argentine named Jorge Luis Borges." Indeed he was so little known in 1963 that a handbook on the major writers of the world listed him as having died in 1959. More importantly it has been noted that "in Europe his reputation is unmatched by that of any American writer except William Faulkner," of both continents, that is. It is also said with justice that his stories echo in the mind as do those of Franz Kafka, that they should be read one at a time slowly to appreciate the baroque imagination and the "carefully wrought, gnarled style." Borges is chiefly important in two areas. He is a poet of some stature. Individual poems in translation appeared every few weeks in *The New Yorker* for some time. And he has developed into a new form what is only clumsily referred to as the short story or the short short-story, part parable, part essay, largely fantasy, the kind first used by Kafka and then by Lagerkvist and, somewhat modified, by such writers as Eudora Welty and E. M. Forster. Moreover in *Ficciones* (1935-1944) he has found a name for it, a Fiction; in his hands it becomes highly cerebral and ironic, the Hermetic, minimal labyrinth.

There are several lines of descent that have been suggested, some of them by Borges himself. André Maurois sums up: "These inventions are described in a pure and scholarly style which must be linked up with Poe, 'who begat Baudelaire, who begat Mallarmé, who begat Valéry,' who begat Borges. It is especially by his rigor that he reminds us of Valéry." But if this is the begetting he was certainly begotten *on* Kafka. And there are more than traces of Joyce, Flaubert, Lewis Carroll, even Unamuno, Kierkegaard, Robert Browning, Rilke. In fact his literature very much depends on precedent literature, as he recognizes in much the way that Michel Butor does. Expressionist and experimenter, he is also a relativist. His characteristic recurrent images are worth recording: mirrors, libraries, labyrinths, dreamtigers. In a reasonable and well-written article, "Tigers in the Mirror," (*The New Yorker,* June 20, 1970) George Steiner refers to his "artistic dreams," his "erudition"—half joke, half serious ("the fabric of bibliographical allusions, philosophic tags, literary citations, cabalistic references, mathematical and philological acrostics . . . is obvious crucial to the way he experiences reality") —"itself a kind of fantasy, a surrealistic construct." But his weaknesses in fiction are two: there are no characters, especially women, in whom we can believe and the "space of action" is mythical but never social. The result may be a strangeness that "makes for a certain preciousness, a rococo elaboration, that can be spellbinding but also airless." His work has created nightmares but also witty and elegant dreams, and we "wake from them, increased."

LIFE: Jorge Luis Borges was born in Buenos Aires August 24, 1899, of a line of native-born Argentinians, with Spanish, English, and Portugese elements in his inheritance. His childhood was spent in the Palermo district of the city and in a summer house in Adrogué. In 1914 the family moved to Geneva, Switzerland, where they stayed during the war years and where Jorge went to school. After the war they traveled to Madrid, and Jorge frequented a vanguard group of poets. Returning to Buenos Aires in 1921 he became active in literary circles, writing and editing, translating (he has done Gide, Kafka, Faulkner, and Virginia Woolf among others), traveling back and forth to Europe, continuing his studies. His first book of poetry *(Fervor of Buenos Aires)* was published in 1923, the first story, "Men Fought," in 1928. For many years Borges held a position as librarian in a municipal library, but denouncing the evils of Nazism and not pleasing the new dictatorship in Argentina was demoted by the government to a position as chicken inspector in 1940. In 1955, after the revolution against Peron, he was appointed Director of the National Library of Buenos Aires and was elected to the Argentinian Academy of Letters. He began to teach as a Professor of English and North American Literature at the University of Buenos Aires. *Ficciones* and *El Aleph,* his most important volumes of "short stories," had already been published in 1944 and 1949. Later for an anthology, six Argentine writers were to choose the best story they knew; Borges chose Hawthorne's "Wakefield," an interesting choice in relation to his own fiction since it's a story that's almost an essay.

In 1961 he went to the University of Texas to give a course on Argentine literature, subsequently lecturing at Columbia University, in London, Cambridge, Oxford, and Edinburgh. Also in 1961 Borges and Beckett were awarded equal shares in the Formentor Prize, an international publishers' recognition. Blind since 1955, he traveled with his mother, Leonor Acevedo, who read to him and took dictation. More recently during his stay in Cambridge, Massachusetts, for the Charles Eliot Norton lectures in 1967-68 he was accompanied by his wife. He has equally enjoyed and been embarrassed by the coterie of writers who say he has "succeeded Joyce and Kafka." He is as talented a linguist as Joyce was, "at home in English, French, German, Italian, Portugese, Anglo-Saxon, and Old Norse, as well as in Spanish," and lives quietly (when not traveling) in Buenos Aires.

REPRESENTATIVE POEMS: "El Otro Tigre" ("The Other Tiger"), one of his favorite poems, according to Borges, is about the futility of art as conveying the reality of life; "the poem is supposed to be endless, because the moment I write about the tiger, the tiger isn't the tiger, he becomes a set of words in the poem. 'El otro tigre, el que no esta en el verso.' " There is a parable but not too obvious. "I think I have three tigers, but the reader should be made to feel that the poem is endless." The poet in South America in a "remote lost seaport" describes and dreams of a tiger on the Ganges but it's made up of "symbols and of shadows," not "the real one, it whose

blood runs hotly, / and today, 1959, the third of August." Naming
it creates a fiction, so we look for a third tiger, and then presumably
a fourth, and so on. "The Golem" Borges considers, with some
justice, his best poem, one where humor has a part, an account of
how the golem was evolved with a kind of parable attached. A
"golem" from the Yiddish and Jewish folklore is an artificial figure
constructed to represent a human being and endowed with life, specifically one created by the cabalist Rabbi Löw of Prague in the
sixteenth century. The rabbi is rather ashamed of the clumsy golem;
and at the end it is hinted that as the golem is to the cabalist so is
man to God. "At the hour of anguish and vague light / He would
rest his eyes on his Golem. / Who can tell us what God felt, / As He
gazed on His rabbi in Prague?" There is the added suggtstion of a
parable on the nature of art: the rabbi as artist intended something
beautiful or important but ended up with a very clumsy doll.

CHIEF FICTIONS: "Tlön, Uqbar, Orbis Tertius" called by Borges
one of his best stories but left out of *A Personal Anthology,* perhaps
because of its formidable title, is a fantasy dealing with a nonexistent
country somewhere theoretically in Asia Minor, Uqbar, found at the
end of Volume XLVI of *The Anglo-American Cyclopaedia* after
Upsala (but only in a certain copy belonging to Borges' friend, Bioy
Casares), and later an unknown, invented planet, Tlön or Orbis
Tertius, details from a book mailed to a dead man, Herbert Ashe,
in *A First Encyclopaedia of Tlön,* Volume XI, *Hlaer to Jangr.* A
secret and benevolent society, once including George Berkeley, with
headquarters in the nineteenth century in Memphis, Tennessee
decided to invent a country, later a world. The cause for alarm in
the nineteen forties occurs when a compass and a very heavy "cone
of bright metal" from the invented planet appear on earth. Fiction
intrudes on reality causing fright.

"Pierre Menard, Author of the *Quixote"* is, as Borges remembers
it, the first story he ever wrote but a kind of essay which produces a
feeling of tiredness or skepticism. Menard (perhaps Borges himself)
comes at the end of a long literary period and doesn't want to en-
cumber the world with more books, so he decides to rewrite a book
that already exists, *Don Quixote,* and in the exact words of Cervantes. His highly implausible but substantial character is revealed to

us in a list of his "visible" works a) through s); Pierre Menard is clearly a twentieth century "writer" because p) is an invective against Paul Valéry ("the exact opposite of his true opinion of Valéry"). Each item in the catalogue points to the parable's meaning. The climax is comparative quotation from Cervantes' *Quixote* and Menard's *Quixote,* precisely the same passage: "truth, whose mother is history, rival of time, depository of deeds, witness of the past, exemplar and adviser to the present, and the future's counselor." In the seventeenth century this was mere rhetorical praise. In the twentieth the idea is astounding, "brazenly pragmatic," and the style being archaic has a certain affectation. As time passes, every time a book is read or reread, the book changes.

"The Circular Ruins" has an epigraph from *Through the Looking Glass* (Lewis Carroll: "And if he left off dreaming about you . . ." Here we have a magician who works hard at his dreams, trying to create a real man as his "son" in dreaming his existence (one could think of Leopold Bloom and his recreation of Rudy in the Nighttown of *Ulysses*) and through and in spite of his hallucinations, succeeding, only to discover that his own existence is merely the dream of another (Unamuno's question in *Mist*). The compactness and the South American circular ruins in the jungle are of course, Borges' own.

"The Library of Babel," which only, perhaps, a long-time librarian could devise (there's an echo of Melville's use of the sub-sub-librarian in *Moby Dick*), conveys the horror of the universe as a library, infinitely extended hexagonal galleries, each with a small closet for sleep standing up and a small closet for physical processes of elimination, a classified collection of human knowledge past and to come, enthusiasms and follies nightmarishly catalogued—with the possibility of God as the Head Librarian, but certainly inaccessible and not particularly efficient. One gets the impression that cataloguers may be in the process of shifting from the dewey decimal classification to the Library of Congress system. In any event the individual traveler is lost in the stacks. The store of knowledge may alternately seem wonderful or spatial accumulation of trash.

There are many other of the "Fictions" that one might choose as favorites: "The Garden of Forking Paths," (a compressed metaphysical-detective-spy story, parody and parable), "Funes the Memorious," (based on the amazing total recall powers of an invalid) "The Immortal," "The Theologians," or "The Zahir"—they are all filled with mirrors and labyrinths, with scraps of real and made-up quotations and authorities, "antique truths and waste conjectures that throng the attic of history," dreams that offer an alternative to "the loud graffiti of erotic and political emancipation that currently pass for fiction and poetry." Borges has written in an essay on H. G. Wells, whom he admires, that "a durable work of literature is always capable of an infinite and plastic ambiguity; it is everything for everybody . . .; it is a mirror proclaiming the reader's features and it is also a map of the world."

Heinrich Böll (German, born 1917)

Heinrich Böll, as a follower of Wolfgang Borchert (1921-1947) who, in writing *Draussen vor der Tür* or *The Man Outside,* was presenting a German version of the Sartrian-Camus' *The Stranger,* existentially alienated in the modern world, may be considered an existentialist. He too feels the anguish of choice, although he would not be as emotionally involved as Borchert. Böll has published widely in the field of fiction since 1949 and is regarded as of equal eminence with Günter Grass.

LIFE: Born in Cologne in 1917 on the 21st of December, the son of a Catholic cabinetmaker, Heinrich Theodor Böll was early apprenticed to the book trade. He was inducted into the German army in 1939, was wounded on the Russian front, and as an infantry corporal became an American prisoner of war in eastern France. After the war he learned carpentry and later worked as a statistician for the city of Cologne. War experiences and family influences led him to be highly critical of professional careerists and of those who, self-satisfied, would cover up the mistakes of the past, particularly of the Nazi regime and the war. His early fiction makes clear his concern. In his novella, *Der Zug war pünktlich (The Train was on Time),* published in 1949, the soldier Andreas reflects: "Pain sits in his throat and he was never so miserable as now. It is good that I suffer." His 1951 novel, *Wo warst du, Adam? (Adam, where art thou?),* shows people infected by war as if it were a disease. Catas-

trophe can serve as an alibi before God: " 'Adam, where are thou?'
'I was in the world war.' "

In 1953 Böll published *Und sagte kein einziges Wort (Acquainted
with the Night* in its English version although it means "And he said
not one word") about lower middle-class domestic life, followed the
next year by the broken families of *Haus ohne Hüter,* which ended
up in English as *Tomorrow and Yesterday.* Böll's major and highly
original novel, *Billiard um halb zehn (Billiards at half-past Nine)*
appeared in 1959. His next novel was *Ansichten eines Clowns (The
Clown,* 1963), closer to the satire and mordant wit of Grass; and
this was followed by *Ende einer Dienstfahrt* in 1966. Böll lives in
Köln-Müngersdorff in the German Federal Republic.

CHIEF NOVEL: *Billiard um halb zehn (Billiards at half-past Nine;*
novel, 1959) is another story of three generations, this time the
German Fähmel family of architects, but the time sequence is
shattered by the history of our time, the first half of the twentieth
century: time past, time present, and the time that never existed save
in the imagination—each permeates the other. We are offered direct
narration, conversations, interior monologues, and recurring symbols.
The grandfather Heinrich Fähmel, a giant in those days, creates the
design for St. Anthony's Abbey in 1907 while the Kaiser is very
much in power; Robert, his son, dynamites the same abbey in the
German retreat at end of the Second World War; Joseph, his grandson revolts against the meaningless cycle of construction, destruction,
and reconstruction which symbolizes and literally represents the
matching historical periods. It is not until the end of the novel that
the reader can piece together the story of the family and that of
central Europe in what has been as chaotic as a nightmare.

The exterior action of the novel covers seven hours on a particular
Saturday, September 6, 1958 ("the perpetual present, moved steadily
on by the second hand"); but the interior action in the minds of the
characters shifts and sifts through the past in an effort to give meaning to the present. Clock time and calendar time and St. Anthony's
Abbey are points of reference in the general incoherence. The family
is as subject to the ravages of time as the abbey. During the war
one son was killed, another son became a Nazi, and a third son was
a passive victim. Böll establishes a firm relationship between victim

and executioner; there are two groups: the People of the Lamb and the Sacrament of the Buffalo, the latter advocating raw power. The existential choice of our time has been Lamb or Buffalo.

One of the central characters and a possible spokesman for the author is the mother of the Fähmel family; events have unhinged her mind but from the advantaged seclusion of the sanitarium she reflects on a world supposed to be sane with integrity and ironic insight: "All of us here know that all men are brothers, even if they be hostile ones. Some have tasted of the *Host of the Lamb,* only a few of us of the *Host of the Beast,* and my name is *got to get a gun, get a gun,* and my Christian name is *forward with Hindenburg, hurrah.* Forget all your bourgeois prejudices for good, your conversational clichés; here the classless society rules. And stop complaining about losing the war. Good heavens, did you really lose two wars, one after the other? You could have lost seven for all of me. Stop your sniveling, I wouldn't give five cents for all the wars you lost; losing children is worse than losing wars." And she continues, "The German future is all pegged out. If you have to weep, don't blubber. . . . But now relax, in this booby hatch they take care of you fine, in this place they go into it every time your soul lets out a squeak, all complexes respected here. Just a question of money: if you were poor, it would be cold water and a good thrashing, but here they cater to every one of your whims."

Mother Fähmel insists that she has never felt such a stranger among people as now, not even in 1935 or in 1942. They are "respectable, without a trace of grief. What's a human being without grief?" Her son Robert stands in the middle between the firmly decent and urbane father and his mother's derangement, between his own "security" and prosperity and the protests of his son Joseph, the only hope of the family's future. In the meantime he seeks stability by playing billiards and never varying from his scheduled games; this is his tranquilizer to lay the memories of the abbey ruins for which he is responsible, the deaths of his brother and wife during the war. A police chief, Nettlinger, who had worked with the Gestapo, wanders through the novel in a sinister way; he is the sadist who covers his evil with sentimentality and charm. For the Fähmels the reemergence of conscience and responsibility thaws the frozen past, floods the present, and gives at least a minimal hope for the future as Robert gives up the routine of his billiard games to face things as they are.

13. NOUVEAU ROMAN OR ANTI-NOVEL

In France after the second World War two important tendencies dominated the novel and spilled over into other genres, even other arts and other nations: first existentialism and then the "New Novel" (Nouveau Roman) or Anti-Novel. In some ways the second grew out of the first; in other ways it revolted against existentialism, particularly against its latent doctrine of commitment, its call to making a choice, to engagement.

Although Sartre did not invent the term *anti-roman* (or anti-novel), as Wallace Fowlie has suggested (Jean-Pierre Faye traced it back to a 1633 book by Charles Sorel, *L'anti-roman*), he did use it for the first time in its new context in his introduction to Nathalie Sarraute's *Portrait d'un inconnu (Portrait of a Man Unknown)* published in 1948 and reprinted in 1956. This is a statement of primary importance: "One of the most singular traits of our literary epoch is the appearance here and there of lively and completely negative works which one could call *anti-romans.* I would place in that category the works of Nabokov, those of Evelyn Waugh and, in a certain sense, *The Counterfeiters.*" Evelyn Waugh seems to be an eccentric inclusion and Vladimir Nabokov a prescient one among the anti-novelists, but Sartre is leading up to Nathalie Sarraute.

He goes on to define the anti-novel as an attempt to undermine the accepted forms of the novel from within. "The anti-romans preserve the appearance and contours of the novel; they are imaginative works which present us with fictive characters and tell us their story. But it is for the purpose of better deceiving us: their aim is to make use of the novel in order to challenge the novel, to destroy it before our eyes while seeming to construct it, to write the novel of a novel unwritten and unwritable, to create a type of fiction that will compare with the great compositions of Dostoevsky and Meredith much as Miro's canvas, 'The Assassination of Painting,' compares with the pictures of Rembrandt and Rubens. These strange and difficult-to-classify works are not a witness to the weakness of the novel form; they only call attention to the fact that we live in an age of reflection and that the novel is in the act of reflecting on itself. Of such is the book of Nathalie Sarraute: an anti-novel that reads like a detective story (*roman policier*). Moreover it is a parody of "quest" novels and she introduces in it a sort of amateur detective who is passionately fascinated by a banal couple—an old father, a daughter no longer very young—and spies on them and dogs their footsteps and sometimes guesses about them from a distance, but never very well knowing what he is looking for nor what they are. Besides that he will find nothing, or almost nothing. He will abandon his inquiry because of a metamorphosis: as if Agatha Christie's policeman, on the point of finding the guilty one, should be suddenly and criminally silent."

The question of destruction and building might have been put in reverse: building a novel in front of us at the same time as seeming to be destroying it. The analogy with painting is well taken (all the arts seem to have become self-conscious); there is discernible a kind of anti-painting today which goes back to cubism and non-representational art for its beginnings. Anti-theatre will be seen in the Theatre of the Absurd. Anti-music and anti-sculpture are also viable terms in the challenge of modern art. Malraux of course has recently written his *Anti-Mémoires*. The anti-poem is the least interesting of them all. In the film, closely connected with the work of Robbe-Grillet and Alain Resnais, the anti-novel becomes the *Nouvelle Vague* (New Wave) as in *L'Année Dernière à Marienbad (Last Year in Marienbad)*.

Of course the attack on novel conventions has concentrated first of all on plot in the old sense; its reduction to a minimum or virtual elimination; then on character, again reducing characters to the minimum, to the nebulous, often without even names for identification (somewhat like one aspect of expressionistic theatre). Time is frequently shattered, or at least traditional chronology. What is left? Place, or at least objects in space ("saying it with things"), phenomenology, epistemology, language, and psychological states. Ultimately reduction can become ridiculous (as in Samuel Beckett's contribution, "Prologue," to the 1969 *Oh! Calcutta!*—rubbish, naked people, a faint brief cry and a sigh: that's all). But some reduction can be intriguing—giving the reader a sort of do-it-yourself novel kit. These novels are often in the nature of puzzles; but there is no "cheating" in them, as may be the case in surrealism, and puzzles can be fun.

Every novel if it's worth much is "new." But the Nouveau Roman, even if not a movement and nobody connected with it seems to want to be in or part of a movement, generally includes centrally the work of Nathalie Sarraute, Alain Robbe-Grillet, and Michel Butor, who are the chief theorists as well as practitioners of the form. What they have in common defines the form; their differences help define them and give them significant individual voices. Often added are Samuel Beckett (see Theatre of the Absurd), Claude Simon, Claude Ollier, and Robert Pinget. Probably now Golding and Durrell and Nabokov should be added as well.

The influences that have created the New Novel are generally recognized by its writers as fundamentally Joyce and Kafka, add Proust, Faulkner, and Gide (and indirectly the filtered-down thinking of Heidegger and Husserl); and there are isolated references to Camus, Sartre's *Nausea,* and John Dos Passos; to Henry Green and Ivy Compton-Burnett, particularly in Nathalie Sarraute's excellent *The Age of Suspicion.* In John Sturrock's study of 1969 he emphasizes as a central proposition that the *nouveau roman* must *never* be read as an exercise in naive realism or naturalism, but as a dramatization of the creative process itself. "What the New Novel is depriving its readers of are the consolations of a mechanistic sequence of events, with its confident marriage of causes with effects, and of an essentialist psychology which lends a spurious coherence to the activity of unknowable other minds." Robbe-Grillet has an essay entitled "Nouveau Roman, Homme Nouveau" (New Novel, New Man), which indicates a thrust toward artistic responsibility. We must face the facts of chaos if we are going to try to order them. The New Novel is subjective and objective both, within specific limitations; the New Novelist is humble (filled with self-doubt, even guilt, according to Nathalie Sarraute) and proud with his "sovereignty of reflective consciousness," which produces an interior monologue as the only area of justifiable reality.

Nathalie Sarraute (Russian-French, born 1902)

Nathalie Sarraute is really the innovator among the French of the Nouveau Roman or Anti-Novel, although the terms did not become current until after Alain Robbe-Grillet had appeared on the scene in 1953 with *Les Gommes (The Erasers)*. Madame Sarraute had published her first work, *Tropismes,* in Paris in 1939 (and had begun writing them as early as 1932). The war intervened and she received little attention until Jean-Paul Sartre "discovered" her in 1947 and prepared a "Préface" for her novel, *Portrait d'un Inconnu*. Not by nature a polemicist like Robbe-Grillet and to some extent Michel Butor, she has been somewhat overwhelmed by the advent of her successors, although she has in the sixties appeared in literary debate, in conferences and interviews, lecturing and broadcasting over much of Europe and in America. Her position and her literary discoveries now seem assured of the considerable attention they deserve.

LIFE: Born July 18, 1902 in Russia of Jewish parents who had met in Geneva, Switzerland (not being at that time welcome in Russian universities) Nathalie experienced a rather divided childhood after the divorce of her parents when she was two, living sometimes with her mother (who wrote popular novels) and sometimes with her father in Russia, Switzerland, or Paris, where from eight on she lived with her remarried father. From her step-mother's mother she learned German (to add to her Russian and French) and at the Sorbonne took a *licence* in English. In 1921-22 she was studying history at Oxford; there followed a year of sociology in Berlin, and law studies at the University of Paris, with admission to the Bar. She married a fellow law student and during the next twelve years had three daughters, practiced law on the side, and began writing. *Tropismes,* her first book, not a novel but twenty-four brief sketches, was written during the thirties and published in 1939. A dictionary defiinition of her title, basically a scientific term, is important to an understanding of what she was trying to do with no predecessor of whom she is aware: Involuntary movement of an organism or any of its parts involving turning or curvature and induced either automatically or in reference to stimuli as in heliotropism or phototropism or geotropism. This produces her distinctive method of writing which she explained in 1961 in *The Listener* as follows: "These movements glide quickly round the border of our consciousness, they compose the small, rapid, and sometimes very complex dramas concealed beneath our actions, our gestures, the words we speak. . . . I had to express them through the rhythm of the style as poetry does, and, as they can hardly be expressed in words, I had to try to find images which could convey to the reader the impression, the feeling of these tropisms produced in the character without his knowing clearly what they really were." As Ruth Tempje says, "This is not stream of consciousness but the sea of the subconscious from which that stream flows. In this sea there are vague tidal movements from and toward the persons and objects of experience." Tropisms are microdramas.

In 1941 and during the Occupation Madame Sarraute lived outside Paris under an assumed name as the pretended governess of her own children and worked on her first novel. Even with Sartre's help it was not a success financially although published in 1948. Upon republication in 1957 by Gallimard *Portrait d'un Inconnu* joined her second novel, *Martereau* (1953), and *L'Ere du Soupçon* (1956) in finding a somewhat wider public. *Planétarium* and *Fruits d'Or* in 1959 and 1963 contributed to the reputation which won for Madame Sarraute a Prix International in 1964. She wrote two radio plays that were produced in Europe and published in 1967, *Le Silence* and *Le Mensonge*. In 1968 appeared another novel, *Entre la Vie et la Mort*. Madame Sarraute now lives and works in Paris. Her photographs have come to resemble those of Ivy Compton-Burnett, whose novels she so much admires.

CHIEF WORKS: *L'Ere du Soupçon (The Age of Suspicion;* Essays on the novel, 1956) is one of the key theoretical documents of the *nouveau roman* movement. The title is misleading for the English reader who does not know French. "Suspicion" may be translated into French as either *mefiance* or *soupcon*. The first emphasizes mistrust or distrust (for example, the suspicion of a husband that his wife may be unfaithful). The second includes these connotations, but even more emphasizes uncertainty, doubt, or ambiguity. Madame Sarraute's title therefore implies, "The era in which we suspect, or guess, that things may be true, but cannot be sure." This is the spirit of the new novel which the essay collection describes.

Although the book consists of four separate essays, two of them originally published in Sartre's *Temps Modernes* and a third in another magazine, they are actually highly unified and together constitute a kind of history of the modern novel, plus a defense of the nouveau roman or anti-novel. The first essay, "From Dostoevsky to Kafka," argues that these two novelists are not antithetically opposed, as some critics have suggested, but instead are the co-founders of the modern novel at is is to emerge after 1945. Another key novel cited is Camus' *L'Etranger;* the *homo absurdus* or Absurd Hero of Camus is the hero (or anti-hero) of the novels of Robbe-Grillet, Butor, and Madame Sarraute herself. And consideration is also given to Proust, Gide, Rilke, Joyce, and Faulkner for their contribution to reduction of character. In addition to its theoretical importance, this book is a masterful piece of prose in its own right, comparable in significance to E. M. Forster's *Aspects of the Novel* or Virginia Woolf's essays on the art of the novel. The fourth essay, with a focus on things, has the fascinating title, "What Birds See."

Portrait d'un Inconnu (Portrait of a Man Unknown; novel, 1948) is Madame Sarraute's best-known work, at least in the United States. The story, in so far as there is one, is related in the first person by a narrator who is nameless and without qualities, although he is evidently male and neither very young nor very old. The two other main characters are a Father and a Daughter who have lived together for years and who continually torment each other with reproaches and recriminations, although it becomes evident as the novel unfolds that they are held together by forces as strong as the hostilities that tend to drive them apart. The Father is miserly and egotistical; the Daughter is self-pitying, masochistic, and passive. From an existentialistic point of view both are guilty of bad faith, and in the end both are weak human beings, held together by their weakness. The Narrator chats in a labyrinthine and apparently confused way about these people to whom he serves as a family friend, perhaps a "double" for the father, possibly a spy, and perhaps more. A particularly effective scene is the one in which the Father, barefooted and in his nightshirt, steals into the kitchen in the middle of the night in order to prove to his own satisfaction that the Daughter has been stealing small pieces of soap. The small mannerisms, habits, and tics of the pair, including the Father's inane conversational peculiarities, are depicted with great skill.

Meanwhile the Narrator himself probes his own problems, although these are even less clear, and more ambiguous, than those of the Father and Daughter. An examination of the Narrator's own pre-occupations, and his comments about himself, will make it clear that the dominant theme of the novel is loneliness, and the desire of human beings to communicate with their fellows. The Father and Daughter had found a kind of "communication," at least, in their constant tormenting of each other. For the Narrator the problem is more difficult. The closest he has ever come to a genuine communica-tion was an experience, some years before, of contemplating a paint-ing in a Dutch museum. The painting had the title *Portrait d'un inconnu,* and the artist was unknown. Something about the glance, the posture, the personality of this figure, spoke in an unmistakable voice to the narrator, ". . . the man's expression gripped me by its determination and authoritativeness. There was no doubt about it, his entreaty was addressed to me, and to me alone. . . ." Here the author is perhaps suggesting that, although human communication is terribly difficult and perhaps impossible, it can be best achieved, or most nearly achieved, in the world of art.

Later in the novel the Narrator tries to explain his fascination with the painting to the Daughter, but with little success. As the novel ends the Daughter becomes engaged to the strong, vigorous, and confident Louis Dumontet, who easily dominates both Daughter and Father. It is significant that he is the only character in the novel who has a name. Although this is a typical anti-novel in technique, its moral system is thoroughly existentialist: Dumontet, the only character in the novel who knows what he wants, and has the will and courage to set out to get it, has made his own world of values and is the only character in the novel untroubled by the problem of communication. As for the Narrator, at the end he is looking forward only to death.

Alain Robbe-Grillet (French, born 1922)

Alain Robbe-Grillet is not as cerebral a writer as Nathalie Sarraute or Michel Butor. But he has been more popular, particularly in

America. Perhaps that is one reason. There are others. He relies even more heavily than his fellow novelists on the *roman policier* for basic structure, and detective stories have a built-in popular fascination. Most of his characters, so far as we can determine, seem to be psychopathological. He is therefore a kind of Alfred Hitchcock of the novel. He has also devoted himself to film writing and film making in association with the *Nouvelle Vague*. His cinema-novels as he calls them rather than film-scripts, *L'Année Dernière à Marienbad* (1961) and *L'Immortelle* (1963), have certainly brought him a wider public exposure than would have been possible with the novels alone. Furthermore his novels have had wide paperback distribution in English translation. But he is an authentic New Novelist and therefore disturbing but not easy. He is reported to have said that he *wants* his readers to feel disappointed (in their expectation of clarification, presumably), that if they feel disappointed he knows he has succeeded in what he was trying to do. At least one critic has placed Robbe-Grillet at "the most advanced point of evolution of the twentieth-century novel and film."

LIFE: Alain Robbe-Grillet was born August 18, 1922 in Brest on the seacoast of Brittany, the son of Gaston and Yvonne Robbe-Grillet, who had moved there from the Jura. As a child he was intrigued by the lichens and rock plants of the coast (perhaps observing their tropisms while Nathalie Sarraute was writing in these terms) and by the gulls on the cliffs of Finistère (which may reappear in *The Voyeur*). Educated at the Lycée Buffon, the Lycée St. Louis, and the Institut National Agronomique in Paris, he became a professional agronomic engineer in the years 1949 to 1951 at the Institute des Fruits Tropicaux in Guinea, Morocco, Martinique, and Guadaloupe; but his interests turned increasingly toward writing which eventually became his full-time career. The banana plantations, verandas, and fronds of Martinique return in *La Jalousie.* Robbe-Grillet's first novel, *Les Gommes (The Erasers),* appeared in 1953; his second, *Le Voyeur,* in 1955; and his career was well launched. In 1957 he married Catherine Rstakian and published his third novel, *La Jalousie,* followed two years later by a fourth, *Dans le Labyrinthe (In the Labyrinth).*

His attention then turned to the cinema, at first in collaboration with the film director Alain Resnais. In 1961 *L'Année Dernière à Marienbad* hit the movie world with an originality that for a time usurped the attention customarily given to the Italian films of Fellini or the Swedish films of Bergman. *Last Year at Marienbad* played long runs in the art film houses in New York and across the United States. Bruce Morrissette in a critique of the film pointed out to less perceptive critics that it represented a continuation of techniques established in the earlier novels: "False scenes and objectified hypothesis as in *The Voyeur,* a subjective universe converted into objective perceptions as in *Jealousy*—with its detemporalization of mental states, its mixture of memories (true and false), of desire images and affective projections—the 'dissolves' found in *The Labyrinth*: all these reach a high point in Marienbad. . . . The spectator's work, like that of the reader, becomes an integral part of the cinematic or novelistic creation." The viewer like the reader was expected to collaborate in creating meaning. *Marienbad* takes place at an ornate Bavarian palace; the action is circular (like *Finnegans Wake,* says Morrissette) beginning with "Once more" as the camera moves through Freudian corridors, empty rooms and a formal garden (with a return at the end); characters emerge as a young woman, A, an older man M (presumably her jealous husband), and a persistent lover X. Fantasies of seduction, resistance, desire, fear, rape, and even murder are projected; but whose they are, A's or M's or X's is never clear. You take your choice.

Robbe-Grillet's second film, *L'Immortelle* (1963), carries the same techniques even further, this time in Istanbul, with a visiting professor N as narrator-protagonist, but the psychic projections this time are all his: an affair with an attractive woman L and the spying on them by an ominous Turk M with two large dogs, a double scene of death by auto accident at high speed. This time it's Robbe-Grillet all the way. In 1963 he also published a collection of essays, *Pour un Nouveau Roman (For a New Novel),* and in 1965 another novel, *La Maison de rendez-vous (The House of Assignation).* He has been living at Neuilly-sur-Seine, an attractive suburb of Paris.

CHIEF NOVELS (or Anti-Novels): *Les Gommes (The Erasers;* novel, 1953) is Robbe-Grillet's first novel and not as radical in style as some of his later experiments. Essentially this anti-novel is an attempt to annihilate the *roman policier* or French detective story through exaggerating its elements and carrying its techniques to an extreme. It is thus possible to regard it as a parody of a typical novel of Georges Simenon, who created the Inspector Maigret stories which made him world-famous. It may be more, of course, with a hidden story of the Oedipus myth running parallel with it; Morrissette thinks Robbe-Grillet attributed the same importance to the parallelism as Joyce to the Ulysses myth, although *Les Gommes* may seek to "erase" the connecting links. The epigraph is from Sophocles: "Time that sees all has found you out against your will."

In any event the novel follows the form of a conventional *roman-policier* exactly and even imitates its style. The plot is as intricate as those of most detective novels. Wallas, an investigator employed by a secret bureau of the Interior Ministry, comes to an "Amsterdam-like" provincial city to investigate the "murder" of Daniel Dupont, a harmless middle-aged professor. Dupont is a very common name in French, something like Smith in English. The Ministry suggests to Wallas that Dupont's murder is part of a widespread conspiracy organized by an anarchist society, which plans to murder a new victim daily at the exact hour of seven-thirty in the evening. It is true that such conspiracy exists, but in actual fact Dupont has not been murdered; his assassin Garinati has only slightly wounded him, and with the connivance of the Ministry he goes into hiding in order to confuse the anarchist organization.

But both Wallas and Laurent, the police commissioner in the provincial city, believe Dupont to be dead, and they begin their investigation. The major part of the novel is devoted to Wallas' prowlings through the city and to his efforts to interview people who have known Dupont or who might have been his assailant. The *gommes* or erasers of the title are a false clue; a half-dozen times in the novel Wallas goes into a shop and purchases "a soft eraser, suitable for drawing," but nothing ever happens with these erasers and at the end of the novel they are presumably still in his pocket. But they are an example of the preoccupation of the *anti-roman* with objects or things (*choses*) which have led to Robbe-Grillet's being called a *chosiste*. If this is a novel about the writing of a novel, the novelist will certainly need an eraser. Other critics find the gum eraser charged with "erotic significance," a clue to Wallas if not to the crime. He is seized with powerful erotic impulses toward the saleswomen from whom he buys them and "one of these is Dupont's second wife, who may be Wallas' step-mother"—shades of Oedipus! Many elements of the classic detective story are parodied, including the master detective's meticulous noting of streets(like the Rue de Corinthe), bridges (*du pont* means "of the bridge"), the contents of shops, conversations overheard on trams, and other clues, all of which come to nothing. Here Robbe-Grillet anticipates the detailed and almost obsessive concern with epistemological minutia which is to dominate his later novels.

The complicated plot comes to a parodistic yet terrifying climax. Returning secretly to his house in search of some papers, the falsely-dead Dupont is shot and really killed by Wallas himself, who is waiting there in ambush for the return of the assassin to the scene of the crime, Wallas who may be, only may be, the real son of Dupont (at least his mother had brought him to this place as a child to see a "relative"). Yet this ludicrously improbable plot, far from being treated humorously or ironically, is related in the flattest possible manner as deadly serious. After finishing the novel one may feel that he has read a detective story that demolishes detective stories (but perhaps no more so than Cervantes demolished tales of chivalry). There are critics like Morrissette who prefer to concentrate on the Oedipus parallels. And there are others like John Sturrock who see Robbe-Grillet having the time of his life dramatizing the conditions under which a novel comes into being, the relationship between the novelist and his material. This also is highly ingenious; the patron of the café in the opening scene at dawn, six in the morning, is the novelist arranging "the stage" with tables and chairs. The novel is "like a play where the curtain has gone up too soon, since it reveals the author, who is also, in this post-Brechtian age, allowed to double as an actor, still at work on his preparations." Time must have a stop, as the wrist watch of Wallas stops at 7:30, time of the supposed murder, and starts when the murder is really done at 7:30. The draw-bridge which fails to close completely, a "mechanical" failure, is also exploited as symbolic of novelistic structure and the "double" closing of "Dupont's" life. One can be sure that Robbe-Grillet is gratified by such multiplicity of interpretation; it is a game in which all can join for the "refreshment" offered at his novelistic café.

Le Voyeur (The Voyeur; novel, 1955) is the novel with a hole in the middle. The main character, and we are made to perceive with his perceptions, is Mathias, a watch salesman and a sadistic psychopath; he visits on business the coastal island where he had been born some thirty-five years ago but had not seen since childhood. While there for a specific time between steamship sailings he rents a bicycle and sets out to cover the territory; some scenes are real and some imagined; there are images related to voyeurism and sadism, windows and ship cords rolled into a figure-eight, similar marks of iron rings on a sea wall, and the same pattern in flights of gulls. "Something" has happened; and through the accumulation of objective description, the perceptions and movements of Mathias, we become accomplices of a homicidal maniac. But the climax, the rape and murder of a thirteen-year old girl Jacqueline thrown over the cliffs, is left out. As Robbe-Grillet has said, "Everything is told before the 'hole,' then again after the 'hole,' and there is an effort to bring together the two edges to eliminate this troublesome emptiness; but the opposite occurs, the 'hole' engulfs everything."

We don't even *know* that these events take place, although we are relatively sure. With chronometric and minute care we follow Mathias on the island, café, shop, street, country, to the farmhouse where he at last sells a watch and learns from the customer that her daughter Jacqueline is keeping sheep near a cliff on one side of the path he must take to reach the other end of the island. At the crossroads he turns his bicycle toward the cliffs. The narrative resumes an hour or so later, back on the main road, where Mathias meets a peasant woman, Madame Marek, and tells her he has been visiting her farm. His lies are "confirmed" by the woman's son, young Julien, to cover his own *voyeur* presence watching the events of the preceding hour. Julien has picked up a cigarette butt and a candy wrapper that Mathias returns to the scene to recover, but although he confronts him he fails to denounce him. Scenes of torture and killing return uncensored to the mind of Mathias which, with his search for the "clues" and the challenge of Julien, justify our assumption of his guilt. But Mathias is revealed increasingly as schizophrenic; and with inversions of chronology, repetitions and variations of the same scene compounded in memory we are hardly sure of anything but the increased flow of adrenalin.

La Jalousie (Jealousy; novel, 1957) is, perhaps, Robbe-Grillet's best-known novel and one of the most successful examples of "pure" Nouveau Roman. The "action" takes place on a banana plantation somewhere in the West Indies, perhaps Martinique where Robbe-Grillet at one time worked as an agronomist. There are only three important characters: the unnamed viewer or protagonist, a banana planter of European extraction; his wife, who is referred to only as "A . . .," and Franck, another planter who lives nearby and is a friend of both husband and wife. The novel opens with a detailed, almost obsessive physical description of the plantation house. The only action in the early part of the novel is the visit of Franck who comes for dinner and first shares a drink with his friends on the veranda. The second section of the narration introduces another of the descriptive or epistemological themes: the exact geometrical alignment and counting of the banana trees which can be seen from the veranda and other parts of the house. There may be a psychic meaning here, referring to the husband's meticulous habits of observation, a withdrawn, perhaps impotent personality; increasingly he shows himself to be psychotic. A little later a third visual image is introduced: the insect, a particular kind of centipede, which frightens the wife and which is crushed to death by Franck with his napkin leaving an ugly spot on the wall of the dining room. The mark left by this insect is described, and the image recurs frequently throughout the novel; the centipede is built up in the mind of the husband to a gigantic creature, distorted with hallucinatory erotic meaning, the crushing an objective correlative of the vision of his tormented jealousy. The whole structure of the novel is rhythmic or repetitious with recurrent, altered images to reflect the neurotic and obsessive state of mind of the husband, who increasingly convinces himself throughout the novel that his wife is betraying him with Franck.

The climactic action in this anti-novel which is almost devoid of action is a visit of Franck and A . . . to a nearby coastal seaport in Franck's blue sedan. Franck goes to the seaport because he has business there, A . . . takes the opportunity to accompany him to do some shopping. Although this episode (as far as we can determine) is completely innocent, a breakdown of the car compels Franck and A . . . to stay overnight in a seaside hotel. When they do not return, the husband's jealousy drives him into quasi-paranoid imaginative reveries in which the adulterous affair of the pair is consummated. Their absence means that they have escaped the field of the narrator's observation and for behavioral facts he will have to substitute fictions, thereby becoming an "unwilling novelist." The husband has become virtually demented; the whole environment around him is filled with images of vague but ominous portent. This novel is not about action at all; it is about non-action, and about the obsessive inward reactions of the husband to actions he imagines but which have probably never taken place.

The word *jalousie* in French has several meanings; it corresponds to the English "jealousy," but it also is used to designate a lattice or venetian blind, of the kind through which the husband might be peering to spy on A . . . as she is combing her hair, writing a letter, or sitting on the veranda with Franck. It should also be noted that Franck is the only one of the three characters to have a concrete name; he is a masculine character and the husband's consciousness is focussed on him with a neurotic and exclusive intensity.

Michel Butor (French, born 1926)

Butor is a more hopeful writer, more openly a moralist, than the other novelists of the "New" school. He started of course just a bit later and somewhat younger than those with whom his name is associated, although his development was completely independent of Sarraute and Robbe-Grillet. He had already written his first novel, *Passage de Milan,* when Robbe-Grillet's first novel appeared, although his own was not published until the following year, 1954. It wasn't until after writing his second novel, *L'Emploi du Temps,* that he discovered and read Nathalie Sarraute. As a moral and optimistic writer he can offer, among the antinovelists, the best antidote to the gloom of Samuel Beckett.

LIFE: Michel Butor was born September 14, 1926 at Mons-en-Baroeul, just outside Lille, an industrial city in northern France, the third of seven children of a white-collar railroad employee. After the family transfer to Paris in 1929, Michel was sent to Catholic schools until the interruption caused by the outbreak of the war. He did return to Paris during the Occupation to study at the Lycée Louis-le-Grand and later at the University of Paris. He became a teacher in 1949 in the lycée at Sens and for the next eight years taught in Egypt, in Manchester, England (1951-53), in Salonika in Greece, and in Geneva. His first novel, written in England and published in 1954, was followed by the second novel with a setting in England (Bleston presumably standing for a fictionalized Manchester), *L'Emploi du Temps* (1956). *La Modification,* perhaps his finest novel to date, appeared in 1957 and his fourth novel, *Degrés,* in 1960; by this time he was a reader for Gallimard, had married Marie-Joseph Mas in 1958, was publishing considerable non-fiction and lecturing. In 1960. he was a visiting professor at Bryn Mawr and Middlebury, and in 1962 at the University of Buffalo.

An urbane lecturer (visiting many other American colleges in the sixties) Butor feels there is no necessary division between criticism and the novel. His own novels, called "the most formidably intellectual of all the fabrications of the *nouveau roman,*" are seen as the end result of all the novels that have been written in the past (at least those the novelist has read). "The new novelist writes a novel because no existent one, so far as he knows, says what he wants to say," correcting or supplementing the literature already written. The creator criticizes by inventing, and the critic invents by criticizing. Léon Roudiez points out that a writer's stature may be seen in his powers of assimilation. "When first reading Butor, one is not tempted to say, This is like Faulkner, or like Joyce, or like Proust." There are analogies and influences, of course, but on the raw materials, "Michel Butor has indelibly stamped the seal of his unique art."

CHIEF NOVELS: *L'Emploi du Temps (Passing Time;* novel, 1965) really refers to the uses of time. The protagonist-narrator-novelist, a young Frenchman named Jacques Revel, having been sent to the English city of Bleston to spend exactly one year working with an English business firm as a sort of apprentice, arriving a stranger on

the night of October 1, decides seven months later to write down
what has happened to him from that moment of arrival. He writes
in order to give meaning to his life in the oppressive city. The time
remembered and the time of remembering are sometimes difficult to
keep discrete. He has developed relationships of a sort with another
clerk at Matthews & Sons, James Jenkins, and his mother; Ann Bailey
and her sister Rose; and another French youth, Lucien, who is more
of an extrovert. Complications are introduced with a thriller, *The
Murder of Bleston,* and its author, the novelist George Burton,
against whom there is an attempted murder. As the diary entries
reach September 30, recording the events of the same day but looking back, we have finally reached a point of convergence from the
initial entry of Thursday, May 1, which recorded the events of the
preceding October 1. Between, we have have had many confusions,
including the intrusion of June on June, the attempt to discuss June
and November in June without losing narrative thread, and more of
same. The artificiality of the detective thriller by Burton, and its
imitation of life in Bleston, inverted when life imitates art, are further
points of epistemological reference. Jacques, however, never seems
to attain the reality or interest of a Leon Delmont in the next novel.

La Modification (A Change of Heart; novel, 1957) is, among
other things, a tale of two cities, Paris and Rome, and a railway
journey between them. The middle-aged man making the trip is
Leon Delmont, a successful business man representing Scabelli's,
an Italian typewriter firm, in its Paris office. The narrative voice is
neither first person nor third, but second, like that in Kafka's "An
Imperial Message." The point of view is Leon's; therefore the second
person formal "you" means either that he's addressing himself as an
alter ego, or an accuser is imagined as probing his sense of guilt and
responsibility. At the beginning of the novel Leon enters the train's
third-class compartment at the Gare du Lyon for almost immediate
departure at 8:10 a.m. At the end of the novel he leaves the compartment at the Roma Termini station at 5:45 a.m. the next morning. The realistic detail of the train trip, the other passengers, the
conductors, the motion, the view from the windows, the fatigue, the
travel posters above the seats, the litter on the floor, becomes hyp-
notic for the reader as well as Leon. The compartment is the reflective

consciousness for us all; when Leon leaves the compartment for any reason, dining car or rest room, he saves his seat with an unread book bought at the station and the narrative of this book stops until his return. He is used to making this trip on business with some frequency and then travels first class on company money, but this is different, a local instead of an express. He has left his wife Henriette and their children in the apartment at 15, Place du Pantheon (a name link with Rome), and is going to meet his mistress Cecile in Rome to tell her of the decision she has been urging on him: that he has found her a job in Paris and that they can live together in an apartment there, a second ménage. But the modification of the decision, a change of plan (more of mind than heart), is what occurs during the journey. Leon reviews his past and present and imagines the future during the long trip. This ride merges with others he has taken, the compartment where he first met Cecile, other trips in both directions, his honeymoon trip with his wife, a later vacation trip. Rome fascinates him; Paris is humdrum. He realizes he is in love not so much with Cecile as with Cecile-in-Rome. He thinks of duties to his sons and daughters. In half-sleep toward morning he slides in and out of hallucinations, but he has examined his past experience and himself so thoroughly that he achieves a new knowledge and some ilumination. "The best thing, surely, would be to preserve the actual geographical relationship between these two cities . . . toward this book." He will go back to Paris without even seeing Cecile. One gets to know Leon as he knows himself, and that is a satisfaction for the reader who finds a real character in an anti-novel.

Vladimir Nabokov (Russian-English-German-French-American born 1899)

If Jean-Paul Sartre was right and possessed clairvoyance when he called Nabokov an anti-novelist in 1948, he probably based his judgment on the tangled publications of the Russian émigré in Russian, French, German, and English of such works as *King, Queen, Knave,* and *The Defense, Invitation to a Beheading, Laughter in the Dark,* **and** possibly *The Real Life of Sebastian Knight.* The world-wide fame of Nabokov had to wait for *Lolita* in 1955. He does share with other writers of the nouveau roman certain reductive techniques and a recurring tendency to parody of the detective story; but then Nabokov parodies everything (himself included at his best). His method seems best described as parody and pastiche. He creates even more puzzles than his fellow novelists, of the double acrostic, New-York-Times-crossword variety; he can be fun for the few, but the decoded message may seem rather thin.

The critics of Nabokov are likely to see him either as worthless or a genius (he himself inclines to the latter view). Even if he is a charlatan, he's an erudite and intriguing one; and his ultimate position in a scale of values will probably lie between the extremes. Some of his devotees consider him the most avant of avant-garde: the only geniuses of new fiction being the three B's (Borges, Beckett, and NaBokov)—which from the perspective of the seventies seems more than a little excessive. He is always spoofing other forms of literature (all of them, biography, poetry, literary criticism as well as fiction) and many of his betters; but he seems to lack the basic good humor and life-saving irony of many of his predecessors in the field, Laurence Sterne, for instance, whose *Tristram Shandy* is often invoked, and James Joyce. It is amusing to see how many of his novels after *Lolita* have been referred to as Nabokov's *Finnegans Wake*. Each one seems more so until *Ada* (1969) leaves the conviction that he can go no further in this direction. But the real "fun at Finnegan's Wake" and its profound insights into the human condition are finally missing; Nabokov has dried out at the pith. His five-finger exercises, however, are not negligible nor completely unoriginal. It is worth putting up with a good deal (even his personality, rebarbative at best, and his own poor literary judgments of his near contemporaries—Faulkner, Mann, and Dostoyevsky will always be more significant than Nabokov) to read some of his work. *Lolita* may be enough; *Pale Fire* and *Ada* are possible for the hardy; the rest is for aficionados.

LIFE: Vladimir Vladimirovich Nabokov was born in 1899 near St. Petersburg in Russia into an artistic, sensitive, and wealthy family with an aristocratic sense of its superiority. His memoir, *Speak Memory* (1951), will fill in the first twenty years of his life, European resorts and country estate living, for those who want them. His father was killed in 1922 in Berlin, shielding a friend from assassination. The revolution had made the family émigrés. Vladimir studied at Trinity College, Cambridge, from 1919 to 1922, his English period. He then spent about fifteen years in Berlin writing, and tutoring students in English and French, and publishing poetry and prose mostly in émigré journals. By 1937 the political situation in Germany had become intolerable for a liberal intellectual with a Jewish wife, Vera; and the family, including son Dmitri, moved to Paris until 1940 when the Nazis again pushed them out, this time in May on the ship *Champlain* to the United States, where in 1945 Nabokov became an American citizen.

From 1942 to 1948 he worked as a research fellow in Comparative Zoolology (specializing in Lepidoptera—butterflies float through all his fiction) at Harvard, teaching Russian grammar and literature at Wellesley, and writing. From 1948 to 1959 he taught Russian and European Literature at Cornell University, but the phenomenal success of *Lolita* (1955) both as a movie and a novel freed him from what he considered an onerous occupation (see *Playboy* interview in January 1964) and he returned to Europe to live in an immense hotel overlooking Lake Geneva. There are filmed interviews taken here; he obviously enjoys the esteem he cultivates; in 1969 he published *Ada or Ardor: A Family Chronicle* as a kind of gift to graduate students who are invited to work out the games and follows the clues.

In 1972 another new novel by Nabokov, *Transparent Things,* appeared and apparently mystified even such a critic and reader as John Updike. Its cleverness is more transparent than opaque. The "hero", Hugh Person (you, person, whoever you are) is the editor of the author "R" (mirror image of the Russian "Я" or "I", presumably Nabokov) who lives in Switzerland and writes poetic "surrealistic" novels, and who "regards the rest of the world as a grotesquely clumsy siege upon his artistic integrity." There is still the hangover of the detective-thriller shadow characteristic of neouveau roman. The style is exuberant, even youthful, but there is hollowness within. When the author writes, "Mr. R., though perhaps not a master of the very first rank," one could see this as modesty or only thinly-cloaked arrogance—at least when compared with the persistent and equally excessive humility of a Borges, who now says he wants only to be forgotten. The real Mr. B. stands a rather better chance of longevity than Mr. R.

CHIEF WORKS: *Lolita* (novel, 1955) is the work of fiction which precipitated the fame of Nabokov in the English-speaking world. The novel becomes a parody of itself in the first paragraph with the introduction of Humbert Humbert, dissolute, erudite European who removes to America for financial reasons, as the main fictional character, emphasis on fictional. Humbert is a middle-aged white widowed male, about forty (but like Prufrock he seems older), with a pathological and Freudian preference for nymphets, girl-children between nine and fourteen sexually attractive (and at least on the threshold of nubility) to much older men, largely through a certain awkwardness, even hermaphroditism. The story is the love, however erotic, sexual, Havelock-Ellisish, of Humbert for Lolita, or Dolores, or Dolly Haze. He even marries her mother, Charlotte Haze, New Englander from the Middle West, in order to be near her, and rejoices in the mother's accidental, if wished-for, death, in giving him the necessary control only apparently incestuous of his newly acquired step-daughter, Humbert and Lolita (far from innocent at twelve) take offf for a year-long American tour in Charlotte's left-over automobile living in Motels. They return to the East and the Beardsley girls' school for Lolita for the next year. Then comes a second motel tour of America, more sinister and melodramatic, with a chase developing and Lolita progressively alienating herself from the loving Humbert until she disappears, presumably abducted by the pursuer. In a fantastic Peter Sellers-Inspector Cluzot ending H. H. finds Lolita pregnant and married, needing money; worms out the identity of the pursuer, Clare Quilty, playwright and pervert; pursues the pursuer and murders him in psychedelic technicolor; and goes to prison, the confessional papers to be published only after Lolita's death.

H. H., even more than the so-called editor John Ray, seems in many ways a stand-in for Mr. Nabokov—often uneasy and as often prolix in his acquired English, American English at that, erudite in a curiously Joycean way, witty and banal, sensitive and insensitive alternately, dropping tag-ends of T. S. Eliot, Joyce, Proust, Browning, and a hundred more in the off-hand way bound to please the reader who recognizes the tags. Mr. Nabokov has pointed out that deliberate lewdness is not inconsistent with flashes of comedy, or vigorous satire, or even the nerve of a fine poet in a wanton mood. All four may be found in *Lolita.*

Pale Fire (novel, or satire on literary criticism, 1962) discusses a poem, "Pale Fire," by John Shade, a joke and not a joke, with the critical apparatus of Foreward, Commentary, and Index. John Shade, deceased, and his poem are not the center of interest; but the half-mad (or is it only half?) Charles Kinbote, commentator and professor at Wordsmith College in New Wye, Appalachia, "friend" of the poet, is the focus. The intricate criticism, a "cryptogrammic paper chase," is part of the pleasure of what Mary McCarthy blurbily called "one of the very great works of art of this country." Others might find the same kind, quality and quantity, of pleasure in the much more accessible and shorter *The Pooh Perplex* of 1963 by Frederick C. Crews.

Ada or Ardor: A Family Chronicle (novel, 1969) is, rather than *Pale Fire* (as Page Stegner seems to think) or any of the earlier "novels," Nabokov's most deliberate approach to *Finnegans Wake.* Alfred Kazin says that in *Ada* the Russian novelist voyages "madly through Time" (and in the mind of Nabokov) with "Lolita's cerebral young successors—a precocious incestuous pair" named Van and Ada; but he says as well that all his characters sound like little Nabokovs. John Updike refers to the "haughty" Nabokov as the best equipped writer in the English-speaking world (but doesn't mention what he's equipped with) and calls the opening of *Ada* intentionally repellant, "bristling erudition, garlicky puns, bearish parentheses, and ogreish winks," and loaded with butterflies. The novel has to do with the marriage of two Durmanov sisters, Marina and Aqua, to two men each called Walter D. Veen (which is perhaps divine, or the French *devine* meaning "guess"), first cousins kept apart only by nicknames, Red (or Dan) and Demon. (Demon Dan is for the common garden-variety reader.) Demon has a love affair with Marina but marries Aqua who goes insane, with one apparent offspring, Van; but Van's real mother is Marina, who "fertile as well as obliging," is also the mother of Demon's other, illegitimate child, Ada—and by her own husband, Red Veen, the well-known art dealer, another daughter, Lucette.

The very incestuous love affair between Van and Ada occupies nearly six hundred pages set on the unique geography of the planet Demonia, or Antiterra, where Terra is only a rumor to be believed or not like heaven. On Antiterra, Canady and Estoty contain large French and Russian territories (this often *sounds* like Terra). The action takes place in the second half of Antiterra's 19th century in a "nulliverse" which represents the author's mind. Tri-lingual puns abound (but not as good as Joyce's): Aqua - Marina—"A l'eau" yourself. Vain, venereal Van Veen verges on V. N.; Nabokov equals Van + book. Ada (rhymes with Nevada) is ardor and art— but not perhaps the Americans for Democratic Action. She is prob- ably Nabokov's wife, Vera, among other things. In *Ada* he has tried to construct, with his **Hades** and Nirvana, an Otherlife. But, born and brought up an aristocrat, rich, healthy, physically successful, Nabokov lacks the tender underside of Proust, Joyce, Kafka, or Mann. *Ada* sounds a little like Henry Miller crossed with Joyce and J. R. R. Tolkien, which for some tastes will be like bird's nest soup, sprinkled with butterflies soaked in formaldehyde.

Gunther Grass (German, born 1927)

One of the youngest and most successful novelists of post World War II Germany Günther Grass has used the approaches of Theatre of the Absurd and the new or anti-novel for an aggressive and polem- ical satire that is as biting as any written in the twentieth century— Sinclair Lewis, Evelyn Waugh, W. H. Auden, Aldous Huxley, and George Orwell included, even Joseph Heller. Nabokov has satiric thrusts but is diffuse compared with the mordant concentration of Grass.

He began a career as a painter and sculptor but before 1957 had written a number of plays in the idiom of absurd theatre, violent and grotesque canvases like Bosch or Goya. Many of them remained in manuscript for a long time: *Onkel, Onkel (Uncle, Uncle)* about a young man Bollin dedicated to murder, always failing because his intended victims are not afraid of him, and finally killed by two children who steal and use his own revolver: *Zweiunddreissig Zähne*

(Thirty-two Teeth) about a schoolmaster for whom tooth hygiene is an overriding passion (similarities to his 1969 novel); *Hochwasser (The Flood)* about a family on the roof of their house during high water meeting a pair of philosophical rats, regretting the loss of excitement and fantasy when the emergency is over—these are examples. *The Wicked Cooks (Die Bösen Köche)*, first to be published, polishes a theme which was a favorite of Strindberg, the vampires who suck the good out of food and life.

But Günter Grass in turning to the novel with *Die Blechtrommel (The Tin Drum)* in 1959 found a major success with a vast and grotesquely lively story and the medium most congenial to his talent. It was the reverse motion of a Samuel Beckett who started with nouveau roman but found himself most brilliantly in the theatre of the absurd.

LIFE: Born in 1927 in the Free City of Danzig (now the Polish city of Gdansk), the son of a German grocer and a mother of Slavonic-Pomeranian peasant stock, Günter Grass has made his native city, seaport and the surrounding area the setting for much of his fiction. He was forced into the Hitler youth movement and drafted as a Luftwaffe aide at the age of sixteen. He was wounded in battle and taken a prisoner of war, released in 1946 homeless and nineteen. Günter found work as a farm laborer in the Rhineland and later various jobs in a mine and with a stonecutter. He studied sculpture in an art academy at Düsseldorf and earned extra money as a jazz band drummer. Beginning in 1953 he lived for three years in Berlin with his Swiss wife, studied painting and began writing poetry and plays.

Sponsored by "Group 47," he went to Paris for two years to work on his novel. *Die Blechtrommel*. Its success enabled him to continue with *Katz und Maus (Cat and Mouse)*, a novella in 1961 and the novel *Hundejahre (Dog Years)* in 1963. As a novel "trilogy" (characters wander from one into the others which follow) these three form a panoramic view of modern Germany and its history "written in its time, looking out of the window and with one's ear turned to the street," according to Grass, who often talks of his works in terms of the epic novel like those of Melville and Alfred Döblin (who in a sense imitated Joyce's treatment of Dublin with his *Alexanders-*

platz for Berlin). Günter Grass has published a fourth novel. *Örtlich Betäubt* (1969) which appeared in English as *Local Anaesthetic* in 1970; here his satire shifts to a broader perspective with barbs that reach as far as America, and the connections with Robbe-Grillet, for example, become even clearer. He has continued to be active in support of the Social Democratic Party, with residence in Berlin.

CHIEF NOVELS: *Die Blechtrommel (The Tin Drum,* 1959) is Grass' best-known work and perhaps the most interesting novel to be produced by the younger generation of German writers who have emerged since the war. In form it is a *Bildungsroman* or traditional German "novel of personal development," but Grass treats this genre with an exuberant irony which in some passages approaches outright parody. In another sense the novel parallels Mann's *Doktor Faustus:*

it can be read as a kind of allegory of German history from the early twentieth century through the Nazi period and the war. Its chief qualities are its verve and exuberance of style, its caustic irony toward middle-class values and toward German civilization in general, and its macabre comedy of the kind sometimes called gallows-humor.

The Tin Drum is narrated in the first person by Oskar Matzerath, of part German and part Polish extraction, born in Danzig in 1924. As he tells his life story he is evidently in a prviate clinic where he is confined as a mental patient, although the reason for this does not become apparent until the end of the novel. Oskar has two "fathers": his legal father Alfred Matzerath, a grocer who marries his mother in 1923, and his mother's cousin Jan Bronski, whom he believes to be his real progenitor. At the age of three Oskar falls downstairs—an accident which is at least partly voluntary—and causes some neurological damage to his head. As a result of this he grows up a dwarf; he remains less than three feet tall until he is twenty-one. An important (somewhat satirical) theme of the novel is that of Oskar's early reading, which is divided between a somewhat scabrous account of the life of Rasputin, the mad and demonic Slavic monk, and Goethe's novel *Elective Affinities,* representing the epitome of eighteenth-century German rationalism. Thus Oskar—and perhaps Germany too—is made up of these two factors: the irrational-Slavic-demonic and the rational-Germanic-liberal. Here the parallel to Thomas Mann is obvious.

Because of his size the gnomelike Oskar has many curious and often gruesome adventures. He hides under the platform while Nazi speeches are made, he is with the defenders of a Polish postoffice when Danzig falls to the Germans in 1939, he visits the Normandy beaches on the eve of the Allied invasion of June, 1944. The symbol which ties all this together is Oskar's tin drum, or rather his many drums. His fascination with drums is a kind a parody of a psychological fetish-complex; but on another level the drums stand for something basic in Oskar's character and therefore basic to German civilization from 1924 to 1945. In one sense Oskar's drumming is a protest againt everything around him: bourgeois respectability, the squalor of his family life, German pompousness, even Nazism itself. But in another sense Oskar, with his half-Slavic or Rasputin-like quality, represents the darker and more hidden forces which produce the neurotic phenomenon of Nazism. The tin drum and its beating is a symbol of these forces, tawdry yet sinister. Here Grass is more like Kafka than like Mann; his symbol is diffuse, ambiguous, and subject to multiple interpretation. If he is different from Kafka it is because he is more superficially comic, while remaining serious at a deeper and more basic level.

After a long series of picaresque adventures, including a circus tour with the clown Bebra (a character associated in personality with the Nazi propagandist Goebbels), Oskar finds himself accused of a murder he did not commit—although he knows in his own mind that he is spiritually guilty of this and many other murders, including that of Jan Bronski and that of his legal father. It is to escape the consequences of this "crime" that he enters the madhouse. Like Mann's Faust-figure Leverkühn, he becomes demonic-creative and ends up mad. But unlike Leverkühn he does not die; instead at the end of the novel he realizes with horror that he will have to leave the security of his hospital room and go out into the real world with its real problems and real relationships. The only way he can deal with these problems, he now realizes, is with his drum. ". . . I will drum out the little ditty which has become more and more real to me, more and more terrifying; I shall call in the Black Witch." And the Black Witch, the spirit to which he willingly gives himself, is really only a reincarnation of Rasputin. On the last page of the novel, at the age of thirty, he comprehends that he is really mad.

In *Katz und Maus* (Cat and Mouse) Oskar appears in the background, but the main character is Joachim Mahlke, disfigured by the "mouse" of an enormous Adam's apple, who constantly feels separated from other normal "cats" but lives through most of the war only to die by a drowning accident which may have been suicide. *Hundejahre (Dog Years)* is the most complex redoing of the same period of German history with parallels to Grimmelshausen's *Simplicissimus* (1669) and to the Cain and Abel story (storm trooper Walter Matern and half-Jew Eduard, or Eddi, Amsel), but the basic metaphor stretched into an allegory of Germany's "having gone to the dogs" is brilliantly handled.

Örtlich Betäubt (Local Anaesthetic, 1969) for its first half presents no characters to be visualized, no action to be followed, but finally adds up to a dialogue on the generation gap and the urge to revolution. The method and metaphor are from television (flipping channels), and the television set is in the dentist's office where a West Berlin schoolteacher, Eberhard Starusch, is having toothache and prognathic bite corrected by capping. His mouth filled with cotton, Starusch as protagonist projects scenes and fantasies from his own life onto the old films, lewd commercials, and panel discussions of the TV—with running prattle by the dentist. The schoolteacher projects several different versions of his "murder" of his ex-fiancée, Sieglinde Krings, who is apparently still alive and married to Schlottau, an electrician. Or under another name has become a pediatrician. For example:

"The soundless picture showed a clerical-looking gentleman who, it being Saturday, wished to say a word about Sunday, although this program is televised after 10 p.m. and never before the Berlin evening news: 'Yes, yes, my son, I know it hurts. But all the pain in this world is powerless . . .'

"(Eased, tapered off, hardly to be remembered. One more twinge —but that may have been a reflex—then silence). Outside it was snowing from left to right on Hohenzollerndamm. (Not the TV, the street side of the office.) The screen was uninhabited. Like myself: all fuzzy and, I may as well say it, deaf. ('I'm told that anaesthetized tongues have been maimed by the experimental bites of incredulous patients.')"

As in other Grass fiction the prose is "gritty," hard to follow, and characters are individualized by physical deformities: Starusch has a prognathic bite, his young antagonist and student Scherbaum the opposite (a distal bite). Scherbaum has decided to burn alive his pet dachshund Max in the Berlin streets as a protest against the Vietnam war, encouraged by a Maoist girl friend and Starusch's colleague, Irmgard Seifert, who feels a guilt complex as a former "Hitler bitch." Starusch tries to dissuade Scherbaum, to teach all his students "to understand the world." The dentist looks forward toward "worldwide Sickcare." The young students, including Scherbaum, score the capitulations of adults (the over-thirty) and want action to make room "for new foundations."

The dentist tells his patient that the tartar on his teeth is "petrified hatred." "Nothing lasts. There will always be pain." But Grass had writen "immer neue Schmerzen," which means "new pains are always coming" (somewhat more optimistic, according to Grass—at least they're not the same old pains). The dust jacket designed by the author, shows a finger over a candle flame as a primitive dental anaesthetic, a symbol of all palliation. Any anaesthetic (or tranquilizer?) is only local and temporary.

14. THEATRE OF THE ABSURD

In the nineteen fifties and sixties a new kind of theatre emerged in Paris and very soon reached out into the rest of Europe, to England and America. It was a part of the general anti-literary movement of our time, but most closely related to the anti-novel or nouveau roman, largely because Samuel Beckett wrote importantly in both areas. The Theatre of the Absurd probably received its name via Albert Camus, although it was hardly his invention and his plays are existential rather than "absurd." But in *The Myth of Sisphus* (1942) Camus had made a classic statement of the absurdity of the universe and man's position in it: "A world that can be explained by reasoning, however faulty, is a familiar world. But in a universe that is suddenly deprived of illusions and of light, man feels a stranger. His is an irremediable exile, because he is deprived of memories of a lost homeland as much as he lacks the hope of a promised land to come. This divorce between man and his life, the actor and his setting, truly constitutes the feeling of Absurdity."

This statement the new dramatists seized on as their own. But the major ideas of Absurdist Drama go back most significantly to Kafka. Eugene Ionesco wrote in an essay on Kafka moving toward a definition of the concept: "Absurd is that which is devoid of purpose. . . . Cut off from his religious, metaphysical, and transcendental roots, man is lost; all his actions become senseless, absurd, useless." Certainly one of the most important events in the theatre itself as an immediate precurser and impetus to Theatre of the Absurd was the collaborative adaptation of Kafka's *The Trial* as the dramatized *Le Procès* by André Gide and Jean-Louis Barrault which was given its première performance on 10 October 1947 at Barrault's Théâtre de Marigny. Joseph K's nightmare of guilt, the arbitrary powers of the Law and the futility of efforts to understand, was given an appropriate staging by Jean-Louis Barrault—not so much a play as a sequence of images, phantoms, cinema, ballet, pantomime-like montage. As Martin Esslin says, *"The Trial* was the first play that fully represented the Theatre of the Absurd in its mid-twentieth-century form."

Of course there had been many precursers in older drama, surrealist, expressionistic, even Shakespeare, who has been claimed by almost every group and movement since the Renaissance. Jan Kott writes of *King Lear* as if it were Beckett's *Endgame* in *Shakespeare Our Contemporary* (1964). But one that must be mentioned is Pirandello, both for the ideas of relativity of truth and the non-realistic techniques of theatre as theatre. Alvin Kernan has made the most unequivocal statement of his importance: *"Six Characters in Search of an Author,* is in my opinion, the pivotal play in the modern theatre. It reveals in the starkest terms possible the meaning of the realistic drama of Ibsen, Strindberg, and Chekhov which leads into it and the theatre of the absurd which leads out of it." This modern theatre is "a small, isolated area located in the midst of an infinitely extended darkness."

But so far all this could be said of existentialist drama as well. An existentialist play, however, is relatively traditional in form; it has characters, plot, setting, theme, exposition, conflict, resolution—

it is almost a well-made play. But the reductive principle that operated on the nouveau roman or anti-novel operates on the theatre of
the absurd: characters are reduced, plot and time reduced. Absurdist
drama goes much further; place is reduced (even *chosist* objects
are fewer and tend to be more trivial) and dialogue or language is
minimized, made absurd, close to being eliminated (actually eliminated in Beckett's *Act Without Words*—which shortens a play considerably). Language is one thing the anti-novel cannot do without;
it would be novella, then short story, then nothing. And unlike
existentialists and Brecht, absurdists and anti-novelists want no political commitment of any kind.

Ionesco's first play, *La Cantatrice Chauve (The Bald Soprano)*
was billed as an "anti-play" and opened on May 11, 1950 at the
Théâtre des Noctambules in Paris. This has been called a satirical
exposure of absurdly inauthentic ways of life. Presenting situation
rather than events in sequence; the author's world rather than objec-
tively valid characters; a devaluation of language dispensing with
logic, discursive thought, and language—communication between
human beings in a state of breakdown. In the true absurdist play
the proper question is not what is going to happen *next* as in earlier
drama, but what *is* happening, if anything? What is represented by
what is happening, or not happening? It has been declared that with
Ionesco, Beckett, Genet, Pinter, Albee, and others the Theatre of
the Absurd has produced some of the finest dramatic achievements
of our time.

Samuel Beckett (Irish-French, born 1906)

When Samuel Beckett received the announcement that he had been
awarded the Nobel Prize for Literature in 1969, he was probably
as surprised as anyone. The press reacted in a generally favorable
way, but some of the comments reviewed his absurdist pessimism
with a critical air. Beckett's titles suggest "civilization with a terminal
cancer." He is a perverse Cartesian: "I stink, therefore I am." He
presents images for the withering away of the soul. It was suggested
that the Swedish Academy had been considering only one other
author seriously, André Malraux, or that in giving the award to
Beckett it was belatedly paying tribute to his master and mentor,

James Joyce. It may be so, and it could also be a kind of recognition for the whole school of nouveau roman and Theatre of the Absurd, those who try "saying it with things" rather than with linguistic concepts.

Especially honored in his total work was the "trilogy of richly introspective novels: *Molloy, Malone Dies, The Unnamable"* and, of course, his greatest success, *Waiting for Godot,* and at least two of the plays that follow, *Endgame* and *Krapp's Last Tape.* Beckett himself, thin, spare, infinitely sad, face riddled with furrows, had very little to say, as he retreats further and further into silence. In dispensing with plot, the psychology of characters, suspense, description, Beckett at his best has distilled his material (in the plays mentioned) to focus on a metaphor of the human condition, proving to be one of the most seminal writers of our time.

LIFE: Born in 1906 in Dublin into a middle-class Irish prottestant family, Samuel Beckett received his education at Portora Royal School and Trinity College with a degree in modern languages in 1927. For a time he taught French in Dublin and English in Paris, where in the late twenties he met and became friends with James Joyce, at that time working on *Finnegans Wake* as yet unnamed, the most important meeting in Beckett's life. You can find Joycean phrases in *Godot, Endgame,* and elsewhere. In 1929 he was one of twelve writers to publish an essay of interpretation on the *Wake* in the book with the weird title, *Our Exagmination Round his Factification for Incamination of Work in Progress.* Joyce gives Beckett a niche in *Finnegans Wake* on page 112: "You is feeling like you was lost in the bush, boy? You says: It is a puling sample jungle of woods. You most shouts out: Bethicket me for a stump of a beech if I have the poultriest notions what the farest he all means." He certainly was to become "lost in the bush."

In 1930 Nancy Cunard of the Hours Press in Paris and Richard Aldington together offered a prize for a poem to be submitted by June 15. On the morning after, they found under the door a poem they liked called "Whoroscope" by Samuel Beckett, a dramatic monologue in free verse and grotesquely pedantic; but Beckett was "launched" as a creative writer with a ten pound award. After more teaching in Dublin and London and some traveling on the continent, he moved permanently to Paris in 1937. His move to French for writing came somewhat later. His early poems and stories and a novel written in English, *Murphy* (1938), attracted almost no attention, although it is reported that Joyce, Dylan Thomas, and Iris Murdoch liked the novel. After the war Beckett shifted to French and published in French the three novels that gave him a place in the nouveau roman, *Molloy* (1951), *Malone Meurt* (1951), and *L'Innomable* (1953). They did not appear in English until 1955, 1956, and 1958, respectively, probably riding on *Godot's* shirttails. In successive novels the names change until they become the Unnamable but it's all the same first person monologue, with "plot" and "character" increasingly reduced. Molloy "goes in search of his mother," Moran (probable alter-ego) in search of Molloy, but Malone is confined to his bed, waiting for death, and the Unnamable in an unidentified Limbo seeks to find behind names and words whatever might be himself—a quest doomed to failure.

But in 1952 Beckett published *En Attendant Godot* and hit the jackpot when it was produced in Paris in the following year. This play rapidly became the classic example of absurd theatre and the masterpiece of the genre. Translating it into English himself, Beckett published *Waiting for Godot* in 1954. After this he had no problems getting attention. Constructive publication continued and included *Fin de Partie, suivi de Acte sans Paroles* (1957) which he translated for us as *Endgame* **and** *Act Without Words; Krapp's Last Tape* (1959); *Happy Days* (1961); and *Play* (1964). Since that time he has been dribbling off into silence, with one horrifying visit to New York City from which he escaped as quickly as possible (see the *Life* magazine account).

In January of 1973 a new play by Beckett, *Not I* (called "his first major work in ten years"), was given production at the Royal Court Theatre in Sloane Square, London. Language has returned, after Beckett's sighs and silences, a flood of it in a compulsive fifteen-minute woman's rapid-fire monologue. The Royal Court production, directed by Anthony Page, follows a presentation of *Krapp's Last Tape* with Albert Finney. The two are effective companion pieces, male and female tormented semi-confessional outcries. Billie Whitelaw as Mouth (that's all you see of her) gives a virtuoso performance.

Beckett is not saying anything new, but he has found a new and startling reductive metaphor for the human condition of despair and dimly sensed guilt and compulsion to communicate, with an equal compulsion to hide—"What? Who? No . . ., SHE!"—in other words, Not I.

CHIEF WORKS: *En Attendant Godot (Waiting for Godot;* play, 1952) is, without much doubt, Beckett's masterpiece and may indeed be a masterpiece on its own without Beckett. Its original Broadway production with Bert Lahr in 1956 did much to establish it in the *commedia del'arte* tradition with brilliant pantomime clowning in relatively low key by Bert Lahr to carry the play over to puzzled audiences. This play has been overexplained; but one can note two simple things: Godot is an apparent diminutive of God, and a more literal translation of "En Attendant" as "While Waiting for" emphasizes the duration of and what is done during the interim, which is all there is.

On the stage is nowhere, or anywhere, a wasteland probably in France with one bare tree (which sprouts a few leaves for the second act) and a mound (which *could* but doesn't have to introduce us to the cross and Job). The names of the five characters are deliberately a mixed bag of nationalities: one Russian, one Spaniard, one Italian, one Anglo-Saxon, and one unnamed—probably French. Vladimir (Didi) with stinking breath and Estragon (Gogo) with stinking feet, two tramps in bowlers, are doing nothing much and saying nothing much in monosyllables for the most part. They are too incompetent to commit suicide; it doesn't work. Pozzo, the master, and Lucky, the slave, roped to each other at a distance, enter; business with boots, hats, and bags. Lucky is goaded into "thinking" and making a speech, a veritable torrent of words including many out of *Finnegans Wake,* which makes little immediately discernible sense and is followed by silence. Lucky and Pozzo move off to the sound of the latter's "Up! Pig! On!" The fifth character, a boy messenger, comes on to announce that Godot won't come this evening but surely tomorrow. Act two repeats almost the same sequence, except for the few leaves on the tree, a "dog" poem that parallels material from *Ulysses;* and Pozzo (blind) and Lucky are in worse shape than ever. Again the messenger with the same message.

What can one do in such a world? To be either master or slave is repulsive. There are no answers. One must wait. But there are remnants of affirmation hidden in the play. Toward the end Didi says in response to Pozzo's cries for help: "Let us do something, while we have a chance! . . . To all mankind they were addressed, those cries for help still ringing in our ears! But at this place, at this moment of time, all mankind is us, whether we like it or not. Let us make the most of it, before it is too late! Let us represent worthily for once the foul brood to which a cruel fate consigned us! . . . It is true that when with folded arms we weigh the pros and cons we are no less a credit to our species. . . . What are we doing here, *that* is the question. And we are blessed in this, that we happen to know the answer. Yes, in this immense confusion one thing alone is clear. We are waiting for Godot to come—" And although they do little (announce going and don't go), Didi can still offer the justification: "We are not saints, but we have kept our appointment. How many people can boast as much?"

This residue of affirmation, the four or five green leaves on the bare tree, probably gives *Waiting for Godot* much of its power. But Beckett, almost as if he regretted having offered so much, spent his subsequent efforts rooting out the vestiges of affirmation and hope and pursuing his leaner theme of "Waiting for Death." The only thing possible against the void will be talk, and then less and less of that.

Fin de Partie (Endgame; play, 1957) takes us to an interior, as bare and forbidding as the outdoor scene of *Godot,* a room with two high, small windows, two garbage cans (don't be confused by the British ashbins or dustbins), a picture hanging face to the wall, a ladder, a telescope, and a wheelchair. The two main "characters" (more like Pozzo and Lucky than like Didi and Gogo) are Hamm, which suggests ham-actor, blind and paralyzed, who can no longer stand but is confined to the wheelchair, nonetheless the "master," and Clov, a kind of clown who can't sit down but is the only mobile character. Two other legless characters, Nagg and Nell, Hamm's parents, are confined in the garbage cans but stick out hands, arms, and heads occasionally until the covers are shoved back on. The world outside is apparently dead, some disaster, possibly atomic, having occurred, these four sole survivors now at the end of the game. All that remains of nature is sand in the cans, a flea, and these ruined human bodies. Hamm says, "But we breathe, we change! We lose our hair, out teeth! Our bloom! Our ideals!" And Clov answers, "Then she hasn't forgotten us," meaning Nature. Everything is grotesque. Time is running out. There is no more painkiller.

Clov asks, "Do you believe in the life to come?" And Hamm says, "Mine was always that." According to Jan Kott, Hamm in the London production was dressed in a faded purple gown and his wheelchair was his throne; like King Lear in Act IV he was a ruined piece of nature. Clov, lifting the lid of the ashcan to find out what is happening to Nag, reports, "He's crying." Hamm adds, "Then he's living." There seems to be a simple equation. Outside through one window is the sea, through the other the land, on which Clov finally sees with the telescope toward the end of the game a small boy, the very slightest threat of renewal, contemplating his navel, a Buddhistic suggestion of nirvana or nothingness. Beckett was particularly fond of a quotation from Democritus: "Nothing is more real than nothing." There is an unflinching honesty and utter integrity in the picture he gives of the end of the world. perhaps not as frightening as sad. But there is another quotation from King Lear that he ought to remember: "Nothing will come of nothing."

Krapp's Last Tape (play, 1959), written in English for a change and later translated into French, is interesting because it introduces into theatre the tape recorder, which since that time has been used for startling effects in Jean-Claude Van Italie's *America Hurrah!* and in some of Sam Shepherd's plays. This time there is one character, talking to himself, Krapp, who in spite of his name is much consti-pated. But there are at least three Krapps, the present one listening to the one who made the tape who is talking about an earlier remembered past including two "intense moments," one with a dog and a black ball, and the other with a girl in a punt. Krapp, in a clown's white boots, purple nose and white face, occupies with his tape recorder a circle of light surrounded by darkness. He retreats not only from this life but from his past life. His grotesque actions are minimal: into the dark to pop a cork, coming back, brooding, eating a banana, slipping on the peel, putting the half-eaten banana into his pocket, eating another. The banana doesn't have to be Freudian, nor any symbol at all; it may be simply a bright and meaningless, particular *chosist* object, like the carrot Estragon munches on. Beckett's plays, even more than those of other playwrights, depend for full effectiveness upon imaginative production. To see and hear can be more meaningful than simply to read. If he disturbs us, that is already a good deal.

Eugène Ionesco (Rumanian-French, born 1912)

Still generally unknown to a large public until 1956, when Jean Anouilh (who had similarly praised Beckett's *Godot*) among others gave high praise to a revival performance of *The Chairs* and precipitated the Ionesco vogue almost overnight; within a few years this playwright was being acclaimed throughout Europe and America as a leading representative of the Theatre of the Absurd. He seems rather more effective in the shorter one-act play form than in his attempts to expand his material into a single full evening's entertainment. The *Rhinocéros,* for example, brilliant in concept, seems padded to make it fill three acts instead of one or two. But he has still made some interesting contributions to the available literature of world theatre.

LIFE: Eugene Ionesco was born in 1912 of a Rumanian father and a French mother in Slatina, Rumania, but grew up in France until the age of thirteen when he returned to Rumania and learned the language. After study at the university in Bucharest he taught French for a time and wrote poetry and criticism. Since 1939 he has lived in France with a wife and a daughter born in 1944.

It was 1948 when he began to write for the theatre in a rather unusual way. Having begun the study of English by the Assimil method (a kind of modern-look Berlitz), he was struck by the conversations of the characters in his lesson book (the Monsieur and Madame Thibault, Voici la plume de ma tante, kind of thing). Instead of learning English he turned the Smiths and Martins of the Assimil book into a play. Ionesco writes, "To my astonishment, Mrs. Smith informed her husband that they had several children, that they lived in the vicinity of London, that their name was Smith, that

Mr. Smith was a clerk, that they had a servant, Mary—English like themselves." Then in lesson five came the Martins. Here was comedy already in dialogue form: two married couples telling each other perfectly obvious things, suddenly becoming empty and fossilized.

Ionesco wrote it down, calling it *L'Anglais Sans Peine,* later *L'Heure Anglaise,* read it to enthusiastic friends who urged it into production. During rehearsals the actor playing the fire chief mistakenly said "cantatrice chauve" for the words "institutrice blonde;" Ionesco immediately seized on this for a title, a brilliantly irrational choice, much better than the *Big Ben Follies* he had also considered. *The Bald Soprano* has nothing to do with the play that follows, although the words were then teasingly inserted into the text.

Although this anti-play, so designated, without plot, with dehumanized and mechanical "characters," and with absurdly exaggerated *non sequitur* and often repetitious dialogue, was followed by a gradual movement toward the more traditional, progress (or retrogression, depending on your point of view) toward moments of lucidity in *The Chairs* (1951) and a more humanly aware character in the Bérenger of four subsequent plays, *Tueur Sans Gages (The Killer,* 1957-59), *Rhinocéros* (1959), *Le Piéton de l'air (The Pedestrian of the Air,* 1962), and *Le Roi se meurt (Exit the King,* or *The King Dies,* 1963), Ionesco subsequently fell into relative silence, broken only by published fragments *(Journal en Miettes,* 1967, and translated as *Fragments of a Journal,* 1968, a collection of almost psychotic "crumbs"), resurrected one-acts, and one attempt at a major play, *La Soif et la Faim* (1966) translated as *Hunger and Thirst* (1968). (An experimental and private theatre group in the Berkshires in Massachusetts apparently produces the most recent plays of Ionesco with his blessing but also with his injunctions against publicity or review.) Although in *Hunger and Thirst* a semi-autobiographical character named Jean takes over for Bérenger and there is some ironic hope in the vision of a luminous garden which is either there or isn't there in the background, Jean is *not* Bérenger; the King is dead. And the silence of death, which could be the prelude to renewal, could also be, like Beckett's retreat into silence, the end of the game. These two friends, with admiration if without warmth for each other, seem to have become philosophically boxed-in, painted into a corner. Even the absurd should leave a mouse hole to crawl through.

Since his election to the French Academy in 1970 and the regular presentation of a number of his plays on the repertory of the national theatre at the Comédie Française, Ionesco seems to have taken a new lease on life, picking up on Shakespearian material in a play called *Macbett* among other things, perhaps duplicating the discovery of Tom Stoppard and Edward Bond that there's gold to be mined there. Jacques Mauclair, artistic director of the Théâtre Rive-Gauche, who has recently restaged *Tueur sans gages,* says confidenty, "Ionesco continues to write, he has written more than thirty pieces, he will write others; it is our hope."

CHIEF PLAYS: *Les Chaises (The Chairs;* play, 1951) with a dilapidated decor, seven doors leading everywhere and nowhere, introduces an Old Man, who has a message for the world, and an Old Woman. As an invisible audience assembles, they bring chairs into the room for them, gradually crowding themselves out; there are murmurs from the invisible assembly. After having greeted and chatted with their guests, the Old Man and Woman introduce a mute orator to deliver the profound message and jump out the windows into the sea which can be heard in the background. The orator grunts, scribbles a meaningless message on the blackboard, and exits. There are left only the murmuring of the sea, mutterings from unseen audience, and the chairs—nothing else but a delayed curtain.

Rhinocéros (play, 1959) is a fuller play, if somewhat thin in the third act. Bérenger (who is probably an alter ego for Ionesco) was played by Jean-Louis Barrault in the Paris production of 1960 and by Zero Mostel in the subsequent New York production. It is the same Bérenger who appeared in *The Killer* yet different, naive, innocent, ill at ease in society, seeking comfort in drink. The setting at least is a small provincial town in France because in the square you see a Café and an Epicerie. Bérenger argues with his stuffy bourgeois friend Jean. The trouble in the play is that the citizens are turning into rhinoceri, as their animal nature overcomes human reason and feelings. This metamorphosis, rhinoceritis, is a perculiarly modern disease, the thick-skinned insensitivity, the herd instinct, which is destructive, rather than individual identity. The individual remarks of those about to turn into the charging beasts are instructive: "The fact that I despise religion doesn't mean that I don't esteem it highly," "There's no clear thinking at the universities," people "disgust me; and they'd better keep out of my way, or I'll run them down," "I'm all for change," "This is an internal affair, it only concerns our country."

Bérenger holds out until the end; Daisy his girl friend is the last to desert him. There is some ambiguity at the final curtain as to whether or not Bérenger was able to hold on to the vestiges of humanity in a world gone madly rhinocerotic. Or is he turning green with a thickening of the skin?

Le Roi se meurt (Exit the King, play, 1963) is the last of the Bérenger plays; the third was the least successful. Bérenger I is the king facing death, his own before the end of the play. His doctor tells him simply, "You will have no breakfast tomorrow morning." Bérenger here is a kind of Fisher King and Prometheus rolled into one; he is all mankind, HCE fashion, having stolen fire from the gods, written the *Iliad, Odyssey,* the plays of Shakespeare, invented steel, plough, automobile, airplane. In fact his death may be the announced death of the human race, although possible renewal of a new world, a new race, is suggested. Bérenger has an old wife, Marguerite, and a young wife, Marie, who represents wish-fulfillment.

Marguerite and Bérenger are pretty well-rounded characters with a real existence; even the others, Marie, the Doctor, the Guard, Juliette, participate in "human" dialogue. The "death" is represented by the "magical" disappearance of "others" one at a time and the decor at the end of the play. Marguerite, wife and mother, nurse and Death, leads Bérenger to face his annihilation, to free himself from attachment to life, his sense of self. As Marguerite is vacuumed away to nothingness in the wings, the walls fall away, the solitary King on his throne in a gray light is swallowed up, and only the empty stage remains. Marguerite's last comment before disappearance was, "Useless agitation, wasn't it?" That could be hard to follow.

Jean Genet (French, born 1910)

Jean Genet from an early age a dedicated thief and homosexual has spent a large part of his life in French prisons, where he has observed the underside of life with a keen eye, lived many experiences in the imagination and a good many in the flesh, and where he spent much of his time in writing, poems and novels woven out of disparate materials: sin, crime, filth, saints, and ectasies. His particular combination of sinner and saint, evil and devotion, sex and sacrifice, is probably closer to parts of Dostoyevsky than to anything else. The novels, if they can be called that, are strange yet haunting works, free-associational in sequence with one "dissolve" after the other, including *Notre-Dame-des-Fleurs (Our Lady of the Flowers),* dated 1942 at the **Prison de Fresnes**; *Miracle de la Rose,* 1943 at the **Prison des Tourelles** and **La Santé**; *Pompes Funebres (Funeral Pomp,* 1947); *Querelle de Brest,* 1947; and *Journal du Voleur (The Thief's Journal,* 1949). Many of the themes and some of the characters reappear in modified form in the dramas.

As a playwright Genet is something more, at least something other, than simply an absurdist writer. His plays are additionally a kind of ritual theatre, with overtones of a theatre of cruelty; they are fully fleshed and quite distinctly original. It was 1952 when Jean-Paul Sartre published his *Saint Genet, comédien et martyr,* biography and critical analysis of this comedian and martyr, which forced the world to hold its revulsion in abeyance and take a long look at Genet's very real artistic accomplishments.

LIFE: "I was born in Paris on December 19, 1910. As a ward of the **Assistance Publique**, it was impossible for me to know anything about my background. When I was twenty-one, I obtained a birth certificate. My mother's name was Gabrielle Genet. My father remains unknown." Genet could have added that he was placed in a foster home in Burgundy, developed no ties of love or hatred with his foster parents, began stealing as a child and was sent to a reformatory, the Colonie de Mettray where he formed his attachments without any reform whatsoever. He subsequently stole cattle in Albania, picked pockets in Venice, smuggled narcotics in Berlin, and spent time in many prisons, preferring those in France as "home."

By 1948 Genet had published two long poems *(Chants secrets),* several novels, and two plays, *Les Bonnes* and *Haute Surveillance;* he was still in prison, this time sentenced for life at the tenth conviction for theft. Paul Claudel, Francois Mauriac, André Gide, Jean-Paul Sartre, and Jean Cocteau among other prominent literary figures petitioned the government for his release; pardon was granted by the President of the Republic, Vincent Auriol. In the outer world, faced by liberty and fame, he wrote no more for a six year period, although his *Complete Works* were being published by Gallimard beginning in 1952. In 1956 Genet came up with a new play, *Le Balcon,* highly esteemed and made into a film of more than routine interest. His dramatic power had grown and was growing; *Les Nègres* appeared in 1958 and *Les Paravents (The Screens)* in 1961. He wrote the script for a film, *Mademoiselle,* starring Jeanne Moreau, directed by Tony Richardson and released in 1966. He stays away from the world as much as possible; it is part of his literary method to attack or scorn his audiences.

CHIEF PLAYS: *Les Bonnes (The Maids;* play, 1947) was commissioned by Louis Jouvet who directed three actresses in its production at the Théâtre Athénée in Paris in 1947. Genet had intended that the parts be played by boys in women's clothing, as in Shakespeare. *The Maids,* in its emphasis upon the ritual of acting roles, is built upon a triangular relationship, Madame and her two maids, Claire and Solange. Although Madame is on stage only briefly, her presence-in-absence is always strongly felt. At the beginning of the play we do not know that she is absent. A "lady" at her dressing table scornfully gives orders to the maid she calls Claire. We become aware that the relationship is more than employer to servant; there are erotic overtones and gestures, sadism and masochism as well as Lesbianism. Dressing and undressing they may be playing roles, reversing parts, the secret rituals that lie behind newspaper scandals.

An alarm clock rings; in panic they drop their roles. Neither is Madame, who is about to return. They tidy up. The more dominant of the two, Solange, has been pretending to be the weaker Claire. Claire had been playing Madame. They both adore their mistress and hate her at the same time. Madame has a male lover in jail, put there on information supplied by Solange, but now released. The haughty Madame returns. The maids have planned to kill her with poison in her tea. But Madame, not drinking it, changes her clothes and hurries away to meet her lover. The masquerade is resumed. They rehearse the "death scene" but it doesn't work. Claire the weaker then becomes the stronger, forcing Solange-acting-as-Claire to bring the tea. Claire-Madame drinks it, leaving Solange to face the audience, her hands crossed as if held by handcuffs.

Le Balcon (The Balcony, play, 1956) involves two basic metaphors for life: sex and revolution. The brothel called The Balcony is the basic setting, and all the world, or most of it, in the play is a brothel, which involves play-acting to give satisfaction to its clients; so all the world's a brothel-stage. And since sex fulfillment is, as in Shakespeare, a "little death," the enactments here are not basically different from the killings of the revolution which is sweeping the city outside The Balcony (there's a French pun in the title). The play, in nine scenes, starts out in three of them with customers pretending to be a Bishop, a Judge, and a General, their acting out their secret desires with mirrors, costumes, settings, and other actors (the personnel of the establishment), mostly sadistic. The "Bishop" in front of blood-red screens and wearing elevated shoes hears the lurid confessions of a young woman; the "Judge" in front of brown screens and similarly elevated orders a half-naked executioner to whip a beautiful girl; in front of dark green screens the "General" rides an almost nude girl wearing a tail as if she were his horse. At the end of each scene machine-gun fire is heard, outside the house of illusions, but getting closer.

The Revolution is taking place. Chantal, a girl who formerly worked for Madame Irma at The Balcony, has joined the revolution, which plans to destroy The Balcony and the Government, the Queen, and the Royal Palace. The Chief of Police, a real official but less important than Bishop, Judge, or General, friend of Irma and cooperator of the establishment, helps put down the revolution after the death of the Queen by substituting Irma as Queen and the fake Bishop, Judge, and General for the real ones who have fled. They appear on the balcony of The Balcony. The Police Chief gets his wish-fulfillment, achieves his "image," when a man finally comes to the brothel who wants to play at being Chief of Police.

The indecent rites of role-playing continue in both the brothel and the real world. Irma is Genet, as playwright, the mistress of illusions. At the end she turns to the audience: "You must now go home,

where everything—you can be quite sure—will be even falser than
here." There is another burst of machine-gun fire. The "dying" in
the brothel is never over; it will recur tomorrow; and so will the
revolution.

Les Nègres (The Blacks; play, 1958) is a play for black actors,
some of them playing white-face, a minstrel show in reverse. It opens
with eight Negroes dancing around a catafalque containing, we are
told, the body of a white woman who has been murdered. We are
to watch a trial. The judges are five white persons, that is Negroes
wearing white masks, who sit on an upper stage. The "facts" of the
murder are presented with imprecision. The descriptions of the victim
and motives change constantly. In a reenactment of the rape-murder,
a masked "victim" goes to the upper stage and reports that "they're
not white, but pink or yellowish." (This is something like E. M.
Forster's "pinko-gray"). The second part of the play is a contest
of strength between black and white on black territory in the African
jungle, featuring Mrs. Felicity Trollop Pardon, an old Negress who
envisions an all-black world, including sugar, rice, hope—a kind of
reversed Melville chapter on "whiteness." The play ends as it began,
around the catafalque; pulling the sheet from it, it is found empty.
Meanwhile a real murder has been committed off stage. The show
is over.

Racial conflict is not the subject but the occasion for the play;
the subject is power, the energy of rituals. As Tom Driver puts it,
"However wild and terrifying, it is 'there;' and it has power not only
to destroy but also to create." Genet's power to grip an audience
in the theatre is an overwhelming fact.

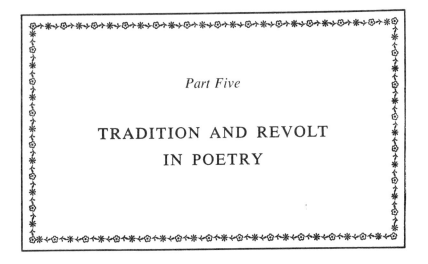

Part Five

TRADITION AND REVOLT
IN POETRY

Like the majority of the intellectuals and artists of their generation, the poets entered the twentieth century in a rebellious mood. The century began in one of those periodic revolts against poetic convention which break out whenever poetry becomes too artificial; similar movements, it will be recalled, took place in the Renaissance and at the time of the nineteenth-century romantic movement. The twentieth-century poetic rebels, however, lacked any single philosophy of rebellion around which to rally; the only quality they all shared was an intense individualism. Thus the twentieth century is an era of schools and movements of great diversity: surrealism, imagism, dada, Symbolism, and a score of movements which are none the less distinct for remaining unnamed.

It is nevertheless possible to group these diverse movements roughly under two headings: (a) the poets who abandon artificiality and preciosity of any kind and seek to return to a natural vernacular idiom; and (b) the opposite group who plunge into various forms of Symbolism, obscurantism, experimental reconstruction of language, and esoteric systems of prosody. For convenience we shall term these two groups "verse naturalism" and "experimental verse" respectively, although the second term especially includes techniques of such variety and diversity as to make it virtually a presumption to speak of them under one heading. This second group, however, is by far the larger and more significant of the two.

15. THE VERSE NATURALISTS

One of the important literary aspects of the Renaissance was its revolt against the stultified Latinism of the late middle ages and its attempt to recreate a popular vernacular literature. In the nineteenth century Wordsworth, one of the focal figures of the romantic movement, was likewise inspired to abandon artificial poetic convention and to return to a diction, if not a content, comprehensible by the ordinary plowman. In America Walt Whitman, in the middle of the century, renounced conventional prosody entirely and wrote simply and sincerely in a sort of unembellished free verse. Each of these attempts represented an experiment in what later came to be known in the twentieth century as verse naturalism. It is noteworthy that all these earlier vernacular revivals were involved with romantic movements. Twentieth-century vernacular poetry is connected to a vastly different literary school: the pseudo-scientific naturalism of the late nineteenth century.

For this reason the twentieth-century verse naturalists share certain qualities with the prose naturalists of the order of Zola, Dreiser, or Hemingway. In diction they shun artificiality or preciosity; their vocabulary is simple, and they avoid bizarre images or highly complex construction. In content they seek to return to the commonplace, although they often disagree on what this commonplace is to be. In the case of Robert Frost and E. A. Robinson it is the simple rural life which had earlier appeared in the poetry of Wordsworth and Hugo, and which appears in twentieth century Europe most charmingly in Juan Ramón Jiménez. For Carl Sandburg and Richard Dehmel the true commonplace of our century is the world of the factory, the locomotive, the metropolis, and the dynamo. In both instances the aim is the same: to abandon the exotic and imaginative themes which so often dominate poetry and to return for subject matter to the interests and activities of the common man.

Richard Dehmel (German, 1863-1920)

Dehmel is a typical naturalist by temperament and inclination who, because of the nature of his literary gifts, turned to poetry instead of to the prose fiction of his naturalistic contemporaries. He is a poet of great simplicity and conviction, a lyricist who seeks to convey his message in the language of everyday conversation. Not only is he a naturalist in diction and technique, but he shares the content of his school: sympathy for human misery, preoccupation with the land and the city as economic ways of life, and a tendency toward personification of natural forces.

Dehmel was a lifetime idealist and enthusiast. Born in the Mark Brandenburg, he retained all his life a love for the vast spaces of this forested plain. As a gymnasium student and in his later university years he showed a fierce independence and a defiance of authority; his life was dominated by a series of "causes" to which he devoted himself with utter disregard of his personal interest or his health. He climbed Mont Blanc at fifty-one; a few months later he managed to get himself accepted as a soldier in the German army to fight in the First World War. He threw himself into the creation of poetry with the same fierce fervor of consecration. His poems are never elegant or contrived, always direct and forceful. His favorite subjects are the power of the city (cf. Carl Sandburg), the overwhelming majesty of the Brandenburg plain, and the terrible forces of passion and repulsion which are released in human sexual relationships.

CHIEF WORKS: Dehmel's chief poetry collections are *Erlösungen* (*Redemptions,* 1891); *Aber die Liebe* (*But Love,* 1893), both studies in the psychology of love; and *Weib und Welt* (*Woman and World,* 1896), poems of autobiographical origin and chiefly of erotic themes. *Zwei Menschen* (*Two Humans,* 1903) is an integrated cycle of poems, a sort of verse novel, concerning the basic relationships between man and woman.

Probably the best-known of Dehmel's single lyrics is "Die stille Stadt" ("The Silent City"), included in *Aber die Liebe.* The poem pictures a sleeping city in which all is smoke, fog, ugliness, and misery; but the image is redeemed through a "hymn of praise" sung by a child. The message is that the human spirit can bring beauty even into the squalor of a modern industrial city.

Juan Ramon Jiménez (Spanish, 1881 - 1958)

The lyricism of Jiménez is associated both with his native region of Andalusia, its natural features and its Moorish and gypsy traditions, in which he shows affinities with Antonio Machado and Federico García Lorca, and with a peculiarly personal withdrawal into himself. Early recognized and influenced by Rubén Darío, he had by 1920 in general critical estimation replaced his predecessor as leading poet of Spanish-speaking peoples. Like Rilke he sometimes expressed his poetic ideas in what is essentially prose poems which in translation make the more elusive poetry available to readers not native to his language.

LIFE: Juan Ramón Jiménez was born in the village of Moguer in the southern region of Spain known as Andalusia in 1881. Educated by the Jesuits, he later began to study law at the university in Seville but soon withdrew in favor of stronger interests in painting and poetry. Perhaps the most striking events in his life and in their significance for his poetry were the death of his father in 1900, so traumatic and dolorous an experience that Juan Ramón had to recover in a sanitarium, and his marriage to Zenobia Camprubí Aymar in 1916, a remarkable woman with a North American background and with a good knowledge of English and American poetry, including Blake, Shelley, Emily Dickinson. She was a cheerful companion and co-worker. Together they lived in Madrid, New York, Puerto Rico, and Cuba, escaping the bitterness of the Spanish civil war in 1936. During his decade in America, Juan Ramón taught and lectured in several American universities, including Duke, Vassar, Maryland, but spent most of his time subsequently in the Caribbean. In 1956 Jiménez was awarded the Nobel Prize for literature. His wife, Zenobia, died shortly afterwards and he himself followed her in 1958, both of them buried in Moguer, the ultimate return to his beginnings. He had published more than twenty volumes of poetry since 1900, of which selections are available in translation.

CHIEF WORKS: *Platero y yo, elegia andaluza (Platero and I;* prose poems, 1914, 1917) is a series of more than a hundred vignettes in a more than usually controlled prose with poetic devices such as the pattern of one descriptive adjective before a noun and one after. Part of the charm of the anecdotes about the poet and his

314 TRADITION AND REVOLT IN POETRY

donkey, Platero, is in frequent *non sequiturs* of action or description. Often compared with *Don Quixote* (in idea as well as popularity), *Platero and I* moves with the donkey and his master-friend through Moguer and the surrounding landscape of Andalusia. But the attitude of the novelist in the Don's wanderings is essentially moral, while the poet in his observations is on the other hand aesthetic. The main characters are the recluse poet and his shaggy donkey who prefer to withdraw from the world of men, but there are sympathetic glimpses of others, of children, of Doctor Darbón the veterinarian, of a village idiot boy, and of course a world of flowers, especially the yellow iris, and white butterflies. The tone is elegiac, quiet lament for vanished childhood and youth in Andalusia and the musical composition of a melancholy air.

Other works of special interest but not yet to be found in complete translation are *Diario de un poeta recién casado* (1916), a combination of prose and verse setting out on the quest for the essence of poetry, *Diary of a Poet Recently Married* (the title was changed in 1948 to *Diary of Poet and Sea* because it records experiences at sea, sailing from Cadiz to New York in January 1916 to the wife waiting for him in the new world; *Españoles de tres mundos: Viejo mundo. Nuevo mundo. Otro mundo. Caricatura lírica.* (1914-1940), "Lyric Caricatures" of Spaniards of three worlds (Europe, America, and "the other world") exaggerate and distort certain attributes and features of the subject to recreate essential personality with loving touch—there are portraits of Unamuno, Ortega y Gasset, Jorge Guillén among the sixty-one; *Animal de fondo* (1949) which can be translated as *Animal of Depth,* a mystical poem seeking equilibrium between poet, art, and the universe, dealing with man as a creature of water, earth, and air, climbing out of sea onto land and wishing to continue his ascension (Carl Sandburg's "Poetry is the journal of a sea animal living on land, wanting to fly in the air" from *Poetry Reconsidered* and Plato's *Phaedrus* both have been suggested as sources).

16. VARIETIES OF EXPERIMENTAL VERSE

Authors, especially poets, developed an increasing tendency after 1850 to write for a limited group of *cognoscenti* rather than for the public as a whole. This tendency, which was enormously accelerated during the Symbolist era of the nineties, rose to a second climax in the period following the First World War. Poetry tended to become the exclusive possession of schools, movements, and cults, each self-sufficient and each believing itself to be struggling in the very vanguard of modern literature.

The poetry produced by these various groups shares at least one quality: it is never obvious, and it is quite commonly difficult or esoteric. It is generally the product of highly educated poets who have a wide background in languages, literary history, and philosophy; Eliot, Rilke, Valéry, Auden, and Spender are all men of a highly erudite culture. (There are exceptions, as in the case of Guillaume Apollinaire.) This is not to say that these poets are academic in attitude; on the contrary they are often antagonistic toward university disciplines and academic criticism. Many of them, it would seem, spend their lives overcompensating for their failure to impress their professors as undergraduates. Their pedanticism, when it occurs, is their own; their allusions and their classic echoes are none the less obscure for the lay reader.

It should be remarked that the most prominent influence on this entire movement is that of the Symbolist school. In the case of the English poets this often means Yeats; in the case of the continentals it is more commonly Mallarmé or Verlaine. From this school the moderns borrowed their interest in sensory associations, which they further refined by the addition of modern Freudian and Jungian psychology. The nineteenth-century Symbolists also share with many modern poets a certain morbidity, apparently deriving from a repugnance toward modern materialism and a disillusionment with the ideals of democracy and science.

It is remarkable as well that an unusual number of modern poets are expatriates for one reason or another. Eliot abandoned America for England, Auden moved in the opposite direction, Rilke lived out his life as a permanent wanderer, and a crowd of American poets established in Paris a little expatriate society complete in itself. This tendency of the avant-garde poet to deny his origins stands in sharp contrast to the nostagia for the homeland of such verse naturalists as Frost, Sandburg, Dehmel, and Robinson.

It is generally felt that Rilke and Valéry are the two most signi-

316 TRADITION AND REVOLT IN POETRY

ficant poets produced by Europe in the twentieth century. The lyric poetry of Unamuno, Lorca, and Brecht, considered elsewhere in this volume, is also of considerable stature.

Rainer Maria Rilke (German-Bohemian, 1875-1926)
Rilke derives essentially from the Symbolist movement of the nineties and from the aestheticism of the Stefan George circle. A strongly personal poet, he altered the principles of these groups in accordance with the needs of his own personality, and emerged with a type of poetry which was distinctly and deeply his own. His early poems, comprising those written before 1899, resemble Heine and the early work of Valéry, who was working out his own poetic technique about the same time. With *Das Stundenbuch* (*The Book of Hours,* 1899) and especially with *Das Buch der Bilder* (*The Book of Pictures,* 1902) Rilke embarked into a technique similar to that of the American imagists: concise descriptions of material sensations more penetrating than mere naturalistic observation. His greatest poems, contained in *Duineser Elegien (Duino Elegies,* 1923) and *Die Sonette an Orpheus* (*Sonnets to Orpheus,* 1923) are personal soliloquies celebrating the poet's intense emotional reaction to his existence. The technique of these later poems, however, is still richly concrete; Rilke is not a metaphysical poet who deals purely in abstractions.

The content of Rilke's early poems is conventional: the despair of the lover, the struggle of the poet, and the impact of natural beauty on a sensitive mind. As time went on he began to evolve a more personal poetic message. Intensely frustrated in his personal life, he developed an antagonism toward the bourgeois virtues, toward physical love, and toward the biological necessity which condemns man willy-nilly to be born, to eat, to make love, and at last to die. His ideal became feminine virginity, the unsullied maiden who appears sometimes in his work as an angel and at other times as the spirit of disembodied ecstasy. There is a religious element in this attitude, but it is far from conventional Christianity. Rilke admired medieval art and the cult of Mariolatry on aesthetic grounds, but in personal attitude he was closer to the transcendental asceticism or Buddhism. His true religion, the religion of his personal devotions, was art, which he worshipped not only in his consecration to his craft but in his adulation of such Titans as Tolstoy and Rodin.

LIFE: Rainer Maria Rilke, born in Prague in 1875, stemmed from an old Bohemian and Alsatian family. His native tongue was German, although he was familiar with most modern European languages. The critical formative factor of his youth was his unhappiness in a series of military academies (1886-91). Condemned to these institutions by a military-minded father, the sickly Rainer was totally miserable; he was nagged and tormented by pupils and instructors alike, and conceived a loathing of athleticism and militarism which lasted him the rest of his life. When his health broke down completely in 1891 his parents removed him to a business college. Here he was happier; he had time for poetry and contemplation, and even managed a desultory affair with a governess. After this incident his father would have nothing further to do with him; but an uncle, Jaroslav Rilke, offered to pay for tutors and books so that Rainer might receive an education. In 1895-96 he attended the University of Prague; during the following academic year he studied art at Munich. His first poems, *Leben und Lieder,* had appeared in 1894. After the appearance of *Larenopfer* (1896) Rilke continued to publish intermittently for the rest of his life.

Rilke was a complete *déraciné;* he lived out his life without ever attaching himself to a particular place. He was a chronic and unhappy wanderer; to him it seemed always that happiness lay in other places. He visited Russia twice (1899 and 1900), met Tolstoy, and declared himself a devoted "spiritual Russian"; for some time he affectedly dressed in a Russian blouse. He spent several years of his life in Paris, but seldom remained there more than a few months at a time. He disliked his native Bohemia, yet was continually drawn back to it; he passed the First World War in Germany and Austria and died in Switzerland. His most famous poems are the elegies conceived at Duino, a castle on the Adriatic coast in what is now Yugoslavia. Another important way-stop was Worpswede, an artists' colony near Bremen where he passed two years (1900-01).

In 1901 Rilke married the sculptress Clara Westhoff, whom he had met in the Worpswede colony. Clara had been a pupil of the sculptor Auguste Rodin; she introduced her husband to the famous artist, and soon Rodin and Rilke were intimate. Rilke served as secretary to Rodin at Meudon for a number of months (September, 1905 to May, 1906), but the two did not get on well together. The older man failed to recognize the young poet's talent, and Rilke for his part alienated the sculptor with egotistical and importunate personal demands. From this relationship, however, came a book, *Auguste Rodin* (1903); and Rilke himself was much influenced by the example of Rodin's personality. As for his marriage, it was hardly more successful; the couple lived together for only a year, and the relationship scarcely interfered with Rilke's succession of highly emotional affairs with young girls.

During the early part of his career Rilke lived mainly through the patronage of wealthy admirers. The most important of these were the Princess Marie von Thurn und Taxis-Hohenlohe, at whose Schloss Duino he achieved the most important poetic inspiration of his life, and Werner Reinhart of Winterthur, who bought Rilke a castle in Switzerland in 1921.

Rilke's death was curiously symbolic. He suffered during his later years from leukemia, which he felt was a disease uniquely conferred upon him in recognition of his isolation from the rest of mankind. In the winter of 1926 he pricked his finger while picking a rose for a young woman he admired; the wound festered, and his weakened blood was unable to fight the infection. He died in December, 1926.

CHIEF WORKS: The *Duineser Elegien (Duino Elegies;* poems, 1923) were begun in 1912 during Rilke's stay at Schloss Duino in Dalmatia and completed in Switzerland in 1922. The poems are written in free verse modified by sporadic dactylic rhythms. There are ten elegies altogether; the general tone is anguished, intense, and pessimistic. The theme is well typified by the opening lines of the first elegy: "Who, if I cried, would hear me among the angelic Orders?" Although the poems are philosophical in meaning, their style is richly concrete, full of images of animals, birds, children, and objects of nature. The most important of the poems is the fifth elegy, inspired by Picasso's painting "Les Saltimbanques"; the family of acrobats are taken as a symbol, "even a little more fleeting than ourselves," of the instability of human existence.

Die Sonette an Orpheus (*The Sonnets to Orpheus;* poems, 1923) were written in a burst of inspiration at the time Rilke was finishing the *Elegien.* In contrast to the *Elegien* the sonnets are exuberant, joyful, and lyrical. An erotic element underlies their content; they may be taken in their whole as a sort of Dionysian hymn to joy. Orpheus, the motif of the book, is not the heartstricken lover who descends to Hades to rescue his mate but the exuberant singer whose lyre was said to charm both animals and men.

An important insight into Rilke's own personality is contained in *Die Aufzeichnungen des Malte Laurids Brigge* (*Notebook of Malte Laurids Brigge;* also translated as *Journal of my Other Self;* novel, 1909). In this semi-autobiographical work Rilke describes his unhappiness as a young poet, especially his aversion to large cities.

Geschichten vom lieben Gott (Stories of God, originally tales "Of God and Other Matters told to Grownups for Children," 1900) is a collection of short stories held together by a village locale, a group of children, and a shy narrator who has to tell his stories by means of intermediaries, notably a neighbor mother, a stranger, the schoolmaster, his lame friend Ewald, evening clouds, and a gravedigger among others. The tales interpret for the German bourgeois myopic vision the exoticism and insights of Russia and Italy and their closeness to God. Although in a deliberately mannered but controlled style and bordering on whimsey and sentimentality, they nevertheless charm the reader and provide clues to the themes that Rilke develops subsequently in his poetry—his own views of the thingness of things (quiddity) so similar to yet distinct from the inscape of Hopkins and the wholeness, harmony and radiance of the Dedalus-Joyce aesthetics; the growth of ideas of God in their dependence on men; the naive, early appearances of the Rilke angels; transmutation of the visible and fleeting into the invisible and permanent; and death as the other side of life.

Die Weise vom Liebe und Tod des Cornets Christoph Rilke (The Lay of the Love and Death of Cornet Christopher Rilke; prose poem, 1904) is a romantic tale of a seventeeth century young Rilke eighteen years old who went to war with western European allies against the Turks and fell in Hungary. Expressionistic imagery bursts through at the climax of the flag-bearer's death as sixteen curved sabers leap upon him as a festival, a laughing fountain. The story is given cohesion by its brevity, by the horsemen riding to the east, the friendship of the Cornet with a French marquis, a brief love affair in a castle near enemy territory, and a nostalgia which is universal with sensitive young men who go to fight and to die in whatever war in whatever time. Part of the effective poetry is in what is not said; the door of quiet remains open.

Paul Valéry (French, 1871-1945)

Although contradictory opinions regarding Valéry abound, one thing is agreed upon: that he is a difficult poet whose work demands careful study for proper understanding. In spite of his stature as the leading twentieth-century French poet, he is read by an infinitesimal fraction of the public even in his native land. He is above all a philosophical poet; his poetry springs from the intelligence rather than from the senses, and it is only after his idea takes shape that the intellectual content is clothed in physical images. The chief problem in his work is the conflict between action and inaction, the active and contemplative lives, the world of matter and the world of spirit. This antithesis proceeds out of a conflict in Valéry's own life, a struggle which led him at one point to abandon poetry for twenty years in fear of the contaminating effects of commercial publication and publicity.

In poetic technique Valéry resembles the fin-de-siècle Symbolists, especially Mallarmé, his early mentor. His images, even his diction, are those of conventional Symbolism. But where the Symbolists were content to demonstrate physical resemblances and affinities in nature, Valéry turns these resemblances into tools for communicating his more profound content. In meter, prosody, and verse pattern he is conventional; he prefers to confine his poetry within a fairly rigid form in order to lend concision to what would otherwise be diffuse and amorphous.

LIFE: Paul Valéry was born in 1871, slightly after his lifetime friend Gide, and died slightly before him. His parentage was thoroughly southern and Latin; his father was French and his mother Italian. Born at Sète, near Montpellier, he was educated at the Montpellier lycée and briefly attended the School of Law at the University of Montpellier. Around 1889 he turned his interest to poetry, at that time dominated by the Symbolism of Verlaine, Mallarmé, and Heredia. The following year he met André Gide and Pierre Louÿs; shortly after this he abandoned his native city for Paris. In the period 1892-98 he was a faithful member of the Mallarmé cénacle, and turned out a number of poems of slight originality but of high quality. Around 1900, at the time of his marriage and shortly after the death of Mallarmé, Valéry abandoned poetry completely; many critics suggest that he was growing weary of the exigencies of the active literary life and wished to consecrate himself to a study of "pure being." For many years he worked patiently at a news-service job, writing almost nothing of a literary quality. At last Gide and Louys persuaded him to write a poetic epilogue to a collected edition of his early work; this short piece eventually turned into the long and difficult *La jeune Parque* (1917) During the following years he wrote his best poetry, the work which earned him his reputation as France's greatest living poet. In 1926 he was elected to the French Academy to occupy the chair vacated by the death of Anatole France. He died only a few weeks after the end of the Second World War, in 1945.

IMPORTANT POEMS: *La jeune Parque* (*The Young Fate;* philosophical poem, 1917) is a lengthy and complex study of one of the basic conflicts of human existence. The narrator or protagonist is a young girl (one of the *parcae* of Greek mythology) hovering in a state between dream and waking. The basic dialogue of ideas is that between chaste contemplation and the active physical and sensual life. At length material life is repudiated ("Each kiss foretells a new agony") and the Fate returns to her immaculate celestial sphere. The poem is remarkable for its subtle and evocative images, for the dream-like mood it pro duces, and for the pervasive manner in which the message is conveyed

"Le Cimetière marin" (translated as "Graveyard by the Sea"; poem, 1920) gives its title to a volume which appeared the same year. The title poem is a sort of elegy; the thoughts of the poet are turned by the proximity of the cemetery to profound and melancholy ideas. The marine cemetery he refers to is to be found in Sète not far west of Montpellier. After an intense vision of the dead who lie beneath him, he goes on to probe the implications of death itself. He rejects immortality, and avoids the truism of Gray that death reduces all men to equality. At length he abandons contemplation on the subject as artificial and useless; he determines to join battle with life and live it in the fullest manner: "The wind rises . . . one must try to live!" The first half of this poem somewhat resembles Baudelaire, but the tone is marked by a greater serenity and assurance.

Guillaume Apollinaire (French, 1880-1918)

Apollinaire, who wrote chiefly before 1914 and died in 1918 still a young man, was nevertheless the founder of the school of surrealism which was to dominate French poetry in the early twenties. His life was as curious as his poetry. He was born in Rome in 1880, the illegitimate son of Angelique-Alexandrine de Kostrowitzky, a Lithuanian adventuress. The blood of his undisclosed father was probably Italian. While he was still a child his mother brought him to Monaco, then to Paris. After 1899, when his mother contracted a semi-permanent alliance with a wealthy admirer, the young man was thrown onto his own resources. He spent a brief period as a tutor in a Rhineland estate, where he fell in love with a governess, only to be separated from her by circumstances. Returning to Paris, he took a job in a bank and set out to invade Bohemian and literary circles; soon his friends included Alfred Jarry, Max Jacob, and Pablo Picasso. His first important collection of verse was *Alcools* (*Liqueurs;* poems, 1913), a small volume which won him wide fame in avant-garde circles. He published only a handful of books before he was mobilized in 1914. Apollinaire was a brave soldier and a competent officer; military life, strangely enough, seemed to suit him. In March, 1916 he was severely wounded in the head in the Château-Thierry sector of the front. He was demobilized after several skull operations, and remained an invalid the rest of his life. He died of influenza in the epidemic of November, 1918.

Although Apollinaire's prestige was considerable among a small circle of devotées before the war, it was during the period of the twenties that his work exerted its main influence. His poetry is half-bantering, half-serious, but always strangely attractive; he creates the identical quasi-whimsical air of mystery which Cocteau and others were to make famous after his death. He departs from normal punctuation and typography somewhat in the manner of E. E. Cummings; indeed the two authors have much in common.

CHIEF WORKS: "Zone" (poem, 1913) is the most famous single piece contained in *Alcools.* The poem consists of a panorama of modern society, with its buses, autos, and buildings. The element of decadence is similar to that portrayed in Eliot's *Waste Land,* except that Apollinaire handles the material with a lighter touch. Most of the poems of *Alcools* are in a similar vein. The usual medium is free verse modified with occasional rhyming endings.

Calligrammes (the word means "handwriting exercises"; poems, 1918) are more radical in technique; here Apollinaire uses the trick typography and bizarre imagery which later became associated with surrealism.

Les Mamelles de Tirésias (*The Mammaries of Tiresias;* farce, 1917) is an amusing plea for an accelerated birth-rate; the war had made Apollinaire deeply conscious of the problem of France's falling population. Tiresias, in Greek mythology a male seer who had once been a woman and thus knew all secrets, becomes a feminist wife who refuses to have children. Her husband valiantly takes over the task, and succeeds in bearing several thousand. It was this play which introduced the word "surrealist" to the French public; Apollinaire uses the term in his introduction.

The Surrealists

The aim of every literary artist should be to reveal the inner forces which operate unseen to mold the external events of our lives. In the tumultuous period following the First World War a group of young French poets, impatient of the usual literary techniques for attaining this end, invented a new style (as they claimed, a new language) which they called surrealism. The roots of this movement are long. It owes something to Baudelaire and to the Symbolists of the nineties; it was especially indebted to the work of Lautréamont (1846-70). It proclaimed as its prophet Guillaume Apollinaire, who had invented the adjective *surréaliste* and who had sketched out the new method in his own work. The surrealists also operated in close contact with avant-garde Parisian painters; Pablo Picasso was a perennial habitué of the circle, and Max Jacob, Matisse, Marie Laurencin, Henri Rousseau, and Braque were all more or less involved with the group. The surrealists were also connected with the cénacle of literary pranksters known as the dadaists, whose code was little more than an impudent and imaginative irrationalism.

In 1919 the surrealists founded *Littérature,* a review devoted to their principles; this magazine was the focus of the movement in its formative period. In 1924 another review, *Révolution surréaliste,* took up the battle. This second review had definite anarchist leanings, which became a militant communism in 1930 when the magazine's title was changed to *Surréalisme au Service de la Révolution.* The surrealists were not temperamentally inclined to serve any organized party for long, however, and the honeymoon of surrealism and communism was brief and tumultuous.

In their efforts to reveal the hidden processes of human existence the surrealists first of all revolted against conventional syntax, grammar, vocabulary, and prosody. They generally write in free verse or in some sort of asymmetric doggerel devoid of metrical beauty; their images are startling, colorful, and often apparently meaningless (e.g., the "soluble fish"). Their cénacle was a highly exclusive one; they established conventions and used forms and techniques deliberately baffling to the outsider. Their use of free association contributes to the generally anarchistic character of their verse. There is usually no single organizing thread in a surrealist poem; the thought wanders from one association, image, or concept to another without apparent motive. The influence of modern Freudianism is apparent; the Oedipus and Electra complexes, the stock Freudian sexual symbols, and the concept of the collective unconscious appear frequently. The surrealists shun poetic diction along with everything else savoring of pedanticism; in its place they borrowed the succinct, salty, and often expressive slang of the Paris streets.

The chief figures in the surrealist movement between the two world wars were Apollinaire, André Breton, Louis Aragon, Paul Eluard, Jacques Vaché, Philippe Soupault, Georges Hugnet, René Crevel, and Jean Cocteau.

Louis Aragon (French, born 1897) joined the surrealist movement in 1924 after experimenting in Symbolism and dada. He is the chief communist member of the surrealist movement. In 1931 he published a poem entitled *Front Rouge (Red Front)* for which he was convicted of sedition in the French courts; he narrowly escaped a prison sentence. When his surrealist companions attempted to rescue his reputation by arguing that the political content of the poem was innocuous and unessential, Aragon repudiated surrealism; he shortly became an editor of the communist daily *Ce Soir* and a militant Soviet sympathizer. With the outbreak of the war in 1939 he joined the army as an "auxiliary doctor" (like André Breton, who wrote Surrealist Manifestoes in 1924, 1930 and an explanation in 1934, he had partially completed a medical education); he fought in Belgium, was evacuated from Dunkerque to England, and returned to France immediately. After the armistice of 1940 he was demobilized; he shortly began to organize underground activities among writers and intellectuals in France. During the Occupation he published frequently, not only in officially censored publications but through such clandestine outlets as the secret *Editions de Minuit.*

Aragon's chief works are *Un Traité du Style* (*Treatise on Style,* 1928); the poem *Front Rouge* (1931); and the novel *Les beaux Quartiers* (translated as *Residential Quarter, 1935*). Since the war he has published additional fiction and verse, including the novel *La Semaine Sainte (Holy Week,* 1958), and *Blanche ou l'Oubli* (1967).

Paul Eluard (French, 1895-1952) was the most profound and the most talented of the surrealists, although not the most typical. He differs from Breton and Aragon chiefly in that he retains definite links with traditional poetry, especially with Baudelaire and Rimbaud. The dominant theme of his work is love; Eluard treats this passion somewhat in the manner of the neo-Platonists, but with greater detachment, almost from a position of isolation. Not only does love serve man as a key to the realms of higher beauty, but it may in its highest forms exalt him to a veritable cosmic position, a station of divinity far transcending the temporal ecstasies of Rimbaud or Baudelaire.

Eluard's attitude toward women is comparable to that of his lifetime friend Pablo Picasso. Two preoccupations are present in the work of both: a tenderness toward woman as an object of mystery, and a seemingly incompatible desire to dissect woman in order to view her inner mysteries.

Eluard's first surrealist work was *Mourir de ne pas mourir* (*To Die of Not Dying;* poetry, 1924). This book contains his chief expression of the nature of woman and of woman's place in man's development. *L'Immaculée Conception* (*The Immaculate Conception;* poetry, 1930) is chiefly devoted to explorations into the subconscious in the Freudian manner. The book was written in collaboration with André Breton.

During the late thirties Eluard became increasingly concerned with politics. *Cours naturel* (*Natural Course;* poetry, 1938) contains "Victoire de Guernica," a poem of liberal sentiments inspired by the Spanish Civil War and by the famous painting of Picasso. His liberal emotions during the Occupation are expressed in *Poésie et Vérité* (*Poetry and Truth,* 1942) and *Au Rendez-vous allemand* (*Rendez-vous with the Germans,* 1945). Active with the French resistance during World War II, he became a communist during the Occupation, and was denied a visa to the United States in 1949. The author of more than seventy books, with Aragon and Picasso for close friends, Eluard died in November of 1952.

Rubén Darío (Nicaraguan-Spanish, 1867-1916)

Darío, a Symbolist and hedonist, is the chief Spanish-language poet of the early twentieth century. Born in Nicaragua, he worked as a journalist in Chile and Argentina before coming to Spain in 1892. He immediately plunged into European intellectual life and attempted to convert himself into a genuine European poet; but he often remarked that he felt himself a European in Latin America and an American in Europe. At the time of his first contact with Europe he was greatly impressed with French Symbolist poetry; he determined to introduce the genre into Spanish literature. This plan was doubly ambitious; Spanish poetry had for centuries been dominated by a rigid classicism, and nineteenth-century European innovations had thus far had little effect on its form. Darío burst the bonds and permanently altered the course of Spanish poetry; thenceforth the modernist element in Spanish verse was to increase throughout the century.

CHIEF WORKS: *Azul* (*Blue;* poems, 1888) was Darío's first book, published before his arrival in Europe. The poems, partly in prose and partly in verse, are permeated by the color blue, which Darío considered the hue of art and dreams.

A much more important book is *Prosas profanas* (poems, 1896). The word "prose" in the title is used in the medieval sense of "poetry in the vernacular" as opposed to Latin poetry. Since the medieval allusion conveys a hint of religious content, the adjective "profane" produces a paradoxical tension. In this book, the most influential of Darío's works, he expresses fully his hedonistic and Epicurean ethics and his admiration of the cult of art. The themes are the usual epigrams of decadence: e.g., the short lyric beginning "Cojamos la flor del instante" repeats the classic *carpe diem* theme.

Cantos de vida y esperanza (*Cantos of Life and Hope;* poems, 1905) is Darío's climactic work. "Sonatina," the best-known lyric from this collection, is a purely musical experiment without discernable content. "Canción de otoño en primavera" ("Autumn-song in Spring") is often held Darío's greatest poem. The theme is the classic melancholy of the poet who feels his youth departing from him.

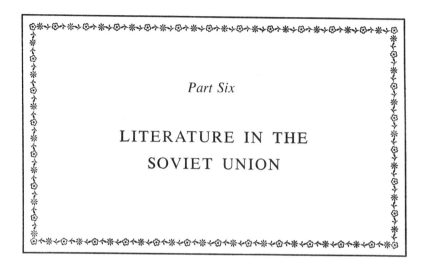

Part Six

LITERATURE IN THE
SOVIET UNION

A considerable amount of literature has been produced in the Soviet Union since 1917, and this literature is homogeneous enough in character to warrant its being treated as a distinct movement. The literature, however, has been produced only under the greatest difficulties and handicaps. The difficulties are so formidable, in fact, that the frequently high quality of the results is remarkable. Two great fears dominate the creative process in the Soviet Union: fear of official censorship, and fear proceeding out of ignorance of the precise attitude the government will take toward literature in the future. The Soviet author is not only harassed, he is harassed for reasons which have not been properly explained to him, and which seem to change constantly and capriciously.

At the same time it is a mistake to assume that everything written in the U.S.S.R. since October, 1917 is mere propaganda, and that authors in the Soviet Union are rigidly controlled in every sentence they write. On the contrary, the author's chief problem in the U.S.S.R. has been the vagueness of the official attitude, which allows him to venture far out on the limb of heresy before condemning him. The history of literary censorship in the Soviet Union is a story of vacillation, of constantly reversing policies, and of the conflict of incompatible

and hostile schools of criticism each ostensibly devoted to the further-
ance of the Revolution and the defense of the communistic system.

HISTORY: The October Revolution of 1917 found Russian letters in
a chaotic state. The chief schools of the time were Symbolism, deriving
from the French movement, and realism, harking back to Tolstoy and
Gogol and centering around Gorky. In addition there were any number
of left-wing, socialist, communist, and Bolshevik literary groups, each
with its magazine or review and its private literary philosophy. This
literary anarchy was for a time encouraged by the attitude of the
government. Lenin gave it as his opinion that literature lay outside
the realm of direct political control, and Trotsky and Bukharin spoke
out specifically for the freedom of the artist. The chief literary cénacles
of the immediate post-war, or "war communism," period, were the
PROLETCULT or movement for proletarian literature, centering around
the critic A. A. Bogdanov; the FUTURISTS, devoted to writing the
poetry of the age of machines and headed by Vladimir Mayakovsky;
and the SMITHY POETS, factory workers and artisans who sought to
instigate a truly popular literature.

With the era of the New Economic Plan (1921-28) this excessively
proletarian emphasis was abandoned; literature tended to become more
"literary" and to return to the principles of pre-Revolutionary realism.
The Futurist group evolved into the LEF (Left Front of Art) and
began to espouse a journalistic or reportorial form of realism; verse
was frowned upon. The NAPOSTOVTSY group formed around the magazine *Na postu* ("At your Post"); the editors of the review called for
a "living, concrete contemporaneity." Numerous other groups with
alphabetical designations flourished, but the *Na postu* circle seemed to
have the blessing of the government. None of these groups, however,
was an official government organization; all were private and independent literary societies.

In 1928, with the inception of the First Five-Year Plan, occurred
another reversal of policy. The government, denouncing the "purely
hot-house proletarian literature" of the literary cults, called for a new
approach to literature to be known as SOCIALIST REALISM. This was
defined as a progressive and communistic viewpoint in politics combined with an intelligent critical attitude; in practice it meant that
details and blunders in the Five-Year Plan might be criticized, but not
the basic soundness of the Plan itself. The focal point of the new litera-

ture was the government-created RAPP (Russian Association of Proletarian Writers), which was to supersede all unofficial organizations. As RAPP got under way it tended to attack the established writers of the pre-Revolutionary generation; by 1930 most RAPP authors were younger men who began to write after 1920.

The next upheaval came in 1932. RAPP, although government-inspired, began to take on certain characteristics of an independent organization. It was dissolved by "vote of the members," and party critics called for a new literature based on PARTIINOST (Party Spirit) —apparently a dogged adherence to the party line. A government censorship office, *Glavlit,* was created, and began to examine all published works. Soviet literature has continued to operate under these conditions up to the present time, although shortly after the Second World War the government again called for helpful criticism of failings and inadequacies at the local level. Much criticism of this type has actually appeared in the Soviet press and in literary works; the government of the U.S.S.R. still appears to approve criticism of weaknesses as long as these do not strike at the heart of the communistic system.

By the early 1950s Russian writers were again experiencing enormous frustration from rigid censorship, but when the Twentieth Congress of the Communist Party in 1956 decided to expose the "cult of personality" of Stalin, there were at least certain features of the past opened to their criticism—the kind of thing that permitted Solzhenitsyn to write a book like *One Day in the Life of Ivan Denisovich,* even if he was to have difficulties with its publication. But there are still boundaries beyond which they must not go, particularly in comment on the contemporary scene, as witnessed by the 1966 court sentence of Andrei Sinyavsky (who wrote under the pseudonym of Abram Tertz) to seven years at hard labor. The scandal caused by the offer of the Nobel Prize to Boris Pasternak in 1958 for *Doctor Zhivago* is somewhat harder to understand, as that novel seems innocuous enough. In any event Pasternak died two years later, a broken and disappointed man.

According to Deming Brown of the University of Michigan in a recent article on Soviet Russian Fiction, "The real leaders of Soviet literature in recent times have been the poets." Poetry apparently is not as easily censorable as prose. Of those leading poets the one best known in the western world is Yevgeny Yevtushenko (born

1933 in Zima, now Irkutzk Oblast), who has traveled considerably outside Russia: two visits to Cuba in 1960-61 which produced *Stikhi o Fidele (Verses about Fidel)*, two visits in 1962 to France, England and Finland. His first work was published in 1949 and his first collection, *Razvedchiki gryadushchego (Scouts of the Future)*, in 1952. He has continued to publish extensively, but the Soviet press has criticized him for "free-thinking" and "over-originality." He's a good man to watch, but effective translations of a large body of his work into English may take some time. Professor Brown feels that recent Soviet fiction has not produced anyone of the stature of Isaac Babel, Yuri Olesha, or Evgeny Zamyatin, but adds that Solzhenitsyn may emerge as "indeed a great writer."

Alexander Blok (Russian, 1880-1921)

Blok is widely acknowledged the greatest Russian poet of the twentieth century. A Symbolist before 1905, he turned thereafter to a bitter realism mixed with a sympathy for the miserable masses of the Russian people. At the time of the Revolution he was acclaimed as the poet of the new Russia, but Blok soon alienated the Bolsheviks by his introspective brooding and by his failure to view the promise of the new Russia with sufficient optimism. In the end all parties repudiated him; yet his popularity in the eyes of the Russian people has remained great throughout the century.

The chief quality of Blok's poetry, especially that written after 1905, is its bitter irony. In this respect he is well compared with Maxim Gorky; his ideas and technique are merely those of Gorky adapted to the vastly different medium of lyric poetry. His early Symbolist poetry was heavy and rich, influenced by the French Symbolist school and by Renaissance lyrics. In his later style he is sparse, even laconic; "The Twelve" is a masterpiece of concision. He gains his best effects through small, carefully-polished images, through ironic understatement and sarcasm, and through juxtaposition of the sublime and the sordid.

CHIEF WORKS: *Verses About the Lady Beautiful* (Russ. *Stikhi o prekrasnoi dame;* poetry, 1904) was Blok's first book-length publication. The poems of the volume are tributes to femininity in the neo-Platonic tradition, heavily influenced by Petrarch and Mallarmé. The work is said to have been chiefly inspired by Liubov Mendeleyevna, daughter of the famous chemist Mendeleyev and later Blok's wife.

"The Twelve" (Russ. "Dvenadtsat"; poem, 1918) is Blok's best-known single lyric. The "twelve" of the poem are Red soldiers who march through the streets of Petrograd in the terrible days of the October Revolution, terrorizing the bourgeois and looting from the rich. The poem is full of street slang, popular quatrains, and deliberately incongruous juxtapositions. The reactionaries—priests, rich old ladies, pompous middle-class citizens, and Czarist bureaucrats—are depicted with colorful sarcasm. At the end of the poem Jesus Christ appears to lead the twelve on their Odyssey through the city. As might be expected, this ending displeased both Christians and Bolsheviks.

"The Scythians" (Russ. "Skify"; poem, 1918) proudly identifies the Russians with the Scythians of classic times who swept down out of the steppes to pillage and destroy the outposts of the Roman Empire. "Yes," says Blok, "we are Scythians; we are Asiatics with slanting and eager eyes." This exuberant outburst of nationalism is well compared with Gogol's famous Troika image in *Dead Souls*. Blok ends by predicting that the Scythians will soon again sweep over a decadent and enfeebled Europe to revive it with regenerated blood.

Vladimir Mayakovsky (Russian, 1893-1930)

According to Guerney, Blok's "The Twelve" was the poem of the Revolution, but Mayakovsky was its poet. Certainly he was a more acceptable Bolshevik than Blok; he continued in intermittent good grace with the regime up to the time of his suicide in 1930. In addition he bitterly attacked the Symbolist school from which Blok sprang; in fact Mayakovsky's Futurism, which he borrowed from Italian and French models, took as its primary mission the attack on the Symbolist movement.

Mayakovsky was the son of a Caucasian forester; he was brought to Moscow by his mother in 1906. He began to engage in underground political activity while still a child, and at the age of fifteen was sentenced to eleven months in prison for working in an illegal printing establishment. As a student in a Moscow art school he met the group of young painters and poets who called themselves Futurists, and in 1912 he published his first Futurist poem. The same year he produced an important and influential Futurist manifesto, "A Slap in the Face of Public Taste." Mayakovsky's "Cubo-Futurism," as he called it, was actually a poetry based on themes from city life and marked by an iconoclastic and whimsical style somewhat resembling French surrealism.

At the time of the 1917 Revolution Mayakovsky plunged into the struggle on the side of the Bolsheviks; he produced thousands of propaganda posters and jingles. Soon he was acclaimed as the official poet of Bolshevism. This triumph lasted only a short while; by 1922 his supremacy was challenged by a score of poets of his generation and before his death he had been discredited through the 1928 reversal in government literary policy. More than any other poet, however, Mayakovsky epitomizes the spirit of the early years of the Soviet Revolution. His work has never been officially banned, and it is likely he will continue to be accepted as a standard poet in Russia.

CHIEF WORKS: "A Cloud in Pants" (poem, 1915) is typical of Mayakovsky's early Futurist work. The poem takes the form of an exhortation to the crowds of the Moscow streets; they are implored to "straighten their backs," to cease cringing before their masters, and to prepare themselves physically and spiritually for the Armageddon ahead. (Mayakovsky believed the Revolution would take place in 1916, and he was not far wrong.) "The Spine Flute," also dated 1915, is similar in tone.

"150,000,000" (poem, 1920) is a good example of Mayakovsky's post-Revolutionary style. Ivan, a symbol of the Russian Revolution, is contrasted to Woodrow Wilson, who crouches in his fortress-palace in Chicago (!) while he pulls the strings of capitalistic puppets the world over.

American Verses (Russ. *Amerikanskiye stikhi;* poems, 1926) is a book of travel verse growing out of Mayakovsky's visit to the United States and Latin America in 1926. The poems consist chiefly of sarcastic attacks on the capitalistic system and its alleged inequalities and persecutions. Typical is "Black and White," a portrait of a downtrodden negro street-sweeper in Havana who naively inquires of his boss why white sugar must be made by black niggers, and has his face punched for his pains—he does not know that "negroes who try such a question to pose / Should address it to Moscow to the Comintern."

Boris Pilnyak (Russian, 1894-1938?)

Pilnyak, deriving in style from the Symbolists and Chekhov, bears little resemblance to a typical Bolshevik writer; nevertheless *The Naked Year* is probably the best novel to come out of the October Revolution. Pilnyak was not a Party member but a fellow traveller. (Note that this term has a pejorative sense in the U.S.S.R. as in America, but for the opposite reason—a "fellow traveller" is a socialist whose sympathies are with the Revolution but who does nothing to aid in its realization.) In his diary for 1923 Pilnyak notes, "In so far as the Communists are with Russia, I am with them . . . The Communist Party is for me but a link in the destiny of Russia." This statement connects him to the Slavophiles of the nineteenth century and especially to Gogol, whose *Dead Souls* he imitated in "Mahogany." It is not surprising that Pilnyak often found himself at odds with the Soviet government.

Pilnyak is not a realist in technique. He resembles the continental naturalists in his treatment of mass humanity, in his thesis that society must be treated in terms of classes rather than as individuals; but the techniques he uses to convey this principle are symbolistic or expressionistic. He feels a kinship with the peasant, whose elemental psychology he finds more sympathetic than the cynicism of the city worker; thus his work is permeated with a sort of elemental animism similar to that of Hamsun and Giono. This cult of the peasant is connected with his adulation of the "Russian soul," crude, powerful, and creative, which will some day sweep over the decadent sophistication of Western Europe. Pilnyak manifests to perfection the qualities which Western readers, rightly or wrongly, consider most "Russian." Of all the Soviet authors he will seem most familiar to the reader of Dostoyevsky, Gogol, and Chekhov.

LIFE: Boris Pilnyak (pseud. of Boris Andreyevich Vogau) was born in a Moscow suburb in 1894; his ancestry included German, Jewish, and Tartar elements. In 1920 he received a degree in business administration from the Moscow Commercial Institute. He had been writing even before the Revolution (he was excused from military duty because of his poor eyesight) and shortly after his graduation he began to write in earnest. *The Naked Year* appeared in 1922; it was the first novel of high literary quality to come out of the Revolution, and won wide acclaim. During the following decade Pilnyak's relations with the Soviet government followed a precarious path: he wrote, found himself attacked in the press, confessed his error publicly, rewrote, and won a grudging approval; then the cycle began over again. The greatest crisis occurred in 1929, when Pilnyak offered a story, "Mahogany," to a Berlin publishing firm which had occasionally published the work of émigrés. He narrowly escaped prosecution in this instance; he revised the tale, which eventually appeared as *The Volga Falls to the Caspian Sea* (1930), but he remained under a taint of suspicion the rest of his life. Pilnyak travelled more widely than most Soviet authors; he visited Germany and England in 1922-23, the Far East in 1926 and again in 1932, and America in 1931. His ultimate fate is uncertain. His name has not appeared in the Soviet press since 1937, and rumor has it he was secretly executed in 1938.

CHIEF NOVELS: *The Naked Year* (Russ. *Goly god;* novel, 1922) is a novel of intricate structure covering the period from 1917 to 1921 and especially the events of the last year. Individuals play only a minor part in the plot; the real protagonists are the peasant class, the working class, and Russia herself. The structure resembles that of Dos Passos' *U.S.A.;* there are flashbacks, vignettes, and closeups of characters involved in the common situation, and these are mixed with press clippings, dispatches, and governmental edicts. The style is often chaotic; Pilnyak attempts to convey the confusion of the era through the use of jumbled language. Words tumble profusely at the reader without apparent sequence; characters and incidents flash by the eye in dizzying succession.

The year 1921 as Pilnyak portrays it was a confused muddle of heroism, cruelty, and destruction. Anarchists and other splinter groups attempt to set up independent colonies and are suppressed; peasants engage in sporadic uprisings, and aristocrats dabble half-heartedly at counter-revolutionary agitation. An often-remarked chapter is "Train No. 58," a chaotic picture of the perils of rail transportation in 1919.

The Volga Falls to the Caspian Sea (Russ. *Volga Vpadayet v Kaspiskoye more;* novel, 1930) centers around the building of a dam at Kolomna, on the Volga, to divert the course of the river. The title is ironic; the Caspian is a dead sea, and the Volga has no outlet to the Mediterranean and world commerce.

The kernel of this novel appeared in the tale "Mahogany" (1929), a story of two brothers who travel about in the provinces attempting to cheat ignorant landowners of their antique furniture. The resemblance to Gogol's *Dead Souls* is obvious. The story is full of "Oblomovism," the traditional defeatism and indolence of the landowning class; even the Communists seem to be infected with the disease. "Mahogany" was promptly banned in Russia, and Pilnyak set about rewriting it. When it reappeared as *The Volga Falls to the Caspian Sea* most of the offensive sections had been removed, although the novel never won wide acclaim in the Soviet press. The theme of the rewritten work is the triumph of human energy and ingenuity over the passive river, a symbol of pre-Revolutionary Russian indolence. As in Pilnyak's first novel, the emphasis is on groups rather than on individuals.

Mikhail Sholokhov (Russian, born 1905)

Sholokhov's novels are gigantic in scope and conception; moreover they are "proletarian" enough to make them acceptable in the Soviet Union, and objective and detached enough to be appreciated by Western readers who would reject mere propaganda. He is not particularly original in technique. Essentially he derives from Tolstoy; *The Quiet Don* is merely *War and Peace* transferred to a later war and adapted to the literary taste of a new generation. This is not to say that Sholokhov is a novelist and moralist of the stature of Tolstoy, merely that the attitudes and techniques of the two authors are similar.

Sholokhov's novels are chiefly concerned with life in the Don Cossack region—with its peasants, its local functionaries, and its vast natural beauties. In the years following the 1917 Revolution this region was cruelly divided in its loyalty; Cossack bands fought the Red army as late as 1923. Although Sholokhov has always been a Communist, he shares the anguish these people felt in the years when they hesitated to accept communism and when villages, even families, were divided by bitter hatreds. It is perhaps this conflict in the minds of his own people which has made Sholokhov into a more penetrating artist of human psychology than most Soviet authors.

In structure Sholokhov, early trained as a short-story writer, has difficulty in adapting himself to the panoramic sweep of the novel; his novels tend to split into small individual narratives only loosely connected to the central plan. Thus, like Pilnyak, he occasionally resembles John Dos Passos; *The Quiet Don* is markedly similar in structure to *U.S.A.* In intent too the two books are parallel; both seek to present an epic picture of an entire land, including every element and class, during a period of transition. Like Dos Passos, Sholokhov often includes official documents, newspaper articles, and dispatches verbatim in his novels to establish authenticity.

Although Sholokhov frankly confesses his loyalty to the Communist ideology, his books are far from mere propaganda; he never gives the impression of seeking to force the reader to agree to his political sentiments. His characters are seldom all black or all white; his best-known hero, the Grigory of *The Quiet Don,* vacillates from the White cause to the Bolsheviks a half-dozen times, and in the end surrenders his loyalty to no one. It is obvious that Sholokhov believes Grigory has been wrong, but author and reader share a sympathy for Grigory which remains independent of the morality of his political actions.

Like his model Tolstoy, Sholokhov has a fine feeling for details. He dwells upon apparently unimportant incidents—the death of a horse, a sexual interlude, an accident on a train—with a perspicacity which at first seems excessive, yet at the end the reader sees that all was a part of the whole.

LIFE: Sholokhov was born in 1905 in the Cossack village of Veshenskaya on the Don. His father was a middle-class lumberman and cattle dealer, and his mother of Turkish extraction. Sholokhov, a gymnasium student, was only twelve at the time of the German invasion of the Don Basin; he fled with his family, and in 1917 joined the Bolshevik cause. He held a number of clerical and bureaucratic jobs in the government from 1918 to 1925; in 1922 he helped to battle White "bandits" in his own Cossack region.

Sholokhov began to write around 1924; the following year he published *Tales of the Don,* a collection of short stories. In 1928 appeared the first part of *The Quiet Don;* the work was an immediate success and went into numerous editions even before the final parts had appeared. In 1940, when the final volume of the Russian version was announced, crowds waited for hours in line for copies. Sholokhov has been widely honored by the Soviet regime; he is the recipient of a Stalin Prize, a member of the Soviet Academy, and a deputy to the Supreme Soviet of the U.S.S.R.

As soon as his success as a writer was assured, Sholokhov returned to his native village on the Don, where he worked at his writing under greater conditions of tranquillity than obtained in the city. The town is said to be a hundred miles from the nearest railroad. Sholokhov emerged from this rustication to serve as a war correspondent in the

Second World War; the Germans again invaded the Don Basin, and his mother was killed by a Nazi bomb. Since 1945 little has been heard from him; rumor has it that excessive drinking has curbed his literary output. But in 1965 Mikhail Sholokhov was awarded the Nobel Prize in literature, which made the Russians feel a little better after the Boris Pasternak affair of 1958, when the Soviet government insisted upon his refusal of the award.

CHIEF NOVELS: *The Quiet Don* (Russ. *Tikhi Don;* novel, 1928-40) is a gigantic work; it was written over a period of fourteen years and published in several sections. The Russian edition comprises four volumes, the last of which appeared in 1940. The Anglo-American edition, slightly abridged, fills over two thousand pages. It was first published in two volumes, *And Quiet Flows the Don* (1934) and *The Don Flows Home to the Sea* (1940); a single-volume version later appeared under the title *The Quiet Don.*

Sholokhov's intent in the novel is to present an encompassing picture of the Cossack people from 1910 to 1920. The structure of the book makes condensation difficult; the novel is a vast and intricate network of characters, incidents, and movements. The chief character, and the thread which holds the action together, is Grigory or Gregor, a young Cossack, like Sholokhov half-Turkish by birth. An important sequence in the novel is the love affair of Grigory and Axinia, wife of Grigory's neighbor. This narrative, a study in the psychology of illicit love, bears comparison with the Anna-Vronsky plot in *Anna Karenina.* Grigory has many other adventures. He serves as a non-commissioned officer on the German front during the war, and becomes indignant at Czarist corruption and incompetence. Yet when the October Revolution breaks out he feels little sympathy for the fanatic Bolsheviks; he assumes command of an irregular White column in southern Russia. When the Whites are beaten, his comrades escape by ship to Turkey, but by this time Grigory feels little kinship with them either; he remains in Russia and joins a Red cavalry column under Budenny. After fighting in Poland he is demobilized; he returns to his native village to find it in the hands of bickering and incompetent Soviet officials. He speaks out against the situation until he is almost arrested; he flees and again joins a band of anti-communist guerrillas. For over six years he continues this underground fight against Bolshevism, but his ideals deteriorate as his experience increases. At the end of the novel he is entirely disillusioned and cynical. His wife and parents are dead, his mistress Axinia has been killed, and he is left with only a son, the last link between himself and the future.

Seeds of Tomorrow (Russ. *Podnyataya tselina;* novel, 1932-33) is a second vast novel-epic, this time concerned with the collectivization of the land in the Don region. Again Sholokhov's head is with the Soviets and his heart with the Cossack peasants; the situation of conflict between government and peasants is drawn with sympathy and objectivity. The chief character is Davidov, a young peasant who becomes a Communist organizer and vigorously fights the kulaks who oppose collectivization of the Don farmlands.

Alexander Solzhenitsyn (Russian, born 1918)

Born in Rostov-on-Don, apparently in 1918, and educated there, Alexander Isaevich Solzhenitsyn joined the Soviet army in 1941, served at the front and was twice decorated for bravery. In February 1945 as a young captain he was arrested by the Soviet armed forces counterintelligence agency (SMERSH) for making derogatory remarks about Stalin in a letter to a friend. He was sentenced and served eight years in labor camps (which gave him material for two novels); he contracted and was cured of cancer (which gave him material for another); he spent three years of exile in Siberia before being officially "rehabilitated" in 1957. Since that time he has been a teacher of mathematics and physics in Vladimir and in the high school at Ryazan. A prolific writer, he has had an almost constant struggle to get published. *Odin den' Ivana Denisovicha (One Day in the Life of Ivan Denisovich)* was published in some form in 1962. Since that time (and in 1968 in English) two other novels have appeared, *The First Circle* (with a reference to Dante's *Inferno*) about a scientific or technical institute near Moscow staffed by the Mavrino Special Prison, and *Rakovyi Korpus (Cancer Ward),* where the hospital for the treatment of cancer becomes a metaphor for the whole diseased world. Yevgeny Yevtushenko, the young Russian poet, has called Soltzhenitsyn "our only living Russian classic." Deming Brown refers to "Matryona's Home" as "perhaps the finest story in recent years."

CHIEF WORK: *Odin den' Ivana Denisovicha (One Day in the Life of Ivan Denisovich;* novel, 1962) uses the "skaz" form, a story told as if orally by a fictive first person narrator with individualized speech patterns. Ivan Denisovich Shukhov is a very ordinary citizen of Soviet Russia, a John Doe (Ivan is Russian for John) who is serving the tenth year of his sentence in a Siberian prison camp. We follow him through one winter day from reveille at 5 a.m. through lights out. The concentration is on the present—food, sick call, work details, clothes and keeping warm—elements of survival. Memories of the past are very thin and the future hardly bears thinking about. The translators apparently feel that a day in the life of an ordinary Soviet citizen outside the camp had much in common with the life inside the prison—on both sides of the fence the same material and spiritual squalor, corruption, frustration, and terror. Allowing for relativity you can even make that statement "on both sides of the curtain." The humble, utterly bewildered plain man, Ivan, is not just a Russian Everyman, but a mid-twentieth century apolitical Everyman in the prison of power politics and bureaucracy —and material and spiritual squalor.

Ivan and numerous fellow prisoners manage to show "the endurance of the human spirit" confronted by deprivation, insult, and torment, which lift this story out of the "social document" category where it undeniably has roots. Its authentic characters and quiet honesty "have caused its publication to be regarded by many Russians as the greatest single event in the literature of recent times." That is Professor Deming's pronouncement.

In 1969 a play by Solzhenitsyn, *The Love-Girl and the Innocent,* appeared in English translation. Whether this play, written apparently in the early sixties and accepted for performance in Moscow in 1962, then banned without being performed, is the same play referred to by the author as *The Reindeer and the Little Hut* in his May 16, 1967 letter to the Congress of Soviet Writers, is a question to which we do not yet have enough information for a secure answer. Titles are often slippery. The action of this play is a love story with an inevitably tragic separation in a Stalinist slave-labor prison compound in the middle forties; Nemov and Lyuba emerge as convincing characters.

In 1970 when the Swedish Academy announced its designation of Alexander Solzhenitsyn as the winner of the Nobel Prize in literature the Soviet Union was apparently faced with the same traumatic experience that they confronted in the case of Boris Pasternak. They have reacted, according to their press, in much the same way; it is to be hoped that Solzhenitsyn as a younger man will also be stronger.

Solzhenitsyn's recent historical novel, *August 1914,* published in America in 1972, has been announced as the first in a major series but is complete in itself dealing with the German destruction of the Russian Second Army in the opening rounds of the First World War. Ambitious as a meditation on Russian history, it bears comparison with Tolstoy's *War and Peace* and Proust's *Remembrance of Things Past;* the author brings to life a great variety of people, some historical, some fictional, rubbing elbows, and deals with events that reflect back on Napoleon in Russia and forward to Stalin's losing nearly a third of the Russian Army in the summer of 1941. Naomi Bliven in *The New Yorker* (October 14, 1972) gives this book its most succinct accolade: "The questions Solzhenitsyn's novel poses are universal as well as Russian, and terrible and inescapable, and probably unanswerable. . . . What is the use of courage? Of loyalty? And why are most people so much better than what happens to them?"

OTHER SOVIET AUTHORS

Fyodor Sologub (pseud. of Fyodor Kismich Teternikov; 1863-1927) is a Symbolist poet and novelist who continued to write after the Revolution but who had little sympathy for the Communists. In the period 1900-1914 he was the acknowledged leader of the Symbolist movement. His best-known work is the novel *The Little Demon* (Russ. *Melki bes,* 1905). Peredonov, the hero, is a malicious and tyrannical school-teacher whose life seems devoted to making himself disagreeable to others. At last the Demon which obsesses Peredonov drives him to murder his best friend.

Another excellent work of Sologub is *The Created Legend* (Russ. *Tvorimaya legenda,* 1908-12), a novel series centering around the mysterious magician Trirodov. The mood of this latter work is dark, fantastic, and decadent. After the Revolution Sologub wrote chiefly lyrics; his models were eighteenth-century pastorals and songs.

Mikhail Zoshchenko (1895-1958) is a chief Russian humorist of the Revolutionary period. A Czarist officer during the war, he joined the Red army in 1917. In 1922 he became an intimate of the Serapion circle, a Petersburg literary cénacle, and soon made himself the chief ornament of this group. Zoshchenko's best works are his short stories or anecdotes, written in a breezy colloquial style and highly condensed in the manner of Voltaire's *contes*. The first of these stories appeared as *Tales by Nazar Ilyich Sinebriukhov* (1922); the book won Zoshchenko instant fame. These tales are narrated by Corporal Sinebriukhov, a rascally wag something like Schnitzler's Anatol.

Zoshchenko, a fellow traveller, incurred the suspicion of the Party around 1930, and his subsequent works hew closer to the Party line. In *Restored Youth* (novel, 1933) he apparently produced what was wanted; the book was favorably reviewed in the Soviet press. "The Adventures of an Ape" (story, 1945) appeared in a post-war collection of Zoshchenko's work. In 1946 a government purge of writers attacked this story with especial vehemence, and it appeared that Zoshchenko had entered a more or less permanent period of disgrace. When some stories by him began to appear in the fifties, it was difficult to recognize the old Zoshchenko, and he died in 1958.

Alexey Tolstoy (1882-1945) is a fellow traveller who began his literary career as a Symbolist. During the First World War he fought in the White army; he subsequently fled to Paris, returning to Russia only in 1922. In the post-Revolutionary period he turned from poetry to the realistic novel. The great work of his career is the novel trilogy *The Road to Calvary* (Russ. *Khozhdeniye po mukam,* 1923-41). This vast work comprises a panorama of Russian society from 1914 to 1921, dwelling especially on the political evolution of the intellectual and educated classes. Tolstoy, as a repentant émigré, was at first viewed skeptically by the Soviet press; his prestige continued to increase between the wars, however, and his intense patriotism during the Second World War aided in his popularity. It is said that Tolstoy, after Gorky, is the most widely-read author in the U.S.S.R. today.

Evgeny Zamiatin (variously spelled Yevgeni, or Eugene, Zamyatin; 1884-1937) was a naval engineer by profession. His early work was strongly influenced by Gogol; his *District Tales* (1911) were written in imitation of Gogol's *Evenings on a Farm Near Dikanka*. Never an orthodox Communist, Zamiatin was frequently in trouble with the Soviet regime. The chief work of his career, and the only one of his works to be translated into English, is *We* (Russ. *My;* novel, 1922), a "nightmare utopia" in the manner of Huxley's *Brave New World* or Orwell's *Nineteen Eighty Four*. This novel was never published in the Soviet Union, although it was read at a 1924 meeting of the Writers' Union. An English edition appeared the same year, and a pirated Russian version was later published by an émigré press in Prague. Naturally this caused Zamiatin no end of trouble in Russia. His utopian novel is one of the best of its genre. It is laid in a collectivist city roofed over with glass to insulate it from the weather. Individuality is totally suppressed; persons are designated by letters and numbers instead of by names, and a special government form, good only for certain days and hours, is necessary before one can make love. As in *Nineteen Eighty Four,* the individual has no privacy whatsoever; all walls are transparent, and "eyes" and "ears" in the streets record everything that goes on.

FOR FURTHER REFERENCE

For Soviet authors see also Maxim Gorky.

BIBLIOGRAPHY

This bibliography is compiled for the convenience of the student of literature who wishes to make further study of the authors and literary movements treated. It does not pretend to be complete; in the case of some authors who published fifty or more separate items during their careers, a complete list would be both inconvenient and confusing. The bibliography includes (a) the most significant or important works of each author, and (b) a selected list of critical or biographical materials for further reference.

Titles are indicated in English except where no translation exists or where the title is untranslatable. Dates listed, however, are those of original publication.

Especially significant or useful works are indicated with an asterisk (*).

* * *

HISTORIES OF LITERATURE AND GENERAL STUDIES

GENERAL

Columbia Dictionary of Modern European Literature, Columbia U. P., 1947; Wm. A. Drake, *Contemporary European Writers,* N. Y., 1928 (good but obsolete); Herbert J. Muller, *Modern Fiction,* N. Y., 1937; Annie Russell Marble, *The Nobel Prize Winners in Literature,* N. Y.,

1928 (good but outdated); David Daiches, *The Novel and the Modern World*, Univ. of Chicago Press, 1939 (novels in English only); William O'Connor, ed., *Forms of Modern Fiction*, Univ. of Minn. Press, 1948.

ENGLISH

*Albert C. Baugh, ed., *A Literary History of England*, N. Y., 1948; J. M. Manly and Edith Rickert, *Contemporary British Literature*, N. Y., 1928 (outdated); J. W. Cunliffe, *English Literature in the Twentieth Century*, N. Y., 1933; Edwin Muir, *Introduction to English Literature*: vol. V, *The Present Age*, N. Y., 1940; *Edward Wagenknecht, *Cavalcade of the English Novel*, N. Y., 1943.

AMERICAN

Carl Van Doren, *The American Novel: 1789-1939*, N. Y., 1940; *Edward Wagenknecht, *Cavalcade of the American Novel*, N. Y., 1952; F. B. Millet, *Contemporary American Authors*, N. Y., 1940.

FRENCH

*Wm. A. Nitze and E. Preston Dargan, *A History of French Literature*, N. Y., 1922-27-28; D. W. Alden, *Bibliography of Critical and Biographical References for the Study of Contemporary French Literature*, N. Y., 1949; Denis Saurat, *Modern French Literature*, N. Y., 1946; René Lalou, *Histoire de la littérature française contemporaine*, Paris, 1947; Marcel Girard, *Guide illustré de la littérature française moderne*, Paris, 1949 (period 1918-49).

GERMAN

*Arthur Eloesser, *Modern German Literature*, N. Y., 1933; *Jethro Bithell, *Modern German Literature*, London, 1939.

RUSSIAN

*D. S. Mirsky, *A History of Russian Literature*, N. Y., 1949 (includes Soviets); Gleb Struve, *Soviet Russian Literature, 1917-50*, Univ. of Okla. Press, 1951; Marc Slonim, *Modern Russian Literature*, Oxford U. P., 1953; Ernest J. Simmons, *Through the Glass of Soviet Literature*, Columbia U. P., 1953.

SPANISH

George Tyler Northup, *An Introduction to Spanish Literature*, Univ. of Chicago Press, 1936; Gerald Brenan, *The Literature of the Spanish People*, Cambridge U. P., 1951; Gonzolo Torrente Ballester, *Literatura Española Contemporánea*, Madrid, 1936.

ITALIAN

*Domenico Vittorini, *The Modern Italian Novel*, N. Y., 1930; Joseph Spencer Kennard, *A Literary History of the Italian People*, N. Y., 1941.

II. THE REALISTIC MOVEMENT

REALISTS AND STORY-TELLERS

THOMAS MANN

Tales: *Tonio Kröger*, 1903; *Death in Venice*, 1913; *Mario and the Magician*, 1930. Also see *Stories of Three Decades*, N. Y., 1936. Novels: *Buddenbrooks*, 1901; *The Magic Mountain*, 1924; *Joseph and his Brothers* (tetralogy), 1933-44; *Lotte in Weimar (The Beloved Returns)*, 1939; *Doctor Faustus*, 1947; *The Holy Sinner*, 1951; *The Confessions of Felix Krull, Confidence Man*, 1955. About: *Henry Hatfield, *Thomas Mann*, Norfolk, Conn., 1951; James Cleugh, *Thomas Mann: A Study*, London, 1933; H. J. Weigand, *Thomas Man's Novel Der Zauberberg*, N. Y., 1933; J. G. Brennan, *Thomas Mann's World*, N. Y., 1942. I. Feuerlicht, *Thomas Mann*, N. Y., 1968; E. Kahler, *The Orbit of Thomas Mann*, Princeton, 1969.

HEINRICH MANN

Novels: *The Blue Angel (Small Town Tyrant)*, 1905; *The Empire* (trilogy), 1914-25; *Young Henry of Navarre*, 1935; *Henry, King of France*, 1938. About: F. Gross, "Heinrich Mann," *Contemporary Review*, CLX (1941); W. Schroeder, *Heinrich Mann*, Vienna, 1932 (German language).

JACINTO BENAVENTE Y MARTINEZ

Works: *Teatro Fantastico*, 1892; *Autumnal Roses*, 1895; *The Evil Doers of Good*, 1905; *Brute Force*, 1908; *La Malquerida*, 1913; *The Bonds of Interest*, 1917. About: *Walter Starkie, *Jacinto Benavente*, London, 1924; John Dos Passos, *Rosinante to the Road Again*, N. Y., 1922.

IVAN BUNIN

Stories in collection: *Ioann the Weeper*, 1913; *The Cup of Life*, 1914; *The Gentleman from San Francisco and other Stories*, 1923; *The Dreams of Chang and other Stories*, 1923; *God's Tree*, 1931; *Grammar of Love*, 1934. Novel: *The Village*, 1923. About: Gleb Struve, "The Art of Ivan Bunin," *Slavonic Review*, XI (1932-33).

SIGRID UNDSET

Works: *Madame Martha Oulie*, 1907; *The Happy Age* (tales), 1908;

Gunnar's Daughter, 1909; *Kristin Lavransdatter*, 1920-22; *The Longest Years* (autobiography), 1934. About: Victor Vinde, *Sigrid Undset, a Nordic Moralist*, Univ. of Wash. Press, 1930; S. U. Winsnes, *Sigrid Undset, a Study in Christian Realism*, N. Y., 1953.

TWENTIETH CENTURY NATURALISTS

HENRIK IBSEN

A Pathfinder

Dramas: *Cataline*, 1850; *The Comedy of Love*, 1862; *The Pretenders*, 1863; *Brand*, 1866; *Peer Gynt*, 1867; *The League of Youth*, 1869; *Emperor and Galilean*, 1873; *The Pillars of Society*, 1877; *A Doll's House*, 1879; *Ghosts*, 1881; *An Enemy of the People*, 1882; *The Wild Duck*, 1884; *Rosmersholm*, 1886; *Hedda Gabbler*, 1890; *When We Dead Awaken*, 1899. About: Edmund Gosse, *Isben*, London, 1907; Otto Heller, *Henrik Ibsen: Plays and Problems*, N. Y., 1912; *Theodore Jorgenson, *Henrik Ibsen, a Study in Art and Personality*, Northfield, Minn., 1945.

GERHART HAUPTMANN

Dramas: *Before Dawn*, 1889; *The Weavers*, 1892; *The Beaver Coat*, 1893; *The Assumption of Hannele*, 1894; *The Sunken Bell*, 1898; *Michael Kramer*, 1900; *Henry of Aue*, 1914; *The Bow of Odysseus*, 1915; *Hamlet in Wittenberg*, 1935; *The Tetralogy of the Atrides*, 1941-48. Fiction: *Stationmaster Thiel*, 1888; *The Apostle*, 1891; *Florian Geyer*, 1895; *The Fool in Christ, Emanuel Quint*, 1910; *The Heretic of Soana*, 1918. About: John J. Weisert, *The Dream in Gerhart Hauptmann*, N. Y. 1949; Camillo von Klenze, *From Goethe to Hauptmann*, N. Y., 1926; Philo M. Buck, *Directions in Contemporary Literature*, Oxford U. P., 1942; Hugh F. Garten, *Gerhart Hauptmann*, New Haven, 1954.

MAXIM GORKY

Prose: *Chelkash*, 1895; *Creatures that Once Were Men*, 1897; "Twenty-Six Men and a Girl," 1899; *The City of the Yellow Devil*, 1906; *Recollections of Tolstoy*, 1919. Drama: *The Lower Depths*, 1902. Autobiography: *My Childhood*, 1915; *In the World*, 1917; *My University Days*, 1923; *Fragments from My Diary*, 1924. About: *Aleksandr Roskin, *From the Banks of the Volga: The Life of Maxim Gorky*, N. Y., 1946; A. Kaun, *Maxim Gorky and His Russia*, N. Y., 1931.

ALEXANDER KUPRIN

Story collections: *The River of Life*, 1916; *A Slav Soul*, 1916; *The Brace-*

let of Garnets, 1917; Novels: *The Duel,* 1905; *Yama,* 1908-15. About:
W. L. Phelps, *Essays on Russian Novelists,* N. Y., 1911; Charles Ledré,
Trois Romanciers russes, Paris, 1935.

JULES ROMAINS

Novels: *Death of a Nobody,* 1911; *The Boys in the Back Room,* 1913;
Men of Good Will, 1932-45 (for breakdown see p. 111). Drama: *Knock,*
1923. About: Milton H. Stansbury, *French Novelists of Today,* U. of
Penn. Press, 1935; Philo M. Buck, *Directions in Contemporary Literature,*
Oxford U. P., 1942. Also see *Saturday Review,* June 3, 1933; December
30, 1939; April 6, 1940.

ROGER MARTIN DU GARD

Novels: *Jean Barois,* 1913; *Les Thibaults,* 1922-36. About: *H. C. Rice,
Roger Martin du Gard and the World of the Thibaults,* N. Y., 1941; *New
Yorker,* March 1, 1941; *Saturday Review,* November 20, 1927; March
25, 1939; D. L. Schalk, *R. M. du Gard, the Novelist and History,* Ithaca,
N. Y., 1967.

PIO BAROJA Y NESSI

Chief translated novels: *The Struggle for Life (The Quest, Weeds, Red
Dawn),* 1904; *Paradox, King,* 1966; *Caesar or Nothing,* 1910; *The Three
of Knowledge,* 1911; *The Restlessness of Shanti Andia,* 1911. About:
Ernest Boyd, *Studies from Ten Literatures,* N. Y., 1925; John Dos Passos,
Rosinante to the Road Again, N. Y., 1922; Salvador de Madariaga, *The
Genius of Spain,* N. Y., 1923.

REGIONALISTS AND RURAL NATURALISTS

KNUT HAMSUN

Novels: *Hunger,* 1890; *Pan,* 1894; *Growth of the Soil,* 1917; *The Ring
Is Closed,* 1936. Essay: *The Cultural Life of Modern America,* 1889.
About: Hanna Astrup Larsen, *Knut Hamsun,* N. Y., 1922; Alrik Gustaf-
son, *Six Scandinavian Novelists,* N. Y., 1940.

SELMA LAGERLÖF

Novels: *Gösta Berling's Saga,* 1891; *The Girl from the Marshcroft,* 1908;
Liliecrona's Home, 1911; *The Outcast,* 1918; *The Ring of the Löwen-
skölds* (trilogy), 1928. Story collections: *From a Swedish Homestead,*
1899; *Christ Legends,* 1904. Juvenile: *The Wonderful Adventures of Nils,*
1906. Autobiographical: *Marbacka,* 1922; *Childhood's Memories,* 1930;

Diary, 1936. About: Walter A. Berendsohn, *Selma Lagerlöf, Her Life and Work*, N. Y., 1931; H. A. Larsen, *Selma Lagerlöf*, N. Y., 1936; Alrik Gustafson, *Six Scandinavian Novelists*, N. Y., 1940.

JEAN GIONO

Novels: *Hill of Destiny*, 1929; *Lovers Are Never Losers*, 1929; *Harvest*, 1930; *Blue Boy*, 1932; *The Song of the World*, 1934; *The Joy of Man's Desiring*, 1940; *Les âmes fortes*, 1949; *Les grands chemins*, 1951; *Le hussard sur le toit*, 1951; *Le bonheur fou*, 1957; *Angelo*, 1958. About: H. Fleming, "Persons and Personages," *Living Age*, April, 1935; *Wilson Bulletin*, October, 1937 (biog. sketch). R. de Villeneuve, *Jean Giono ce solitaire*, Avignon, 1955; P. de Boisdeffre, *Giono*, Paris, 1965; W. D. Redfern, *The Private World of Jean Giono*, Durham, N. C., 1967.

II. THE REACTION TO REALISM

LITERATURE OF PSYCHOLOGY AND ANALYSIS

PSYCHOLOGY IN LITERATURE, GENERAL

Joseph Collins, *The Doctor Looks at Literature*, N. Y., 1923; Joseph Wood Krutch, *The Modern Temper*, N. Y., 1929; *Frederick J. Hoffmann, *Freudianism and the Literary Mind*, Louisiana S. U. P., 1945. Also see article, "Psychoanalysis in Modern Literature," *Columbia Dict. of Mod. European Literature*, N. Y., 1947 (pp. 651ff).

ALBERTO MORAVIA

Novels: *The Indifferent Ones* (in English *The Age of Indifference*), 1932; *The Wheel of Fortune*, 1935; *Angostino*, 1944; *Luca*, 1948 (these two publ. together in Engl. as *Two Adolescents*, 1950); *The Woman of Rome*, 1949; *The Conformist*, 1951; *The Fancy Dress Party*, 1952. *A Ghost at Noon*, 1954; *Two Women*, 1957; *The Empty Canvas*, 1960; *The Lie*, 1965; *Una cosa è una cosa*. 1967. About: S. Hughes, "Notes on Moravia," *Commonweal*, January 20, 1950; G. Dego, *Moravia*, London, 1967; D. Heiney, *Three Italian Novelists: Moravia, Pavese, Vittorini*, Ann Arbor, 1968.

JEAN ANOUILH

Drama collections: *Pièces roses*, 1945; *Pièces noires*, 1945; *Nouvelles pièces noires*, 1946; *Pièces brillantes*, 1951. Separate dramas: *Eurydice*, 1942;; Antigone, 1944; *L'Invitation au château* (adopted as *Ring Around the Moon)*, 1947; *The Waltz of the Toreadors*, 1951; *The Lark* (Christopher Fry's translation of *L'Alouttte)*, 1955; *Poor Bitos*, 1956; *Becket, or the Honor of God*, 1960; *The Rehearsal*, 1961; *The Cavern*, 1961; *The Orchestra*, 1962; *Le boulanger, la boulangère et le petit mitron*, 1968; *Le Directeur de l'Opéra*, 1972. About: E. O. Marsh, *Jean Anouilh*, London, 1953; Unsigned, "Anouilh: Dramatist of Wit and Style," *Christian Science Monitor Magazine*, November 25, 1950. L. C. Pronko, *The World of Jean Anouilh*, Berkeley, 1961; John Harvey, *Anouilh: A Study in Theatrics*, New Haven, 1964.

ARTHUR SCHNITZLER

Drama: *Anatol*, 1893; *Light O' Love*, 1895; *The Green Cockatoo*, 1899; *Reigen (Hands Around)*, 1900; *The Lonely Way*, 1903; *Young Medardus*, 1910; *Professor Bernhardi*, 1912. Novelettes: *Sterben (To Die)*, 1895; *Lieutenant Gustl*, 1901; *Fräulein Else*, 1925; *Casanova's Homecoming*, 1918. Novel: *The Way to Freedom*, 1908. About: Sol Liptzin, *Arthur Schnitzler*, N. Y., 1932; Archibald Henderson, *European Dramatists* N. Y., 1926.

HUGO VON HOFMANNSTHAL

Works: *The Death of Titian*, 1892; *Death and the Fool*, 1893; *Alkestis*, 1895; *The Adventurer and the Singer*, 1899; *The Mine of Falun*, 1899; *Elektra*, 1904; *Der Rosenkavalier*, 1911; *Ariadne on Naxos*, 1912. About: See introduction by Herman Broch to *Selected Prose of Hugo von Hofmannsthal*, N. Y., 1952. Also Jethro Bithell, *Modern German Literature, 1880-1938*, London, 1939 (pp. 236ff).

JULIEN GREEN

Novels: *The Pilgrim on the Earth*, 1924; *Avarice House*, 1926; *The Closed Garden (Adrienne Mesurat)*, 1927; *The Dark Journey*, 1929; *The Dreamer*, 1934; *Midnight*, 1936; *Then Shall the Dust Return (Varouna)*, 1940; *Le Malfaiteur*, 1955; *Each in His Darkness*, 1961; *Minuit*, 1967. About: See *Saturday Review of Literature*, February 5, 1949 and November 24, 1951. S. E. Stokes, *Julien Green and the Thorn of Puritanism*, N. Y., 1954; P. Brodin, *Julien Green*, Paris, 1957.

HERMANN HESSE

Novels: *Posthumous Writings and Poetry of Hermann Lauscher* (not translated), 1901; *Peter Camenzind*, 1904; *Rosshalde*, 1914; *Demian*, 1919; *Siddharta*, 1923; *Der Steppenwolf (Wolf of the Steppes)*, 1927;

Unterm Rad, 1906 (translated as *The Prodigy,* 1957); *Gertrud,* 1910; *Die Morgenlandfahrt,* 1932 (translated as *The Journey to tht East,* 1957). *Narcissus and Goldmund,* 1930; *Das Glasperlenspiel* (in translation *Magister Ludi),* 1945. About: *Thomas Mann, "Hermann Hesse: Liberator of a stifling provincialism," *Saturday Review of Literature,* January 3, 1948; *Publisher's Weekly,* November 23, 1946; R. Pick, "Nobel Prize Winner Hesse," *Saturday Review of Literature,* December 7, 1946; Hugo Ball, *Hermann Hesse,* Zurich, 1947 (in German). T. Ziolkowski, *The Novels of Hermann Hesse,* Princeton, 1965; Mark Boulby, *Hermann Hesse: His Mind ad Art,* Ithaca, N.Y., 1967; F. Baumer, *Hermann Hesse,* N.Y., 1969.

THE NEO-ROMANTIC MOVEMENT

EDMOND ROSTAND

Drama: *Les Romanesques* (untranslated), 1894; *La Princesse lointaine* (untranslated), 1895; *The Samaritan,* 1897; *Cyrano de Bergerac,* 1897; *L'Aiglon,* 1900; *Chantecler,* 1910. About: Edward Everett Hale, Jr., *Dramatists of Today,* N. Y., 1911; Barrett H. Clark, *Contemporary French Dramatists,* N. Y., 1915.

STEFAN GEORGE

Poetry: *Hymns,* 1890; *Pilgrimages,* 1891; *Algabal,* 1892; *Pastorals and Eulogies,* 1895; *The Year of the Soul,* 1897; *The Tapestry of Life,* 1899; *The Seventh Ring,* 1907. Prose: *Days and Deeds,* 1903. In English see Stefan George, *Poems,* rendered into English by Carol North Valhope and Ernest Morwitz, N. Y., 1943. About: C. M. Bowra, *The Heritage of Symbolism,* London, 1947; also introductory essay to Valhope-Morwitz translated cited above.

MAURICE MAETERLINCK

Drama: *La Princesse Maleine,* 1889; *The Blind,* 1891; *Pelleas and Melisande,* 1893; *Monna Vanna,* 1902; *Joyzelle,* 1903; *The Blue Bird,* 1908. Prose: *The Treasure of the Humble,* 1896; *The Life of the Bees,* 1901. About: Jethro Bithell, *The Life and Writings of Maurice Maeterlinck,* N. Y., 1913; Montrose J. Moses, *Maurice Maeterlinck: A Study,* N. Y., 1911; C. Burniaux, "The Life and Death of Maurice Maeterlinck," *Books Abroad,* Autumn, 1949.

GABRIELE D'ANNUNZIO

Poetry: *Primo Vere,* 1880; *Canto Novo,* 1882; *Odi Navale,* 1892. Novels:

The Child of Pleasure, 1889; *The Triumph of Death*, 1894; *The Flame (of Life)*, 1900. Drama: *The Dead City*, 1898; *The Daughter of Jorio*, 1904; *Francesca da Rimini*, 1902. About: *F. V. Nardelli, *Gabriel the Archangel*, London, 1931; J. S. Kennard, *A Literary History of the Italian People*, N. Y., 1941; *Saturday Review of Literature*, June 11, 1938.

FERENC MOLNÁR

Works: *The Devil*, 1908; *Liliom*, 1909; *The Swan*, 1920; *The Red Mill*, 1923; *The Guardsman*, 1924: *The Play's the Thing*, 1924. About: *S. N. Behrman, "Playwright," *New Yorker*, May 25, June 1, June 8, 1946; I. Brody, "Molnar," *American Mercury*, April, 1945; J. W. Krutch, "Made in Czecho-Slovakia," *Nation*, November 11, 1925.

LEONID ANDREYEV

Works: "The Little Angel," 1899; "The Wall," 1901; "In the Fog," 1902; "The Abyss," 1902; *The Red Laugh*, 1905; *The Seven Who Were Hanged*, 1908; *Anathema*, 1909; *The Life of Man*, 1914. About: A. Kaun, *Leonid Andreyev: A Critical Study*, N. Y., 1924; Maxim Gorki, *Reminiscences of Leonid Andreyev*, N. Y., 1928; W. L. Phelps, *Essays on Russian Novelists*, N. Y., 1911.

ANTOINE DE SAINT-EXUPÉRY

Novels: *Southern Mail*, 1933; *Night Flight*, 1931. Autobiographical: *Wind, Sand, and Stars*, 1939; *Flight to Arras*, 1942. Juvenile: *The Little Prince*, 1943. About: *New York Times Book Review*, January 19, 1941; "Missing in Action," *Publisher's Weekly*, December 23, 1944; L. Galantière, "Antoine de Saint-Exupéry," *Atlantic*, April, 1947.

PIERRE LOUŸS

Translation: *Poésies de Méléagre de Gadara*, 1893. Poetry: *The Songs of Bilitis*, 1894. Novels: *Aphrodite*, 1896; *The Adventures of King Pausole*, 1901. About: *Wm. A. Drake, *Contemporary European Writers*, N. Y., 1928 (pp. 192ff); *Paul Valéry, "Pierre Louys," *Dial*, January, 1926; J. T. Shipley, Pierre Louys of Hellas," *Poet Lore*, December, 1926.

JEAN COCTEAU

Poetry: *La Lampe d'Aladin*, 1909; *Poésies*, 1920, 1924, 1947. Novels: *Le Potomak*, 1919; *Les Enfants terribles*, 1929. Drama: *Le Boeuf sur le Toit* (with D. Milhaud & R. Dufy), 1920; *Orpheus*, 1927; *Antigone*, 1928; *The Infernal Machine*, 1934; *The Knights of the Round Table*, 1937. Films: *The Blood of a Poet*, 1932; *The Eternal Return*, 1944; *Beauty* and the Beast, 1945; Orpheus, 1951. About: *Roger Lannes, Jean Cocteau, Paris, 1948 (in French); Wallace Fowlie, "Jean Cocteau," in The Age of Surrealism, N. Y., 1950; Francis Fergusson, "On Cocteau's Infernal Machine," in Alan S. Downer, editor, English Institute Essays, Columbia U. P., 1949; K. Campbell, "And Now It's the Cocteau Touch," N. Y. Times Magazine, January 11, 1948. N. Oxenhandler, Scandal and Parade; the Theater of Jean Cocteau, New Brunswick, N. J., 1957; A. Fraigneau, Cocteau, N. Y., 1961; W. Fowlie, Jean Cocteau; the History of a Poet's Age, Bloomington, Ind., 1966; J. M. Magnan, Cocteau, Paris, 1968.

MICHEL DE GHELDERODE

Plays: Ghelderode Seven Plays, vol. 1: The Women at the Tomb, 1928; Barabbas, 1928; Three Actors and their Drama, 1926; Pantagleize, 1929; The Blind Men, 1933; Chronicles of Hell, 1929; Lord Halewyn, 1934. Ghelderode Seven Plays, vol. 2; Red Magic, 1931; Hop, Signor!, 1935; The Death of Doctor Faust, 1925; Christopher Columbus, 1927; A Night of Pity, 1921; Piet Bouteille, 1918; Miss Jairus, 1934. About: Pol Vandromme, Michael de Ghelderode, Paris, 1963; Vernon Mallinson, Modern Belgian Literature (1830-1960), N. Y., 1966.

IMPRESSIONISM AND STREAM-OF-CONSCIOUSNESS

MARCEL PROUST

Collections: Les Plaisirs et les Jours, 1896; Pastiches et mélanges, 1919. Novel: A la Recherche du Temps perdu (Remembrance of Things Past), 1913-27 (sub-novel titles in English: Swann's Way, 1913; Within a Budding Grove, 1918; The Guermantes Way, 1920; Cities of the Plain, 1921-23; The Captive, 1923; The Sweet Cheat Gone, 1925; The Past Recaptured, 1927). About: Edmund Wilson, Axel's Castle, N. Y., 1932; Georges Lemaitre, Four French Novelists, Oxford U. P., 1938; Harold March, The Two Worlds of Marcel Proust, U. of Penn. Press, 1948; *André Maurois, Proust, a Portrait of a Genius, N. Y., 1950. J. W. Krutch, Five Masters, Bloomington, Ind., 1959 (paperback); G. D. Painter, Proust The Early Years: Proust The Later Years, Boston, 1965.

EXPRESSIONISTS AND EXPERIMENTERS

GENERAL

*Richard Samuel and R. Hinton Thomas, Expressionism in German Life, Literature, and the Theatre, Cambridge U. P., 1939; K. F. Reinhardt, "The Expressionistic Movement in Recent German Literature," Germanic Review. VI (1931).

AUGUST STRINDBERG: A PREDECESSOR

Drama: *In Rome*, 1871; *Master Olaf*, 1872; *The Father*, 1887; *Comrades*, 1888; *Miss Julia*, 1888; *The Inferno*, 1897; *To Damascus*, 1898-1904; *The Dance of Death*, 1901; *The Dream Play*, 1902; *The Ghost Sonata*, 1907. Fiction: *The Red Room*, 1879; *Married* (two series). 1884-85. About: Johan Mortensen, "Strindberg's Personality," *American-Scandinavian Review*, X, 289-95 (1922); C. E. W. L. Dahlström, *Strindberg's Dramatic Expressionism*, N. Y., 1930; V. J. McGill, *August Strindberg the Bedevilled Viking*, N. Y., 1930.

FRANK WEDEKIND

Drama: *The Awakening of Spring*, 1891; *The Earth-Spirit*, 1895; *The Marquis of Keith*, 1901; *Pandora's Box*, 1903; *Hidalla*, 1904; *Schloss Wetterstein*, 1910; *Der Kammersänger (Heart of a Tenor)*, 1899. About: F. W. J. Heuser, "Gerhart Hauptmann and Frank Wedekind," *Germanic Review*, XX (1945); J. Altmann, "Mephisto's Emissary," *Theatre Arts*, March, 1951; E. Muir, "Frank Wedekind," *Freeman*, October 10, 1923.

GEORG KAISER

Drama: *The Jewish Widow*, 1911; *Koenig Hahnrei*, 1913; *The Burghers of Calais*, 1914; *Europa*, 1915; *The Centaur*, 1916; *From Morn Till Midnight*, 1916; *Rector Kleist*, 1918; *Gas* trilogy *(Coral*, 1917; *Gas I*, 1918; *Gas II*, 1920). Novel: *A Villa in Sicily*, 1940. About: M. J. Fruchter, *The Social Dialectic in Georg Kaiser's Dramatic Works*, Phila., 1933; H. F. Königsgarten, *Georg Kaiser*, Potsdam, 1928 (in German); Ludwig Lewisohn, "From Morn to Midnight," *Nation*, June 14, 1922.

ERNST TOLLER

Drama: *Transfiguration*, 1919; *Man and Masses (Man and the Masses)*, 1920; *The Machine-Wreckers*, 1922. Poetry: *Gedichte der Gefangenen*, 1921. Autobiography: *I Was a German*, 1933. About: *W. A. Willibrand, *Ernst Toller, Product of Two Revolutions*, Univ. Okla. Press, 1941; A. Dukes, "Ernst Toller," *Theatre Arts*, May, 1924; Ludwig Lewisohn, "Masse Mensch," *Nation*, April 30, 1924.

KAREL CAPEK

Drama: *R.U.R.*, 1921; *The Insect Play (The World We Live In)*, 1921; *The Makropoulos Secret*, 1925; *Power and Glory*, 1938. Stories: *Money and Other Stories*, 1921. About: René Wellek, "Karel Capek," *Slavonic Review*, XV (1936-37), pp. 191ff; obit. by W. Schlamm in *Saturday Review of Literature*, January 7, 1939; Erika Mann, "Last Conversation with Karel Capek," *Nation*, January 14, 1939.

Franz Werfel

Poetry: *Der Weltfreund*, 1911; *Einander*, 1915. Drama: *The Trojan Women* (adaptation), 1914; *The Mirror-Man*, 1920; *Not the Murderer, the Murdered Is Guilty*, 1920; *Jacobowsky and the Colonel*, 1944. Novels: *The Forty Days of Musa Dagh*, 1933; *The Song of Bernadette*, 1941-42. About: Wm. A. Drake, *Contemporary European Writers*, N. Y., 1928; G. O. Arlt, "Werfel As His Translator Saw Him," *Saturday Review of Literature*, March 2, 1946; H. Smith, "Franz Werfel," *Saturday Review of Literature*, September 8, 1945.

Franz Kafka

Tales: *The Judgment*, 1913; *Metamorphosis*, 1916. Novels: *The Trial*, 1925; *The Castle*, 1926; *Amerika*, 1927. In English also see: "In the Penal Colony," *Partisan Review*, VIII, pp. 98ff; *A Franz Kafka Miscellany*, N. Y., 1940; *Selected Short Stories*, N. Y., 1952. About: *Max Brod, *Franz Kafka, A Biography*, N. Y., 1947; Angel Flores, editor, *The Kafka Problem*, N. Y., 1946 (anth. of criticism); Paul Goodman, *Kafka's Prayer*, N. Y., 1947; *Charles Neider, *The Frozen Sea: A Study of Franz Kafka*, Oxford, U. P., 1948; Herbert Tauber, *Franz Kafka: An Interpretation of His Works*, Yale, U. P., 1948; Flores and Swander, *Franz Kafka Today*, Madison, Wisc., 1962, including an extensive bibliography.

F. García Lorca

Poetry: *Libro de poemas*, 1921; *Romancero Gitano*, 1928; *The Poet in New York*, 1940. Drama: *The Love of Don Perlimplin*, 1933; *The Prodigious Shoemaker's Wife*, 1930; *Blood Wedding*, 1933; *Yerma*, 1934; *The House of Bernarda Alba*, 1936. In Engl. see *From Lorca's Theatre; Five Plays*, N. Y., 1941. About: Arturo Barea, *Lorca, the Poet and His People*, N. Y., 1949; Edwin Honig, *García Lorca*, Norfolk, Conn., 1944; F. de Onís y Sanchez, *Federico García Lorca* (in A. M. Fiskin, editor, *Writers of Our Years*, N. Y., 1950).

Par Lagerkvist

Poetry: *Angest (Anguish)*, 1913. Drama: *Sista mänskan (The Last Man)*, 1917; *The Difficult Hour*, 1918; *The Hangman*, 1933. Fiction: *The Eternal Smile*, 1926; *Onde Sagor (Evil Tales)*, 1924; *The Dwarf*, 1945; *Barabbas*, 1950; *Pilgrim at Sea*, 1962-64; *The Holy Land*, 1964-66. Nonfiction: *Modern Theatre: Points of View and Attack*, 1918. About: T. R. Buckman, Introduction to *Modern Theatre Seven Plays and an Essay*, Lincoln, Nebraska, 1966; R. B. Vowles, Introduction to *The

Eternal Smile, N. Y., 1954; A. Gustafson, *A History of Swedish Literature,* Minneapolis, 1961.

FRIEDRICH DURRENMATT

Fiction: *Die Stadt,* 1952; *The Judge and his Executioner,* 1950; *Der Verdacht,* 1951; *The Trap,* 1956; *The Pledge,* 1957. Plays: *Es steht geschrieben (Thus Is It Written),* 1947; *The Blind Man,* 1948; *Romulus the Great,* 1949; *The Marriage of Mr. Mississippi,* 1952; *An Angel Comes to Babylon,* 1594; *The Visit (Der Besuch der alten Dame),* 1955; *The Physicists,* 1961. About: G. Rogoff, "Mr. Dürrenmatt Buys New Shoes," *Tulane Drama Review,* Oct. 1958; A. Klarmann, "Friedrich Dürrenmatt and the Tragic Sense of Comedy," *Tulane Drama Review,* May, 1960; M. W. Askew, "Dürrenmatt's *The Visit of the Old Lady,*" *Tulane Drama Review,* June 1961; E. A. Wright and L. H. Downs, *A Primer for Playgoers,* Englewood Cliffs, N. J., 1969.

III. THE REALM OF IDEAS: INTELLECTUAL AND IDEOLOGICAL LITERATURE

THE RETURN TO TRADITION AND FAITH

FRANÇOIS MAURIAC

Novels: *The Child in Chains,* 1913; *Flesh and Blood,* 1920; *Préséances (Ranks of Society),* 1921; *The Kiss to the Leper,* 1922; *The River of Fire,* 1923; *Genitrix,* 1923; *The Desert of Love,* 1925; *Thérèse Desqueyroux,* 1927; *The Viper's Knot,* 1932; *L'Agneau,* 1954. Poetry: *Joined Hands,* 1927. Essay: *The Suffering and Joy of the Christian,* 1929-31. Drama: *Asmodée,* 1938. Other Prose: *Bloc-notes, 1952-1957,* 1958; *Second Thoughts: Reflections on Literature and on Life,* 1961; *Cain, Where Is Your Brother,* 1962; *De Gaulle,* 1964. About: *Elsie Pell, Francois Mauriac in Search of the Infinite,* N. Y., 1947; Milton H. Stansbury, *French Novelists of Today,* Philadelphia, 1935; Nelly Cormeau, *l'Art de Francois Mauriac,* Paris, 1951 (in French); M F. Moloney, *Francois Mauriac, a Critical Study,* Denver, 1958; P. Statford, *Faith and Fiction, Creative Process in Greene and Mauriac,* Notre Dame, Ind., 1964; C. Jenkins, *Mauriac, N. Y.,* 1965.

PAUL CLAUDEL

Poetry: *Five Great Odes,* 1910; *This Hour Between the Spring and the Summer,* 1913. Drama: *The Golden Head,* 1889; *The City,* 1890; *The*

Exchange, 1893; *The Hostage*, 1910; *The Tidings Brought to Mary*, 1910; *The Satin Slipper*, 1929; *Partage du Midi* (translated as *Break of Noon*, 1906); *Christopher Columbus*, 1930; *Jeanne d'Arc au Bûcher*, 1939. About: Henri Peyre, "The Work of Paul Claudel," *Living Age*, November, 1932; "Sequences of Claudel," *Saturday Review of Literature*, November 27, 1943; P. d'Estournelles, "The Poet as Playwright," *Theatre Arts*, May, 1946, Louis Perche, *Paul Claudel, Paris*, 1952 (in French). J. Chiari, *The Poetic Dramas of Paul Claudel*, N. Y., 1954; L. Chaigne, *Vie de Paul Claudel et genèse de son oeuvre*, Tours, 1961; L. Chaigne, *Paul Claudel: the Man and the Mystic*, N. Y., 1961; R. Berchan, *The Inner Stage*, East Lansing, Mich., 1966.

LIBERALS AND HUMANITARIANS

GENERAL

Max Eastman, *Artists in Uniform*, London, 1934; C. Y. Harrison, "Proletarian Literature Sans-Culottes," *Nation*, March 22, 1933; Edmund Wilson, "Marxism and the Historical Interpretation of Literature," in *The Triple Thinkers*, N. Y., 1948.

ANATOLE FRANCE

Works: *The Crime of Sylvestre Bonnard*, 1881; *Thaïs*, 1890; *l'Histoire contemporaine* (novel tetralogy incl. *The Elm on the Mall*, 1896; *The Wickerwork Mannequin*, 1897; *The Amethyst Ring*, 1899; *M. Bergeret in Paris*, 1901); *Crainquebille*, 1901; *The Gods Are Athirst*, 1912. About: E. Preston Dargan, *Anatole France*, N. Y., 1937; Haakon M. Chevalier, *The Ironic Temper: Anatole France and His Time*, Oxford U. P., 1932; Jacob Axelrad, *Anatole France: A Life Without Illusions*, N. Y., 1944.

ROMAIN ROLLAND

Novels: *Jean-Christophe*, 1905-13; *Colas Breugnon*, 1919. Drama: *Le Jeu de l'Amour et de la Mort*, 1925. Essays: *The Triumph of Reason*, 1899; *Above the Battle*, 1915. About: Albert L. Guérard, *Five Masters of French Romance*, N. Y., 1916; *Stefan Zweig, *Romain Rolland: The Man and His Work*, N. Y., 1921; C. Sénéchal, *Romain Rolland*, Paris. 1933 (in French); A. R. Levy, *L'Idealisme de Romain Rolland*, Paris, 1946; W. T. Starr, *Romain Rolland and a World at War*, Evanston, Ill., 1956.

EUGÈNE BRIEUX

Drama: *Ménages d'Artistes*, 1890; *Blanchette*, 1892; *The Three Daughters of M. Dupont*, 1897; *The Cradle*, 1898; *The Red Robe*, 1900; *Les Avariés (Damaged Goods)*, 1902; *La Femme seule (Woman on Her Own)*, 1913; *Maternity*, 1913. About: P. V. Thomas, *The Plays of Eugene Brieux*, London, 1913 (also Boston, 1915). Also see preface by G. B. Shaw to *Three Plays by Brieux*, N. Y., 1911.

JEAN GIRAUDOUX

Drama: *Siegfried*, 1928; *Amphitryon 38*, 1929; *The Trojan War Will Not Take Place*, 1935; *Electra*, 1937; *Undine*, 1939; *The Madwoman of Chaillot*, 1945. Novels: *Simon the Pathetic*, 1918; *Suzanne and the Pacific*, 1921; *Siegfried and the Limousin (My Friend from Limousin)*, 1922. About: Georges Lemaitre, *Four French Novelist*, N. Y., 1938; Milton H. Stansbury, *French Novelists of Today*, Phila., 1935; Laurence Le Sage, *Jean Giraudoux, Surrealism, and the German Romantic Ideal*, Univ. Illinois Press, 1952.

ANDRÉ MALRAUX

Novels: *The Conquerors*, 1928; *The Royal Way*, 1930; *Man's Fate*, 1933; *Days of Wrath*, 1935; *Man's Hope*, 1937. About: Milton H. Stansbury, *French Novelists of Today*, Phila., 1935; *Haakon M. Chevalier, "André Malraux: The Return of the Hero," *Kenyon Review*, II (1940), pp. 35ff; *W. M. Frohock, *André Malraux and the Tragic Imagination*, Stanford U. P., 1952. Other Prose: *The Voices of Art*, 1953; *The Metamorphosis of the Gods*, 1960; *Malraux par lui-même*, 1961; *Antimémoires*, 1967. About: W. M. Frohock, *André Malraux and the Tragic Imagination*, Stanford, 1952; Janet Flanner, *Men and Monuments*, N. Y., 1957; W. Righter, *The Rhetorical Hero*, N.Y., 1964; D. Boak, *André Malraux*, Oxford, 1968.

E. M. REMARQUE

Novels: *All Quiet on the Western Front*, 1929; *The Road Back*, 1931; *Three Comrades*, 1937; *The Arch of Triumph*, 1946. *Spark of life*, 1951; *A Time to Live and a Time to Die*, 1954; *The Black Obelisk*, 1957; *Heaven Has No Favourites*, 1961; *The Night in Lisbon*, 1964. About: Wilhelm K. Pfeiler, *War and the German Mind*, Columbia U. P., 1941; *Literary Digest*, July 15, 1933; *Saturday Review of Literature*, March 27, 1937 (biog. sketch); *Publisher's Weekly*, January 3, 1953.

IGNAZIO SILONE

Novels: *Fontamara*, 1933; *Bread and Wine*, 1936; *The Seed Beneath the Snow*, 1942; *A Handful of Blackberries*, 1953; *The Fox and the Camelias*,

1961. Dialogue: *The School for Dictators*, 1938. Drama: *And He Hid Himself*, 1946. About: Malcolm Cowley, "The Man Who Lived Twice," *New Republic*, August 24, 1942; Edmund Wilson, "Two Survivors: Malraux and Silone," *New Yorker*, September 8, 1945; Nathan A. Scott, "Ignazio Silone, Novelist of the Revolutionary Sensibility," in *Rehearsals of Discomposure*, N. Y., 1952.

ARTHUR KOESTLER

Longing, 1951; Arrow in the Blue (autobiographical), 1952; *The Trail of the Dinosaur*, 1955; *The Sleepwalkers*, 1959; *The Lotus and the Robot*, 1960; *The Act of Creation*, 1964; *The Ghost in the Machine*, 1967; *Drinkers of Infinity*, 1968. About: W. Phillips, "Koestler and the Political Novel," *Nation*, August 26, 1944; M. Fischer, "Koestler's Longing and Despair," *Commonweal*, June 1, 1951; Maxwell Geismar, "From a Westward Europe," *Saturday Review*, September 27, 1952; S. Brown, "Arthur Koestler," *American Mercury*, October, 1952; J. Calder, *Chronicles of Conscience* (about Orwell and Koestler), Pittsburgh, 1968.

BERTOLT BRECHT

Poetry: *Bertolt Brechts Hauspostille (Domestic Breviary*, 1927); *Bertolt Brechts Gedichte und Lieder*, 1956; in English, *Bertolt Brecht, Selected Poems*, 1947; Plays: *Baal*, 1918; *Trommeln in der Nacht (Drums in the Night*, 1918); *Im Dickicht der Städte (In the Jungle of Cities*, 1923); *Die Dreigroschenoper (The Threepenny Opera*, 1928); *Aufstieg und Fall der Stadt Mahogonny (Rise and Fall of the City of Mahagonny*, 1929); *Die Heilige Johanna der Schlachthöfe (St. Joan of the Stockyards*, 1930); *Furcht und Elend des Dritten Reiches* (An English version, *The Private Life of the Master Race*, 1938, 1945); *Mutter Courage und Ihre Kinder (Mother Courage and Her Children*, 1939); *Leben des Galilei (Galileo*, 1939); *Der Gute Mensch von Sezuan (The Good Woman of Setzuan*, 1940); *Die Gesichte der Simone Machard (The Visions of Simone Machard*, with Lion Feuchtwanger, 1943); *Der Kaukasische Kreidekreis (The Caucasian Chalk Circle*, 1945). Essays: *Kleines Organon für das Theater (Little Organon for the Theatre*, 1948, 1951, 1953). About: J. Willett, *The Theatre of Bertolt Brecht*, N. Y., 1959; M. Esslin, *Brecht, the Man and his Work*, N. Y., 1960; R. Brustein, *The Theatre of Revolt*, Boston, 1962; D. I. Grossvogel, *The Blasphemers: the Theatre of Brecht, Ionesco, Beckett, Genet*, Ithaca, 1962; F. Ewen, *Bertolt Brecht; his Life, his Art, and his Times*, N. Y., 1967; M. R. Turner, *Bluff Your Way in the Theatre*, London, 1967; C. R. Lyons, *Bertolt Brecht; the Despair and the Polemic*, Carbondale, Ill., 1968.

RELATIVISM AND EXISTENTIALISM

ANDRÉ GIDE

Works: *The Notebooks of André Walter*, 1891; *The Voyage of Urien*, 1893; *Marshlands*, 1895; *Fruits of the Earth*, 1897; *Philoctetus*, 1899; *Prometheus Ill-Bound*, 1899; *The Immoralist*, 1902; *The Return of the Prodigal Son*, 1907; *Strait Is the Gate*, 1909; *Lafcadio's Adventures (The Vatican Swindle)*, 1914; *The Pastoral Symphony*, 1919; *Corydon*, 1924; *The Counterfeiters*, 1926; *If It Die* (autobiog.), 1926; *Return From the U.S.S.R.*, 1936; *Theseus*, 1946; *Imaginary Interviews*, 1946. About: Leon Pierre-Quint, *André Gide, His Life and Work*, N. Y., 1934; *Klaus Mann, André Gide and the Crisis of Modern Thought*, N. Y., 1943; Mischa Harry Fayer, *Gide, Freedom, and Dostoevsky*, Burlington, Vt., 1946; Van Meter Ames, *André Gide*, Norfolk, Conn., 1947.

JEAN-PAUL SARTRE

Novels: *Nausea*, 1938; *The Roads to Freedom (The Age of Reason*, 1945; *The Reprieve*, 1945; *Troubled Sleep (La Mort dans l'Âme)*, 1949; *The Last Chance*, unpubl.). Stories: *Le Mur (The Wall)*, 1939. Drama: *The Flies*, 1943; *No Exit*, 1944; *The Respectable (Respectful) Prostitute*, 1947. *Le Diable et le Bon Dieu (Lucifer and the Lord)*; 1951; *Kean*, 1954; *Nekrassov*, 1955; *Les Sequestres d'Altona (The Condemned of Altona)*, 1959. Philosophy: *Being and Not-Being*, 1943. About: A. J. Ayer, "Novelists-Philosophers: Jean-Paul Sartre," *Horizon*, XIII (1945); R. McLaughlin, "Private Dramas," *Saturday Review of Literature*, December 6, 1947; Marjorie Grene, *Dreadful Freedom, a Critique of Existentialism*, Univ. Chicago Press, 1948; I. Rosenfeld, "Sartre's Underground," *New Republic*, May 19, 1952; H. E. Barnes, *An Existentialist Ethics*, N. Y., 1967; D. McCall, *The Theatre of Jean-Paul Sartre*, N. Y., 1969.

ALBERT CAMUS

Fiction: *The Stranger*, 1942; *The Plague*, 1947; *The Fall*, 1956; *Exile and the Kingdom*, 1957. Drama: *Caligula*, 1944; *The Misunderstanding*, sometimes called *Cross Purposes*, 1944; *State of Siege*, 1948; *The Just Assassins*, 1950. Essays: *Noces (Wedding Feasts)*, 1938; *The Myth of Sisyphus*, 1942; *Man in Revolt*, 1951. About: P. Thody, *Albert Camus*, N. Y., 1957; A. Maguet, *Albert Camus, the Invincible Summer*, N. Y., 1958; J. Cruickshank, *Albert Camus and the Literature of Revolt*, London, 1959; R. de Luppe, *Albert Camus*, Paris, 1960; Germaine Bree, *Albert Camus, N. Y.*, 1964; E. Parker, *Albert Camus, the Artist in the Arena*, Madison, Wisc., 1965; E. H. Falk, *Types of Thematic Structure*, Chicago, 1967.

LUIGI PIRANDELLO

Novels: *The Late Mattia Pascal*, 1904; *The Old and the Young*, 1913. Story collections: *Passion Without Love*, 1894; *Tricks of Life and Death*, 1902; *Black and White*, 1904. Drama: *If Not Thus*, 1915; *Think, Giacomino!*, 1916; *Right You Are If You Think You Are*, 1916; *The Pleasure of Honesty*, 1917; *It's Not a Serious Matter*, 1919; *Six Characters in Search of an Author*, 1921; *Henry IV*, 1922; *Clothe the Naked*, 1922; *As You Desire Me*, 1930. About: *Walter Starkie, *Luigi Pirandello*, N. Y., 1926-37; Philo M. Buck, *Directions in Contemporary Literature*, Oxford U. P., 1942; Domenico Vittorini, *The Drama of Luigi Pirandello*, N. Y., 1935; Lander MacClintock, *The Age of Pirandello*, Bloomington, Ind., 1951.

MIGUEL DE UNAMUNO

Works: *The Life of Don Quixote and Sancho*, 1927; *Mist*, 1928; *The Tragic Sense of Life*, 1921; *Three Exemplary Novels and a Prologue*, 1930; *The Agony of Christianity*, 1928; *The Christ of Velasquez*, 1951; *Poems*, 1952; *Abel Sanchez*, 1956; *Saint Emmanuel the Good, Martyr*, 1956. About: Arturo Barea, *Unamuno*, New Haven, 1952; Julian Marias, *Miguel de Unamuno*, Cambridge, Mass., 1966.

NIKOS KAZANTZAKIS

Novels: (Note: All dates are of publication in English) *Zorba the Greek*, 1953; *The Greek Passion*, 1954; *Freedom or Death*, 1956; *The Last Temptation of Christ*, 1960; *The Rock Garden* (translated from the French), 1963; *Toda Raba*, 1964; *The Fratricides*, 1964; *Saint Francis*, 1965. Epic poem: *The Odyssey: A Modern Sequel*, 1958. Meditations and Memoires: *The Saviors of God: Spiritual Exercises*, 1960. *Report to Greco*, 1965. Plays: *Christopher Columbus, Melissa, Kouros*, 1969. About: P. Prevelakis, *Nikos Kazantzakis and His Odyssey*, N. Y., 1961; Helen Kazantzakis, *Nikos Kazantzakis: A Biography Based on His Letters*, N. Y., 1968.

JORGE LUIS BORGES

Poetry: *Fervor de Buenos Aires*, 1923; *Poemas* (1923-1958), 1958, Fiction: *Historia universal de la infamia*, 1935; *El Jardin de senderos que se bifurcan (The Garden of Forking Paths*, 1942); *Ficciones*, 1944; *El Aleph*, 1949, In English the best basic collection of prose is *Labyrinths*, 1962; and a selection of prose and poetry, *A Personal Anthology*, 1961-1967. About: A. M. Barrenechea, *Borges the Labyrinth Maker*,

N. Y., 1965. R. Burgin, *Conversations with Jorge Luis Borges*, N. Y., 1968; L. A. Murillo, *The Cyclical Night: Irony in James Joyce and Jorge Luis Borges*, Cambridge, Mass., 1968; C. Wheelock, *The Myth-maker*, Austin, Tex., 1969.

HEINROCH BOLL

Fiction: *Der Zug war pünktlich (The Train was on Time*, 1949); *Wo warst du, Adam? (Adam, Where art Thou?*, 1951); *Und sagte kein einziges Wort (Acquainted with the Night*, 1953); *Haus ohne Hüter (Tomorrow and Yesterday*, 1954); *Billiard um halb zehn (Billiards at half-past Nine*, 1959); *Ansichten eines Clowns (The Clown*, 1963); *Ende einer Dienstfahrt*, 1966. About: Siegfried Mandel, *Contemporary European Novelists*, Carbondale, Ill., 1968.

NOUVEAU ROMAN OR ANTI-NOVEL

General: J. Bloch-Michel, *Le Present de l'indicatif*, Paris, 1963; M. Nadeau, *Le Roman Francais depuis la Guerre*, Paris, 1963; J. Ricardou, *Problems du Nouveau Roman*, Paris, 1967; J. Sturrock, *The French New Novel*, N. Y., 1969.

NATHALIE SARRAUTE

Fiction: *Tropismes*, 1939; *Portrait d'un Inconnu (Portrait of a Man Unknown)*, 1948; *Martereau*, 1953; *Le Planétarium*, 1959; *Les Fruits d'Or*, 1963. Other Prose: *L'Ere du Soupcon*, 1956; *Le Silence suivi de Le Mensonge*, 1967. About: R. Z. Temple, *Nathalie Sarraute*, N. Y., 1968.

ALAIN ROBBE-GRILLET

Fiction: *Les Gommes (The Erasers)*, 1953; *Le Voyeur*, 1955; *La Jalousie (Jealousy)*, 1957; *Dans le Labyrinthe (In the Labyrinth)*, 1959; *Instant-anés*, 1962; *La Maison de Rendez-vous*, 1965. Cine-romans: *L'Année Dernière à Marienbad*, 1961; *L'Immortelle*, 1963. Other Prose: *Pour un Nouveau Roman (For a New Novel)*, 1963. About: B. Morrissette, *Les Romans de Robbe-Grillet*, Paris, 1963; O. Bernal, *Alain Robbe-Grillet: le Roman de l'Absence*, Paris, 1964; B. Morrissette, *Alain Robbe-Grillet*, N. Y., 1965; B. Stoltzfus, *Alain Robbe-Grillet and the New French Novel*, Carbondale, Ill., 1964.

MICHEL BUTOR

Fiction: *Passage de Milan*, 1954; *L'Emploi du Temps (Passing Time)*, 1956; *La Modification (A Change of Heart)*, 1957; *Degrés*, 1960. Other

Prose: *Le Genie du Lieu*, 1958; *Mobile*, 1962; *Réseau aérien*, 1962; *Essais sur les Modernes*, 1964; *Portrait de l'artiste en jeune singe*, 1967. About: R-M. Alberes, *Michel Butor*, Paris, 1964; L. Roudiez, *Michel Butor*, N. Y., 1965.

VLADIMIR NABOKOV

Fiction: *Despair*, 1937; *Laughter in the Dark*, 1938; *The Real Life of Sebastian Knight*, 1941; *Bend Sinister*, 1947; *Speak Memory: A Memoir*, 1951; *Lolita*, 1955; *Pnin*, 1957; *Invitation to a Beheading*, 1959; *Pale Fire*, 1962; *Ada or Ardor: A Family Chronicle*, 1969; *Transparent Things*, 1972. About: F. Kermode, *Puzzles and Epiphanies: Essays and Reviews*, N. Y., 1962; P. Stegner, *Escape into Aesthetics: The Art of Vladimir Nabokov*, N. Y., 1966.

GUNTER GRASS

Fiction: *Die Blechtrommel (The Tin Drum*, 1959); *Katz und Maus (Cat and Mouse*, 1961); *Hundejahre (Dog Years*, 1963); *Ortlich Betäubt (Local Anaesthetic*, 1969). Drama: *Die Bösen Köche (The Wicked Cooks*, 1964); *Four Plays*, 1968. About: S. Mandel, ed., *Contemporary European Novelists*, Carbondale, Ill., 1968; M. Esslin, *The Theatre of the Absurd*, N. Y., 1961.

THEATRE OF THE ABSURD

General: M. Esslin, *The Theatre of the Absurd*, N. Y., 1961; W. Fowlie, *Dionysus in Paris*, N. Y., 1960; M. Beigbeder, *Le Théâtre en France depuis la Libération*, Paris, 1959; R. Brustein, *The Theatre of Revolt*, Boston, 1964.

SAMUEL BECKETT

Fiction: *Murphy*, 1938; *Molloy*, 1951; *Malone Dies*, 1951; *The Unnamable*, 1953. Drama: *Waiting for Godot*, 1952; *Endgame*, 1957; *All That Fall*, 1957; *Krapp's Last Tape*, 1959; *Happy Days*, 1961; *Play*, 1963. About: R. Cohn, *Samuel Beckett: the Comic Gamut*, New Brunswick, 1962; H. Kenner, *Samuel Beckett, a Critical Study*, N. Y., 1961; F. J. Hoffman, *Samuel Beckett, the Language of Self*, Carbondale, Ill., 1962; W. Y. Tindall, *Samuel Beckett*, N. Y., 1964.

EUGENE IONESCO

Plays: *La Cantatrice Chauve (The Bald Soprano*, 1949); *Les Chaises (The Chairs*, 1951); *Tueur Sans Gages (The Killer*, 1957-59); *Rhinoceros*, 1959; *Le Piéton de l'Air (The Pedestrian of the Air*, 1962); *Le*

Roi se meurt (Exit the King, also *The King Dies,* 1963); *La Soif et la Faim,* 1966 *(Hunger and Thirst,* 1968). Prose: *Fragments of a Journal,* 1968. About: G. E. Wellwarth, *The Theatre of Protest and Paradox,* N. Y., 1964; L. G. Pronko, *Eugene Ionesco,* N. Y., 1965.

JEAN GENET

Fiction: *Notre-Dame-des-Fleurs* (Our Lady of the Flowers, 1942); *Miracle de la Rose,* 1943; *Pompes Funèbres (Funeral Pomp,* 1947); *Querelle de Brest,* 1947; *Journal du Voleur (The Thief's Journal,* 1949). Drama: *Haute Surveillance (Deathwatch,* 1949); *Les Bonnes (The Maids,* 1948); *Le Balcon (The Balcony,* 1956); *Les Nègres (The Blacks,* 1958); *Les Paravents (The Screens,* 1961). About: J.-P. Sartre, *Saint Genet, Actor and Martyr,* N. Y., 1963; J. H. McMahon, *The Imagination of Jean Genet,* New Haven, 1963; T. Driver, *Jean Genet,* N. Y., 1966.

IV. TRADITION AND REVOLT IN POETRY

THE VERSE NATURALISTS

RICHARD DEHMEL

Poetry collections: *Redemptions,* 1891; *But Love,* 1893; *Woman and World,* 1896; *Fair and Savage World,* 1913. Verse Novel: *Two Humans,* 1903. About: R. T. House, "The Life and Poetry of Richard Dehmel," *Poet Lore,* XXXVIII (1927); Harry Slochower, *Richard Dehmel, der Mensch und der Denker,* Dresden, 1928 (in German).

JUAN RAMÓN JIMÉNEZ

Poetry: *Rimas,* 1902; *Diario de un poeta recién casado,* 1916; *Animal de fondo,* 1949. Prose: *Platero y yo, elegia andaluza,* 1914; *Espanoles de tres mundos,* 1914-40. In English: *Fifty Spanish Poems,* 1950; *Platero and I,* 1957; *Selected Writings,* 1957; *Three Hundred Poems,* 1962. About: H. T. Young, *Juan Ramón Jiménez,* N.Y., 1967.

VARIETIES OF EXPERIMENTAL VERSE

R. M. RILKE

Poetry: *Life and Songs,* 1894; *The Book of Pictures,* 1902; *The Book of Hours,* 1899-05; *New Poems,* 1907; *The Duinese Elegies (The Duino Elegies),* 1923; *Sonnets to Orpheus,* 1923. Novel: *The Notebook of Malte Laurids Brigge,* 1909. Prose-poetry: *Stories of God,* 1900-04; *The Lay of the Love and Death of Cornet Christopher Rilke,* 1906. Biography:

Rodin, 1903. About: W. Rose and G. C. Houston, *R. M. Rilke*, London, 1938; E. C. Mason, editor, *Rilke's Apotheosis*, Oxford, 1938 (anthol. of criticism); *E. M. Butler, *Rainer Maria Rilke*, N. Y., 1941; C. M. Bowra, *The Heritage of Symbolism*, London, 1947. W. L. Graff, *Rainer Maria Rilke - Creative Anguish of a Modern Poet*, Princeton, N. J., 1956.

PAUL VALÉRY

Poems: *La jeune Parque (The Young Fate)*, 1917; *The Graveyard by the Sea* (title poem of volume), 1920. Poetry collections: *Odes*, 1920; *Album of Ancient Verses*, 1920; *Charmes*, 1922. Novel: *An Evening with M. Teste*, 1925. About: William A. Drake, *Contemporary European Writers*, N. Y., 1928; *Edmund Wilson, *Axel's Castle*, N. Y., 1931; Theodora Bosanquet, *Paul Valéry*, London, 1933; C. M. Bowra, *The Heritage of Symbolism*, London, 1947.

GUILLAUME APOLLINAIRE

Poetry: *Liqueurs*, 1913; *Calligrammes (Handwriting Exercises)*, 1914. Novels: *The Poet Assassinated*, 1916; *The Seated Woman*, 1920. Drama: *The Mammaries of Tiresias*, 1917. About: William A. Drake, *Contemporary European Writers*, N. Y., 1928; André Billy, *Apollinaire*, Paris, 1947 (in French); C. M. Bowra, "Order and Adventure in Guillaume Apollinaire," in *The Creative Experiment*, London, 1949; Leroy C. Breunig, "The Chronology of Apollinaire's 'Alcools,' " *PMLA*, December, 1952.

SURREALISM, GENERAL

Milton H. Stansbury, "The Surrealists," in *French Novelists of Today*, Phila., 1935 (pp. 121ff); *Wallace Fowlie, *The Age of Surrealism*, N. Y., 1950; Georges Lemaitre, *From Cubism to Surrealism in French Literature*, Harvard U. P., 1941; Herbert Read, *Surrealism*, London, 1936; André Breton, *The Situation of Surrealism Between the Two Wars*, Yale U. P., 1948.

RUBÉN DARÍO

Poetry collections: *Blue*, 1888; *Prosas Profanas*, 1896; *Poems of Life and Hope*, 1905. About: Isaac Goldberg, *Studies in Spanish-American Literature*, N. Y., 1920; Pedro Salinas, *La Poésia de Rubén Darío*, Buenos Aires, 1948 (in Spanish); Gerald Brenan, *The Literature of the Spanish People*, Cambridge, U. P., 1951.

V. LITERATURE IN THE SOVIET UNION

ALEXANDER BLOK

Poetry: *Verses About the Lady Beautiful*, 1904; *Earth's Bubbles*, 1905; *The City*, 1906; *"On Kulikova Battlefield,"* 1908; *The Mask of Snow*, 1908; *Faina*, 1909; "The Twelve," 1918; "The Scythians," 1918. About: *C. M. Bowra, *The Heritage of Symbolism*, London, 1947; Maxim Gorky, *Reminiscences*, N. Y., 1946; Marc Slonim, *Modern Russian Literature: From Chekhov to the Present*, Oxford U. P., 1953.

VLADIMIR MAYAKOVSKY

Poetry: "A Cloud in Trousers," 1915; "The Spine-Flute," 1915; "Chelovek" ("Man"), 1917; *American Verses*, 1926. Drama: *Mystery Bouffe*, 1918; *The Bedbug*, 1928; *The Bathhouse*, 1930. About: Max Eastman, *Artists in Uniform*, London, 1934; *C. M. Bowra, "The Futurism of Vladimir Mayakovsky," in *The Creative Experiment*, London, 1949; D. S. Mirsky, *A History of Russian Literature* (rev. ed.), N. Y., 1949; Marc Slonim, *Modern Russian Literature: From Chekhov to the Present*, Oxford U. P., 1953.

BORIS PILNYAK

Novels: *The Naked Year*, 1922; *Machines and Wolves*, 1925; *The Tale of the Unextinguished Moon*, 1926; *The Volga Falls to the Caspian Sea*, 1930; *The Ripening of the Fruit*, 1935; *Birth of a Man* (novelette), 1935. Story collections: *Spilled Time*, 1924; *Tales of the Wilderness*, 1924. About: George Reavey, *Soviet Literature Today*, Yale U. P., 1947; "Scenes From the New Russia," *Nation*, October 7, 1931; "Mirage or Miracle," *Living Age*, April 10, 1936.

MIKHAIL SHOLOKHOV

Stories: Tales of the Don, 1925; *The Azure Steppe*, 1926. Novels: *The Quiet Don (And Quiet Flows the Don* and *The Don Flows Home to the Sea)*, 1928-40; *Seeds of Tomorrow*, 1932-33. About: Philo M. Buck, *Directions in Contemporary Literature*, Oxford U. P., 1942; "Beside the Quiet Don," *Time*, February 9, 1948; Gleb Struve, *Soviet Russian Literature: 1917-50*, Univ. Oklahoma Press, 1951; Marc Slonim, *Modern Russian Literature: From Chekhov to the Present*, Oxford U. P., 1953.

ALEXANDER SOLZHENITSYN

Fiction: *One Day in the Life of Ivan Denisovich*, 1963; *Cancer Ward*, 1968; *The First Circle*, 1968; *August 1914*, 1972. Drama: *The Love-Girl and the Innocent,* 1969. About: D. Brown, "Soviet Russian Fiction," *Contemporary European Novelists,* ed. by S. Mandel, Carbondale, Ill., 1968.

INDEX

367

Introducing
Barron's Book Notes
The Smart Way to Study Literature

Everything you
need for better
understanding, better
performance in class,
better grades! Clear
concise, fun to read –
Barron's Book Notes
make literature come alive.

101 titles to choose from:

THE AENEID
ALL QUIET ON THE WESTERN FRONT
ALL THE KING'S MEN
ANIMAL FARM
ANNA KARENINA
AS I LAY DYING
AS YOU LIKE IT
BABBITT
BEOWULF
BILLY BUDD & TYPEE
BRAVE NEW WORLD
CANDIDE
CANTERBURY TALES
CATCH-22
THE CATCHER IN THE RYE
CRIME AND PUNISHMENT
THE CRUCIBLE
CRY, THE BELOVED COUNTRY
DAISY MILLER &
    TURN OF THE SCREW
DAVID COPPERFIELD
DEATH OF A SALESMAN
THE DIVINE COMEDY: THE INFERNO
DOCTOR FAUSTUS
A DOLL'S HOUSE & HEDDA GABLER
DON QUIXOTE
ETHAN FROME
A FAREWELL TO ARMS
FAUST: PARTS I AND II
FOR WHOM THE BELL TOLLS
THE GLASS MENAGERIE &
    A STREETCAR NAMED DESIRE
THE GOOD EARTH
THE GRAPES OF WRATH
GREAT EXPECTATIONS
THE GREAT GATSBY
GULLIVER'S TRAVELS

HAMLET
HARD TIMES
HEART OF DARKNESS &
    THE SECRET SHARER
HENRY IV, PART I
THE HOUSE OF THE SEVEN GABLES
HUCKLEBERRY FINN
THE ILIAD
INVISIBLE MAN
JANE EYRE
JULIUS CAESAR
THE JUNGLE
KING LEAR
LIGHT IN AUGUST
LORD JIM
LORD OF THE FLIES
THE LORD OF THE RINGS &
    THE HOBBIT
MACBETH
MADAME BOVARY
THE MAYOR OF CASTERBRIDGE
THE MERCHANT OF VENICE
A MIDSUMMER NIGHT'S DREAM
MOBY DICK
MY ANTONIA
NATIVE SON
NEW TESTAMENT
1984
THE ODYSSEY
OEDIPUS TRILOGY
OF MICE AND MEN
THE OLD MAN AND THE SEA
OLD TESTAMENT
OLIVER TWIST
ONE FLEW OVER THE
    CUCKOO'S NEST
OTHELLO

OUR TOWN
PARADISE LOST
THE PEARL
PORTRAIT OF THE ARTIST
    AS A YOUNG MAN
PRIDE AND PREJUDICE
THE PRINCE
THE RED BADGE OF COURAGE
THE REPUBLIC
RETURN OF THE NATIVE
RICHARD III
ROMEO AND JULIET
THE SCARLET LETTER
A SEPARATE PEACE
SILAS MARNER
SLAUGHTERHOUSE FIVE
SONS AND LOVERS
THE SOUND AND THE FURY
STEPPENWOLF & SIDDHARTHA
THE STRANGER
THE SUN ALSO RISES
A TALE OF TWO CITIES
THE TAMING OF THE SHREW
THE TEMPEST
TESS OF THE D'URBERVILLES
TO KILL A MOCKINGBIRD
TOM JONES
TOM SAWYER
TWELFTH NIGHT
UNCLE TOM'S CABIN
WALDEN
WHO'S AFRAID OF
    VIRGINIA WOOLF?
WUTHERING HEIGHTS

Only $2.50 each!
On sale at your local bookstore

BARRON'S
250 Wireless Boulevard
Hauppauge, New York 11788